Hardball on the Home Front

Hardball on the Home Front

Major League Replacement Players of World War II

CRAIG ALLEN CLEVE

McFarland & Company, Inc., Publishers
Jefferson, North Carolina, and London

LIBRARY OF CONGRESS CATALOGUING-IN-PUBLICATION DATA

Cleve, Craig Allen.
 Hardball on the home front : major league replacement players of World War II / Craig Allen Cleve.
  p.   cm.
 Includes bibliographical references and index.

 ISBN-13: 978-0-7864-1897-8
 (softcover : 50# alkaline paper) ∞

 1. Baseball players—United States—Biography.
 2. Baseball—United States—History—20th century.   I. Title.
 GV865.A1C48   2004
 796.357'092'2—dc22   2004017516

British Library cataloguing data are available

©2004 Craig Allen Cleve. All rights reserved

No part of this book may be reproduced or transmitted in any form or by any means, electronic or mechanical, including photocopying or recording, or by any information storage and retrieval system, without permission in writing from the publisher.

On the cover: Lefty Lefebvre with the Senators in 1943 (©Brace Photograph)

Manufactured in the United States of America

McFarland & Company, Inc., Publishers
 Box 611, Jefferson, North Carolina 28640
  www.mcfarlandpub.com

To my father, Al Cleve, for September 1, 1971

Acknowledgments

Writing a book about events that happened over a half-century ago requires the efforts of more than one individual. I was most fortunate to have the help and support of many people along the way. Foremost in this group are the seventeen former ballplayers and their families who shared their stories with me. I thank each of them for their letters, phone conversations, encouragement, and confidence.

Much research was required for this book. I haunted the microfilm department at the Harold Washington Library here in Chicago. When articles from *The Chicago Tribune* and *The New York Times* proved insufficient, I turned to other sources. One of the most reliable was Steve Grietschier. A senior editor at *The Sporting News*, Steve provided me with photocopies of files for most of the players included in the book. These contained photos, press releases, player profiles, and period articles from *TSN* and other sources.

George Brace was one of the most prolific sports photographers in the history of the genre. For parts of six decades, George photographed nearly every major league baseball player who passed through the Windy City. In the process, he compiled what stands as one of the largest, most complete photographic records of major league baseball in the twentieth century. George passed away in 2002, but his daughter Mary keeps the family business in full swing. Using her father's old negatives, Mary recreated most of the photos used in this book—a fitting contribution to her father's remarkable legacy.

During the writing process, I frequently referred to a small book aptly titled *How to Do Baseball Research*, edited by Gerald Tomlinson and published by the Society for American Baseball Research (SABR). Written by a savvy collection of baseball writers, the book offers tips on style and research and suggestions on how to get published.

Thanks to the entire SABR staff for continually providing encouragement for prospective authors, as well as maintaining a forum for showcasing and discussing their work.

Thanks are also due to Pat Doyle and the folks at Old-Time Data, Inc., who are responsible for the fine player statistical profiles contained at the end of each chapter.

Not surprisingly, my family has been my staunchest support. My wife Laura is my proofreader and—in one of the great miracles of the cosmos—she thoroughly understands my single-minded pursuit of baseball knowledge. Thanks, honey.

It is only fitting that this book be dedicated to the man who first introduced me to the game of baseball. I was most fortunate to share this process with my father, Al Cleve. "How's the book going?" became the first order of business for almost every conversation over the last three years. We shared a roadtrip to Lebanon, Missouri, to visit with Ed and Marilee Carnett. My chapter on Eddie Basinski moved Dad to write his own letter to Eddie, and Dad was both tickled and proud to get a response from him.

I am more than three decades removed from my first visit to Wrigley Field. It's a blessing to know that some things still bring fathers and sons together and make their hearts pump like that first glimpse of the green grass of the playing field.

Table of Contents

Acknowledgments	vii
Introduction	1
1. Frank Mancuso	7
2. Ford Mullen	24
3. Ed Carnett	36
4. Lee Pfund	54
5. George Hausmann	70
6. Cy Buker	90
7. Bill Lefebvre	104
8. Eddie Basinski	119
9. Nick Strincevich	142
10. More Wartime Players	161
Appendix: Statistics	173
Notes	187
Selected Bibliography	193
Index	195

Introduction

> Let me say one thing before we start. At the first part of the war, it didn't look too good for us on either side. I think one of the greatest things that President Roosevelt ever did was to say, 'I want Major League Baseball to keep playing.' Let me tell you, not only did it uplift the morale of our people—we had a lot of people working 'round the clock on wartime efforts—but it also did a hell of a job beating down the morale of our enemies. [They] couldn't understand how we could still be playing baseball and taking the lumps that we were taking. That was probably one of his greatest decisions.
> Frank Mancuso
> Houston, Texas
> September, 2000

In the wake of the terrorist attacks of September 11, 2001, Major League Baseball announced that it would suspend play for seven days—a move made partly out of respect for a nation in mourning and partly so that major league franchises across the country could rethink their security protocols. Going to a ballgame—or any massive public gathering—would never be the same.

The attacks left America reeling. The absence of baseball contributed to the disruption of the American rhythm. In one of the darkest moments in the history of our nation, Americans did not have their pastime to pull them away from the news reports.

There is no question that Major League Baseball's decision to suspend play was the necessary choice. But, for a brief period, Americans didn't have a pennant race to divert their attentions from a world that had suddenly become all too threatening.

Imagine for a moment that during the most cataclysmic episode of the twentieth century—the Second World War—Americans did not have baseball to boost their morale. What if Roosevelt had ordered baseball's commissioner, Judge Kenesaw Mountain Landis, to suspend play "for the duration?" What effect might the absence of baseball have had on the American countenance?

This book does not seek answers to those questions. Rather, it is a celebration of the fact that Roosevelt chose to keep baseball going, in spite of the fact that every able-bodied ballplayer of draftable age was not exempted from military service. More than 5,000 major and minor league ballplayers served in the military between 1942 and 1945. The void created by their absence sent clubs across the country scrambling in search of serviceable talent.

Major league rosters remained relatively unscathed in 1942, with notable absentees including Bob Feller of the Cleveland Indians and Hank Greenberg of the Detroit Tigers. By 1943, when progressively more players were called into the service, it became anybody's ballgame. In baseball, it sometimes doesn't hurt to be in the right place at the right time.

More than 400 ballplayers made their big-league debuts between 1943 and 1945—the years which saw the largest concentration of departing players. The majors saw a glimpse of their future with the arrivals of Sal Maglie, Billy Pierce, Early Wynn, Andy Pafko, Whitey Lockman, Red Schoendienst, Stan Musial, and many others. But the true story of wartime baseball rests mostly with those players whose careers were not so well remembered or documented.

Sixty percent of those players making their debuts during the war never played another game in the major leagues after the war ended. *Hardball on the Home Front* tells the stories of nine ballplayers who had the opportunity to play major league ball during World War II. They came from sandlots, schools, and the most remote regions of the low minors. Some were coaxed out of teaching assignments and jobs in defense plants—jobs that kept them out of the service—for the prospect of realizing a dream they had tucked away somewhere years before.

For the most part, they were minor league baseball players, a few of whom had made it to the big leagues for a cup of coffee in the late 1930s. Only two or three could have been considered true big-league prospects, and at least three of them had abandoned professional baseball altogether. In some cases, the war hastened their arrival into the majors. For others, it created an opportunity where none existed, either presently or prospectively.

Frank Mancuso was a top catching prospect in the St. Louis

Browns system. He volunteered for the paratroops in 1943 and was nearly killed on a training jump. His injuries earned him a medical discharge, but he recovered sufficiently enough to become the opening day catcher for the Browns in 1944.

Ford Mullen was a scrappy second baseman who had risen to the level of the Pacific Coast League. He abandoned baseball for teaching after the 1942 season, but wartime shortages led to his arrival in the major leagues in 1944.

Ed Carnett began his big-league career as a pitcher with Casey Stengel's Boston Bees in 1941. A series of arm injuries forced him from the mound and the majors, but he returned in 1944 as an outfielder with the White Sox.

Lee Pfund believed in keeping the Sabbath holy and did not play ball on Sundays. He pitched well enough the other six days of the week to break into the Dodgers' starting rotation in 1945.

Diminutive George Hausmann started all 155 games at second base for the New York Giants in 1945. Not impressed with his club's offer in 1946, he and eight of his teammates left the majors for the promise of higher salaries in Mexico.

Cy Buker thought his 7–2 record with Brooklyn in 1945 was good enough for a decent raise in 1946. When Branch Rickey offered him an insufficient increase, he tore up the contract and mailed it back to his boss. He never saw the majors again.

After two years pitching for the Red Sox in the late 1930s, Bill Lefebvre spent four years in the minor leagues trying to get back. He latched on with the Washington Senators in 1943 and 1944 before the army claimed him.

Eddie Basinski was a mechanical engineer, a virtuoso violinist, and quite possibly one of the best defensive second baseman in baseball during the 1940s and '50s. Plucked from the sandlots of Buffalo, New York, without a day in the minor leagues, he helped turn the 1945 Brooklyn Dodgers from bums into winners.

Nick Strincevich learned how to pitch on mill teams in his native Gary, Indiana. He did his best work for another steel city—Pittsburgh. A crafty side-armer, he became one of the most effective pitchers of the war.

Every newspaper and newsreel of the day reminded these players of the harsh realities of Europe and the South Pacific. They were in a position for which most men would have given their right arms, and it happened during a time when young men were literally sacrificing their limbs and lives in service of their country. They were lucky to be playing baseball, and they knew it.

But wartime baseball has always carried with it a certain stigma as insidious as the asterisk that haunted Roger Maris after his record mark of 61 home runs. Wartime baseball's asterisk comes with the conspicuous presence of players who were either too young, too old, or physically unfit for military service. Every team had its share.

Four of the nine players profiled in *Hardball on the Home Front* served in the armed forces during the war. Three were approved for service but were never called to active duty. Only two of the nine were classified as "4-F"—one for a chronic knee injury, and the other for asthma.

It doesn't help that the player most closely associated with baseball during the war is Pete Gray, the one-armed outfielder who played a generous hitch with the Browns in 1945. Gray was the Southern Association's player of the year in 1943. He was a tremendous gate attraction and a symbol of hope for a legion of amputees returning home from the war. He was also incapable of hitting a change-up and wound up batting just .218.

It is a simple truth that the quality of play in the majors during the war was a notch below that of baseball before or after the war. Gray's presence contributes strongly to this notion and, over time, has led to the erroneous conclusion that wartime baseball was a hastily assembled product that survived as much on buffoonery and shenanigans as it did on talent. If a one-armed outfielder could play in the big leagues, heck, *anybody* could. But there are other simple truths about wartime baseball that have often gone unnoticed or unmentioned.

Wartime baseball was fiercely competitive. Four of the eight pennant races during the war were decided by a margin of three games or less—one on the last day of the season. As progressively more players were taken by the draft, the war had a great equalizing effect on the major leagues.

And wartime baseball was not without its stars. Besides Wynn, Musial, and those players mentioned previously, stellar performances were turned in by Hall of Famers as well as unknowns whose careers lasted only a season or two. Not surprisingly, it was from this latter group that some of the most exciting, touching, and somber stories of the era came.

In the summer of 2000, I began writing letters to and receiving replies from former major league ballplayers whose careers began or were revived during the war. I was discriminating in my pursuit, con-

Introduction 5

centrating my efforts mostly on players who were on a major league roster for at least one full season. Each profile follows the player along what was often a meandering but memorable path to the major leagues. To a man, each of the nine proved his major league mettle, sometimes in a single game or over the course of a well played season.

Which begs the question: If they played so well while they were in the major leagues, why didn't they stick after the war ended? This question is not so easily answered. Suffice to say that the circumstances surrounding baseball's first postwar season of 1946 provided ample fodder for further adventures.

Although four of the nine players saw major league action after 1945, most banged around the minor leagues and points beyond looking for another major league opportunity that never materialized. After their playing careers ended, they mostly disappeared from the baseball stage. They returned to their homes, got regular jobs, helped raise their families, and subtly reached a point where only a handful of close friends and relations knew that they had once played major league baseball.

Fortunately, the memories of that time never faded. At this writing, the average age of the players profiled in *Hardball on the Home Front* is 86 years. The very act of "talking baseball" resurrected images and faces, names and stories, that had been stored away for more than 50 years. It was my privilege to hear them recount their trials and triumphs on the field, as well as their experiences with some of the game's greatest players during one of baseball's most important periods.

True history is always available for those who are willing to search for it. It is my hope that the stories contained in *Hardball on the Home Front* will contribute to a more accurate, enjoyable history of major league baseball during the war.

North Riverside, Illinois
Summer 2004

1
Frank Mancuso

The story of Frank Mancuso's journey to the major leagues conflicts strongly with the notion that wartime ballplayers lacked something which their pre- and postwar counterparts possessed. One of the St. Louis Browns' best minor league prospects, Frank would likely have joined the club as a catcher in the spring of 1943. Instead, he volunteered for the army and became a paratrooper with the 101st Airborne Battalion. An accident on his final training jump nearly cost him his life. His injuries were serious enough to earn him a medical discharge, but not before he spent five months in an army hospital.

Had he escaped injury, he would have joined his battalion during the Allied invasion of Normandy on June 6, 1944. Instead, he went back to catching, where his luck continued. The Browns made him their opening day catcher in 1944, which was to become their greatest season. In 1944 the Browns achieved their only pennant-winning season, to which Frank contributed a great deal in spite of the constant repercussions of his injuries.

It would surprise no one that Frank, a true patriot and genial Texan, spent much of his post-baseball life in the political arena. He served for thirty years as a city councilman in his home of Houston, Texas.

Indeed, Frank's life seemed to leap from the storyboard of a motion picture—each scene as preposterous as it was inspiring. And although Hollywood might not have dared script his life as it actually occurred, Frank lived it all the same.

Frank Mancuso
St. Louis Browns, 1944–1946
Washington Senators, 1947

Frank Octavius Mancuso was born in Houston on May 23, 1918, the youngest of seven children. His father died when he was ten years old, but Frank didn't have to look far for role models in his youth. Each of his four brothers played baseball, and one, Gus, made it all the way to the big leagues.

Gus Mancuso was born in Galveston in 1905. Along with his parents, he survived the Galveston Flood of 1906, his father carrying him over his head as he waded through waters up to his neck. Gus went on to become an All-Star catcher who played seventeen seasons in the National League. He was a mainstay on the New York Giants teams of the 1930s, where he caught the great Carl Hubbell during his string of five consecutive twenty-win seasons.

Less than a year after his paratrooper accident, Frank Mancuso was the Browns' Opening Day catcher in 1944. ©Brace Photograph.

Frank looked upon his big brother with the kind of awe and admiration only a kid brother can bestow.

"He was thirteen years older than me. Gus was one of the greatest catchers of all time, and I think other people will say the same thing. He was, you might say, my hero. He was certainly the big influence on me being a catcher."[1]

His education took precedence over baseball, an ethic that was instilled in him by his mother. There were no days where lessons took a back seat in favor of pickup baseball games. In fact, throughout his school days, Frank could recall missing school on only two occasions—once for illness, and the other when his mother gave him permission to stay at home and listen to Gus play in the 1933 World Series.

Frank followed in his brother's footsteps behind the plate. By the time he finished high school, baseball scouts had begun to take interest in the younger Mancuso. In 1937, he was asked to sign a pro contract with the Houston Buffaloes, a St. Louis Cardinals affiliate in the Texas League. Not sure how to proceed, he called Gus for advice.

Gus was clearly taken aback by his brother's dilemma. He knew that Frank had talent, but he was surprised to learn that he was being courted by professionals. He advised against signing with Houston and told his brother to wait until he told the Giants about him.

"That would have looked kind of bad—to have a brother that was good enough to have the Cardinals sign, and he didn't tell the Giants about me."[2]

Gus did tell the Giants about his kid brother. Frank signed with New York in the spring of 1937 and reported to spring training with Jersey City, their top farm club. He was ultimately sent to the Blytheville Giants, a Class D affiliate in the Northeast Arkansas League. He turned heads in his first pro season, batting .297 with 13 home runs and 88 RBIs. His performance earned him a promotion in 1938 to the "Three-I" League, so named because its teams hailed from Illinois, Indiana and Iowa. Playing for the Cedar Rapids Raiders, he hit just .237 in 39 games. The Giants decided to move him, although it was not immediately clear where he was going.

"That was the year I was in five different leagues. Three-I, Evangeline League. They sent me up to the Eastern Shore League. I got there one Monday, and was gone the next Monday. I didn't play a game there."[3]

Eventually, he landed with the Fort Smith Giants in the Western Association. The frequent changes of venue left him no worse for the wear. He finished the season with Fort Smith, batting a robust .419 in 23 games. That outburst caught the attention of the parent club.

Things were changing in New York, and the long-range effects of those changes would eventually find their way down to Arkansas. Still with the Giants, Gus Mancuso had been relegated to a backup role behind Harry Danning, a younger, harder-hitting catcher. In December of 1938, Gus was traded to the Cubs in a six-player deal that brought catcher Ken O'Dea to New York. O'Dea had split catching duties with Gabby Hartnett the year before, and he hit a two-run homer off the Yankees' Red Ruffing in the final game of the World Series. With both

O'Dea and Danning, the Giants looked solid behind the plate for the 1939 season.

Apparently, the only person who thought otherwise was the only person whose opinion mattered. Bill Terry, the Giants' manager and general manager, decided he needed some insurance down the line. The last man to hit .400 in the National League, Terry eyed the names of Giants farmhands and settled on a familiar name.

Frank was just twenty years old in the spring of 1939. Once again, he was slated for duty with Fort Smith. Terry dispatched Hank DeBerry, a former major leaguer and Terry's right-hand man, to meet with Frank in Arkansas.

DeBerry approached Frank during a spring training workout and asked, "How soon can you get packed?" Perhaps recalling his travels of the previous year, Frank responded, "Aw, hell. I'm always packed." "Well," said DeBerry, "you're going to New York!" By evening he was aboard a train, about to become a major leaguer, or so he hoped.

Thoughts of his brother accompanied Frank as he walked through the Giants' clubhouse and took his position behind the plate for his first workout at the Polo Grounds. He just wanted to give a good account of himself and measure up to the expectations he was sure Gus's old teammates must have had.

As it turned out, Bill Terry had other plans. Frank spent the entire '39 season with the Giants, although his official playing record lists him as "inactive."

"I was the bullpen catcher. That was it. Bill brought me up there, and I knew I wasn't going to play. Of course, I didn't expect to go no games at all. I was wide-eyed, you know? I'd like to have played, but it was good to be in the big leagues."[4]

Terry realized that he had no room for his young catcher. Rather than reassign him to a minor league club, he gave Frank his outright release, giving him the opportunity to get picked up by another major league ball club. He was signed by the Cubs and sent to Missouri to play for the St. Joseph Saints, a Class C farm club in the Western Association. As he had done with Fort Smith, he flourished at St. Joe, batting .310 with seven homers and 103 RBIs. The following year, he hit .303 with 18 homers and 97 RBIs.

"Baseball was little tougher back then. Money was a little tougher to come by, even for club owners. Like in '40, we won the pennant with St. Joe. We just didn't draw very many people. The owner just had nothing [and] had to move. In '41, we started the year in St. Joe, but then they moved the franchise down to Carthage. I finished the year there. The Browns had a working agreement with Carthage, [and] that's how I got into the Browns' organization."[5]

Frank went to the San Antonio Missions in 1942, a top Brownie farm club in the Texas League. He hit just .252 there, but his 11 home runs were the fourth highest total in the league. At the end of the season, St. Louis placed him on their major league roster.

The Browns were in desperate need of a good catcher who could produce at the plate. Brownie catching duties were shared by two men in 1942. The first was Rick Ferrell, who at thirty-seven could manage just a .223 batting average, the lowest in his Hall of Fame career. The other was Frankie Hayes, the erstwhile catcher for the Philadelphia A's. Hayes usually hit around .280 and had some power. He hit 20 home runs with 83 RBIs in 1939, but his power numbers had fallen off over the last several seasons. He had just two home runs during the '42 season, while batting .252.

Placing Frank on their big-league roster was a strong vote of confidence on the part of the Browns. Had things turned out as planned, he would have battled both Ferrell and Hayes for one of the catching spots in 1943. Frank, however, had plans of his own.

He was single with no dependents and fit for military service. The armed forces had not yet called, but he had resolved to enlist at the conclusion of the '42 season. In spite of his decision, the Browns kept him on their major league roster for the entire '43 season. Frank spent all of 1943 in the service, but he received an extra year toward his baseball pension all the same. It was an act of remarkable benevolence on the part of the Browns, but it also ensured that if Frank came back from the war in one piece, he would trade in his khakis for a St. Louis uniform.

"I had a unique war experience," he says, and that is truly an understatement.[6] He first enlisted in the Naval Air Corps and began training to become a navy pilot. When the university-level courses necessary for his flight training proved too difficult for his high school education, he was sent back to Houston with no hard feelings.

He tried next to enlist in the Marine Corps, but was told that their quotas had been met. He could try again in two months. Instead, he enlisted in the army and went through Officer Candidacy School. He was commissioned a second lieutenant and assigned to a tank destroyer unit. A short time later, enticed in part by the extra $50 per month, he volunteered to become a paratrooper.

"I was the biggest man in the paratroops at the time. Back then all paratroopers were kind of small. They had weight limits. I think it was about 160 to 170 pounds. I went through there, and I weighed about 185 to 190 pounds. I'll never forget the doctor giving me the examination. He hit me on the ass and said, 'Lose fifteen pounds!'"[7]

Paratrooper training in 1943 consisted of three stages: physical training, ground school, and jump training. A new recruit could count on spending much of the first two weeks in physical training, which consisted of daily five-mile runs, calisthenics, and strength training with dumbbells. Later, in ground school, recruits learned how to correctly pack their own parachutes. They also learned how to lead and guide an open chute.

Last came jump training, where the wheat was separated from the chaff. Jumping out of C-47 transport planes, recruits made five practice jumps—often on five consecutive days—under varying conditions and altitudes. The chutes were tied with pieces of common string and attached to the static line, which was hooked to the inside of the plane. After hooking up, a trooper waited for a signal and jumped out feet first. The line played out about fifteen or twenty feet, clearing the jumper from the plane's tail. The line pulled the parachute, and chute and line were separated when the trooper's weight broke the connecting string. The trooper fell free of the plane and guided the chute to earth. Recruits who successfully made all five jumps received their Airborne wings and earned the right to blouse their pant cuffs into their boots—a paratrooper trademark.

The first four jumps were made from about 1,500 feet—a relatively high altitude. If a recruit made it through the first four jumps, he made a final "action jump" complete with rifle and other gear.

"It was only from about 450 feet. That parachute—you swing about twice, and you're on the ground. That's the one I got hurt on."[8]

As an officer, Frank had to stand in the door of the plane. His job was to locate the jump site so that all of his men would land in the same area. Above the door were two lights—one red and one green. A red light indicated that the pilot was not yet over the jump site. Recruits began their jumps immediately after the green light appeared. Frank was the first jumper out of the plane.

"I was looking down, and the red light was on. I was trying to recognize the site down there. Then I looked back up, and the light was green. The first thought that went through my mind was, 'Well, I've got to go!' If I don't, my last man isn't going to hit the field. Over there in Georgia, if that last man don't hit the field, he lands in the Chattahoochee River."⁹

In his haste to make his jump, Frank committed a critical error. Instead of jumping out feet first, he led with his head. His body position was upside-down, and in consequence, the chute opened around his feet and the lines wrapped around his left leg.

Done properly, the chute will open around a jumper's chest, where the body's thick trunk absorbs most of the shock. When Frank's chute opened, the force created by chute and line snapped his leg just below the knee and twisted his upper back. Realizing he had only a few seconds before impact, he reached up with his right leg and managed to separate the damaged left leg from the tangled lines. His legs dropped free, and he braced himself for landing. Having had no time to guide the chute as it opened, he landed awkwardly in a grove of shrubs.

Doctors were quick to arrive on the scene. His injuries were severe, but considering the nature of the accident, they could have been much worse. In addition to the fractured leg left, X-rays revealed damage to the cartilage surrounding two of his upper vertebrae. The latter injury was enough for a medical discharge.

"I was five months in the hospital getting over everything, and I was about as healed as I was every going to get. But there were things wrong that I couldn't do. Even to this day, I can't look up. If I looked up, it would cut off the oxygen to my brain, and I'd black out. If I go outside and look up, I have to be holding on to something."¹⁰

After he recovered from his injuries, the army retired him from service in the winter of 1944. Hoping he could still play ball at some level, Frank contacted the Browns, on whose roster he still remained.

By the spring of 1944, St. Louis still had not found a solution to its catching woes. Ferrell and Hayes did not rebound from their dismal performances in 1942. The following season, Ferrell hit just .239 with no home runs. Hayes offered a feeble .188 with five home runs. Both players were gone prior to the start of spring training.

The only other catching prospect in the Browns' system was Myron "Red" Hayworth, himself the younger brother of venerable major league catcher Ray Hayworth. Red had kicked around the minor leagues for eight seasons. He wasn't much on power, having hit a total of six home runs during his entire career. He had played for the Toledo Mud Hens in 1943, the Browns' top farm club, where he hit a respectable .278. Perhaps exhibiting a faith in genetics that was years ahead of its time, the Browns invited both Frank and Red to spring training at Cape Girardeau, Missouri.

"When I went to [Cape Girardeau] I was still in uniform. I came home for a while, and then I went to spring training. I didn't have any civilian clothes. I remember I had to go down into town there and buy me a couple pairs of pants and a coat. All I had were my military clothes."[11]

Frank quickly found an ally in Browns manager Luke Sewell. The two had a lot in common. Sewell had been a major league catcher himself. In fact, he was the starting catcher for the Washington Senators during the 1933 World Series, the one for which Frank's mother had allowed him to skip school. Sewell had a famous older brother, too: Hall of Famer Joe Sewell. He didn't pressure Frank and was supportive from the start.

"I never will forget Luke Sewell. He was a college graduate and a very intelligent fellow. He realized, coming out of the service like I was, that I would have problems."[12]

As it turned out, one of the most conspicuous problems involved pop fouls. Frank's back injury prevented him from pursuing popups from behind the plate. The act of bending his neck to track the flight of the ball would cause him to black out. Sewell alerted only his pitching staff and his infielders to the unusual circumstances. He told no one else.

"Luke gave me every chance. He liked me, and in all reality, I think he was just hoping that I would be able to do it. Luckily, I came through enough for him. My case was a little unique with me being a paratrooper and all. It drew a little interest. The sportswriters gave me pretty favorable write-ups, due to the fact that I was a veteran. I appreciated that."[13]

On March 30, *The Sporting News* ran a front-page article on Frank, with the heading "Paratrooper Mancuso Lands with Brownies."[14] The article was accompanied by a large, obviously staged photo of Frank behind the plate in full catcher's regalia, except for his mask. The caption read, "Frank Mancuso, No. 1 catching prospect of Browns," and he lived up to the billing. By the end of spring training, Sewell had chosen him as the opening day catcher. Less than six months after his accident, Frank was starting for the St. Louis Browns.

Whether he leaped head first or feet first this time, he was about to plunge into one of the wildest seasons in baseball history. The Browns truly embodied the term "underdog." They had been in the American League since 1902, yet over the course of forty-two seasons, they had never made it to the World Series. They came close to winning an AL pennant in 1922 but lost to the Yankees by one game. More often than not they finished in the second division, and since 1929, they had finished better than .500 only once.

On paper, the Browns of 1944 were not much different from the 1943 edition, which had finished eight games under .500. A month into the '44 season, they lost their best pitcher, Steve Sundra. A 15-game winner a year before, Sundra was gone with the draft. But the Browns benefited from the arrival of pitcher Jack Kramer, who was discharged from the navy at the end of '43. They also took a risk in signing Sig Jakucki, a hard-drinking, thirty-four-year-old, semipro pitcher who had had a cup of coffee in the big leagues in 1936.

Returning from the 1943 squad were the starting infield of George McQuinn at first, Don Gutteridge at second, Vern Stephens at short, and Mark Christman at third. Also back were outfielders Al Zarilla, Chet Laabs, Milt Byrnes, and Mike Kreevich. They were joined by Gene Moore, who was acquired when Ferrell was traded to the Senators. Denny Galehouse, Nelson Potter, and Bob Muncrief rounded out the starters. Veteran George Caster performed a yeoman's duty in the pen.

On opening day in Detroit, the Browns defeated the Tigers, 2–1. Frank had one hit in three at-bats—a single off the great Dizzy Trout. Surprising everyone, St. Louis went on to win its first nine contests.

"A lot of them, especially sportswriters back then, expected us to fold at any time. We jumped out there and won the first nine games of the season. We had a darn good ball club. Junior Stephens had a good year. Don Gutteridge was always a good ballplayer. George McQuinn was the best first baseman I ever saw. Of course, we had good pitching too.

"We had Nelson Potter, who won 19 games. He was a darn good pitcher. Nelson was a right-handed pitcher, and he had a damn good right-handed screwball. He'd get left-handers out with that, boy. He'd love to see clubs put up left-handed pinch hitters against him because he'd get them out with screwballs.

"Kramer won 17 games. Jakucki was a good pitcher, but he also drank too much. When he was due to pitch, he was OK. Bob Muncrief had the best curveball I guess I ever saw. And then, we had good relief pitchers, like George Caster."[15]

But it was a hard season for Frank. He struggled both at the plate and behind it. The year's layoff from baseball had wreaked havoc on his timing. There were some good moments, though. On June 3, in a game against the Athletics at Sportsman's Park, he drove in six runs with a double and a home run. But for most of 1944, Frank struggled to keep his average above .200.

As difficult as it was to hit, it was behind the plate that he most felt the effects of his paratrooper injuries. His left leg wasn't ready for a long season of crouching and barked at him constantly. And as Luke Sewell had feared, pop fouls were an adventure. Not surprisingly, Frank led all AL catchers with 17 errors, in spite of splitting duties with Hayworth.

On one occasion, he did manage to chase down a popup and park himself under it. He raised his glove above his head and caught the ball. When he looked around, he found himself surrounded by Christman, McQuinn, and Caster, each with his glove beneath Frank's catcher's mitt.

The Browns led the American League for most of the season, but were closely pursued by both the Tigers and Yankees. Detroit took a one-game lead over the Browns into the season's final weekend. Because of rain earlier in the week, both teams played a Friday doubleheader. Detroit split theirs with Washington. The Browns swept the Yankees. The Tigers won on Saturday, but lost the final game of the season on Sunday. The Browns won on Saturday and clinched the pennant on Sunday, a 5–2 victory behind Jakucki.

"Our celebration was pretty mild. None of us had any money to spray champagne all over each other!"[16]

The Browns' opponents in the World Series were none other than the St. Louis Cardinals, with whom they shared a home—Sportsman's Park. The Cards were making their third consecutive Series appearance and were heavily favored against their hometown rivals. The Browns had batted just .252 during the regular season, third lowest in the American League. Their bats were no match for the Cardinals' pitching in the Series, which boasted the likes of Max Lanier, Mort Cooper, and Harry "The Cat" Brecheen. The Cardinals beat the Browns, four games to two.

By the end of the season, Red Hayworth was doing the lion's share of the catching. Sewell favored Hayworth going into the Series, with Frank in reserve. It wasn't until late in the second game that Frank was called upon to pinch hit.

The Browns had been stymied by the crafty pitching of Cardinal left-hander Max Lanier. Lanier carried a 2–1 lead into the seventh inning. Hayworth, batting in the eighth slot, had doubled off the fence. Nelson Potter was due to hit next.

"Red was standing on second base. Luke was standing over there in the coach's box. Back in those days, the manager always coached third."[17]

Sewell looked into the dugout and pantomimed the stance of a right-handed hitter. Frank's heart jumped. "You mean me?" he asked. "Yes!" said Sewell. "Grab a bat and get up there!"

All games of the '44 Series were played at Sportsman's Park, home to both teams during the regular season. Needless to say, every seat was filled, including those in straightaway center field. The weather was warm, and many of the patrons were dressed in white shirts. This put hitters at a strong disadvantage.

Good hitters look for the point at which a pitcher releases the ball. As a deception, some pitchers vary their release points, coming at a hitter with a three-quarter or side-arm delivery instead of an overhand delivery. From a hitter's perspective, most release points are on the same visual plane as the center field bleachers. Consequently, when the bleachers are filled with people, the ball appears to emerge suddenly from the stands—a blurry white projectile from a sea of white shirts. All modern parks have a "hitting background" in center, preventing this advantage to the pitcher. Batters in 1944 had no such luck.

"I kept hearing our guys come back to the bench saying, 'Geez, I can't see that ball!' Well, when Luke told me to go up and hit, the thought that came to my mind was, 'I got to take a pitch to see if I can see it.' Ol' Maxie threw me a good curveball. It just snapped right over. The umpire said, 'Strike one!' 'Well,' I thought, 'I can *see* it!'"[18]

On the next pitch, Lanier came back with a fastball. Frank hit it as hard as he ever hit a ball in his life. It was a single to center field that scored Hayworth and tied the game, 2–2. The game lasted eleven innings. The Cardinals prevailed on a run-scoring pinch single by Ken O'Dea and four innings of scoreless relief pitched by Blix Donnelly.

Sewell called on Frank once again in Game 4, this time to pinch-hit for Hayworth. He singled off Brecheen, who went the distance in a 5–1 Cardinals victory.

"I could have had three hits. The third time I was up, I hit a ball to right that Stan Musial made a good catch on. I could have had three hits out of three."[19]

Frank's two hits in three at-bats matched Hayworth's total output for the Series. Red managed just two for 17, and even that figure was better than Mark Christman (two for 22) and Mike Kreevich (one for 10). Only two Brownies—George McQuinn (.438) and Frank (.667) hit better than .250 for the six games.

Frank had batted just .205 during the regular season. His paratrooper injuries had prevented him from playing for long stretches during the summer, and they contributed significantly to his error total. But Luke Sewell spent the winter months thinking about Frank's clutch hitting in the Series. With a long off season to regain his strength, Sewell expected better things from his catcher. Frank didn't disappoint him.

1945 was Frank's best season in the major leagues. After reclaiming his starter's role from Hayworth that spring, he went on to catch 115 games during the season. His defense improved dramatically; his error total dropped to six. In addition, he batted .268—best among all regular catchers in the American League.[20]

Despite having most of the '44 lineup intact, the Browns were unable to defend their title and recapture the pennant. Although they stayed near the top of the pack all season long, they ultimately finished third behind the Senators and the Detroit Tigers' who would go on to win the World Series.

One of Frank's teammates on the '45 squad was Pete Gray. His arrival sparked controversy both in the press and on the team itself. With the Memphis Chicks in 1944, Gray had won Player of the Year honors for the Southern Association after hitting .333 with 63 stolen bases. Still, Sewell had difficulty justifying the one-armed outfielder's presence on the club, especially when the Brown's began to falter.

"I have to say this about Pete: He was a remarkable fellow, the things he could do with one arm. The harder you threw the ball to Pete, the more you were doing him a favor. I remember some of those guys like Bobo Newsom and Red Ruffing. When they'd see Pete up there

Though he hit just .205 during the season, Frank Mancuso's seventh-inning single tied the second game of the 1944 World Series. ©Brace Photograph.

with one arm, the first thought they must have had in mind was, 'I'll knock that bat out of his hand!' They'd rear back and throw that fastball in there, and Pete would hit it. He could hit a fastball better than anything, and he could catch a fly ball as good as anybody."[21]

But pitchers soon discovered Gray's Achilles' heel. With one arm, Gray lacked the bat speed necessary to hit a big-league fastball. To make matters worse, he swung a heavy bat and had to start his swing early to compensate. This strategy left him particularly vulnerable to off-speed pitches. American League pitchers ate him alive. He had to be constantly vigilant of fastballs, but could not adjust quickly enough for change-ups. Although he only struck out 11 times in more than 200 at-bats, he hit just .218 and did not return in 1946.

"Pete could do just about everything, but he couldn't tie his own shoes. Believe it or not, I was the only guy that he would ask to tie his shoes. Nobody else would do it, [and] he wouldn't ask them. I dressed right next to him all the time, and I got along with him fine."[22]

The average wartime ballplayer didn't return to play in the big leagues in 1946. Most were lost in the melange of returning veterans and saturated lineups. The vast majority of players whose careers began during the war never saw the major leagues again. There were, however, exceptions to this rule. Billy Pierce began his career during the war. So did Whitey Lockman, Gene Woodling, Gene Mauch, Ed Miksis, Cal McLish and several others.

Frank Mancuso had several reasons to be optimistic looking ahead to the 1946 season and his place on the Browns' roster. First, Frank had been the Browns' top catching prospect before the war. With the exception of Hayworth, no one else had mounted a serious challenge for the position, and Hayworth had hit just .194 in 1945. Second, Frank had demonstrated convincingly that he could play at the major league level. For proof, one need look no further than his fine performance in '45.

In addition, Frank was in the singular position of having served in the army and returned safely—albeit, slightly damaged—a feat that earned him a tremendous amount of respect around the league and in the press box. Finally, he had a manager who liked him and if necessary was willing to fight to keep him. For a variety of reasons, most wartime players never received that vote of confidence.

He hit .240 as the Browns' first-string catcher in 1946. The Browns were one team that did not seem to benefit from the return of players back from the war. They slipped back into the second division, finishing seventh in 1946. In December of that year, looking to shake things up on their roster, they traded Frank to the Senators in exchange for catcher Jake Early.

"I felt pretty good about [the trade] because Jake was an All-Star catcher. After a year there, they sent me to Toledo, back in the Browns' organization."[23]

He had batted just .229 with Washington, but rebounded at Toledo, hitting .273 with 13 homers and 61 RBIs. The following year, he went to Baltimore of the International League, where he hit .258 with 17 homers. In spite of his resurgent power numbers, no call came from the parent club in St. Louis.

"Then the Brownies asked me to go back down to San Antonio, which I did. I was glad to get back down here, because I was married. It was nice to get back into the Texas League."[24]

He played two seasons in the Texas League before accepting the job as playing manager for the Wichita Falls Spudders of the Big State League in 1952. The Spudders, a Boston Braves farm club, finished with a 77–70 record, but finished sixth in a very competitive league. The top six teams finished within eight games of each other. Frank was not offered a contract to return as manager in 1953, and instead returned to Houston and the Texas League.

About halfway through the '53 season, he was asked to join the Omaha Cardinals of the Western League. Their catcher had gone down with an injury, and the team was in dire straits. Frank obliged, and in appreciation, he was offered the helm of the Ardmore Cardinals, a St. Louis affiliate in Oklahoma's Sooner State League.

He continued as playing manager with Ardmore, guiding them to the championship series, where they lost to the Lawton Braves in four games. Frank managed and played his final season with Ardmore in 1955. He enjoyed managing, but he decided that eighteen seasons in professional baseball were enough. Besides, he had already decided to make a move to another arena and try his hand there.

"I always liked politics. Even when I was starting out in baseball, some of the local guys that were running for office would come asking for help to endorse them and talk for them. I had a good friend at that time who was a councilman running for office. I'd go on the radio and talk for him. That was the way I got interested in it. I just decided, 'Well, hell, I'll just try it for myself!'"[25]

After two unsuccessful bids for a seat on the Houston City Council, Frank was appointed to finish out the term of a councilman who had died while in office. That was in April, 1963. He went on to serve thirty years on the council, elected to fifteen consecutive terms.

So respected was Frank as a Houston politician that he spent much of his political career as the city's mayor pro tem. As mayor pro tem, Frank was essentially the city's acting mayor, running the city when the actual mayor was ill or out of the city for an extended period.

"When [the mayor] would leave town, I'd have all the executive power of the mayor. Quite a few times, there were things happening that I was caught up in."[26]

In 1970, while Houston mayor Louie Welch was vacationing in Europe, Frank found himself in the middle of an angry dispute over garbage. The city had decided to open a landfill in a section of Houston populated almost exclusively by African Americans. The site would receive garbage from all over the city. Demonstrators argued that the choice for the site was racially motivated, and they attempted to block city garbage trucks from delivering garbage to the new site.

"If I live to be a hundred, I'll never forget that. We had 300 policeman over at this landfill site, and there were a thousand black protesters. There was a face-off. Late at night, I called a meeting with the public works director, the chief of police, and the city attorney. I made an executive decision to pull all the garbage trucks back and then pull all the police out of there."[27]

During the "cooling off" period of the next several days, Frank devised a fair alternative plan: The city would be divided into quarters, each with its own landfill. No single quarter would receive garbage from all the others. That satisfied the demonstrators.

"I'm real proud of the record I had there. I don't think you'll ever find anything bad written about me. I had one writer come up to me when I retired, and he said, 'Frank, I've been looking to get something on you for ten years!' Just like that, you know? But the thirty years will never be broken because they have term limits now. I think that was a bad mistake. The longer a person's in office, that's how he gets skilled. 'Course, if you're a bad politician you're going to get beat anyway."[28]

Sometimes politics had its lighter side, and baseball was often at the root of the humor. At a dedication ceremony at a convention center in Houston, Frank, acting as mayor pro tem, approached former President George Bush. "I just wanted you to have my card, Mr. President," he said. From his breast pocket, Frank drew his baseball card. The former President, a onetime first baseman at Yale, was very pleased.

He retired from political life in 1993. Bypass surgery several years ago has slowed him, and the recent loss of Marian, his wife of more than fifty years, was a difficult blow. He still enjoys emeritus status in Texas politics, recently named a senior advisor to the governor of Texas. To this day he still remains a baseball fan, though he admits that the game is different today.

"I was just watching the Yankees and Mariners tonight. I watch a lot of baseball now. The things I notice now is that ballplayers today just don't run out ground balls to first base like we used to. I guess the union's too strong, or the managers can't get on them for it. Only one time can I ever remember Luke Sewell getting on my butt, and he was right when he did it.

"We were playing in Yankee Stadium in '46, and I hit just a little fly ball to center field. Joe DiMaggio came in and was just casually standing there. I didn't even hardly run down to first base. I was just watching DiMaggio, and *damn!* He dropped the ball! It wasn't even a tough chance.

"I'm still standing on first base. Luke got on my butt good, and you can bet that was the last time I ever did *that*. If we'd done like these guys do today where they just trot down to first base, or they stand at home plate to see whether it's going out of the park, hell, our teammates would've been all over our butts good."[29]

2
Ford Mullen

In an odd way, Ford Mullen is the whole reason for this book. While flipping through the pages of *The Baseball Encyclopedia* one day, I happened upon his brief entry. He is listed as "Moon" Mullen, corrupted from the comic strip character "Moon Mullins"—the panels of which I encountered time and again each time I searched newspaper archives for old box scores. *Ford* Mullen played a single season at second base with the Philadelphia Blue Jays, who were the Phillies by another name for two seasons during the war. The first time I read his stats, I knew I wanted to find out more about him.

He played in 118 games for Philadelphia, batting .267 in 464 at-bats. Of his 124 hits, only 13 were for extra bases—nine doubles and four triples. He had no home runs. He struck out just 32 times that year and was a better than average glove at second base. By his own admission, there was nothing extraordinary about his performance during the '44 season, except for the fact that it was his only season. Although he was the regular second baseman for the Blue Jays and had a respectable batting average to boot, he never returned to the major leagues.

Most wartime ballplayers came to and departed from the big leagues under similar circumstances. It was their individual performances that distinguished them from one another. Ford Mullen was one player who truly showed his mettle during his lone season in the majors. When I first spoke to him, I told him that I had just returned from the library, where I had been researching his major league career. "I bet it didn't take you long!" he quipped. On the contrary, my research took considerably longer than a single trip to the library. The box scores from 1944 told a remarkable story that was both typical and timeless.

Ford "Moon" Mullen
PHILADELPHIA BLUE JAYS, 1944

In the autumn of 1942, Ford Mullen figured he had gone about as far as he could go in professional baseball. In his four pro seasons, he had compiled a .307 batting average, mostly for Class B and C ball clubs.

He was signed out of the University of Oregon in 1939, where he had played both baseball and basketball. On the latter team, he was a reserve guard, in spite of his 5' 7" frame. The Ducks, under the guidance of coach Howard Hobson, won the first-ever NCAA championship that year, defeating the Ohio St. Buckeyes, 46–33. Because of Mullen's size, professional basketball wasn't in the cards. Instead, he signed a baseball contract with the Detroit Tigers in the spring of 1939.

He played first for the Jacksonville Jax, a Class C ball club in the East Texas League. The Jax finished last in their league, but Ford hit .327 in his first season. He stayed in the East Texas League in 1940, but the Tigers moved him to the Henderson Oilers, a club that also had Tiger ties. He hit .340 at Henderson and earned a promotion to Class B ball in 1941.

The Tigers sent him to the Winston-Salem Twins, then a new franchise in the Piedmont League. The Twins were an awful ball club, finishing nearly thirty games out of first place. But Ford made the most of his first season in Class B ball, batting .277 and earning the interest of other clubs.

By the spring of 1942, he was with a new team and a new organization. He was sent to the Vancouver Capilanos, a Chicago Cubs affiliate in the Western International League. The move sent Ford closer to home—a good thing, since his wife was expecting their first child. In July of that year, fans and teammates joined together to hold a baby shower honoring his daughter's arrival. Ford showed his gratitude by hitting .293 and earning yet another promotion.

At the end of the '42 season, he had the opportunity to close out the year with the Seattle Rainiers of the Pacific Coast League. Ford was a native of Olympia, Washington, and the Rainiers were his boyhood favorites. The chance to play with them was a rare treat. He played in Seattle's final three games and went two for four.

In spite of his progressive rise through the minor leagues, Ford privately felt that he had risen about as far as he could in pro ball. The quality of play in the Coast League was a far cry above that of the Western International League, or any other stop he had made along his career path. His family was growing, and the war was on. It was time for other things. It had been a good run, and he decided that his brief trip to the Coast League was a good note on which to end his career.

He took a teaching position at Eugene High School in Eugene, Oregon, the site of his alma mater and his basketball triumphs just a few years before. Surrounded by familiar faces, he coached both baseball and basketball, assisted with football, and also did some teaching. He was not in any immediate danger of being drafted. He was married and had to sign a special affidavit swearing that he was not getting married to dodge the draft. A wife and child would have made Ford 3-A in the draft. Even so, married men with children were indeed being called to service. It's likely that Ford's teaching position gave him an additional deferment.

Professional baseball remained mostly intact in 1942, losing only a handful of patriotic volunteers along with single men who had no deferments. Joe DiMaggio played a full season in '42. So did Ted Williams. By the close of the '43 season, more than 200 players who had been on major league rosters were in the service. By the end of the war, more than 5,000 major and minor league players served in the armed forces.

In the spring of 1943, Ford was contacted once again by the Rainiers. Seattle had lost six position players to the draft after the 1942 season, including their second baseman, Al Niemiec. Hoping to add a good glove up the middle, they asked him if he would be willing to join the team.

Ford was already in the

Ford Mullen with the Phillies Blue Jays in 1944 (note the blue jay emblem on the sleeve). ©Brace Photograph.

middle of a baseball season of sorts, this time at the helm of the Eugene High School team. He asked if the Rainiers would be willing to wait until his school contract ended in June. Seattle agreed, and he caught up with them on a road trip to Hollywood, California.

Ford played extraordinarily well for a player who had hung up his cleats just a few months before. He played as the Rainiers' regular second baseman almost from the time he joined the team in June after the school year ended. In 110 games, he batted .272 in 426 at-bats. The Coast League of 1943 was not the powerhouse it had been just a season or two before but even stripped down by the draft, the league boasted the likes of Babe Herman and Charlie Root, plus young comers like Andy Pafko. Throughout the war, the Coast League remained a primary pool of talent for the major leagues.

One morning in late August, Ford got a surprise with his breakfast. "I woke up one morning and read the Seattle paper: 'Ford Mullen Sold to Phillies.' It happened just that fast. Needless to say, I was ecstatic!"[1] He signed a contract for $5,000 a year and was told to report to training camp that spring.

"In those days, we didn't know what an agent was. You either signed [the contract] or you didn't play ball. You had to be liked, for some reason or other. Your performance meant something if you were a star, but if you were a mediocre or average ballplayer, it was a little rough."[2]

Ford did not return to teaching after the '43 season. Instead, he took his family back to his hometown of Olympia, Washington, where he worked in a veneer factory during the off season.

Danny Murtaugh had been Philadelphia's regular second baseman in 1943, but now he was gone with the draft. The Phillies spent the spring of 1944 in Hershey, Pennsylvania, which was well within Judge Landis's 100-mile restrictions.

The second base job was Ford's from the get-go, with no other true candidate in camp. The Phillies had bought the contract of infielder Charlie Letchas from Toronto of the International League, but Letchas spent the bulk of his spring playing at third and short. By the time the team broke camp and headed for Philadelphia, Ford was the starting second baseman.

The Phillies had finished last in the National League for six of the last seven seasons. They had not had a winning season since the days of Chuck Klein, over a decade earlier. And with the Athletics serving as perennial American League doormats, baseball attendance in Philly was flagging.

In the spring of 1944, Phillie management designed a publicity stunt to help bring fans to the ballpark and jump-start morale. They announced a contest to rename the club, choosing from a pool of suggestions submitted by fans. The winning suggestion came from Mrs. Elizabeth Crooks, who received a season pass to all 1944 home games for submitting the name "Blue Jays." The Philadelphia uniform bore a blue jay patch on the chest and sleeve during the 1944 and 1945 seasons.

The Blue Jays opened the '44 season at home against the Dodgers on April 18. Ford led off the ballgame against Brooklyn's Hal Gregg and popped out in his first trip. He managed two singles, one of which drove in a run. The story in the *New York Times* credited Mullen and several of the other new faces on the team with the victory:

> Opening day was a marked success for the Phillies and a crowd of 11,910, said to be the largest ever to witness a curtain raiser for the Phils. The Blue Jays beat the Dodgers, 4–1, rather easily, with Kewpie Barrett scattering six hits, only one for extra bases.
> Andy Seminick, Ted Cieslak, and Ford Mullen, a trio with whom Shibe Park fans scarcely are acquainted, contributed most in the victory.
> In the sixth, with Les Webber pitching, Seminick opened with a single to left, Cieslak sacrificed and, with two out, Mullen, young second baseman, singled Seminick home.[3]

The Blue Jays were skippered by "Fat" Freddie Fitzsimmons, a venerable pitcher and winner of 217 games during his major league career. Fitzsimmons pitched well into his forties, in part because he threw a knuckleball requiring more finesse and less physical effort than a fastball. Like so many players-turned-managers, Fitzsimmons was never able to translate his success on the field into victories from the dugout. He compiled a .367 career winning percentage in one full season and parts of two others for Philadelphia. While it's true that his teams sported very little talent, he also may not yet have been ready to close out his playing career. Both may have contributed to his poor managing record.

"I never saw anything like him. You know, that son of a gun would throw knuckleballs in batting practice and try to get us out! If we were gonna face a knuckleball pitcher—I could understand it then. Not during regular batting practice, though."[4]

On one occasion, Fitzsimmons's tactic seemed to pay off, at least for Ford. In the first game of a doubleheader on April 23, the Blue Jays faced knuckleballer Jim Tobin of the Boston Braves. Tobin was nearly perfect that day, yielding a base on balls and one hit—a single off the bat of Ford Mullen.

"I hit three balls on the nose against him. All three were to left field. The left fielder caught two of them, and the other one was a line drive that dropped. It wasn't any big deal."[5]

Or was it? Four days later, on April 27, Tobin no-hit the Brooklyn Dodgers, 2–0, the first wartime no-hitter in the majors. Had it not been for Ford's sixth-inning single on April 23, Tobin might have thrown no-hitters in consecutive starts, a feat accomplished only once in the history of major league baseball. Cincinnati's Johnny Vander Meer threw consecutive no-hitters on June 11 and 15, in 1938.[6]

After denying Tobin his share of history, Ford's performance became inconsistent. Against Boston on June 15, he drove in the winning run in a 5–4 victory with a single (off Tobin) in the eighth inning. But he struggled just to keep his batting average above the .200 mark. In fact, for several weeks in June, Ford lost his starting role to the right-handed-hitting Charlie Letchas, who played as many games at short and third as he did at second. Fitzsimmons began to use Letchas against left-handed pitching. After a couple of multihit games early in July, Ford resumed his place at second, but by the All-Star break on July 13, he was only batting .226. That was about to change.

On July 14, he collected two hits off the Giants' Harry Feldman. Two days later, he went four for eight in a doubleheader against New York. Against the Pirates on July 19, he had two hits off Pittsburgh starter Nick Strincevich. The following day, he went three for five in the first game of a doubleheader which the Pirates won, 4–1. He went two for four in the nightcap, and in the bottom of the eleventh, with the scored tied at two and the bases loaded, he singled off Strincevich to drive in the winning run.

He was shut down by the Pirates' Max Butcher on July 21, but he

Ford Mullen got the only hit off Jim Tobin on April 23, 1944. Four days later, Tobin no-hit the Dodgers. ©Brace Photograph.

went four for five against the Reds' Jim Konstanty the following day. He managed just one hit in eight at-bats in a doubleheader vs. Cincinnati on the 23rd, but rebounded on July 26 with a four-for-six performance against the Cardinals that included a triple and an RBI.

In the 14 games he played after the All-Star break, Ford went a combined 24 for 60, good for a .400 clip. His average rose 42 points to .268 in less than two weeks. As for his sudden plate prowess, Ford had no clear explanation.

"I just gained a little confidence, is all. I never struck out that much, and I didn't try to hit the ball out of the ballpark, like they do now. I tried to watch the pitchers prior to going up to bat. I tried to see where they released the ball and watched that spot. I never guessed. I was a punch hitter. I would just hit to left and center quite a bit. I'd drag [bunt] the ball to the second baseman a lot. I never really hit the ball hard."[7]

By 1943, the war was perceived by many as having a sort of equalizing effect on major league baseball. Teams in both leagues lost top-drawer talent and were sent scrambling in search of ballplayers who could fill voids left on big-league rosters. Also-rans like the St. Louis Browns and the Washington Senators suddenly rose to become pennant contenders during the war. Such was not the case in Philadelphia. Fresh faces and a new team name were not enough to keep the Blue Jays from playing like the prewar Phillies. Philadelphia finished the '44 season 44 games behind the pennant-winning Cardinals.

Ford recalled management's often futile search for new talent: "We were having batting practice in Philly about an hour before a game started. They used to bring in players from the outlying area. There was one boy there who was batting. He was probably 6' 3" and husky as the dickens. Merv Shea was pitching batting practice. The kid swung at about five pitches and never hit one of them. Chuck Klein was one of the coaches. He was in back of the cage checking the kid out. He said, 'Son, one more pitch and run it out to second base.'"

"By golly, he swung at another pitch and topped it about ten feet down the third base line. Klein yelled, 'Run to second!' He took off running, but instead of running to first, he ran straight over the mound toward second base. Merv heard him coming. He reared back like he was being attacked! I was in back of the cage and I happened to witness all of this. I sure thought it was funny."[8]

Rookies and rubes were not the only players guilty of misplays afield. According to Ford, even Hall of Famers were prone to the occasional lapse in judgment. One incident involved Giants catcher Ernie "Schnozz" Lombardi. At the Polo Grounds, the Blue Jays' Ron Northey hit a pop foul, with Lombardi behind the plate.

"Lombardi threw off his mask, looked up, and thought he saw the ball traveling toward the stands in back of first base. He took off after it. It wasn't a ball he saw, but a pigeon flying from the third base side of the stands to the first base side. By the time he realized his mistake, it was too late. The ball dropped about three feet behind home plate!"[9]

And on a Sunday afternoon in St. Louis:

"Stan Musial was playing center field that day. Northey hit a high fly to center field. Stan tried to shade his eyes from the sun, but lost the ball. Instead of covering up, he held his glove where he thought the ball was coming down. The ball missed his glove and hit Stan on top of the head! It bounced about fifteen feet in the air and went towards the center field fence. [The right fielder] had moved over to cover him, and when he saw what happened, he stopped and actually fell to the ground, doubled over in laughter. Needless to say, Ron was able to round the bases for an inside-the-park homer!"[10]

The riddle as to why Ford did not play in 1945 is easily solved. By trading his teaching position for the second base job in Philadelphia, he forfeited his draft deferment. He was drafted into the army after the '44 season and served throughout 1945 and '46. He spent the duration of his army days at Ft. Lewis in Washington State, where he played on the baseball team with a host of other pros.

"We just clicked. I think we won 76 straight games. Most of the players were former major leaguers: Dom Dallesandro, Danny Litwhiler, Bill Fleming, Hank Camelli and many others. We played other service teams on the West Coast and exhibition games against several of the Coast League teams.

"The servicemen supported us real well. They came out in force. We had good crowds all the time. I was fortunate in having stayed at Ft. Lewis the entire time. In fact, the following year I managed the team. We had no major league ballplayers on the club, but we had a fairly good team and did quite well."[11]

Ford was discharged from the army in August of 1946. He was contacted by the Phillies (no longer the Blue Jays) and reported to spring training in 1947 to try to win back his old job.

But second base was not to be had. That job now belonged to Emil Verban, whom the Phillies had acquired in a trade with the Cards early in the '46 campaign. Verban had hit a solid .275 for the Phils and had a tight hold on the position going into the spring.

The third base job was a different story. Jim Tabor, who had played seven years with the Boston Red Sox, was the incumbent at the hot corner for Philadelphia. Tabor had performed well in '46, batting .268 with 10 homers, but it was clear that his skills were waning. Additionally, Tabor was a right-handed hitter. Manager Ben Chapman toyed with using Ford (who was a right-handed fielder) at third as another left-handed bat in the lineup.[12]

Phillies management had a difficult decision to make, and Ford's all-around play that spring didn't make it any easier. He worked hard at his new position, taking ground ball after ground ball. As expected, Tabor got most of the playing time at third and was one of the team's most productive hitters early on. Ford played with a sprained ankle, but managed a few starts early in April as the team left Clearwater, Florida, and journeyed back to Philadelphia, stopping along the way to play games in the Carolinas and Virginia.

In Greensboro, North Carolina, on April 11, Ford started at third in an exhibition game against the Washington Senators. He managed three hits, including a triple off Milo Candini that drove in two runs. In the field, he handled every chance cleanly and started three double plays. When the game ended, the Philly trainer pulled him aside and said, "You're in. You're in there!" Ford was beginning to believe that it just might be so. He continued on to Philadelphia with the team and even went so far as to rent a house.

On the day before the season opened, Ford was called to report to the Philly front office. He learned that he was being traded to the Yankees for first baseman Nick Etten and would be assigned to their minor league club in Kansas City. Etten had been one of the most productive offensive players in the American League during the war, leading the league in home runs and RBIs in different seasons. The Phillies had purchased Etten from the Yankees for the waiver price of $10,000. The Yankees were solid at third and second with veterans Billy Johnson and Snuffy Stirnweiss, respectively. A return to the majors via New York would be a remote chance, at best. Ford was stunned.[13]

"It was one of the most disappointing things that happened to me. They sent me directly to Kansas City. I was there for two or three weeks."[14]

Try as he might, he could not get himself on track with his new team. In his fourteen games with Kansas City, he batted just .178. The Yankees decided to send him to Memphis in the Southern Association, but Ford protested. He was still getting over the shock of being traded from Philadelphia. Now they wanted to send him somewhere else? He suddenly felt a long way from home, and he asked management if they could try to make a deal with one of the Coast League teams.

The Yankees relented and sent him to Portland of the PCL, where he would remain for the next three seasons. As had been the case four years earlier, he found that he was well suited to the Coast League's level of competition. He batted .323 with Portland after the Kansas City debacle. In three seasons there, he hit a combined .285. After hitting just .226 in 1949, he decided to pursue another baseball interest.

He was 33 years old in the spring of 1950 when he became the playing manager of the Boise Braves, a Class C team in the Pioneer League. He played his first full season since Philadelphia and put up some of his best professional numbers, including 26 stolen bases and 112 walks. But when Boise finished last under his direction, he abandoned any future managerial aspirations and ended his professional baseball career.

He returned to teaching, this time in his home town of Olympia, Washington. Over a twenty-seven-year career, he taught biology and zoology, and also coached baseball and basketball. He retired in 1977.

He still watches baseball these days and thoroughly enjoyed the Seattle Mariners' 116-victory season in 2001. He was particularly pleased by the play of Ichiro Suzuki, whose ability to put the ball in play no doubt made Ford think of his own style of play. It has been more than fifty years since he played professional baseball, and he finds it difficult, at times, to revisit his playing days. There has been a lot of living since then, and the game he once knew is very different.

"I enjoyed every minute of my ten years in pro ball and the two years in the army. We were treated with respect by players, management, and fans. We all hustled the entire ballgame, and unlike many of the 'stars' of today, we ran every ball out full speed. We played because we loved playing baseball—heavier bats, no helmets, wool suits, one pair of game shoes, one mud pair, small gloves, and not much money.

"After I retired from teaching and coaching, my wife and I did a lot of fishing for salmon. We had nineteen real good years fishing, and we haven't fished now for about five years. We've just given it up because the fishing hasn't been that good. Baseball is the same way. Some people reminisce. I enjoy baseball, but I don't reminisce too much. I had a lot of fun in those days. What the heck. Those days are gone, and there's no sense in reliving that stuff."[15]

3

Ed Carnett

Like many of his contemporaries, Ed Carnett never considered himself to be merely a "wartime ballplayer." He was one of the first players I tried to contact because his major league career was unique. There was an inauspicious beginning with the Boston Bees in the spring of 1941, where he pitched in just two games and nearly came to blows with Boston manager Casey Stengel. He returned to the majors in 1944, this time as a converted outfielder with the Chicago White Sox. After a full season in Chicago, he was traded to the Cleveland Indians and played there until the navy took him away just 30 games into the 1945 season. He is part of a very short list of major leaguers—among them, Smoky Joe Wood, Lefty O'Doul and Babe Ruth—who made their debut as pitchers, but stayed in the big leagues because they could hit.

Nearly three months after my initial letter, I received a call from Ed from his home in Lebanon, Missouri. He was tickled that someone should be interested in "the old guys." He is eighty-five years old, but talks a mile a minute in a voice that would suit a man half his age. A gregarious soul, Ed seemed to know everyone and everything in baseball during that marvelous era, and the privilege of hearing his stories was well worth the wait.

Ed Carnett
BOSTON BEES, 1941
CHICAGO WHITE SOX, 1944
CLEVELAND INDIANS, 1945

---

3. Ed Carnett

In baseball parlance, Ed was a "good-hitting pitcher." For any other ballplayer under any other circumstances, such an enviable combination of skills should have made him an asset. Yet over the course of a twenty-year professional career, his abilities on the mound and at the plate were the source of a dilemma that was never fully resolved: Was he a pitcher or a hitter?

As a youngster growing up in Ponca City, Oklahoma, there was no question. Ed was a pitcher, and he closely followed the exploits of Carl Hubbell, a fellow Oklahoman and left-hander. Ed admired Hubbell's great talent and unshakable concentration on the mound. He was drawn by the ballplayer's apparently genuine, unassuming nature.

Pitcher-turned-outfielder Ed Carnett left the majors as a pitcher and returned as a position player. ©Brace Photograph.

In 1933, he had the rare treat of watching his idol pitch in the World Series. The manager of Ed's American Legion baseball club was Joe Vance, a former pitcher with the St. Louis Browns. Through various contacts, Vance arranged for Ed and another player to travel with him by train to Washington, where they would watch three World Series games at old Griffith Stadium.

Ed set about collecting autographs before one of the games and had no trouble getting them from the hometown Senators. When he went to the Giants, however, nobody would sign. At one point, he called out to Carl Hubbell. Hubbell came by, and Ed quickly pointed out their Oklahoma connection. He also told Hubbell that he couldn't get anyone from his team to sign.

"He took my scorecard, and in about fifteen minutes, I had autographs of everyone on the team. I hung the moon that night, I guarantee you!"[1]

Although he never developed a screwball like Hubbell, Ed pitched well enough to earn the interest of professional scouts by the time he finished high school. He enrolled in junior college in the fall of 1934, but by the following spring, he had signed a contract with the Chicago Cubs.

The Cubs had a working agreement with the Los Angeles Angels of the Pacific Coast League. After going to spring training with the Angels, Ed was assigned to their Class C farm club, which happened to be in his home town of Ponca City. He had been courted the year before by Ponca City's manager, Roy "Hardrock" Johnson, a former major leaguer and longtime Cubs coach.

His first year in professional baseball was memorable and, by his own account, couldn't have been scripted any better. Ed won 19 ballgames with an earned run average of 3.20. He won in the All-Star game that summer and won three other games in the playoffs. In 256 innings, he struck out 160 batters. And beginning a pattern that would continue throughout most of his early career, he played an additional 23 games as an outfielder and pinch hitter, batting .271. The Angels invited him to spring training in 1936.

The Pacific Coast League was a competitive league filled with major league talent. In its prime during the 1930s and '40s, the PCL was considered by many to rival the majors in talent and was without peer as a proving ground for a young ballplayer. The DiMaggio brothers rose to the majors through its ranks, as did Ted Williams.

Ed pitched well during spring training and earned himself a spot in the Angels' starting rotation. Shortly before breaking camp, he was involved in a freak accident during a "pepper" game that cost him his year at Los Angeles and seriously affected the course of his career.

In pepper, three or four players take turns tossing a ball to a batter, who stands a short distance away and taps the ball back to the players. It is a simple drill designed to improve a player's reflexes. It is often discouraged, however, since the risk of injury is great, especially when players become too zealous or lackadaisical.

Ed was playing pepper alongside another squad. He bent over to retrieve a batted ball, picking it up with his bare hand. While in the act of throwing, he locked arms with Don Lang, the Angels' third baseman, who was picking up a ball from an adjacent game.

"When we did, I pulled a muscle way down deep in my left shoulder. Man, I'll tell you, I couldn't break a pane of glass. I had the team made, but I couldn't throw. I started three games at Los Angeles. I wanted to dig a hole and hide, because those baseballs came back like buckshot!"[2]

He was sent back to Ponca City. Dejected by the demotion, and with his shoulder still aching, he lost ten ballgames in a row. The night of his tenth defeat, he lasted only into the third inning, already having surrendered 10 runs. Ed's manager at Ponca City was Mike Gazella, a former utility infielder with the Yankees. Rather than send his pitcher to the clubhouse, Gazella made an extraordinary move.

"Instead of taking me out, he put me in right field. He took out the right fielder, who was hitting about .320. I expect that if he'd sent me to the clubhouse, I'd have hung myself from the rafters. I didn't pitch any for about a month and a half."[3]

The moved paid off. Ed hit .258 with two home runs and 33 RBIs. Relieved for several weeks from the constant strain of pitching, his shoulder slowly mended. He might have made a fine outfielder, but Gazella wasn't convinced that his pitching days were over. Just prior to a game in Springfield, Missouri, he gave the ball to his young southpaw. "You're gonna find out tonight whether you're gonna be an outfielder or a pitcher!" Ed protested, claiming his arm still didn't feel right, but he took the ball anyway.

He was encouraged during his warmup tosses. His arm felt better. His confidence began to loosen up with the arm. The ballgame went into extra innings, with Ponca City winning in the tenth. Ed pitched all 10 innings, striking out 15 batters. It was his first pitching victory of the season and the first in a remarkable streak.

Amazingly, his record at Ponca city in 1936 was 16–10: 10 consecutive losses followed by 16 consecutive wins. After his horrendous start, he finished with an ERA of 3.81, with 155 strikeouts in 215 innings.

"I'll tell you one thing—it taught me how to lose. It's easy to go when you're winning, but then that adversity crops up. Sometimes it's hard to cope with, but I was fortunate. I think I learned early, and that helped me."[4]

The following year, he was promoted to Tulsa, a Class A1 farm club in the Texas League. He finished the year with a 15–6 record made all the more remarkable in that, as with Ponca City, his pitching duties were interrupted. Tulsa's manager-first baseman went down with an injury. Ed became the starting first baseman, batted .304, and did not pitch for two months. When he returned to the rotation, he pitched all 12 innings in a 6–5 victory over Dallas. The Angels called for him again in the spring of 1938.

He was given a second chance to show the PCL what it had missed prior to his injury in the spring of '36. For the first time in three seasons, he was not called upon to play a position in addition to pitching.

At that level of play, if a position player went down with an injury, another was generally available to take his place. Even though he was allowed to focus on pitching alone, his record was not impressive. He pitched in "hard luck," finishing at 3–6, with an ERA of 4.15. It was a frustrating year. His arm was sore again. He knew that all eyes were watching, and he hadn't given a good account of his abilities. Baseball, however, is a fickle calling.

Although Ponca City and Tulsa were essentially Angels farm clubs, Ed was the property of the Chicago Cubs. The Cubs had a working agreement with the Angels, a common practice in the PCL and other leagues. The Cubs had won a tight race in the National League in 1938, barely beating the Pittsburgh Pirates to capture the pennant. They were swept by the Yankees of Gehrig and DiMaggio in the World Series.

Not possessing an overpowering offense, the Cubs won with pitching. "Big Bill" Lee and Clay Bryant were their best, winning 22 and 19 games, respectively. They even enlisted the services of Dizzy Dean, who was trying to come back from a devastating shoulder injury suffered when he was with the Cardinals. It proved to be a fine move. Dean was practically unhittable down the stretch, going 7–1 with a 1.81 ERA.[5]

The Cubs had just one left-hander on their staff. Larry French had won 10 games for the pennant winners, but he had lost 19. By most accounts, he pitched better than his record indicated. He did not start during the Series, seeing action only out of the bullpen. French was 31 years old, and his role on the '39 version of the Cubs was not clear. Chicago appeared to be looking for some left-handed help when they invited 22-year-old Ed Carnett to spring training on Catalina Island in 1939.

"That was something. You see, Mr. Wrigley owned that island, and they had this beautiful hotel there—St. Catherine's. They had a great, big ballroom where all the big bands played: Artie Shaw, Guy Lombardo, Jan Garber. It was just 27 miles from the mainland, but it was just like another world over there. We had a beautiful ballpark. It was right next to a golf course. When we'd get through practicing ball, we'd go and play golf."[6]

Spring training marked a number of "firsts" for Ed, the most important being his first real chance to make a major league roster. In addition, Mr. Wrigley's island afforded him his first opportunity to enjoy some of the accommodations of major league life. Also in 1939 came the first in a series of uncanny coincidences.

When he reported to camp, Ed learned that he would be sharing quarters with none other than Dizzy Dean. Roommate assignments were often handled alphabetically, so it wasn't unusual to find a "Carnett" with a "Dean." What is unusual is the fact that Ed seemed to be a sort of "star magnet." During the course of his major and minor league career, he would room with Dean, Eddie Lopat, Allie Reynolds, Warren Spahn, Phil Rizzuto and Johnny Lindell.

Dean's success in 1938 proved to be an aberration. His injury had forced him to become a "finesse" pitcher, relying on craft and guile as opposed to power.

"It hurt him to go out there when he couldn't defend himself. He was such a competitor. He was just like a little kid. He'd come around and ask the rookies, 'How's my arm look?' He called me 'Pistolhead.' He'd say, 'Hey, Pistolhead! How'd I look?'"[7]

Dean pitched a portion of the year with the Cubs. After the '39 season, he was sent to Tulsa to rehabilitate his shoulder. While in Oklahoma, he paid an impromptu visit to the home of Carnett's parents, greeting Ed's mother at the door with "Are you Pistolhead's mama?"

"He was just like one of the home kids. Just a lot of fun. He made a special effort to go out and see me. That's just the kind of a guy he was."[8]

The Cubs took a good look at Ed that spring. He appeared quite frequently in exhibition games as spring training neared its end. On March 21, he pitched three innings of no-hit relief against the Pirates. Three days later, on March 24, he relieved starter Bill Lee and retired the Pirates in order in the sixth, seventh, and eighth innings. With one out in the ninth, he gave up walks to Bill Brubaker and Bob Elliott, followed up with singles by Fern Bell and Arky Vaughan. Pittsburgh notched three runs in the inning, but Ed managed to finish the game.

He felt certain that he had made the club, perhaps as one of the starting pitchers. It was a tough rotation to crack, considering that the Cubs were the defending National League champions and had all of their pitchers returning. Near the end of spring training, Ed was approached by the Cubs' player-manager, Gabby Hartnett.

Hartnett looked at his returning veterans and suggested to Ed that he consider going to Milwaukee of the American Association. Ed told him he thought he could pitch in the major leagues, and Hartnett concurred. But he also felt that he'd be wasted on the bench for much of the season.[9]

"I said, 'OK, if that's where you want to send me, that's where I'll go.'"[10]

It was bittersweet. In one respect, Ed was encouraged by the fact that the Cubs thought he could pitch at the major league level. He did not, however, relish another year in the minor leagues. He had cause to rue Hartnett's decision. After starting the year on the mound for Milwaukee, he quickly found himself in a familiar situation. The Brewers' roster had more than its share of aging veteran players who had done a tour in the major leagues over the years. When one of their outfielders when down with an injury, Ed replaced him and did not pitch for more than a month. He hit .274 in 53 games as a position player with the Brewers, but his pitching suffered. He won only four ballgames while losing 11. As a result of his hiatus from pitching, he never felt comfortable on the mound. The Cubs did not bring him up at the end of the '39 season, though he managed an afternoon of good-natured revenge.

On June 26, Milwaukee played the Cubs in a wild exhibition game. Ed started the ballgame and trailed 6–2 after just four innings. He held the Cubs scoreless for the next four innings. Meanwhile, the Brewers rallied with five runs in the sixth to take the lead, 7–6. The Cubs loaded the bases in the ninth inning, and with two outs, Gabby Hartnett came to bat.[11]

"It was wild. I had the bases loaded in the top of the ninth inning, and I struck out Gabby Hartnett on a high fastball to end the game! I beat 'em, 7–6. He was the first guy to grab me and give me a big hug."[12]

That fall, Ed was traded by the Cubs to the Yankee's organization in exchange for catcher Clyde McCullough. He reported to spring training with Newark of the International League, the Yankees' top farm club. He pitched with three different Yankee ball clubs in 1940 and played with some of the top prospects in baseball along the way. He started with Double-A Kansas City in the American Association, where he went 2–2 in eight games with a 3.86 ERA. He was promoted to Newark, where he pitched poorly in four outings. His arm was still hurting, and he watched with dismay as so many of his teammates—among them Rizzuto, Gerry Priddy, Lindell, Snuffy Stirnweiss, Hank Borowy, Ernie Bonham, Hank Majeski and Tommy Byrne—left Kansas City and Newark to become the Yankees of the 1940s.[13]

After his poor performance at Newark, Ed was sent to Binghamton, a Yankee Class A farm club in the New York State League. He was still just 23 years old in the summer of 1940. He may have been heading to upstate New York, but it was clear that his career was going south.

Binghamton was the turning point. They were managed by Bruno Betzel, who had been a Yankee catcher. Binghamton was in the midst of a pennant race, and Ed's pitching couldn't have come at a better time. He flourished at Binghamton, going 6–3 with a 2.77 ERA. He won on the last day of the season, pitching on just two days' rest.

"Sometimes you can just throw your glove out there and win. That's about what happened. We just beat the hell out of them so everybody could go home. We beat Hartford, which was a Boston Bee farm club."[14]

Unknown to Ed, Casey Stengel, the Boston Bees' manager, was in attendance that day, hoping to scout some talent for next season. Boston was in need of left-handed pitching, and Stengel was impressed by the efforts of the young Binghamton pitcher. Later that year, Boston drafted Ed and invited him to spring training at San Antonio. As with the Cubs in '39, he pitched well enough to make the opening day roster. Boston, however, was not coming off a World Series appearance in 1940. They had finished next to last and were not expected to fare much better in '41. When the Bees broke camp and headed north, they took Ed with them.

Stengel immediately put him in the bullpen, no doubt hoping to use him against left-handed hitting. He entered his first game on April 19, the second game of a doubleheader against the Dodgers in Boston. Bee starter George Barnicle had allowed just one run through the first six innings, but the Dodgers scored four times in the seventh. Ed replaced Barnicle with two outs in the seventh and struck out Pete Reiser—the National League batting champ that year—to end the Dodger surge.

He retired Joe Medwick to open the eighth, but gave up singles to Cookie Lavagetto and Dolf Camilli. After striking out Alex Kampouris for the second out, Dodger catcher Mickey Owen doubled Lavagetto home. Pitcher Whitlow Wyatt followed with a long single to right center that scored Camilli and Owen. Pee Wee Reese walked, and Paul Waner flied out to right, ending the inning. Stengel sent Tom Earley in to pitch the ninth inning.

Ed did not pitch again until April 24 in Boston—a cold, blustery day at Braves Field. Every player spent a few extra minutes warming up. Boston led the Giants 3–1 in the sixth inning, when starter Dick Errickson ran into trouble. After Errickson gave up a single and a double that scored a run, Ed got up in the bullpen and started to throw.

"We got into trouble, and I started to warm up. Stengel sent one of the guys down there to say, 'Don't warm up. Casey'll tell you when he wants you to warm up!'"[15]

Errickson walked two batters and, with two outs, gave up a single to Joe Orengo that scored two. Suddenly, Stengel emerged from the dugout and signaled for a left-hander out of the bullpen.

"It's cold up there in Boston at that time of the year. I was a hot-weather pitcher anyhow. I didn't have a chance to warm up. (Stengel) sent me out there, and they had a man on first and third."[16]

Deprived of a proper warmup, Ed began to throw over to first baseman Babe Dahlgren. Orengo, the runner on first, stole just one base over the course of the season. The umpire had seen what had happened, but tried to move the game along nonetheless.

"Well, kid, you gotta throw over to home plate sometime!"

He did. He walked Giants shortstop Billy Jurges to load the bases. Next, he walked Joe Bowman, the pitcher, scoring the runner from third base. Mercifully, Stengel called for Al Javery, who *had* been given a chance to warm up. Javery retired the next hitter to end the inning.

Ed was beside himself with anger. He couldn't believe that Stengel had let him enter the game on a cold day without the benefit of warming up. He couldn't protect himself on the mound. Later, in the clubhouse, he made his feelings known.

"I said something like, 'Well, cripes! It looked to me like you got a chance to warm up in this damn league!'"

Stengel was unmoved. "Aw, that's just like you rookies. Makin' a damn excuse!"

"And boy, when he said that, I went for him! I was gonna clean his clock good."[17]

Before Ed could lay a hand on Stengel, several Boston players intervened and carried him out of the clubhouse. He figured correctly that his outburst had earned him a trip back to the minor leagues. The following day, Stengel sent a coach to give him the news that he was being shipped to Kansas City. As he went into the clubhouse to retrieve his belongings, he found Stengel there.

"Hey, kid! You still mad at me?" he asked.

"You're damn right!" Ed answered. "I won't kiss anybody's butt to stay in the big leagues, and if that's the way the big leagues are run, I don't want any part of it!"

He spent the remainder of the '41 season with Kansas City, once again in the Yankee organization. Both starting and working out of the bullpen, he finished at 4–2 with a 4.91 ERA. The year had begun with such promise in the major leagues. Now it seemed as if a return was nowhere in sight.

He started the next season at Binghamton, but after a poor start, the Yankees shipped him to Seattle in the PCL. He pitched mostly with the Rainiers, going 4–6 with a 3.54 ERA. At the plate, he batted .258. The Seattle pitching staff had a number of former major leaguers. Dick "Kewpie" Barrett, their ace, won 27 games in 1942. When Barrett was called up to the Cubs the following season, Ed took his place in the starting rotation.

In 1943, Ed's career took an unexpected turn. His arm was still bothering him, and he lacked the good stuff he had had when he first broke into professional ball. Every ballgame was a struggle, and the stress and strain of going to the mound every third or fourth day was beginning to wear him down. As usual, he played outfield whenever the team was short-handed.

His team provided him with little or no run support. Their most productive power hitter managed just six home runs all season. He lost several one-run decisions, one of which was decided by a late-inning home run off the bat of Babe Herman. During his last start, he led Sacramento 1–0 going into the top of the ninth inning. With two outs and a man on, he gave up a home run to Ray Mueller and lost the game, 2–1.

Ed stormed into the clubhouse and threw his glove. He turned to manager Bill Skiff and told him he was finished as a pitcher. Skiff let his player vent his frustration and didn't say anything. After a day of cooling off, a more sedate Ed sought out Skiff and apologized for his outburst. Skiff told him not to worry about it and surprised Ed by naming him as his new left fielder. He had, indeed, pitched his last game for the Rainiers.

He flourished in the outfield as never before. At one point, his average reached .330, threatening the league leaders. He sustained an injury to his left hand while catching a fly ball in a game at Oakland. After making a catch near the fence, he used his left hand to cushion his collision. His hand found a protruding nail, a portion of which pierced his hand and remained within the tissue until a doctor found it nearly a week later. He played every day with the injury, but his average fell to .290. After the nail was removed and his hand stitched, he brought his average back up to finish at an even .300.

No one seemed more pleased than Skiff by the performance of his pitcher-turned-outfielder.

"I'll give you one thing," he said. "You played hard for me and you played hurt for me. I'll get you your shot at the big leagues!"

He was true to his word. Shortly after returning home from Seattle, Ed was contacted by the Chicago White Sox. Skiff had phoned White Sox manager Jimmy Dykes and told him he had a ballplayer who was as tough as, well, nails. The White Sox drafted Ed and brought him to Chicago in the spring of 1944.

The young man who had tried to emulate Carl Hubbell was back in the big leagues, not as a pitcher, but as an outfielder. Ed was one of only a handful of major leaguers during the last century who started their careers as pitchers, but managed to play at least one full season as a position player. Ruth, O'Doul, Wood and Rube Bressler had done it prior to 1920. Johnny Cooney did it in the 1930s. Willie Smith and Bobby Darwin accomplished the feat in the '60s and '70s.[18]

"I was fortunate enough where I was fast, and I was a pretty good hitter. I never had a good arm in the outfield, so left field was good for me because I didn't have to throw so far. I know I could have pitched and would have just loved to, but I never really got the chance when my arm was right."[19]

Ed started his renaissance season as a utility player. On paper, the White Sox had a solid outfield going into the '44 season. Wally Moses was the right fielder and had stolen 56 bases the year before. Thurman Tucker was an All-Star center fielder who stole 29 bases himself. Guy Curtright had hit .291 a year earlier and seemed likely to stay in left field. Ed spent the first month of the season spelling each of them when he could. After Tucker went down with a severe cold, Ed played a few games in center field. Later, he filled in for Hal Trosky at first base.

Trosky had been one of the premier sluggers in the American League during the 1930s. With Cleveland in 1936, he batted .343 with 42 home runs and 162 RBIs. Besieged by migraine headaches, he retired at the end of the '41 season, when he was just 28 years old. Lacking a power-hitting first baseman, the White Sox convinced him to return that spring.[20]

"We had only eight teams in each league, and the competition was pretty fierce. We were afraid not to play if we got hurt. I was afraid to get out of the lineup once I got in a Chicago. Somebody else was sitting on the bench who was maybe as good, or maybe better. That's how I got in. Curtright got heavy. I was afraid to get back out, 'cause I was afraid he'd get back in."[21]

Regardless of where Jimmy Dykes played him, Ed batted second for most of the season. He made the most of his playing time, hitting safely in 17 of his first 18 games. By mid–June, he was among the leading hitters in the American League. On June 22, *The Sporting News* ran a brief article on him describing, among other things, how he "gave up" pitching in Seattle. The headline read: "Hill Sit-Down Lifted Carnett to White Sox as Handyman."[22]

A photo shows a smiling Trosky ceremoniously presenting Ed with his first baseman's glove.

"I was a different kind of hitter then. I was one of those line drive hitters, like George McQuinn—the kind that would just make you mad as hell when you pitched against them. I hit a lot of doubles and triples. I legged a few out."[23]

Ed hit .276 in 457 at-bats. He drove in 60 runs, second on the club to Trosky's seventy. He had 18 doubles and eight triples, and he struck out just 35 times. On July 22, he connected off the Yankees' Walter "Monk" Dubiel for his first and only major league home run.

"I was just protecting the plate. When I hit the ball, I knew I'd hit it good. I didn't hit it high, and I knew that wind comes in from right field off of Lake Michigan. The first thing I knew, it was over the fence."[24]

He enjoyed playing for the White Sox and was happy to fill in wherever he was needed. Even when Jimmy Dykes asked him to pitch in relief on two occasions, he did not complain. He gave up two earned runs in two innings of work. He participated in various pregame contests and fund-raising events typical of wartime baseball. On one occasion, he was chosen to run a foot race against the Senators' George Case, who had led the American League in stolen bases for each of the last five seasons.

"George Case—I guess he was the fastest in baseball. It was before a game, and we were to run the proportions of the old ballpark, from the right field line to the left field line. I did pretty well for about the first thirty yards!"[25, 26]

Some occasions were more somber. Not long after the Allied invasion of Normandy, Ed and a few other White Sox players visited Valley Forge Hospital in Philadelphia. They moved through the rows of beds and visited with wounded veterans. At one point, Ed and Trosky were ushered into a room and introduced to a soldier who had lost both eyes to shrapnel. Learning that one of his visitors was the great Hal Trosky, the soldier rose, grabbed an imaginary bat, and perfectly affected Trosky's stance at the plate.

"I mean to tell you, that was one of the toughest things I ever went through. I can still see that big Swede standing up there with no eyes.

If that wasn't a tear-jerker, there's nothing that ever was. Trosky stayed right there with him, too. He didn't go any further."[27]

Ed was physically fit for military service. He was married and had a family to support, but was willing to go if and when the War Department came calling. He was traded to the Cleveland Indians in the fall of 1944, in exchange for outfielder Oris Hockett. He lasted just 30 games with Cleveland before he was inducted into the navy. He did his basic training at Great Lakes Naval Base just north of Chicago.

The baseball team at Great Lakes was considered one of the best "professional" teams in 1945 in that most of its players were taken from major league rosters. Walker Cooper was the catcher. Johnny Groth played center. Pitchers included Clyde Shoun, Denny Galehouse and team captain, Bob Feller.

Feller had been one of the first major leaguers to enlist after Pearl Harbor. He spent much of the war aboard the USS *Alabama* and routinely saw action in the Pacific. With the war nearly over, he was shipped stateside where he rejoined the Indians before the end of the '45 season. While at Great Lakes, Feller began to tinker with a slider, hoping it would complement his remarkable fastball. He sought advice on how to throw the pitch from anyone who could give it.

Through one source or another, Feller found out that Ed could throw a slider. Ed's basic training had not yet ended, and he was not a member of the Great Lakes team. Still, Feller arranged to have him driven from basic training to the ballpark. He tutored the great pitcher on the basics of the pitch. Since there was no available catcher, Ed put on the gear and caught him. Feller added the pitch to his repertoire, where it stayed for the rest of his career.[28] Ed played first base for Great Lakes for several months until he was assigned to a naval air station in Norman, Oklahoma, just twenty miles from his wife and daughter.

Upon his release from the navy, Ed spent several weeks on the Cleveland roster, a gesture made to most ballplayers returning from the service. Cleveland gave Ed his release, and he was signed once again by Seattle. He split his time between the outfield and first base, but he struggled at the plate, batting just .204 in 52 games.

In June of 1946, a bus crash killed nine members of the Spokane Indians of the Western International League. In a compassionate move, the league president allowed teams to assign players conditionally to Spokane for the remainder of the season. Teams from the WIL and Coast League responded, mostly sending their dregs to the crippled team. In the process, team rosters in both leagues were effected.

3. Ed Carnett

Amid all the chaos, Seattle manager Jo Jo White approached Ed with a proposition. While on a road trip to Oakland, White asked Ed if he would be interested in managing the Vancouver Capilanos in the WIL. He hadn't really considered it. In fact, he wondered if White's offer wasn't a polite way of saying that Seattle wasn't happy with his play. Thinking he might be released if he declined, Ed accepted the offer.

News of the transaction passed from player to player at the hotel, eventually reaching the ear of an old nemesis. Casey Stengel was the manager of the Oakland Oaks and resided at the hotel where Seattle was staying. He hunted Ed down and began to bend his ear.

"We sat down and had a talk. He gave me a few pointers. He finally said, 'You were pretty mad at me up at Boston that day, weren't you?'

"I said, 'Yeah, Case, I was. I like you, but I think you were wrong. You didn't give me a chance to warm up, and it wasn't fair to me.'

"He said, 'You woulda really tried to whoop me?'

"I said, 'Well, I'da tried. I don't know if I woulda or not.'"[29]

Neither Ed nor Stengel harbored any resentment toward the other. Stengel offered a few pointers on managing, a gesture that Ed most appreciated. The two parted company, having made their peace.

As things turned out, the fanfare preceding the Vancouver job was for naught. Ed went north to manage the Capilanos, a Boston Braves farm club, and stayed for several months. The team's owner loved Ed and wanted him to stay on to manage for as long as he wanted. But by season's end he was back in Seattle. Earl Torgeson, the Rainiers' first baseman, went down with an injury.

"They called me back down to Seattle. I played first base. One Sunday afternoon I slid into second base and ripped up my knee. I had to crawl off the field. I went home, and they released me that fall. That's one thing about baseball back then before guaranteed contracts: you could get your pink slip any time. Everybody got them at one time or another."[30]

After a brief stint back with Tulsa in the Texas League, Ed landed with the Wichita Falls Spudders in the Class B Big State League. Even after hitting better than .350, he still had a difficult time keeping a job.

"We had a lot of good times, and we had times that were tough. It's pretty tough when you're going real good and they release you because you got a bonus coming. That happened down at Wichita Falls. I signed up for a small bonus that wasn't too good. The guy that was running the club was a good friend of mine.

"One day he called me up to the office just before the ballgame started. Somebody had bought the club. He fidgeted around, and I figured what was happening. I knew [the new owner] wasn't going to pay me that bonus when he had another kid out there [who] was a pretty good ballplayer. I said, 'Just give me the pink slip, Bob. I'll get my stuff so I can go home.'"

"The Paris ballclub was coming over. The manager came over and said, 'What's the matter? You hurt?'

"I said, 'Naw, I got my release.'

"He said, 'Hey, call me after the game!'

"I called him, and I guess I was out of a job for about four hours. I played for Paris for the rest of the year. But it's things like that [that] make you go back and look over it. My wife cried like a baby. She was pregnant. I had to tell her [that] sometimes it's pretty tough. You laugh about it later, but it wasn't so funny at the time."[31]

The Wichita Falls GM felt so bad about releasing Ed that he got him a job with the Borger Gassers of the West Texas-New Mexico League. He was back in the low minors (Class D), but he was managing again, as well as playing.

"Oh, that was a good town! The wind blew out and the parks were all small. That was one of those kinds of years where you can't do anything wrong, even if you try."[32]

The West Texas-New Mexico League was a Class C adventure that lasted for parts of three decades and provided one of the only sources of entertainment for ranchers and oil roughnecks. The combination of warm desert air and notoriously poor pitching created a haven for hitters. Some of the most auspicious offensive numbers in the history of professional baseball were posted in the WT-NM during the late 1940s. Ed Carnett was right in the thick of it.

He had his best offensive season in 1948 with Borger, batting a remarkable .409 with 230 base hits in 563 at-bats. He had 59 doubles and 33 home runs, scored 158 runs and drove in 161. Incredibly, his average was only good for fourth best in the league. Thirty-nine-year-old Hersh Martin, once an outfielder with the Cardinals and Yankees, hit a whopping .425 to lead the league. Ed's 33 home runs were the sixth highest total in the league, but less than half the total of the league leader, Bob Crues.

Ed Carnett hit .276 for the White Sox in 1944 and later hit over .400 in the minor leagues. ©Brace Photograph.

Crues never played major league baseball, but through his exploits in the low minors, he became something of a legend. Much like Ed Carnett, Crues failed as a pitcher but continued to find work as a hitter. After the war, he came to the West Texas-New Mexico League and split time between Lamesa and Amarillo. In his first season as a regular position player, Crues batted .341 with 29 homers and 120 runs batted in.

He answered that year with a .380 effort in 1947, socking 52 home runs and driving in 178.

As impressive as those statistics might appear, Crues's 1948 season was one for the books. Playing for Amarillo, he batted .404 and finished sixth behind Ed Carnett. But he led the league with 69 home runs, tying what was then the existing home run record for organized baseball, held by Joe Hauser since 1933. Moreover, he established organized baseball's all-time record for runs batted in with 254, 63 RBIs more than Hack Wilson's seemingly unbreakable major league total of 191. And he did it within the cozy confines of a 140-game schedule.

On one occasion, Ed crossed paths with Crues. In addition to managing the Borger team, Ed played outfield and occasionally took the mound to rest his staff or rescue a shell-shocked youngster from further abuse. Starting a game against Amarillo one afternoon, Ed surrendered three home runs to Crues, but atoned for the offense by clubbing three of his own.

"When I went into managing, I was more of a power hitter. I changed my batting style a little bit. We had a good hitting ball team. We didn't have too many pitchers, but we had a lot of fun.

"We would be down six or seven runs with two outs in the ninth inning, and we'd win some ballgames. I enjoyed it. I had a chance to work with a bunch of young kids, [and] some of them I sent up a little higher.

"It was kind of a renegade league. You signed for five or six hundred dollars a month, and then you'd have three or four hundred dollars more in that envelope every month."[33]

There were other "perks" that were unique to baseball in the southwest. It wasn't unusual for players to receive cash rewards for home runs—a gesture provided by the fans in the stands.

"If you hit a home run in a close ballgame, why, they'd stick money through the fence. Hell, I got about $350 one night for hitting a home run to win a ballgame. They did that all over the league.

"I had one guy hit a home run off me to win a ballgame. I think he got $460. I told him he should split it with me! They were all pretty good sports down there. They didn't rawhide you too much."[34]

In 1950, Ed hit .361 with 24 home runs and 135 RBIs. His pitching arm came back that year, and he went 13–6 with a league-best 3.15 ERA. He spent six seasons in the WT-NM and held just about every position that existed. In addition to pitching, playing the outfield and first base, and managing the ball club, he spent several seasons as

Borger's general manager. He even made an extra $100 each month by driving the team bus. A *Sporting News* article in 1951 called him "Mr. Five Jobs."[35]

He continued in professional baseball as a player until 1955, when he was released as playing manager of Ponca City, still a Cubs farm club. In twenty professional seasons, he had come full circle.

Not long after, the Cubs asked him to become the general manager of the Burlington Flints in the Class B Three-I League. Ed met with Flint owner Paul Bonewitz, and the two hit it off immediately. Ed took the position, and by 1957 he was Burlington's executive vice president.

He resigned that post in the fall of 1957 to become the club manager of the Burlington Golf Club. Bonewitz was the club president. He stayed on at the club for four more years, eventually leaving to work for Bonewitz Chemical Services, rising to the level of vice president in charge of sales and marketing. He retired to Lebanon, Missouri, and is active in many local affairs, keeping a pace that would tire men and women half his age.

"I always liked to play ball, and I probably would have played for nothing. In fact, we did! But it was all right. It was good money back in those days. I don't begrudge those guys who get all the money they can get. The public is fickle. They forget about you pretty quick. I don't miss playing the ball so much as I do seeing all of the people.

"I missed the pension by a couple of months. I never lost anything there neither, 'cause, hell, I never had any to start with. You can be bitter, or you can take things as they are. You can be tickled to death that you met a lot of fine people and fans. I always conducted myself where I could always go back to where I came from. That probably was the most important thing for me."[36]

4

Lee Pfund

In the summer of 1941, Lee Pfund was in the middle of his first season of professional baseball, pitching in Albany, Georgia, a St. Louis Cardinals affiliate in the low minors. He and his wife-to-be were planning to marry after the season was over. But the bride's sister announced that her own wedding was being moved up to August to accommodate her fiancee's teaching schedule. The sisters' mother was a widow. To save on the cost of two weddings, both couples decided to condense them into one affair.

Lee was 22 years old and a regular in Albany's starting rotation. He now had the dubious task of asking his manager's permission to leave the club for a week and, more importantly, to miss his next scheduled start.

Lee was already in Dutch with his ball club, though not for any offense or lack of responsibility on his part. A religious young man, he agreed to play professional baseball on the condition that he would not play on Sundays. His family had always honored the Lord's day. To play baseball on Sunday would be to denigrate it. Throughout his professional career, Lee stayed true to his convictions and never played on Sundays.

Although his teammates admired his commitment to his faith, he knew that there were also mutterings about his loyalty to the team. The fact that he was going to leave them for a week—even for something so noble as marriage—did not bode well for his future at Albany.

The manager was not unsympathetic to Lee's case. He adjusted his rotation to accommodate his player's beliefs. But when the rookie approached him and asked permission to return to Chicago for his wedding, he decided to have a little fun with him all the same.

"What would you do if I told you no?," he asked. Then, in response to the look of utter despair of Lee's face, he placed a paternal hand on his shoulder and said, "You go with my blessing. I'll pitch you when you get back."

That August, Lee jumped on a train to Chicago—a redeye that departed Albany well after midnight. In spite of the late hour, seats aboard the train were assigned. Lee took his place next to a young woman who was headed to New York. They chatted to pass the time.

> "She asked, "What do you do in Albany?"
> I said, "I play on a professional baseball team."
> She responded, "That's what my father does. He's in professional baseball."
> I said, "Oh, yeah? Where?"
> She said, "He's the general manager of the St. Louis Cardinals."
> I said, "He's my boss!"[1]

The young woman's father turned out to be Branch Rickey, then the general manager of the Cardinals and in charge of their vast farm system, which he had created a decade earlier. Lee was a little taken aback by the identity of his traveling companion, but her revelation ignited their conversation.

"We talked all the way to Atlanta. She was going on a train to New York, and I was going to Chicago. I don't think I ever saw her again. But she went home and told her dad about this conversation with this person who was going home to get married. It just seems [like] that conversation led to other things."[2]

Although Branch Rickey would be an ongoing presence in Lee's career, it was Lee's own father who steered him in the direction of baseball. In spite of the hardships of the times, he encouraged his son to pursue the game. In 1933, he took him to see baseball's first All-Star game, played at Comiskey Park. They stood and cheered when Babe Ruth socked the first-ever All-Star home run.

"My dad loved the game. He never got to play. He was from a big family—eleven kids. He had to quit school after fourth grade to help in the family business. Imagine, at that age.

"I was the one. I had to have a chance. Any time I talked to him about going into his business with him, he'd say, 'No, no. You've got something you can do that's very good. You stay with that.' That was a big thing for me to have that opportunity. In those days, it wasn't the money."[3]

After attending the University of Illinois for two and a half years, Lee began his professional career at Albany in the Georgia-Florida League. His was like so many other rookie seasons—occasional brilliant flashes, but mostly many, many learning experiences. He finished the season with a respectable 10–10 record, but he gave up a whopping 186 hits in just 157 innings, and his ERA was 5.16.

"I probably threw fairly hard then, but they didn't measure speed. I turned out to be a sinkerballer pretty much—the ball that was natural for me to throw, even up here [overhand]. The ball would spin down and in. And then, if I dropped down a little bit, it was like a screwball, although I never really threw it like they throw a screwball, where they'd turn it over. But I came close to that.

"A guy I pitched with in the 1940s, Slick Coffman, used to say, 'There are some nights your fastball isn't working [and] you have to stick it in your back pocket. Some nights your curveball isn't working; you have to stick it in your back pocket. Some nights your change-up isn't working. Stick it in your back pocket.'

"He was talking to me about this after I had been taken out of a game where I didn't have any of that! Some nights you don't have any of 'em, and you don't belong out there!"[4]

Lee wanted to show that he belonged in professional baseball and set out to improve on his first erratic year. He returned to Albany in the spring of 1942 and managed to turn a few heads in spring training. He would have likely returned to Albany in '42, but he asked to be sent to a team closer to home. His wife was expecting their first child, and the doctor had warned that the pregnancy would be a difficult one. It was at this point that Lee had his first personal experience with Branch Rickey.

"He was wonderful to be around. If you try to put me back to what I thought of him back then, leaving out all that I've read about him since—it's hard to separate those two things. The guy was so articulate. He had such a great vocabulary. He could have been a judge, which, in a sense, he was in baseball—a judge of talent. He could have been a doctor, a lawyer. He could have been a great evangelist! But I can remember after talking to him on several occasions, when you think of it—that a man of that stature would talk to a lowly farmhand!"[5]

Rickey called Lee into his office, already briefed on the young player's request. "We have several teams that want you as a result of your spring training," Rickey told him. "Where do you want to play?" Lee chose the Decatur Commodores of the Three-I League. They were closest to home.

"On the Decatur club, I think we had fifty ballplayers on the roster during the whole year. Guys were coming and going all year because of the war. It was only probably a seventeen-man roster."[6]

Lee's first year at Decatur was similar to his previous season at Albany. He won six games while losing 10. He gave up 176 hits in 163 innings, and he walked more batters than he struck out. He did manage to lower his ERA to 4.86.

He stayed out of professional ball for the entire 1943 season. His wife was expecting again, and her questionable health during her pregnancy delayed Lee's draft examination until later that summer. He continued to play ball, latching on with a semipro club in Alton, Illinois. He was ultimately rejected for military service because of a floating bone chip in his left knee—a remnant from an old injury.

That fall, he accepted a teaching position in Wheaton, Illinois, where he and his wife would eventually settle. But in the spring of 1944, the Cardinals organization called him and asked him to report to spring training with the Columbus Red Birds of the American Association.

"I don't know if I would have got that opportunity, except that it was during the war time. I had a bad cold when they called me. I said, 'I'll get there, but I don't think I'll be any use to you until I get over this cold.' I really didn't do any spring training. I just went to Columbus. Then it rained in Columbus for about a week, and we didn't do anything except sit around and wait for the rain to stop. I treated this cold and got pretty well over it."[7]

Still a little weak from the cold, Lee was hammered in his first outing for Columbus. His manager decided not to start him in a regular-season game until his health and good stuff returned. His next appearance was in an exhibition game—a relief appearance against the navy's fine team at Great Lakes Naval Base.

The Great Lakes Bluejackets might have won the pennant in either league in 1944, due mostly to the conspicuous presence of top-drawer major league players who were serving in the navy. At various times during the war, Johnny Mize, Ken Keltner, Dick Wakefield, Denny Galehouse, Bob Feller, and many others played for Great Lakes. The 1944 team was managed by former Detroit Tigers catcher Mickey Cochrane and included erstwhile Tiger pitchers Schoolboy Rowe and Virgil Trucks. Other players included Johnny Gorsica, Gene Woodling, and Hall of Famer Billy Herman.

Great Lakes played a fifty-game schedule, split between major and minor league clubs, colleges, and other military teams. They played and defeated all sixteen major league clubs in 1944 and won 33 games in a row, finishing with a 48–2 record overall.

For a young player looking for an opportunity to prove his worth, there was no truer opponent. And it was onto this stage that Lee Pfund walked for his second appearance with Columbus.

"I went in relief. The first guy I faced flew out to left field, and they scored a run from third base. So that made the second out of the inning. The next hitter was Billy Herman, who had played with the Cubs. Kind of an idol of mine. My highlight was I struck him out on a sidearm curveball, and everybody's eyes kind of opened up! That was my pitch when I was a kid coming up. I wouldn't throw it until I had two strikes on the hitter. So that was like a feather in my cap."[8]

Lee earned a start with that performance and pitched five innings against the Kansas City Royals. He drove in all of the Redbirds' runs with a double and a triple. Red Barrett relieved him with two outs in the sixth inning, and Columbus held on to win. He pitched in nineteen games with the Redbirds, winning four and losing four.

In August, he received word that he was being sent to the Mobile Bears. Mobile was a Cardinal team—a Class A1 affiliate in the Southern Association. Mobile was Lee's turnaround as a pitcher. The Bears were managed by Bill "Buddy" Lewis, a journeyman catcher who had spent time in the big leagues. Lee found a true ally and baseball mentor in Lewis.

"He always said, 'I'll send you to the big leagues!' He would say to me, 'I'm not going to catch you tonight. I'm going to have Harry Chozen catch you.'

"I'd say, 'You said *you* were the one who was gong to send me to the big leagues!' and he would write his name in and catch me. He had more to do with stabilizing my pitching so that I knew what I was doing."[9]

Lee pitched in just 10 games with Mobile to finish the 1944 season. He enjoyed his best success in professional baseball there, notching a 6–2 record with a 3.06 ERA. Lewis did his best to deliver on his boast and send Lee to the majors.

In the fall of 1944, Lee crossed paths once again with Branch Rickey. Rickey had become the president and general manager of the

Brooklyn Dodgers in November of 1942. Cardinal teams he had helped create would win National League pennants in 1943, 1944, and 1946. But Rickey loved the lure of the much larger Brooklyn market.

Lee had been a minor leaguer for three seasons without making the trip to the major leagues. He was eligible to be drafted by another big-league club in the minor league draft. Impressed by Lee's performance at Mobile, the Dodgers selected Lee in the minor league draft of 1944.

The Brooklyn Dodgers of 1944 were a good offensive team, ranking near the top in team batting average and runs scored. Their pitching, however, was the worst in the National League. Brooklyn finished with a 61–93 record. Pitching was Rickey's principal off-season objective. He acquired veteran Tom Seats from the Coast League. He brought up rookies Cy Buker and Ralph Branca. He snatched up Vic Lombardi when he was mustered out of the armed forces. Rickey remembered Lee from his days in the Cardinal organization. He invited him to spring training and looked to use him as a starter during the '45 season.

The Dodgers trained at the Bear Mountain Resort in upstate New York. Even before breaking camp, Leo Durocher seemed high on Lee. In a newsreel filmed for servicemen overseas, the Dodger skipper spoke of his hopes for his pitching staff in '45:

"We acquired some new, young fellas, and I look for them to be much better than what we had last year. The old mainstays are Hal Gregg and Curt Davis, and there'll be a new kid named Pfund."[10]

Lee made his major league debut on April 21, the Dodgers' fifth game of the season. He relieved starter Ben Chapman in the seventh inning and finished the game, a 3–2 loss to the Giants at the Polo Grounds. The first batter he faced was Giants outfielder Steve Filopowicz, who spent two years as a fullback for the football New York Giants. No doubt experiencing some rookie jitters, Lee drilled him in the back with his first pitch. Filopowicz was erased in a double play. Lee retired Phil Weintraub, Ernie Lombardi, Johnny Kerr, Napoleon Reyes, and Bill Voiselle in succession to end the game. In two innings of work, he gave up no hits and no runs.

He credited Mickey Owen and some of the older players with

helping him in the early going. Lee came at hitters from several different angles and used a big windup. Owen helped him with his pitching motion.

He also got help from Dixie Walker, the Dodgers' right fielder and Flatbush favorite. Walker emphasized the need for a pitcher to change speeds regularly, throwing hitters off balance and forcing them to think while they were batting.

"In today's terminology, a guy's throwing at 92 mph, then you see him put it up there at 88. Then you see one at 83. They call them all fastballs. That's what Dixie was saying. He'd hate it when a guy throws one of those at a different speed. He'd say, 'I don't know whether he knows that he did it. Was it an accident? The fact that they make me think is what helps you as a pitcher. If you can make a batter think, he doesn't hit naturally.'"

He helped me out with things like that."[11]

Lee made several other relief appearances in April and early May. As was his custom, he took Sundays off, and he had Branch Rickey include in his contract a "No Sundays" clause. Rickey no doubt felt a certain kinship with his young pitcher. He was a devout Methodist and he had played under a similar arrangement early in his career.

The "No Sundays" arrangement created an unusual advantage for Lee. Sundays were traditionally "getaway" days for major league ballclubs. Doubleheaders were often played on Sunday, and clubs used Mondays for transit to their next destination on a road trip. By not pitching on Sundays, Lee ensured himself of at least two consecutive days of inactivity in any given week. Even Durocher saw the advantage.

"By May 14, we had an eight-game win streak. I'd been off on Sunday. We'd had a doubleheader. We were down in our pitching some. I had not yet started a game. I was in the outfield, and Durocher sent one of the coaches out to get me. He said, 'Leo wants to see you in the box seats.'

"He wasn't even in uniform. He was still in his street clothes. This was 'early workout,' and he had just come to the ballpark.

"He asked, 'Were you throwing any this morning?'

"I said, 'No, just throwing the ball back in from the outfield.'

"He said, 'I want you to pitch today. You're the starting pitcher.'

"He didn't give me much time to think about it. He said, 'Get ready for the game.'"[12]

The game was played at Ebbets Field against the Pittsburgh

Pirates. Preacher Roe, who would later become one of Brooklyn's "Boys of Summer." pitched for the Pirates. Dixie Walker singled, doubled, tripled, and managed to pick off a runner who had strayed too far off first after a base hit.

"But even all these stellar performances." said the New York Times the following day, "were somewhat overshadowed by the 25-year old Roy [sic] Pfund, Leo Durocher's non–Sunday pitcher, who made his initial major league start a seven-hit triumph against as tough a batting line-up as the National League boasts. The youngster, who doesn't play ball on Sunday 'because our family believes that the seventh day was made for rest, just as it says in the Bible,' showed remarkable poise throughout his winning effort."[13]

Lee Pfund offers a few tips to young hopefuls shortly after signing with the Dodgers in 1945. Lee's "No Sundays" clause put him in street clothes on Sundays when his teammates were in uniform. Courtesy of the Wheaton College Archives, Wheaton College, Illinois.

After starting off sharp, Lee gave up a triple to Pirate second baseman Jack Saltzgaver in the third. Center fielder Johnny Barrett followed with a single, and the Pirates broke a scoreless tie. The Dodgers tied the score in the fourth and took the lead for good in the seventh. Lee encountered trouble only one other time during the game.

"With two outs in the eighth inning, I walked two guys on eight pitches. Obviously, I was getting a little tired. I had not gone more than two innings before that. I don't know how many pitches I'd thrown. At that point, we're leading four to one, and somebody got up in the bullpen. In those days, we didn't do that too much. They expected you to go the distance. But I saw the guy get up in the right field bullpen. They called time."[14]

Durocher emerged from the dugout and began a slow walk to the mound. Mickey Owen was catching, and he made it to the mound before Durocher. Pittsburgh first baseman Babe Dahlgren, a right-hander who had gone hitless in the game, was due to bat. Pirates manager Frankie Frisch called him back to the dugout in favor of left-handed pinch hitter, Frank Colman.

"Owen said, 'We can curve him and get him out of there.'"

"Well now, here comes Durocher from the dugout. I don't want to come out of the game. This is my opportunity to show him I can do something. I even turned my back on him. When he got to the mound, he was just sort of scratching around. I just figured he was waiting for the other guy to get warm in the bullpen."[15]

At last, Durocher asked, "Lee, did Mickey tell you how to pitch to this guy?"

"Yes, he did," Lee answered.

"I guess I'll get back in the dugout," said the Dodger manager. "I don't know what in the hell I walked out here for!"

"The language didn't bother me, but what he did say was, 'I believe in you. You go ahead and finish this out.'"[16]

The Ebbets Field crowd cheered Durocher for leaving the young pitcher in the game. Colman saw nothing but curveballs and, on an 0-2 pitch, popped up to Eddie Stanky to end the threat. Lee pitched a scoreless ninth and won the ballgame.

"Durocher was a lot like Dr. Jekyll and Mr. Hyde, but he treated me like an uncle would treat a nephew. I couldn't ask for better treatment. Whether Rickey told him that this guy's of a different ilk—he won't understand it if you use a lot of profanity or whatever—he just never did. He challenged me. He encouraged me. He patted me on the back, but he never reamed me out. Never. I heard him do it something terrible, so I know there was a difference. Whether he thought I was that good a prospect in his eye, I don't know. He was a hellraiser, to use the common term. Guys had all kinds of speculations as to where he spent his time. But on the ball field, he was all business."[17]

Lee found that Durocher looked after his players, too, and he wasn't afraid to stick his neck out when he felt they were being slighted or unnecessarily harassed.

"I had a situation that happened to me in Cincinnati. I was relieving on a Saturday, since I wasn't going to pitch on Sunday. They would use me then in short relief, sort of to mop up. The guy I was going to pitch to had three hits and was coming up for the fourth time. Back then, they'd say that if you're going to throw at somebody, or you're going to knock them down, don't tell anybody about it. We knew we were supposed to back people off the plate."[18]

Lee tested the reflexes of the hitter on his first two pitches, brushing him back off the plate each time. He eventually bounced out to second for the third out of the inning.

"Bill McKechnie was the Cincinnati manager, and he coached first base. Before I could get into our dugout, he timed his walk so that he'd meet me as I came across the line. He said, 'A fine thing for a preacher, doing that to a great hitter!' I was never a preacher, but he knew about the Sunday thing. I didn't answer him back. I went over to the dugout, and both Durocher and Dressen were on the dugout steps. 'What'd he say? What'd he say?' I told them."[19]

From the top step of the dugout, Durocher and Dressen serenaded McKechnie with their own brand of music until he reached the Reds' dugout.

After the complete-game victory against the Pirates, Lee was a regular in the Brooklyn starting rotation. Just four days after his victory, he squared off against the Cubs at Ebbets Field. The Cubs treated him to a rude awakening, knocking him out in the second inning. He was saved from a loss in part by the hitting of Luis Olmo, who both homered and tripled with the bases loaded—the last time anyone has accomplished the feat. Brooklyn won, 15 to 12.

Durocher kept him in the rotation, and he bounced back nicely against the Cardinals when the Dodgers went on their next western road trip. In front of his wife and son, both of whom he hadn't seen since spring training, he went the distance once again in an 11–2 victory. He gave up a run-scoring single to Whitey Kurowski and a solo home run to center fielder Buster Adams. But three Dodgers homered in the game, including another grand slam by Olmo.

Lee helped his own cause with an RBI single. On the mound, he gave up eight hits, while walking one and striking out five. He was 2–0, with two complete-game victories in the month of May. His stock within the Dodger organization was starting to rise.

Rickey liked to look in on his ballplayers from time to time. Not long before the victory against the Cardinals, he called Lee into his office. The press called Rickey's office "the cave of the winds," mostly because of its occupant's affinity for long-winded sermons on any topic that was handy. When Lee arrived, Rickey was multitasking as usual, chewing on a trademark cigar and talking over his shoulder to his secretary about a flight he had to catch in an hour. When he found a spare moment, he asked, "Well, my boy, how are you getting along?"

By now, Lee had met with Rickey on several occasions. He felt that he could speak candidly with the man, and he told Rickey that he was having trouble making ends meet. He couldn't find an apartment near the ballpark that was within his means, and as a young man with a family, he had other expenses.

He was looking more for advice than cash, but Rickey didn't see it that way. The fatherly facade disappeared, and he proceeded to read the riot act to his young pitcher. He did not renegotiate contracts in midseason. "You negotiated this contract at the *beginning* of the year!"

"Well, we went on the road, and I won the game in St. Louis. We went to Pittsburgh, and I got credit for the win. We came back, and in my box at the St. George Hotel were two envelopes."[20]

The first envelope contained Lee's paycheck. The second contained a note from Rickey. He said that the ball club had decided to retain Lee's services for the remainder of the season. Rosters would be trimmed in June, but Lee's job was safe for now. Rickey also said that he wanted Lee to have a bonus, and he included a draft for $700.

"That was his answer to my request—enough money to get along. That's the way he operated. He treated you like he wanted to treat you for what you were doing. I had three contract negotiations with him, [and] he knew what he was going to pay you."[21]

Perhaps Lee's best game came on June 20 in a night game at Ebbets Field against the Giants. Lee and Giants starter Harry Feldman traded scoreless innings into the eighth, when Lee was removed for a pinch hitter. Clyde King took over for Lee and pitched the next four innings. Brooklyn won the game in twelve by the score of 2–1.

"I pitched in fifteen games [ten starts] from May 14 til July 10. It was so much better than any other place I played. I saw and/or pitched in the old ballparks: Ebbets Field, the Polo Grounds, Braves Field in Boston, Shibe Park, Crosley Field, Sportsman's Park, Wrigley Field, and Forbes Field."[22]

He was treated roughly in each of his next four starts, and he did not start again after June 30. He tended to pitch in extremes — either masterfully or horribly. Durocher wanted more consistency, and he used him in the bullpen to see if he could find the stuff he had thrown earlier against the Pirates and Cardinals. He was still in the pen at the All-Star break in July.

"If you go back and look, 1945 was the only year there was no All-Star game since 1933. What we were doing was playing Red Cross benefit games against a matchup. The Cubs played the White Sox. The two Philadelphia teams played each other, and the two Boston teams. Cleveland played Detroit. The Giants played the Yankees. We played Washington.

"I was the starting pitcher, but just before the game was supposed to start, we had a downpour. A real deluge. They covered the mound and home plate, but they never had a chance to cover the infield, and everything got soaked. It was a benefit game, so we couldn't walk off the field and say the game was canceled. You know — the people contributed their money, and we're not going to play?"[23]

In the second inning, Lee faced Jose Zardon, a Cuban outfielder who was very fast on his feet. Zardon topped a sinker — a swinging bunt that died on the wet turf as it rolled toward third. Lee ran for the ball and bent to pick it up. When he did, his left knee — the one with the bone chip — locked, causing him to shift all his weight on his right leg. The leg slipped on the wet grass, and he felt something twist in the knee. He went down on the turf and grimaced in pain. His day was over, and he had to be helped from the field.

"They put heat on my leg, and it swelled up like a football. They didn't use ice. I was in the hospital in Washington for two days, and then I went back to New York. Apparently, it didn't tear the cartilage. I just had a weak knee for a long time."[24]

He might have returned later in the '45 season, but Rickey had other plans. "I don't want you to come back this year," he said. For effect, he harkened back to his Cardinal days and told the story of Dizzy Dean.

In the 1937 All-Star game, Dean broke his toe when a line drive off the bat of Earl Averill struck his foot. It was a simple foot injury, but Dean came back too soon. The toe still bothered him, and he changed his pitching style to compensate. Not long after, he developed arm trouble and never pitched with his pre-injury dominance again.

"You're not going to come back with this type of injury," Rickey told Lee. "I'll give you the rest of the summer, fall, and winter to get over it."

He finished the season with three wins and two losses, with a 5.20 ERA. In spite of his inconsistency, Brooklyn fared remarkably well with Lee on the mound. The Dodgers won eight of his ten starts. They also saved some of their best offense for Lee, scoring eight or more runs in seven of his starts. But prior to the injury, he hadn't won since May 30, and his last good outing was against the Giants, nearly a month before.

"I don't know to this day if they were going to send me to St. Paul after that [benefit] game. That happened sometimes after pitching an exhibition game. I was having a little trouble with my control right before that time.

"Anyway, they were very anxious to keep up with me all through that season, although I was never in uniform for them again. They didn't do anything to get me any kind of therapy program. They just didn't do that. You were under contract for five months. I don't mean to say that they didn't care what you did in the off season, but they didn't give me anything to do."[25]

Following the advice of his doctor, he rode a bicycle and did other exercises for strength and flexibility. Feeling confident, he began to play basketball to help pass the long winter months. During a pickup game, he collided with another player and took a direct hit on the knee. This time the injury was serious enough to require him to wear a knee brace during physical activity, including pitching.

"I might have been all right if I hadn't got hit again. That kinda did it in. From then on, I pitched with a knee brace, and I'm sure it effected what I was doing with my arm. I had arm trouble after that."[26]

The Dodgers sent him back to Mobile in the spring of 1946. The injury notwithstanding, Lee's 1946 season was his most productive. He pitched in 38 games, most of them as a starter. The Bears, however, did not produce runs as the Dodgers had a year earlier. Lee lost more ball-games than he won, and many were one-run decisions.

"I pitched several ballgames in '46 where it had been a two-one loss, and I'd pitched all the way. One thing or another usually happened. An error. I walked a couple of batters."[27]

Even so, his chances of returning to the Dodgers in '46 were quite good, due largely to the fact that he had pitched better than his record indicated and that Brooklyn was in the thick of a pennant race. After a strong effort in a loss against the Memphis Chicks, Rickey, by proxy, let Lee know that he wanted him to return.

"One of the Dodgers' scouts came down to see me in Memphis, and he said, 'Mr. Rickey wants to bring you and [catcher] Bruce Edwards back, but we've got to bring you back on a win.' He had seen me pitch, and he said to me, 'You pitched a great ballgame, but tonight's the night.'"[28]

With a clear purpose at hand, Lee bore down harder than usual. He worked two quick innings without allowing a hit. In the third inning, he began to feel a twinge in his right shoulder. It was an unusually hot night, and the shoulder didn't stiffen as it might have on a cooler evening. He worked through the discomfort and finished the inning without allowing a hit. He repeated the effort for the next four innings.

"I went to the eighth with a no-hitter. But in the eighth, whether it was my arm, or I just gave out—I don't remember the circumstances—they got two or three hits in a row. I just couldn't go the distance. That was the end of my going back. It turned out I couldn't even raise my arm the next morning. Whether it was the rotator cuff or not, I don't know. I missed almost three weeks, and I finished up at Atlanta. I really had a sore arm, but I had a pretty good ball game. I think we lost the game, three to two, on an umpire's decision in the ninth inning.

"At the time, I was really disappointed. I wasn't going around bragging to the other players that I was going back. In fact, I didn't even think any of the other players knew it, except for Bruce Edwards. They took him after the ballgame. That was in '46, and they were in the World Series in '47, the next year."[29]

At the end of the 1946 season, Lee's contract was sold to the Montreal Royals of the International League. The Royals and Saints joined the Dodgers in Cuba for spring training in 1947. The three teams played exhibition games with each other in preparation for the trip north. Clearly, the Dodgers did not handle Lee like the hot prospect he had been prior to his shoulder injury. Montreal played seven exhibition games against the Dodgers that spring. Lee saw action in none of them. The Dodger higher-ups were focusing most of their attention on Lee's teammate, Jackie Robinson. Branch Rickey waited until one week before opening day before adding Robinson to the Dodger roster.

"I got to know him. I lockered next to him. A lot of guys shied away from him. It wasn't my nature to do that. I had little idea of how good he was and what the future was for him. He was just an African American ballplayer and was friendly, so I befriended him.

We were almost exactly the same age. I would ride the bus into the stadium with him. We talked about our faith together—about what the Bible said about salvation in Christ.

"I talked with him after he was brought up with the Dodgers in the Ebbets Field clubhouse. So I got to know him pretty well. In the '50s, I took all three of my boys to Cubs games when the Dodgers were there. Jackie was the one who would invite us up to the clubhouse. In those days, we didn't think as much about autographs as they do now. Our whole thing was just to be with him and the others we knew."[30]

Lee would split the 1947 season between Montreal and St. Paul, where he would compile a 6–7 record. All the while he fought pain in his knee and subsequent arm trouble. He played two more seasons of professional ball before leaving the game in 1950.

He eventually went back to Wheaton College, where he remained a fixture in intercollegiate athletics for three decades. He coached baseball and basketball at Wheaton. In 1957, he led his Crusaders to a College Division NCAA National Championship (later Division II schools). They defeated Kentucky Wesleyan, 89–65.

His son, Randy, whom Lee coached at Wheaton in the early 1970s, went on the coach the Los Angeles Lakers for two seasons and is now president and general manager of the Miami Heat organization. When the Lakers won an NBA championship while he was an assistant coach, he gave his championship ring to his dad.

Lee's legacy is long and fruitful. A lectureship and a basketball tournament bear his name at Wheaton College. He has influenced the lives of dozens of young men and women over the years. The memories are abundant and mostly pleasant. He still harkens back to his lone season in the big leagues—a special time worthy of quiet, reflective moments.

"Playing in the big leagues was the culmination of a boyhood dream and goal. We traveled by train—sleepers overnight to Boston, Chicago, and St. Louis—stayed in the best hotels, had quality uniforms and altogether had an exciting, fun time.

"We were treated very well by fans, players, and management. I never heard the words 'replacement players' until the years of the recent strikes, though that is an easy description now, 55 years later. I never felt anything but great respect from Branch Rickey, Leo Durocher, Charlie Dressen—our team, opponents, and fans. All those kinds of experiences were good for me for what I hoped to do in my life when my baseball career was over."[31]

5

George Hausmann

George Hausmann readily confides that had it not been for the war, it is unlikely the major leagues would have had much demand for a 5'5" second baseman. Understandably, he is fiercely proud of his time in the majors, and rightly so. After earning the starting second base job for the Giants early in the 1944 season, he started every game at second through the last game of 1945. He distinguished himself in the field as well as at the plate, earning the right to play major league ball even when so many regular players came home from the war.

He was a perennial little guy—a self-effacing Everyman, confident of his skills and triumphant in scenarios where he seemed likely to fail. On the field, he controlled his own fate. But the Goliaths of Major League Baseball lurked everywhere—as plentiful off the field as on it— and were quick to remind Hausmann and his contemporaries just how little power they had. 1946 was arguably baseball's most chaotic season since the Black Sox scandal, historically overshadowed by the heroics of Jackie Robinson just one year later. George Hausmann's role in it all was not unlike the man himself: small, but compelling.

In 1937, George was working at his summer job at an insurance firm in his hometown of St. Louis when he received word of a tryout camp held by the Browns. He was known around St. Louis as a good "little" ballplayer—quick on his feet, good with the glove and a tough out at the plate. He called Lou Magualo, his American Legion coach and later a scout in the Yankees' organization. Magualo encouraged him to attend the camp, going so far as to offer to drive him across town to Sportsman's Park.

George joined the camp on the last of three days. Magualo had pulled a few strings with contacts he had as a bird dog scout in the Browns' organization, and they agreed to give a look to the young second baseman.

5. George Hausmann

By his own recollection, George stood about 5'4" and weighed a slight 120 pounds in the summer of 1937. After participating in various drills, the coaches staged a scrimmage to test the players' abilities in a game situation. On the very last play of that game, the diminutive Hausmann hit a deep, fly ball that one-hopped the left field wall. As he motored around second base, he caught sight of the third base coach, who motioned for him to keep running. The left fielder threw a strike to the third baseman, who tagged a sliding Hausmann for the final out.

George figured correctly that the coach was just trying to gauge his speed by sending him, but he was still a little dejected at having made the game's final out. Magualo approached him afterwards and invited him up to the front office. The coaches and scouts *had* been impressed with his performance and, at Magualo's urging, signed him to a professional contract at $60 a month.

The following spring, the Browns' front office asked if he'd be willing to go down to Laredo, Texas. The second baseman for the Corpus Christi Spudders of the Texas Valley League had decided to quit three weeks into the spring camp. Leagues in the deep south routinely began play earlier than others, and Corpus Christi had just a week to go before their regular season would begin. Expecting to have to fight for a job at a Class D affiliate in Mayfield, Kentucky, George readily agreed to the offer and boarded a train the following day.

He arrived in Laredo and set about finding his hotel. At the front desk, he asked who he should get in touch with on the ball club. Charlie DeWitt, he was told.

DeWitt turned out to be the traveling secretary of the St. Louis Browns and the younger brother of Bill DeWitt, the Browns' general manager. George found him and introduced himself. DeWitt shook his hand and called over Rod Whitney, the Corpus Christi manager. Whitney was a small man himself, standing about 5'8" tall—still considerably taller than George. He was a career minor leaguer—a tough catcher, about 35 years old.

"Here's your new second baseman!" DeWitt said.

Whitney took one look at Hausmann, and his face fell.

"He looked at me like I wasn't there," George remembered.[1]

Whitney offered him a dead-fish handshake and engaged him in polite, but brief, conversation. After George went upstairs to his room, Whitney turned to face DeWitt.

"You son of a bitch!" he roared. "I'm ready to start the season, and you send me a batboy!"

Whitney's reservations toward his second baseman were quickly set aside. George produced robust statistics in his first professional season. In just 131 games, he had 198 hits, good for a .355 average, fifth best in the league. In addition to his 14 home runs, he added 14 triples, 38 doubles, 157 runs scored and 120 RBIs. When he returned home to St. Louis that fall, he found nearly every scout in town taking credit for his discovery.

He made the jump to Class B ball in 1939, playing with Springfield in the Three-I League. Against stiffer competition, he managed a .316 batting average, although he hit just five home runs and drove in 57. Within a year, he was playing second base for the San Antonio Missions of the Texas League. He would play three seasons with San Antonio and was always around .300 at the plate.

In 1943, he was sent to New Orleans of the Southern Association, another Class A1 ball club with a working agreement with the Brooklyn Dodgers. At New Orleans, George was able to boast that he was not the smallest member of the squad. At 5'4½", shortstop Pat Ankenman stood just one half-inch shorter than George. The two made a formidable double play combination. Hausmann batted .298 and Ankenman hit .316. New Orleans manager Ray Blades begged Branch Rickey to bring both players to the big leagues. Ankenman did play briefly for the Dodgers in 1943 and 1944.

George would not get the call to Brooklyn. Instead, he was drafted by the New York Giants in the spring of 1944. The Giants had lost their second baseman, Mickey Witek, to the Coast Guard. Witek had played all but one game for the Giants, batting .314. To fill the void, New York purchased the contract of Hugh Luby, a veteran of the Pacific Coast League who had hit better than .300 in each of his last three seasons for the Oakland Oaks. For his services, the Giants were willing to pay the Oaks the princely sum of $25,000. Picked up in the minor league draft, George was offered $5,000, primarily as insurance for Luby. He expected to start the season at Jersey City, the Giants' top farm club.

One of the special circumstances of wartime baseball had a direct impact on the New York Giants' second base job in 1944, with George Hausmann the beneficiary and Hugh Luby the casualty. To relieve the strain on the nation's railroads created by the war effort, Judge Kenesaw Mountain Landis announced that all major league baseball teams would train north of the Mason-Dixon line and no more than 100 miles from their base of operations. The New York Giants would spend the spring of 1944 at Lakewood, New Jersey, on the estate of John D. Rockefeller.

Hugh Luby lived in California and did not relish the idea of a cold, damp, New Jersey spring. He asked the New York front office if he could remain in California to train, then join the ball club after two or three weeks. The Giants assented, Luby got his wish, and George got an opportunity he hadn't banked on.

Although not long on praise, Giants player-manager Mel Ott was impressed by George's hustle. Luby's absence made George's spring performance all the more conspicuous. By the time Luby arrived in camp, George had already earned a spot on the roster and became the frontrunner for the second base job when the Giants broke camp in April. On opening day at the Polo Grounds, Ott penciled George's name in at the top of the order.

He singled in his first big-league at-bat, off the Braves' Al Javery. Leading off the game, his hit was the first of the season by a New York Giant. By early June, George had won the battle for second base. He would start every game at second for the Giants from June of 1944 until the close of the '45 season.

"One of the sportswriters up in New York about the middle of the season had written that Steve Filipowicz and myself were the only guys who ran on and off the field between innings. We didn't walk. We didn't trot. We ran on and off the field. I guess that's one of the things that impressed Ott. I wasn't what you'd consider a good hitter, but I was consistent, always around .270."[2]

George played in 131 games during his rookie season. He batted .266 with a single home run. He scored 70 runs while driving in 30. Almost always putting the ball in play, he struck out just 25 times in 466 at-bats.

He managed just one home run in 1944, but it was an amusing one. The Giants were playing the Cincinnati Reds, and George found himself mired in a slump. He had been unable to get a ball out of the infield during the previous day's game, and he was getting discouraged.

Before the game he approached umpire Babe Pinelli. Prior to umpiring, Pinelli had hit .276 during his major league career, most of which was spent with the Reds.

"Babe, what in the hell am I doing wrong? I haven't had a hit in a long time."

"You're not swingin' through," offered Pinelli. "Take a good cut!"

George took Pinelli's advice. He faced Reds left-hander Clyde Shoun during the game. In the third inning, he took Shoun's first two offerings, then took a good cut, lining the ball to right field. It rolled

George Hausmann led the Giants in hits in 1945. ©Brace Photograph.

all the way to the wall, giving George the chance to circle the bases for an inside-the-park home run. When he crossed home plate, George winked at Pinelli, who winked back. He went three for four on the night.

Unlike most rookies who were traditionally hazed and sometimes ignored by their teammates, George was lucky enough to have a mentor both on and off the field in veteran Giants catcher Gus Mancuso. George had played minor league ball with Gus's younger brother, Frank, with the San Antonio Missions. The elder Mancuso took George under his wing and became one of the biggest influences in his life.

George and his family followed Mancuso down to Houston in the off season. Gus had arranged for George to take a job working in the

Houston shipyards, a job that was good enough for a wartime deferment. He had been approved for "limited service," but without the deferment he felt certain he would be called as the Allied offensive swept through Europe in the early part of 1945. Prior to the start of spring training, he had privately made the decision to continue working in Houston rather than play major league ball. The fact that he had two small children sealed the deal.

The Hausmanns occupied the downstairs apartment of the house in Houston. The couple who lived upstairs had the building's only phone. A call came through for George one evening in early spring. "Hey, George! Got a call for you! A guy by the name of Mel Ott!" George went upstairs to talk to the Giants' manager. He had already told Ott of his plans to continue working at his defense job, but he listened to Ott's deal. He had played for $5,000 in 1944, and Ott offered to up the ante to $6,000. George declined.

Ott phoned again the following evening. "We want you to play, George," he said.

"Yeah, but I can't jeopardize my family. I got two kids. If I play ball, I'll end up in the service."

Ott offered $7,000 for the '45 season. After a little more haggling, he agreed to pay for the cost of transporting George's family back to New York. As it turned out, George caught a bad cold in the spring of 1945, which caused an infection in his ears. He was eventually rejected for military service because of a perforated eardrum. Hugh Luby went back to the Coast League and played for the San Francisco Seals. There was no pressure when he returned in the spring of 1945. The second base job belonged to him.

Had the National League fielded an All-Star squad in 1945, George Hausmann may very well have played on it. His performance that season gives credence to the claim that the wartime ballplayer was more than just a fill-in for the "real" players. He played every game for the Giants that year. In 623 at-bats, he had 174 hits and scored 98 runs. His .279 batting average was second best among regular National League second basemen.

He appeared on the cover of the Giants' home program and scorecard for the 1945 season. The program bore the Giants' insignia as well as a circle containing a black and white photo of George making the pivot on a double play.

He had a 14-game hitting streak in June, and he wowed Giants fans with brilliant performances in consecutive doubleheaders at the end of the month.

In the first game of a doubleheader on June 24, he drove in what would turn out to be the winning run with an eighth-inning single off Phillies pitcher Dick Coffman. *"Hausmann was the heaviest contributor to the Giants' 12-hit output in the opener by coming up with four blows, including a double."*[3] He added a single and a triple in the nightcap to go six for eight on the day. The Giants won both games.

After two days off for travel and a rainout, the Giants played another doubleheader on June 27, this time against the Pirates. George reprised his performance in the first game of the Phillies twin bill, with four hits in five at-bats. The Giants won, 10–4.

They trailed 2–0 in the ninth inning of the second game, but looked like they might pull off another sweep. After loading the bases with nobody out, Giants catcher Ernie Lombardi grounded to third. Pirates third baseman Lee Handley gloved the ball, stepped on third for the force, and threw to catcher Bill Salkeld, who tagged a sliding Billy Jurges for an unlikely 5–2 double play. Jim Mallory followed with a single that drove in the runner from third. Lombardi was lifted for a pinch runner, and George followed.

"Georgie, who had a triple and three singles in four [sic] attempts in the opener and who had collected two singles, a pass and a sacrifice in the second contest, worked the count to 3 and 2 and as both runners started to run Hausmann broke up the ball game with a long drive to left center. It was quite a day for Hausmann, who made seven hits in eight trips to the plate and drove home four runs, as his club's winning streak reached four."[4]

And it was quite a performance over the course of two days and four games. In the consecutive doubleheaders, George went a combined 13 for 16 with six RBIs, two triples, and a game-winning double off the Pirates' Preacher Roe.

He doubled his home run output in his second season, clubbing two in 1945. His most memorable round-tripper came on June 19. It wasn't so much the hit, but the circumstances surrounding the day that were special.

"I hit one off knuckleballer Jim Tobin. It was kind of a spectacular day because General Eisenhower was at the ballpark. He had just arrived from Europe by plane. The Yankees and Dodgers were out of town, and we happened to be playing against Boston. They say he came directly from the airport to the ballgame. I hit a home run against Tobin in that game. Felt pretty good hitting a home run with General Eisenhower sitting there watching the game."[5]

Like many so-called "wartime ballplayers," George wasn't quite sure what the future held for him after the war. He knew that the competition for jobs in the spring would be hot—a veritable hodge-podge of talent created by returning veterans and those wartime players who were good enough to stick. He hoped that he would be one of those who earned that privilege. And why not? He had started every game at second base and led the team in hits, at-bats and runs scored. If any wartime player had distinguished himself at the big league level, surely it was George.

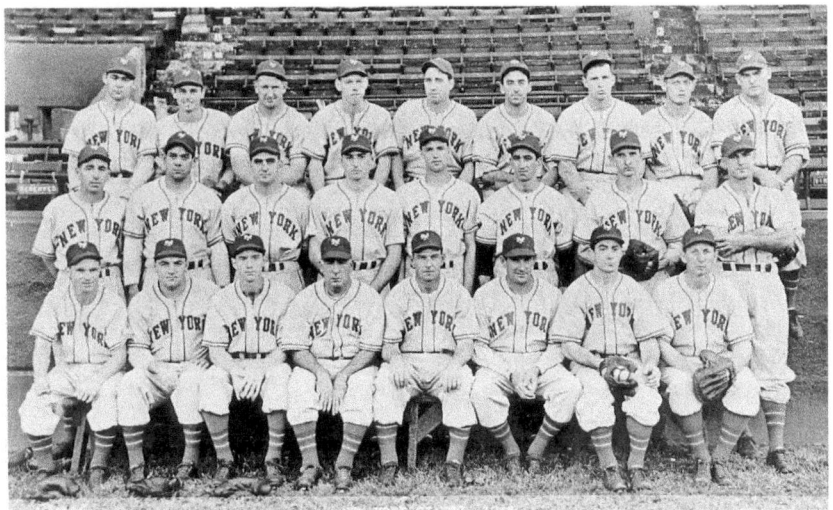

The 1945 New York Giants. Top row: Rube Fischer, Jack Brewer, Ernie Lombardi, Buddy Kerr, Van Lingle Mungo, Sal Maglie, Bill Voiselle, Roy Zimmerman, Don Fisher. Middle row: Johnny Hudson, Nap Reyes, Clyde Kluttz, Harry Feldman, Johnny Rucker, Adrian Zabala, Slim Emmerich, Billy Jurges. Front row: George Hausmann, Ace Adams, Red Treadway, Adolfo Luque, Mel Ott, Bubber Jonnard, Danny Gardella, Ray Berres. In the spring of 1946, Maglie, Zimmerman, Reyes, Feldman, Zabala, Hausmann, Adams, Gardella, and coach Adolfo Luque jumped to the Mexican Leagues in search of higher salaries. All were banished from the major leagues for three seasons. Courtesy *The Sporting News*.

The returning veterans were not the only presence felt in big league camps during the spring of 1946. Ballplayers across the country were beginning to make the acquaintance of one of the game's least known, but most original characters. Jorge Pasquel was a Mexican entrepreneur and insatiable baseball aficionado. He dreamed of transforming the lackluster Mexican League into a baseball superpower, rivaling the major leagues in every way.

Pasquel's plan was simple enough. To lend legitimacy to his league, he needed talent. In spite of the grand return of players like Feller, Williams and DiMaggio, the '46 season was a tumultuous one. Spring rosters were saturated with returning veterans and wartime players—the former of whom claimed a right to a job by virtue of the Veterans Act, and the latter because they felt they had earned that right based on their performance. Simply put, there were more players than jobs, and Pasquel could pick from the surplus.

But Pasquel wasn't about to content himself with the dregs of major league baseball. Possessing a swaggering bravado and very deep pockets, he set about a meticulous courtship of big-league stars and castoffs. He began planting the seeds of his new league among major leaguers who played winter ball in Cuba after the '45 season. By February of '46, just weeks before the start of spring training, he had his first convert.

Danny Gardella was coming off his first full season as an outfielder for the New York Giants. Had the designated-hitter rule existed in the mid–1940s, Gardella might have been a star. He had batted .272 with 18 home runs and 71 runs batted in, but his ineptitude afield often overshadowed any heroics at the plate. It seemed that every fly ball was an enigma to him, causing one New York writer to quip that Gardella had caught a ball "unassisted."

Gardella was displeased with the Giants' offer for the '46 season. In spite of his outfield adventures, he felt he deserved a raise. He had met Alfonso Pasquel, younger brother of Jorge, at a New York City health club earlier that winter. Pasquel assured Gardella that the Mexican League would more than double the $5,000 he had played for a year earlier. On February 19, Gardella agreed to a contract with the Mexican League for $9,000 and a $5,000 bonus. More importantly, the offer came with a two-year option, something that did not occur in major league baseball under the specter of the reserve clause. As was his custom, Pasquel paid Gardella in cash.

5. George Hausmann

For George Hausmann, the first bit of bad news came when his '46 contract arrived in the mail. "I didn't ask for a raise. I just figured they'd offer me one. When I got my contract, it was the same as it was the year before: $7,000. I sent it back, and I told them that I thought I earned at least *some* raise."[6]

George eventually accepted the Giants' offer, but he had more bad news waiting for him when he reported to spring training. The Giants had divided their team into two spring squads, one composed of returning veterans and shoe-in starters, and the other made up of those players who were less likely to make the opening day roster. It didn't take long for him to realize that he had been relegated to the B squad. Among those players in the same boat as Hausmann were reserve infielder Roy Zimmerman and pitcher Sal Maglie.

Zimmerman was a hard-hitting first baseman who had batted .276 with five home runs in just 97 at-bats. Maglie was the least known of the group. He was already 28 years old when he completed the 1945 season, his first in the major leagues. He won five games and lost four, with a 2.35 ERA and three shutouts. Each of the three found their position with the Giants to be tenuous, at best.

In spite of starting all 154 ballgames at second base for the Giants in 1945, George didn't start any of the first six spring games. Although Mickey Witek had returned from the service, the Giants were giving the early nod at second to Buddy Blattner, a Coast League veteran who had put up impressive power numbers before the war.

"We played our ballgames, and I was always the second one to go in. Blattner was the main prospect. He started all the ballgames until about the sixth or seventh game in spring training. I was getting dressed, and Ott came up to me. "You're playing second today!" he told me. I thought, "Oh boy, finally got a chance here!" As he walked away I looked across the room, and there was Blattner taping up both his legs. He had Charley horses so bad he couldn't hardly walk. That's the only reason that I got to play. That tipped me off, then."[7]

George began to think of Gardella in Mexico, wondering if the promises of higher salaries and multiyear contracts were legitimate. When he returned to the hotel that evening, he and Maglie gave the issue some serious thought. Maglie had made Pasquel's acquaintance while playing winter ball in Cuba. He had reported to spring training in Miami immediately following the conclusion of the Cuban winter season. At George's urging, Maglie called a number provided him by Pasquel and soon found himself talking things over with Danny Gardella.

Maglie and George had two conversations with Gardella over the course of two evenings. The first evening consisted of amiable talk between former teammates with Maglie barely intimating that he and a few other ballplayers might be persuaded to play in Mexico. The following evening, Gardella brought Pasquel into the conversation.

"I got a couple of ballplayers for you," Maglie told him.

"Who?" asked Pasquel.

"George Hausmann and Roy Zimmerman," he replied.

"How much do they want?" he asked.

Maglie covered the phone with his hand and looked across the room at his teammate. George had already told him that if Pasquel was willing to offer a $10,000 salary with a $5,000 signing bonus, he would be willing to go down. Maglie smiled, an idea working in his head. He returned to Pasquel.

"They want a *$13,000* salary, and a $5,000 bonus." George winced at Maglie's $3,000 ad lib, but grinned from ear to ear when Pasquel answered, "OK, send them down." Maglie negotiated the identical agreement for himself, which was considerably more money than Pasquel had been offering a few weeks before in winter ball. He and George told Zimmerman the good news, and word of their deal with Pasquel gradually made its way among the other Giants players.

On the second to last day of spring training, George, Maglie, and Zimmerman were summoned by the Giants brass. Not knowing precisely what was to happen, they were ushered into a room where Mel Ott, traveling secretary Eddie Brannick and Giants owner Horace Stoneham were waiting. Ott wasted no time in getting to the point.

"The first thing Mel said was, 'Are you guys going to Mexico?' We said, 'Yep!' Stoneham says, 'You're all fired! You don't play for New York anymore!' Of course, they can't fire you. They have to give you your release. Then Stoneham said, 'Get out of the hotel. We're not paying your bill anymore!'"[8]

Fortunately, the hotel manager ignored Stoneham's bluster and allowed the three players to remain in their rooms for the two remaining days of spring training. The two days were sufficient time for them to begin plans for the trip down to Mexico, but with them came the dark realization of what had just taken place. They were no longer members of the New York Giants. They were pulling up stakes to play baseball in a another country and had no idea what teams they would play for once they arrived. They were broke and, despite assurances from Gardella, they had no more security than a verbal agreement with a man only one of them had met.

Maglie placed another phone call to Pasquel asking for some advance cash to make the trip to Mexico. Pasquel told him he would wire $1,000 to them by the end of the business day. George, Maglie, and Zimmerman headed to the Western Union office at the appointed time to pick up the cash.

The voucher was in Maglie's name, and the clerk needed some form of identification to turn over the money. He asked Maglie for his driver's license. Maglie didn't have one. In fact, he didn't have any form of identification on him. There was a frantic scramble as the trio tried to find someone who could vouch for them. They finally found a military officer who was known to the Western Union office and could confirm Maglie's identity.

The Western Union gaffe was not the only obstacle they would encounter. Try as they might, the three could not seem to find seats on any train going from Miami to San Antonio. George remembered a pal from New York City and gave him a call.

"I said, 'I know somebody.' He was a lieutenant commander in New York and was in charge of military transportation in and out of New York City. His name was Horgan. He and I became good friends. I called him and told him, 'Hey, Horg. I got a problem.'"

"He said, 'Yeah, I read about it in the paper.'"

"He told us to see a guy at the train station and mention his name. We went down there and told them who we were.

"He said, 'Oh, yeah. Horgan just called me. Here's your tickets to San Antonio!'

"All we wanted was to get a seat on this thing, and they were drawing room tickets! Just goes to show what a little influence can do!"⁹

George spent a night at his home in San Antonio before making the final journey down to Mexico. They crossed the border at Laredo and met with yet another Pasquel brother who headed up the ball club at Nuevo Laredo. Zimmerman stayed on at Nuevo Laredo to play with that team. George and Maglie were flown down to Mexico City to meet with Jorge Pasquel and receive their assignments. Maglie was sent to the Puebla ball club to the north. George spent the evening at Pasquel's home in Mexico City. The following day, he received a uniform from the Torreon Lagunas, which was beginning a series with the Mexico

City Reds later that day. That morning, he started his first game at second base in his new league.

Major League Baseball had been slow in reacting to the "jumpers"—the term that was used to describe those professional ballplayers who "jumped" their contracts in 1946 to play baseball in Mexico. Even after the departure of Gardella, Hausmann, Maglie, and Zimmerman, Pasquel and his brothers aroused only a minimal amount of concern among baseball owners and executives. By the end of March, that indifference was replaced with genuine anxiety.

Other ballplayers began to take Pasquel's money. Vern Stephens, who had led the American League with 24 home runs a year earlier, left the St. Louis Browns to play for Pasquel's own Veracruz team. Dodgers catcher Mickey Owen agreed to become the playing-manager of Torreon. Luis Olmo, who drove in 110 runs for the Dodgers in '45, would soon follow his teammate, Owen.

In early April, new baseball commissioner Albert "Happy" Chandler announced that all players who jumped to the Mexican League would be given a "grace period" to return to their teams that would end at the opening of the 1946 regular season. But he warned them that failure to return prior to the season opener could result in their lifetime banishment from organized baseball. Stephens immediately returned to the Browns after having played several games for Veracruz.

Speaking at Crosley Field, site of the season's opening game between the Cincinnati Reds and the Chicago Cubs, Chandler made good on his promise to suspend those players who had not returned to honor their '46 contracts, although he reduced the suspensions from life to five years. Even so, Chandler's threat of immediate ostracism from organized baseball did not stop more players from jumping.

In all, eight New York Giants would go down to the Mexican League. Joining Hausmann, Maglie, Zimmerman, and Gardella were pitchers Harry Feldman and Ace Adams on April 26, just ten days after Chandler's announcement. Cuban first baseman Napoleon Reyes would follow. Even the great Adolfo Luque, a Cuban pitcher who had won 193 games in the majors and taught Maglie how to pitch inside, left his coaching job with the Giants to manage at Puebla. Asked how he felt about losing nearly a third of his '45 roster, Mel Ott declared, "It was different in the days when we often didn't know when we would be able to put nine men on the field. But now we have a camp full of fine players. I don't think any of the others will be missed."[10]

Other major league clubs couldn't afford Ott's stoicism. The Cardinals found themselves without third baseman Lou Klein and two of their pitchers, Fred Martin and Max Lanier. Lanier had been a St. Louis mainstay, winning 13, 15, and 17 games in 1942, 1943, and 1944, respectively. He began the '46 campaign by winning his first six decisions, each a complete game. Pasquel offered him a $20,000 salary for five years and threw in a signing bonus to boot. Asked by reporters why he was leaving the major leagues in light of Chandler's threats, Lanier responded that twenty grand per annum was "a sum a North Carolina farm boy couldn't refuse."[11]

The war years saw the greatest influx of Cuban ballplayers into the major leagues to date. Now, Pasquel's coffers created a mass exodus: Nap Reyes, Bobby Estalella, Tommie de la Cruz, Alex Carrasquel, and Rene Monteagudo all left their big-league ball clubs to join the revamped league in Mexico.

Pasquel's ambitions knew no bounds. He even made a play for Stan Musial, sending one of his brothers to make him a tantalizing offer. By one account, Bernardo Pasquel laid five certified checks—each for $10,000—before the Cardinals star. Another had a Pasquel brother emptying a valise containing $100,000 onto Musial's hotel bed. Both stories end with Stan's polite refusal. Although he never managed to lure the top-drawer talent he felt he needed to jump-start his new league, Pasquel did entice twenty-three major and minor league players to abandon their 1946 contracts and play baseball in Mexico.

Most of the now "former" major leaguers were scattered thoughout the league. Pasquel's own Veracruz ball club had the largest contingent of major leaguers, with Gardella, Zimmerman, Adams, Feldman, Klein, Olmo, Owen, Estalella, and Carrasquel. Ironically, they would finish the season with a losing record.

Rene Monteagudo, an outfielder and sometime pitcher with the Senators and Philadelphia Blue Jays, was the only other player with big-league experience at Torreon. George did not speak Spanish, relying at times on the bilingual Monteagudo to translate for him.

There were advantages to playing in Mexico that the major leagues did not offer. Pasquel's money was the most obvious one, but the baseball schedule was less vigorous than that of the majors. Most teams played just over 100 games, including the postseason, and seldom played more than three or four ballgames in a week. In effect, players were getting more money for less work. In addition, the Mexican League was integrated and had been for years.

George went hitless in his first game with Torreon, but it was the play of one of his teammates which he recalled most vividly. Torreon's manager was Hall of Famer Martin Dihigo, a Cuban ballplayer considered "too dark" for the major leagues. Dihigo was a phenomenal pitcher who could play any position in the field and was nearly as proficient at the plate as he was on the mound. In one season, he led the Mexican League in wins and batting. On this particular day, Dihigo, now in his early 40s, was the starting pitcher.

"Dihigo was a good pitcher. In this ballgame, we were leading two to one going into the bottom of the ninth. I'm playing second base, of course, and I'm moving to where I think I should be. They got a man on second with two men out. The left-handed cleanup hitter came up, and Dihigo steps off the mound, kinda looking around. He looks at me, and he takes his hand and motions for me to move toward first base. I moved about two or three steps. He motions me over a little more. I thought, 'Holy cow! We're giving him a hole right through the middle!' About the second pitch, this guy hits a shot right at me. I wouldn't have been able to move my feet, he hit it so hard. Dihigo knew what he was doing."[12]

Still, life in the Mexican League was a far cry from the Polo Grounds. The largest ballparks held no more than 15,000 to 20,000 spectators, and by George's recollection, none were much better than those found at the Class B level. Teams traveled by bus over unforgiving terrain made worse by an unusually rainy Mexican summer. Ballgames began at 11:00 in Mexico City to avoid conflicts with the popular bullfights held later in the day on the same grounds. Players dressed at their hotels because few ballparks contained facilities for them.

Pasquel's grand plan was doomed to failure from the word "go," done in mostly by a poor infrastructure of ballparks, a grossly lopsided distribution of talent across the league, and Pasquel's own overestimation of his fan base. By early summer of 1946, he and his brothers had ceased their efforts to sign top major league talent. The league would continue through the 1948 season, but was no longer in direct competition for talent with the major leagues.

George hit .306 in his first season in the Mexican League. He kept busy during the off season, playing winter ball for the Almendares team in Cuba, where he earned the nickname "La Ardilla"—"Squirrel." After that, he barnstormed south to north with a team thrown together by Lanier, aptly tagged "The Max Lanier All-Stars." The team mostly consisted of players who had gone to Mexico the previous spring. In addition to George and Lanier, there were Klein, Zimmerman, Gardella, Maglie, and several others. They played mostly local semi-pro teams, since Chandler's suspension included a promise of swift retribution for any players who played with or against the "jumpers." The Max Lanier All-Stars won every ballgame they played and made very little money.

George returned home to San Antonio, where his wife was due to have their third child. He had not been in contact with the Mexican League for some time and decided to call the league office. He was surprised to learn that his salary was being cut from $13,000 to $9,000. It was still considerably more money than the Giants had offered him a year earlier, but it was clear that Pasquel's league was suffering major setbacks. The manager of the Monterrey ball club called and asked if he would be willing to play for his team. George agreed, and set off for Monterrey.

He felt more than a little guilty about leaving his pregnant wife, despite her assurances that she'd be fine. The morning after his first game, he paid a visit to the cathedral in Monterrey to say a few prayers for her and their unborn child. From there, he went to the ballpark.

"As I was getting ready go to bat, this kid ran up to me with a telegram. It said, 'Gregory John born at 11:01 A.M. San Antonio time.' That was the time that I was in the cathedral."[13]

George put the telegram in his pocket and took his turn at bat. Feeling considerably less burdened, he proceeded to sock a triple, and as he slid into third base, he heard the public address announcer share the good news with the crowd. "It was my third boy, and I topped it off with a triple!"[14]

George wasn't the only ballplayer concerned about his growing family and the distance that separated them. Danny Gardella had hit .275 with 13 home runs in his first season in the Mexican League. After barnstorming with Lanier and company, he returned home to New York to remain with his wife, who was expecting their first child. He had been the first major leaguer to accept Pasquel's money. Now, just one year later, he would be the first to truly feel the far-reaching consequences of Chandler's suspensions. To a blacklisted player, all major league ballclubs and their affiliates were off-limits. He played semipro ball with a local team and supplemented his income by working as a hospital orderly for $36 a week. He was still a young man, confident of his baseball skills. He believed that he could still compete at the big-league level, and he began to look for a way to be reinstated.

In reality, Gardella wasn't a true "jumper." He had rejected the Giants' offer for 1946 and accepted Pasquel's more impressive figure. He never signed a contract with New York and, therefore, never ran out on one. In the fall of 1947, Gardella filed suit against Chandler and the baseball establishment, seeking damages totaling $400,000. The target was baseball's ancient reserve clause, which Gardella's attorney referred to as a vehicle "to further a conspiracy in restraint of trade and commerce."[15]

The reserve clause was created in the early years of professional baseball as a means for club owners to "reserve" the services of their best players for subsequent seasons. Eventually, the contract of every player fell under its auspices. Owners agreed not to try and lure players from other teams with promises of higher salaries. A player was bound to his team until released, traded, or sold to another team. Players did not sign multiyear contracts, but rather one-year deals with their own clubs. They were free to negotiate a deal with their club, but they were not free to seek a better offer from another team. The reserve clause saw to it that there were no other offers.

Gardella's case dragged on for nearly two years and was eventually slated for trial in the New York State Appellate Court in November of 1949. One month prior to the trial, Gardella settled out of court for a reported $60,000, but perhaps the most important consequence of the case had already occurred several months earlier.

On June 5, 1949, Commissioner Chandler announced an immediate amnesty for all players who were suspended for violating their 1946 contracts. After three years of exile, he urged them to contact their former teams for immediate reinstatement.

George was struggling through the 1949 season in Nuevo Laredo when he got word that he and the others were reinstated. He contacted the Giants' front office and was told to join the team on their western road trip. George caught up with them in Cincinnati. Almost everyone from the 1945 squad was gone, including Mel Ott, who had quit playing and managing. When Hausmann arrived at the team's hotel on Thursday, he received a message from the Giants' new skipper, Leo Durocher.

"You ready to play?" Durocher asked when George came to his room.

"No, not really," he said. "We only played in three or four games a week down there. I need at least a week to get in shape."

Durocher pumped him for information about the Mexican League. Who were the good players who were still down there? Was there anyone worth bringing up? George told Durocher about Adrian Zabala, a Cuban left-hander who had been particularly dominant in the Mexican League. Durocher would bring him to the Giants later that season. He also urged Durocher to bring up Sal Maglie, who had won 20 or more games in each of his seasons at Puebla, easily the league's best pitcher. Maglie would join the Giants for the 1950 season and become one of the National League's most effective and intimidating pitchers.

Durocher wasn't specific with regard to his plans for George, who assumed he would act as a reserve infielder while he got back into shape. The team traveled to Pittsburgh, where they were to play against the Pirates on Friday night. George fielded grounders during the pregame drills, working up a good sweat while trying to find his rhythm at his old position. He managed to take a few swings in the batting cage after the regulars had taken theirs. He was rusty, no doubt, but he was back in the big leagues. A week's worth of workouts sounded about right, and he'd be able to show Durocher what he could do.

Not long after he arrived at the ballpark on Saturday, he was pulled aside by Red Kress, a longtime American League shortstop who had recently signed on as a Giant's coach. Kress told him that Durocher had written him into the lineup—leading off and playing second base. George was beside himself.

"What?! I'm not ready to play!" he said to Kress, who told him that based on what he had seen the day before, he was in good shape and more than ready. George still thought otherwise, but he went into the

Giants' clubhouse and dressed for the game. Afraid that he wouldn't have enough stamina to make it through the game, he took just a few ground balls at second, and a round of swings in the batting cage.

"Just my luck, my first time at bat I hit a line drive just inside the first base bag, and it goes all the way out to the fence in right field. I wind up sliding into third with a triple, and I'm just all out of breath. I couldn't hardly stand up. I stayed in the whole ballgame, which we won, three to one. In the seventh inning, Durocher looked at me and said, 'Had enough?' I said, 'Yeah, I think I've had enough.'"[16]

Durocher played George every day for two weeks, during which, by his own account, he got worse and worse. He continued to avoid the pregame workouts, certain they would sap his strength for the game. Consequently, he never found his footing at second, nor his timing at the plate. He managed just six hits in 47 at-bats. The triple in his first plate appearance was his only extra-base hit. By the end of the two weeks, Durocher sat him down.

"I never got back into the lineup again. He never even talked to me. I just sat on the bench. I know that once I got into shape I would have been a better second baseman than what he had."[17]

George would learn later that other ball clubs had been interested in him. At least one ball club in the Pacific Coast League inquired about him, but considered the Giants' asking price too high. Incredibly, the Giants seemed finished with him, but still wanted an unreasonable sum to part with his services.

George approached Durocher on the team's next western road trip. If Durocher wasn't going to use him, why not let him go home? "Yeah, sure," he said. "You can go home."

"I left the club in Cincinnati, the same place I had joined them. That was the end of my career in the major leagues."[18]

The Giants sold Hausmann's contract to Houston, a St. Louis Browns affiliate in the Texas League. At Houston, he was briefly reunited with Danny Gardella, who by then had returned to the majors for his one and only at-bat, a flyout to left field. Both players struggled in their first full seasons back from the Mexican League. George hit .218 in 95 games. Gardella hit just .211. After an awful showing in the outlaw Provincial League in 1951 where he hit just .178, Gardella left the game for good.

George remained in professional baseball into the mid–1950s, never playing for one team for very long. He made a nice showing with Class B Anderson in 1952. His .329 batting average was good enough for a top ten finish. He accepted a managing position with York, Pennsylvania in the Piedmont League, a St. Louis Browns farm club. After a fifth-place finish, he accepted a playing-manager position with Austin, Texas in the Big State League. After an injury forced him from the field, he juggled his lineup and managed to pull his team from eighth to fourth place. He earned Manager of the Year honors for the Big State League in that 1954 season.

After a second year at the helm in Austin, he was contacted by the Yankee organization. Lou Magualo, his old American Legion coach, was now a top scout in New York's remarkable baseball system. Magualo recommended George as manager of Winston-Salem, a new team in the Carolina League, and the Yankees offered him the job.

For any player or coach toiling in the low minors in the mid–1950s, the idea of joining the Yankee organization must have had a melodious ring to it. George accepted the offer and was quickly treated to a rude awakening. He began the season with fewer than nine players on his roster, breaking training camp with a relief pitcher and a utility infielder. Eventually, his players drifted in, but they proved to be a poor collection of talent and a difficult bunch to manage. He complained to the Yankees' front office about their shoddy handling of the situation and was fired in midseason. Although New York would try to get him to manage a Latin American ball club later that year, he was done with professional baseball.

"I know I would never have made it to the major leagues because of my size. Just playing in the big leagues was a thrill every day. I felt I held my own, against all odds."[19]

6

Cy Buker

Between 1943 and 1945, 405 ballplayers made their debuts in the major leagues. When the war ended, 237 of them—a full sixty percent—never saw the majors again. Cy Buker was one of those players, although it wasn't for lack of performance.[1]

Joining the Dodgers late in the spring of 1945, Cy compiled a 7–2 record with a 3.30 ERA. Pitching mostly in relief, he gave up just two home runs in over 87 innings of work. He also saved five games, the fourth best total in the National League. Along with Ace Adams of the Giants and Andy Karl of the Phillies, he was one of the most effective relievers in the National League for the 1945 season.[2]

That was his only season in the big leagues. Invariably, whenever the subject of his playing career arises, the question is asked: Why only 1945? How could someone who pitched so well one season be passed over the next? The answer lies where one might expect, amid conflicts over personalities and paychecks.

By the spring of 1944, Cy Buker had made the sober realization that there were two things a man needed to rise through the ranks of professional baseball: talent and luck. He had plenty of one, but almost none of the other.

Cy had given professional baseball a go, signed to a pro contract right out of college by Giants scout Heinie Groh. He was sent to Clinton in the Three-I League in 1940 and pitched a three-hitter in his first outing. The next week, he hurt his elbow and did not pitch again all season.

He stayed out of pro ball completely in 1941, but played with a semipro team in his native Wisconsin. He convinced the team to let him play second base, hoping that the throw to first wouldn't wreak havoc on his sore arm. The arm got stronger as the season wore on. His manager asked him to pitch a game near the season's end, "and behold! By golly, I could throw! The curveball didn't bother me, and I had a pretty good fastball."[3]

But by the end of the season, Cy had decided that his glass arm was going to keep him out of professional baseball for good. He took a job coaching football at a high school in Eau Claire, Wisconsin. He kept his baseball ties alive, playing semipro in the town of Medford, forty miles to the north.

"I finished the season with [Medford], and I got a telephone call from the manager of Wisconsin Rapids in the Class D Wisconsin State League. He asked me if I couldn't come down. He was having horrible problems with his pitching. They couldn't get the ball over. He knew me from college, and he asked me if I couldn't throw well enough to get the ball over the plate.

"Remarkably, as the season went on, I got stronger. I ended up .500 with just a miserable team. The season ended and the war had broke out. The league blew up, and everybody was declared a free agent. Well, once again I gave up. I didn't even attempt to play in '43."[4]

Cy was making $2,000 a year coaching at Eau Claire. It wasn't that he didn't aspire to play professional ball. He continued to play semipro when school was out, and he tossed two no-hitters for Medford in the summer of 1943. But the security of his off-season job contributed to his shoulder-shrug approach to pitching.

"I was fairly well contented. I figured, what the heck. That's the end of it. But spring came around in '44, and they gave me baseball to coach, too."[5]

Cy looked forward to coaching baseball, but he wasn't prepared for the surprise awaiting him when he began throwing to his young charges. For the first time since he signed his first pro contract, he was able to throw without pain. Not only that, the velocity had returned to his fastball.

News travels fast in a small Wisconsin town. It didn't take long for Cy to finally become the beneficiary of some of the luck he had lacked earlier in his career. Word of his resurrected arm began to circulate beyond Eau Claire. About two weeks before the end of the school year, Cy received a phone call from Bob Carlton, the general manager of the St. Paul Saints, a top Dodgers farm club in the American Association.

"He said, 'I've heard of you. Will you come up and pitch a little batting practice?' I talked it over with my wife, and I decided to take

Saturday and Sunday and go on up there. I hadn't any more than finished up with a couple of rounds of hitting and [Carlton] is out there on the mound with a contract."[6]

He was still obligated to finish the school year and did not join the Saints until the first week of June. He pitched the rest of June and all of July and August before he had to adjust his schedule once again to accommodate the new school year.

"When football started I was commuting. I would coach a few days of football and jump on the train, go to St. Paul and pitch a game. Then I'd jump on a train and coach a few days. That last game of the season, we played at Kansas City on a Sunday. I got a ride on a train, and there were no bunks. I had to ride sitting up backwards all the way to Kansas City. I got down there on Sunday, and I pitched that ballgame. We needed that game to get into the playoffs, [and] I beat 'em, two to zero. After the game, I got back on the train and went back to Eau Claire."[7]

Cy finished his regular season with an impressive 11–3 record, in spite of missing the first two months of the season and enduring a commute that would drive even the most stouthearted traveler daffy. He capped off the season by winning two times in the playoffs, twice defeating the Toledo Mud Hens in the first round, which St. Paul won four games to three. The Saints were swept in four straight by the Louisville Colonels in the second round. Cy did not pitch in that series.

"In the process, Branch Rickey purchased my contract at the end of the season. That was the end of St. Paul, for then. Come springtime, I wasn't too hot on going up there to Brooklyn. Rickey sent me this great, big contract—$5,000, which was about two and a half times as much as I was making at coaching. I talked it over with my dad and my wife."[8]

If he went to the Dodgers, there was no way he could continue coaching. It wasn't the money that was important. Rickey's contract took care of that. But teaching was considered an essential wartime occupation, for which Cy received a deferment. Cy was classified as 3-A, which meant that he was physically fit, but with dependents. He might go later in the draft than the 1-As, but forfeiture of his deferment might hasten Uncle Sam's call.

"I was teaching, and not in trouble with the army. I had two little kids. My dad said that the first day I set foot in New York, I would be thrown 1-A into the army."[9]

It didn't quite work out that way. Cy accepted Rickey's contract and reported to the Dodgers' spring camp at the Bear Mountain Resort in upstate New York. It was March, 1945, and all teams trained north of the Mason-Dixon line, most about 100 hundred miles from their base of operations.

It was a cold spring across the country, nowhere more so than at Bear Mountain. "I didn't do very much in spring training. Nobody else did, either. You couldn't. They had to chisel ice off the field just to have infield practice. It was a joke, really."[10]

Nevertheless, when the Dodgers broke camp and headed to Brooklyn, they took Cy along as a relief pitcher. However, before he could pitch a single game for Brooklyn, the army came calling. A chronic physical ailment left him in limbo throughout the months of April and May. Cy had asthma, and army doctors could not seem to decide on whether it was serious enough to classify him as 4-F.

Cy Buker as the Dodgers' relief ace in 1945. ©Brace Photograph.

"They finally decided to put me in Governor's Island for a three-day observation. Well, lucky for me, as far as asthma's concerned, that was the most humid place in the United States. I got out there, and I wheezed like a steam engine. They had me there for three days, and they turned me loose. It didn't hurt my feelings too much. I wasn't about to try and dodge anything. I just went along with it."[11]

The army distraction had cost him about a month and a half of the season. The Dodgers, like most clubs in 1945, were lean on pitching, and they hoped that Cy could flash some of the brilliance he had shown a year earlier at St. Paul.

He first saw action on May 17 against the Pirates, a jittery affair in which he walked four batters in a little more than two innings of work. He finished the ballgame, which Brooklyn lost, 12 to 6. He didn't work another game for nearly three weeks.

But by mid-June his control returned, and Leo Durocher began to use him more consistently. He pitched two scoreless innings of relief against the Braves on June 16, then worked both games of a doubleheader the following day. Before a Sunday ballgame at Ebbets Field, on June 21, he got a surprise from Durocher.

"It was hot as the dickens. I had just finished a thirty-minute run in the outfield at the end of [coach] Charlie Dressen's bat. He would take a fungo bat every day and run us back and forth in the outfield. He'd always hit us fungoes where you just couldn't quite get to them. It was about 105 degrees, [and] I'm in the back changing shirts, wringing wet.

"Durocher comes up to me, hands me the ball, and says, 'You're starting today!' Art Herring had come down with the stomach flu at game time. I had run my duff off in the hot sun for thirty minutes, and I'm expected to go out there and pitch a ballgame? Christ, I'd already done *two* days' work!

"But that's a little indication of how Durocher operated. He'd use you as long as he could get something out of you."[12]

Durocher got quite a bit out of his rookie pitcher that afternoon. Cy worked seven innings against Philadelphia. His mound opponent was a 34-year-old Cuban ballplayer by the name of Isidoro Leon, also making his first career start. Both pitchers left after the seventh with the score tied, 2–2. Brooklyn rallied for five runs in the eighth inning, and Cy had his first major league victory.

He would win twice more before the end of June, picking up a relief victory just two days after his start on June 23, and his first of three victories against the Chicago Cubs on June 29. He didn't start again until the middle of July, but by then he had established himself as the Dodgers' most consistent relief pitcher. He only had two primary pitches, but he left National League hitters befuddled.

"Dixie Walker told me he'd never seen a better curveball—the 'downer,' straight from the top. Started at about the waist and ended at about the shoe tops. He said it looked just like [Detroit Tigers great] Tommy Bridges. I had a fastball that moved all the time. When your ball moves, [hitters] just can't hang down there, dig in, and hit the long one. It wasn't any 95 mph job, but that's why you don't see too many home runs hit against me.

"When the weather was hot, I'd hold the ball off the seams. I threw what they call a 'dry spitter.' It'd come up like a knuckleball, only I threw it just as hard as a fastball. I had tons of guys who would reach around and want to take a look at the ball. They swore I was doping it up!"[13]

What seemed like a good thing—namely, a regular role out of the Dodger pen—was in fact a nerve-wracking situation for Cy. It turned out that Durocher had no real method for using him. He went as long as two weeks without being used, then would pitch in three or four consecutive games.

"From there on in with Durocher, it was a nightmare. I never knew when I was going to pitch. He had some hard-throwing kids on that club: Branca, Hal Gregg, LeRoy Pfund, and a couple of others. They had real bad control. I was cranking up every day! He'd tell me to start throwing in the first inning, right along with 'em. He said he didn't know how long they could go.

"Now, to warm up, you can't just go out there and play lollipop. You gotta be ready to go into the ballgame. You put as much energy in warming up down there as you would going out and pitching a couple of innings. This went on the entire season."[14]

Durocher couldn't seem to go without him. On three separate occasions, he used Cy in both legs of a doubleheader. Twice after starts of more than six innings each, Durocher had him back in the bullpen and pitching relief within two days. After saving both games of a doubleheader against the Cardinals on July 22nd, his record stood at 4–0 with three saves. He finally lost to the Cardinals two days later after having appeared in four consecutive games.

Perhaps Cy's most impressive outing came in a doubleheader against Cincinnati in September. In the first game, he relieved starter Herring after seven innings, with the score tied, 3–3. He worked scoreless eighth and ninth innings before Reds second baseman Kermit Wahl opened the tenth with a single. He advanced on a fielder's choice and went to third when second baseman Eddie Stanky let a grounder go between his legs. After an intentional pass to Dick Sipek, right fielder Al Libke singled in the winning run. Cy lost for just the second time, but his day wasn't over yet.

"I'm in the clubhouse changing clothes and getting a shower. It was brutal hot. That old Crosley Field was in kind of a hole. The fences were up on a hill all the way around. When that sun got in there, it was brutal.

"The [second] game must have been twenty or thirty minutes going on. So, here comes Charlie Dressen, stormin' in. 'Hurry up! Get your uniform on!'

"I said, 'What the heck is going on here?'

"He says, 'Leo wants you in the pen! Right away!'"[15]

Cy had started the first game of the Cincinnati series just two days before, going seven innings. That outing had come after a relief appearance of five-plus innings against the Pirates earlier in the week. His arm ached constantly, and it shook so badly that he had trouble holding a glass of water. But he put on his uniform as Dressen had demanded and headed back out to the pen.

He entered the second game in the fourth inning, with the Dodgers trailing, 5–3. He worked the next six innings, giving up just one hit while striking out six. He allowed just one run in the fourth on a wild pitch with a man on third. The Dodgers scored four times in both the fifth and sixth innings and won the game 11–6. Cy helped his own cause, driving in a run with a single over second base in the fifth.

On the day, he had pitched eight and one third innings. He gave up two runs on five hits, with six walks and eight strikeouts. He had lost the opener, but he won the nightcap. Over the course of seven days from September 5–11, he had worked in four ballgames and pitched a total of twenty and two-thirds innings, nearly a fourth of his season total.

Durocher's tactics notwithstanding, Cy was easily one of the most effective relief pitchers in the National League that year, and he was certainly among the least heralded. He beat the Chicago Cubs—eventual pennant winners and season-long Brooklyn nemesis—three times. In just over 87 innings pitched, he allowed only two home runs—one each to the Cardinals' Whitey Kurowski and the Cubs' Andy Pafko.[16]

"I see Andy once in a while. Andy and I played in the old Wisconsin State League. He was with Green Bay. He hit one off me in Brooklyn—the only home run that was hit off me in Ebbets Field. I think it's still going! It went up into the upper deck, and it rattled around there until the ninth inning. Of course, he reminds me of it!"[17]

His performance earned him the respect and admiration of the Brooklyn press and fans. However, on at least one occasion, the affection of the fans was somewhat misdirected.

"We played a Sunday afternoon doubleheader. Eddie Stanky and I were walking out of Ebbets Field. We were the last ones out. We used to hang around at least an hour and hope to heck that everybody was gone, you know? Eddie had just bought a brand-new sport coat. A beautiful thing. Cost him seventy-five dollars. Luckily, all I had on was a polo shirt.

"Well, here comes a bunch of hoodlums! They tore Eddie's coat off, and they ripped my [shirt] all to shreds. They let Eddie go, but they sure took care of his coat! Eddie felt pretty mad. He was kind of a hot-headed little fella anyway."[18]

By the close of the '45 season, fans and sportswriters alike began to speculate which players would lose their jobs to returning veterans and which were likely to stay. An article in *The Brooklyn Eagle* in September portrayed Cy as a shoo-in to return in 1945. The article praised his exemplary work in the bullpen, noting that his performances were directly responsible for saving at least twenty ballgames. Surely Durocher and company had big plans for him in the coming season.

"I had pretty good luck. With starting late in the year and everything, I still ended up 7–2. It was a terrific year."[19]

But for all his effort over the course of the long season, he was only offered a $500 dollar raise when his '46 contract arrived in the mail that winter.

"That's about a three dollar-a-day raise. I was real mad. When I got the contract, I tore it up in little pieces, put it in an envelope, and sent it back!"[20]

Branch Rickey had a reputation for being one of the most parsimonious men in baseball. He was also one of the game's most powerful figures, having become the principal shareholder of the Dodgers in August of 1945. Rickey had an ego to match his lofty position, and he wasn't about to be shown up by a first-year holdout. Cy's "message" succeeded in infuriating Rickey, who remembered the gesture and bided his time.

Meanwhile, Cy returned to his teaching job at Eau Claire and did not hear from the Dodgers throughout the winter and into early spring. Spring training had already begun in Daytona Beach in March of 1946 when he received another letter. Cy was asked to join the Dodgers at spring training. If he broke camp with the Dodgers and stayed on their big-league roster through the June roster cut-downs, he would receive a $1,500 bonus in addition to his regular salary. It was a tantalizing offer.

"I went and signed the darn thing. I had plenty of confidence that I would be around. I went down there three weeks late. Now get this: when I got there, nobody talked to me. None of the (Dodger) authorities. I was assigned to the B-squad immediately."[21]

On the off chance that his pitcher didn't get the message, Rickey played out his retribution over the entire '46 season. Cy broke camp with the Dodgers and headed to Brooklyn without having pitched to a single batter. Rickey waited until June—just before the cut-down date named in Cy's contract—to send him back to the minors. There would be no bonus for Cy, and considering the circumstances leading up to his demotion, it appears that the offer was a ruse all along.

"I sat on the bench, and I have slivers yet. I was up at Brooklyn until the final dog was hung. That's the way it went. Without pitching a single inning anywhere, to anybody, I stayed there on the bench until the final hour of cut-down time. And without any ceremony, I was shipped to Montreal. You just didn't cross Rickey. I got nothing."[22]

He had signed a regular-season contract, so there was no going home to Wisconsin, though the thought must have crossed his mind. He traveled north to Canada in June of '46 and joined the Montreal Royals of the International League. Well over a third of the season was already gone. He had missed all of April and May, when he knew the hitters were still soft. For the moment, at least, he forgot about Rickey and Brooklyn and returned to the business of pitching.

He probably had no inkling of what he was about to get himself into. The 1946 Montreal Royals were one of the greatest minor league teams of the twentieth century, known both for their fine play as well as their historic significance.

With regard to the former, the Royals destroyed their International League competition, winning 100 regular season games and finishing eighteen and a half games ahead of their closest pursuer. For the most part, the Royals did not possess superior talent. Only two position players would go on to play more than two full seasons in the majors. And aside from veteran Curt Davis and a young Jack Banta, no other Montreal pitcher would play more than a two or three seasons at the major league level.

They were a prime example of a baseball team that came together at the right time and proceeded to play stellar ball.

"That was one hell of a ball club. We had everything you need: Spider Jorgensen on third, Al Campanis at short, and a guy by the name of Les Burge played first. Herman Franks was catching. We had another catcher by the name of Dixie Howell, and I just didn't like him back of the plate. We didn't think alike. Herman caught me, and he always came through with a long one for me every doggone time. Herman was the real heart of that ballclub. (Manager) Clay Hopper could have stayed at home.

"In the outfield we had Red Durret in right, Earl Naylor in center, and Tom Tatum in left. They could all go get 'em. We had guys who could run 'em down, and we still had guys who could hit 'em out, too."[23]

They won with terrific pitching, too. Steve Nagy was the ace of the staff and came in with 17 victories. After him, everybody got into the act. Chet Kehn, John Gabbard, and Glen Moulder each finished with 10 or more victories. Banta had nine. Davis was 43 years old when the season ended, but he still managed a 5–3 record and a 3.00 ERA.

But it was the presence of one player in particular that spurred the Royals' offense and made them a team for the ages. In December of 1945, Branch Rickey signed Jackie Robinson to a minor league contract. He sent Robinson north of the border to Montreal, hoping that he might have an easier go in International League cities like Syracuse, Rochester, Toronto, or Buffalo. It took Robinson a while before he succeeded in impressing his own teammates.[24]

"Then, of course, Jackie Robinson came out. In all fairness to him and everybody else, when he first came onto the field, he wasn't adept at anything. He couldn't throw and he couldn't bat. He had no idea how to play second base. Had he been a white man, he never would have been held on the ball club. He would have been released."[25]

Beginning a pattern that would repeat itself at the major league level a year later, International League pitchers brushed Robinson back or knocked him down at every opportunity. But as would happen in 1947, Robinson quickly learned how to use such tactics to his own advantage.

"He was one of the most intelligent people I ever saw. He learned so quick! There was a lot of resentment about him coming in. About every time he came to bat, he would be decked at least once. They did everything they could to get him out of there.

"He'd take his knockdowns, and he got to be a better hitter as the season went on. Pretty soon, the pitchers wised up. They quit throwing at him. They were getting beat once he learned how to run bases. They'd put him on, [and] first thing, they'd look up and he was on second.

"Everything that was out there to learn, he picked it up as quickly as you could shake a hat. He was right there. He was great at turning the double play. Campanis was good at it, too. As the season progressed, any ground ball that was hit between first and second with a man on base—you walked to the dugout. It was two.

"But there were scuffles. The first time [the team] went into Baltimore, they wouldn't let Jack stay in the hotel. They hired 125 extra cops to quell any uprising that came about. We played in the old football stadium there. The clubhouse we dressed in was the football dressing room way down in center field. When the game was over, we had that long run down to the doggone dressing room. The crowd came on the field, and there was a lot of hitting and slugging going on. Herman Franks and I each grabbed a bat and started to high-tail it. We made it with no trouble.

"There were a lot of hard feelings. Toward the end of the season, they calmed it down. They knew [Jack] was coming, and I guess they kinda accepted it."[26]

For Cy, Montreal turned out to be a proving ground of sorts, as well. After a relief appearance in June, he joined the starting rotation and never looked back. He won ten of his first twelve decisions and had two shutouts. His two losses were both one-run affairs. One came against the Newark Bears on a ninth-inning home run by Yogi Berra.

The 10–2 record was a great moral victory for Cy. He couldn't help but recall the cold reception he had received at spring training, as well as Rickey's snub at cut-down time. Such a phenomenal start for such a remarkable team was, in its way, the sweetest form of revenge. Surely the Dodgers would have to acknowledge such an effort.

The Brooklyn Dodgers, meanwhile, were spending their first postwar season in the thick of a pennant race. Back from the service were regulars like shortstop Pee Wee Reese, left fielder "Pistol" Pete Reiser, starting pitcher Kirby Higbe, and relief ace Hugh Casey. They also got help from former servicemen who were making their major league debuts. These included pitchers Joe Hatten and Hank Behrman and outfielder Carl Furillo.

The Dodgers led the National League for most of the season, but were pursued closely by the St. Louis Cardinals. The league lead seesawed several times in late August, but the Dodgers clung to a slight lead throughout September. They lost to the Boston Braves on the final game of the season and finished in a tie with the Cardinals. The two teams played the first-ever best-of-three playoff series, which the Cardinals took in two straight.

Durocher proved no less ambiguous in his approach to his pitchers than he did a season earlier. He began the '46 campaign by starting, in succession, seven different pitchers. In all, fourteen different pitchers would start ballgames for Brooklyn that year. Those used most consistently were Hatten (30 starts), Higbe (29), and Vic Lombardi (25). Durocher used seven other pitchers in the role of fourth or fifth starter. These included Hal Gregg (16 starts), Rube Melton (12), Behrman (11), Ralph Branca (10), Rex Barney (9), and Ed Head (7). Only injury or Durocher's intuition dictated when they were used.

Casey reclaimed his position as bullpen specialist and was spelled by Art Herring, who had been used mostly as a starter the year before.[27]

But the Dodgers sought help from their minor league affiliates, as well. They brought up Harry Taylor from St. Paul, Paul Minner from Mobile, and three pitchers from the Montreal Royals — Glen Moulder, Jean-Pierre Roy, and veteran Curt Davis.

Taylor, Minner, and Moulder were rookies who had pitched well with their respective teams. Davis was a twelve-year major league veteran who had been a reliable starter during the war. Roy was a Montreal native and fan favorite who surrendered lots of runs, but managed a winning record. None of the five pitched more than four games for the Dodgers, and only Taylor pitched effectively.

Despite a 10–2 start with Montreal, Cy was not asked back to the Dodgers in 1946.

"There I sit on 10–2, with an ERA around two-something, and I did not get called back. To this day, that eats on me more than anything there is. Does that tell you something? It told me a lot, and that kinda changed my year. I wasn't very happy."[28]

Although he was not one to vent his frustration in public, Cy's displeasure over this and other Dodger snubs was common knowledge around the league for those who cared about such things. On one instance in Baltimore, the depth of his discontent was tested.

"I was approached by gamblers in Baltimore. They offered me money to go out there and throw a ballgame. They were gangsters, sure as hell. They were traveling around in groups of three and four. That was when I was sitting there with all the chips on the table, you know? Great record?"[29]

Ironically, the gamblers offered him $1,500 to throw the game, the very same figure Branch Rickey had dangled before him that spring. For Cy, however, there was only one response.

"I told them to get lost. I didn't want any part of it. I was scared! I won my ballgame that night, so they can't accuse me of taking any money. I know who did join the ranks. I saw two guys miss balls that night that they could've put in their jock straps. It was pretty obvious what was going on. One of those ballplayers came with three new $100 suits after the next few days. I turned down $1,500, and that was a mint in those days."[30]

Neither Cy's integrity nor his fine pitching record could save him from the bad luck that followed. While leaving the train station at Toronto one evening, Cy and Herman Franks were assaulted by a drunk.

"I had a little radio in my hand, and I threw it to Herman. I turned around to defend myself, and I clocked him good."[31]

But the blow cost him a broken bone in his pitching hand. It also took put him out of action for the next five weeks. When he returned, he found that he didn't have the same stuff as before.

"I ended up winning only two more games. I ended up 12–7, and I still had a fair earned run average [3.81]. Hell, if things would have kept going like I was before I got hurt, I would've come in with twenty [wins], I know it. Easy."[32]

Montreal walked away with the best record in the International League, then beat Louisville, the American Association champions, in the Little World Series. Cy appeared in one game in the series, but pitched poorly. He returned home to Wisconsin and pondered his future.

He had quit his teaching job by then. Eau Claire had asked him to make a choice, and he had opted for baseball. He could always go back to teaching, but he might never have another chance to pitch in the major leagues. But when his 1947 contract arrived in the mail, he had decided that he would not return to the Royals.

"I got a contract from Montreal again at a fair salary, but I didn't want to go back. By then, I had three little kids. I didn't want to go that far from home. I talked them into trading me back to St. Paul, which is only 140 miles from home."[33]

He opened the '47 season by winning his first four starts, showing the same form he had shown in the first half of the previous season. Not long after that, though, his body began to betray him in the form of leg injuries. Hamstring. Achilles tendon.

"I kept pitching all the way through this. In those days, there was no 'injured reserve.' If you let on that you were hurt, you just got pushed aside, and somebody else got your job. It was dog-eat-dog. I did the best I could, and I finished up 8–8."[34]

He became a journeyman from that point on. He was traded to Milwaukee at the end of '47, sold to Kansas City in '48, then sold to the Texas League in 1949. This time he refused to report, again citing that the distance from home was too hard on his family. In response, the president of the minor leagues' National Association of Professional Baseball Leagues, George Trautman, suspended him without pay for the duration of the '49 season.

"I couldn't play anywhere. I ended up that year pitching semipro around the country, picking up the hard money."[35]

He managed to get reinstated in 1950, but by that time his arm was dead. He had short stints with teams in Little Rock, Colorado Springs, Sioux City, and Lincoln, and although he enjoyed tutoring the younger pitchers on those clubs, he knew his own career was finished. By 1952, he had had enough.

Luckily, he still had coaching to return to. He became a fixture in Wisconsin high school athletics into the 1970s. In 1987, he was named to the Wisconsin Football Coaches Association Hall of Fame. He continues to live in Greenwood, Wisconsin, with his wife of more than sixty years.

"The older I get, the better I was. What little bit I did is something and, by golly, I'm proud of it. I got the good guys out—Stan Hack, Phil Cavarretta, Bill Nicholson. Hank Sauer never hit a ball out of the infield off me. Tommy Holmes, Ernie Lombardi—all these guys that swung the big bats. What little bit I did, I got to think back on the good part."[36]

Could he have had a successful career in the majors after the war? Sadly, we'll never know the real truth. Over the years, however, Cy has developed his own answer.

"The way I could throw in '44 and '45, I could play with anybody. I had people tell me that. Dixie Walker was one. I asked myself that question several times, and I asked those guys the same question. Anyway, that's the way they saw it, and it made me feel that I saw it that way, too."[37]

7

Bill Lefebvre

Although he never became a star, Bill Lefebvre managed to live out a scenario that has been played time and again in back yards and sandlots for generations. Just four days after graduating from Holy Cross College in June of 1938, he signed a professional contract with the Boston Red Sox and found himself pitching in a major league game. The Red Sox were getting clobbered by the White Sox that day, and Bill wasn't able to curtail the damage. In four innings of work, he gave up six earned runs.

Interestingly, it wasn't his pitching performance that anyone would remember. Stepping in against the White Sox' Monty Stratton, he deposited the first pitch he ever saw in the big leagues over Fenway Park's fabled left field wall. He was the first American Leaguer to accomplish the feat and one of only sixteen players to do so throughout baseball's long history. It was an auspicious beginning, but a tough act to follow.

Ironically, the homer off Stratton was the only home run of Bill's career. He would play parts of two seasons with the Red Sox, and after four tough years in the minors, he eventually pitched his way back to the big leagues. He worked two seasons with the Washington Senators during the war and managed to steal the spotlight on several occasions. The first-pitch home run may have been a fluke, but every inning of every game after that was earned.

Bill "Lefty" Lefebvre
BOSTON RED SOX, 1938–1939
WASHINGTON SENATORS, 1943–1944

7. Bill Lefebvre

Bill Lefebvre was a college-educated ballplayer—a rare occurrence in the depression-ridden years of the late 1930s. He was the ninth of ten children, and the fiscal realities of family and the American economy did not offer much hope for advanced education. Baseball enabled some young athletes to seek and receive a college education. During his high school days, Bill played in the leagues in and around his native Rhode Island. His catcher during the summer of his senior year was Joe Cusick, who played minor league ball in the Cardinals organization and later served as a major league scout for various teams. Cusick was already playing at Holy Cross College in Worcester, Massachusetts. What Notre Dame was to football during the 1930s, Holy Cross was to baseball. Bill was already committed to play for nearby Providence College, but Cusick arranged a tryout for Bill with Holy Cross.

Lefty Lefebvre with the Red Sox in 1939. ©Brace Photograph.

The two young players drove with their fathers to Worcester to meet with Jack Barry, the manager of the Holy Cross team. Barry had been a major league shortstop for eleven seasons split between the Philadelphia A's and the Red Sox. He was part of Connie Mack's famous "$100,000 infield" in the 1910s. He maintained a close friendship with his double play partner, Hall of Famer Eddie Collins. It was through Collins that Bill Lefebvre would eventually find his way to the Boston Red Sox.

Barry watched Bill throw to Cusick for about fifteen minutes before saying, "Yes, I'll take him." He sent Bill to the dean of admissions, where he was given a half scholarship. Tuition at Holy Cross was $800 per annum in the 1930s. Bill was responsible for $400, and the university would pay the rest.

Like most ballplayers of the era, Bill played amateur ball during the summer months. In the summer after his freshman year, he played in the Cape Cod League.

"At the end of the season, [the Red Sox] brought in about 25 players from the league. They took about four or five guys from every team. We worked out at Fenway Park in the morning and watched the Red Sox in the afternoon."[1]

At the end of the workout, Bill was approached by Eddie Collins. He asked him if he was interested in playing pro ball. Bill said that he was, but that he still had three years to go at Holy Cross. Collins told him that if he wanted to sign with the Red Sox, he would take care of his tuition at Holy Cross. Bill told Collins that he still owed for his freshman year. When Collins asked him how much that was, Bill told him, "*Five hundred* dollars."

"He peeled five one-hundred-dollar bills right in front of me. I had never seen a hundred-dollar bill in my life. I paid the $400 I owed and kept the [extra] $100. That was my bonus!"[2]

True to his word, Collins took care of Bill's half of the tuition for the next three years. And true to his word, Bill went up to Boston three days after graduation to sign a major league contract with the Red Sox. The following day, June 14, 1938, he was in uniform for a game against the Chicago White Sox at Fenway Park.

Not expecting to see action his first day in the big leagues, Bill took a seat at the far end of the dugout bench where he could soak up the atmosphere. There was plenty to see. White Sox hitters made short work of three Red Sox pitchers in the first five innings. To make matters worse, Boston hitters could not seem to solve the pitching of Chicago starter Monty Stratton.

Stratton was en route to winning 15 games for the second consecutive season with the White Sox. It was also his last season in the major leagues. In November of that year, while hunting rabbits near his Greenville, Texas home, his shotgun accidentally discharged, severely damaging his right leg. The leg had to be amputated the following day. Remarkably, he would pitch his way back into pro ball, winning 18 games for Class C East Texas in 1945. On that day in June of 1938, however, he was at the top of his game.

With his team trailing 9–1 in the sixth inning, Boston manager Joe Cronin decided to give his latest arrival a baptism by fire.

"Cronin got up, and he hollered at me. 'Hey, Lefebvre! Go warm up!'

"I said, 'Who, me?'

"He said, 'Yeah! Hurry up!'"[3]

Bill trotted down to the bullpen, where he was greeted by backup catcher Moe Berg. Berg was a veteran of fifteen major league seasons and was a true baseball character. He was conversant in several languages and would spend part of the war working as a spy for the OSS, precursor to the CIA. No doubt sensing Bill's anxiety, he decided to loosen him up a bit.

"He started talking to me in French! I speak French, [but] I was surprised."[4]

Bill entered the game in the sixth inning and surrendered eight hits in four innings of work, good for six earned runs. In the eighth inning, he stepped into the batters' box to face the right-handed Stratton.

"The first ball pitched I hit over the left field wall. It was a high, outside pitch. I'm a left-handed hitter, so I was a little late!"[5]

Clise Dudley and Eddie Morgan, two National Leaguers, had hit first-pitch, first at-bat home runs prior to 1938. Bill was the first American League player and one of six pitchers to perform the feat.[6] Ultimately, the home run was an anomaly. Bill had been hired to pitch, after all, and his first outing with Boston left something to be desired.

The Red Sox left on a western road trip after the game. While in Chicago, Cronin asked Bill to come see him.

"He called me up to his room. Donie Bush was the manager at Minneapolis, and he was looking for a left-handed pitcher. [Cronin] said, 'It'll be a good chance for you to pitch regular.' If I'd stayed with the Red Sox, I would have been used just as a cleanup guy. If they were getting beat pretty bad, I'd go in."[7]

Bill decided that Cronin was right. He accepted the demotion as an opportunity to hone his skills. By the end of June, he was pitching for the Minneapolis Millers, the Red Sox' top farm club. The Millers were an odd collection of career minor leaguers, upstart youngsters and crafty veteran pitchers, like Belve Bean, Walter Tauscher and Roy Parmelee. Bill was the fourth starter on the Millers and posted an 8–8 record with a 4.25 ERA.

The '38 Millers were also a crucial stop for one of the game's greatest players. After two years in the Pacific Coast League, Ted Williams played one season with the Millers prior to joining the Red Sox in 1939. Just twenty years old, Williams gave the American Association a glimpse of the future, becoming the league's first triple crown winner with a .366 batting average, 43 home runs and 142 RBIs.

After a scary moment during the '38 season, Bill could boast that he replaced Ted Williams in right field for two games. In a game against Milwaukee, Williams was beaned by pitcher Bill Zuber. Donie Bush removed a groggy Williams from the game and put Bill in right. He started the next game in right field and faced pitcher Whitlow Wyatt.

"I replaced Ted and batted third, for cryin' out loud. The first three times up, [Wyatt] struck me out. He had a hell of a curve. The fourth time up, I finally got a base hit. I was Ted Williams's caddy!"[8]

When the season ended, Bill joined Williams and several of his teammates on a barnstorming tour arranged by Andy Cohen, a former major leaguer and Miller mainstay. The tour traveled across western Minnesota and South Dakota, playing fifteen games in as many days.

"We played one night, and the next night we'd go someplace else. We'd play in the twilight, from 5:30 til seven o'clock. They'd always throw a big bash for us after the game. We'd stay up pretty late after that."[9]

Bill, Williams and Stan Spence piled into Walter Tauscher's car and drove from game to game. Bill road in the back seat with Spence. Williams rode up front with Tauscher. Between Williams's legs were a shotgun and a case of shells, the latter a gift from one of the Millers' radio sponsors.

"They told Ted that there were a lot of jackrabbits out there. As we were traveling, all of a sudden Ted would pull out the shotgun and POW!, he'd shoot. I'd be sitting in the back seat with Stan Spence, and we'd jump right up trying to see what the hell was going on! Teddy emptied out that whole case of shotgun shells by the time we got through those fifteen days. Yeah, he was a wild man."[10]

It had been an interesting first year in professional baseball for Bill, and he seemed to figure conspicuously in Boston's future plans. The following year, the Red Sox organization transferred some of its key talent to the Louisville Colonels of the American Association, recently purchased by the Red Sox organization. Bill joined Parmelee and Spence on the Louisville roster, which included a young shortstop named Harold "Pee Wee" Reese.

A press release from early in the '39 season touted Bill as one of the "newcomers worth watching in the American Association":

"In addition to having a tricky name, Lefebvre also has a tricky southpaw delivery which has been causing enemy batters no little trouble this season. As Lefebvre gains experience he is apt to become one of the outstanding hurlers of the league."[11]

The Colonels finished at .500 for the year, and in spite of a subpar 6–10 record, the Red Sox brought Bill back to Fenway in August. There was no pennant race in 1939, the Yankees having clinched the flag in early September. Second place, however, was up for grabs, with Boston, Cleveland and the Chicago White Sox in contention.

Boston's strength was in its offense, which included no less than four future Hall of Famers in Cronin, Williams, Bobby Doerr and Jimmie Foxx. Beyond the performance of pitcher Lefty Grove (15–4, 2.54 ERA), Boston's pitching left much to be desired. Only one other starter could boast a winning record. In addition, Grove was 39 years old and made just 23 starts on the season. No doubt Cronin believed that the addition of another left-hander would be a prudent move down the stretch.

After more than a year's absence, Bill made his first major league start against Washington on August 19. He shut out the Senators for the first four innings before surrendering three runs over the next two innings. He left after the sixth and did not earn a decision.

He would not pitch again until August 29 when he started against the Indians. Aided in part by a Ted Williams's grand slam in the fifth inning, Bill gave up just one run through seven. He ran into trouble in the eighth and yielded to a relief pitcher. Boston held on to win the game, 7–4, and Bill got the win.

The league didn't give him much chance to bask in the glory of his first big-league victory. He lasted into the seventh inning once again in the second game of a doubleheader versus the Senators on September 4. This time, Washington got the better of Bill, tagging him for three runs in both the sixth and seventh innings, and sending him to the showers with his first big-league loss.

Undeterred, he relieved starter Fritz Ostermueller just three days later in a loss to the Yankees. He gave up an earned run in his first inning of relief, then proceeded to shut out the pennant winners for the next five innings, allowing just four hits.

He would pitch just one more time for Boston—a mop-up job in a loss to Cleveland. He finished the game, but not before giving up three runs, including a home run off the bat of Ben Chapman. The Red Sox finished the season in second place, two games ahead of the Indians. Bill finished with a 1–1 record and a 5.81 ERA, with most of the runs coming in the loss to Washington.

In November of 1939, the Red Sox purchased the contract of Dominic DiMaggio from the San Francisco Seals of the Pacific Coast League. As partial compensation for the youngest DiMaggio, Boston sent outfielder Johnny Barrett, pitcher Frank Dasso, and Bill Lefebvre.

"I was only there for about two or three months. They weren't drawing worth the beans. Finally, the owner called me into the office and said, 'We gotta send you back to Boston.' I wasn't doing too well, anyway."[12]

After losing four of five decisions for the Seals, Bill was shipped back to the Red Sox organization. He finished the season with Little Rock, a Class A1 affiliate in the Southern Association. Pitching for a poor team—Little Rock finished the season at 61–92—Bill compiled a 6–13 record, although his 3.62 ERA was the best on the staff. His performance did not go unnoticed by the Red Sox brass, who sent him back to the American Association the following season.

1941 found him back in Louisville, this time posting much better numbers than his previous stint there. Bill went 12–7 with a 3.51 ERA for the Colonels, but he did not receive a call from Boston at season's end. Beginning in '41, he would spend each of the next three seasons in the American Association, or the "big minors," as it was sometimes called. Competition was particularly stiff, both from fellow hurlers trying to break into a starting rotation, and from the hitters.

He went back to Minneapolis in 1942. The Millers were no longer the Red Sox proving ground as in years past, but they kept a working agreement with the Washington Senators, among others. He went 9–11 with Minneapolis—not a bad record, but certainly not worthy of big-league consideration. Four other Millers pitchers won more games than Bill in '42.

1943 was easily Bill's best year in professional baseball. Once again with the Millers, he won 12 games and lost eight. He pitched far better than his record indicated, as his league-leading 2.22 ERA suggests. He lost two ballgames by the score of 3–1, one by the score of 2–1, and an eleven-inning affair where he gave up only three runs.

"I had good control for a left-hander. I hit spots, you know? I was never overpowering. I probably threw in the 88 to 89 mph range. I had a slider, which was supposed to be a curveball, but I never had a big curveball. I threw a palmball, like Satchel Paige. You put the ball in your hand, and you let it drop between your little finger and the thumb. It's a floater, you know? Change of pace."[13]

Although Bill was mostly a starter, Millers manager Tom Sheehan used him quite frequently in relief. Seven of his 22 appearances were out of the bullpen. On several occasions, Sheehan used Bill in relief within two days of a complete-game start. Sheehan had suggested to Bill that these relief appearances would amount to no more than a few batters late in a game. In fact, they averaged more than two innings.

Two days after a complete-game loss to Toledo, Bill pitched four and a third innings of relief versus Louisville—and won the game. After a win against St. Paul on June 25, he pitched two innings of relief against Milwaukee on June 27. He repeated the effort the following day, then fired a six-hitter against Kansas City on July 1.

He pitched 13 complete games, and in one amazing twelve-day stretch, from July 11 to July 22, he pitched *four* complete-game victories, capped by a three-hit shutout of Indianapolis. That was enough for Washington. The Senators purchased his contract from Minneapolis on July 28.

It was also enough for *The Sporting News*, which ran an article on Bill's exploits in early August. Under the verbose heading "Fine Grind on Hill for Millers Lifts Lefty Lefebvre to Majors," the article noted his consistency in years past, with a nod to the future:

"The steady, slightly better than average left-hander of other years has become the best southpaw and one of the three best pitchers in the American Association.

"This year, well-pitched games have rolled off his left arm in a steady stream. Now he gets his reward."[14]

Bill picked up right where he had left off with the Millers and American Association hitters. Making his first start in the majors in nearly four years, he pitched a complete-game victory against the Indians in Cleveland on August 16. He scattered nine hits over nine innings while striking out seven and walking just one.

After surrendering three runs in the first four innings, he shut out Cleveland for the final five frames. Washington scored three runs in the eighth and won the game, 6–3.

Incredibly, Bill's first trip to the plate in his renaissance season was almost a reprisal of his first big-league at-bat. Facing Indians ace Jim Bagby in the third, he connected on the first pitch, sending a drive to deep right.

"We were playing at old League Park. There was a short right field. The regular wall was about ten feet high, and they had a wire fence above that. There was a board along the top of that fence, and I hit the board. Another three inches, and I would've had a home run. Instead, I doubled."[15]

He fared almost as well in his second start against the White Sox on August 21. After giving up two runs in the first inning, Bill shut down Chicago for the next six innings. Leading 3–2 in the eighth, he gave up a two-run single to White Sox third baseman Tony Cuccinello, which gave Chicago a 4–3 advantage. Bill singled in the ninth inning (he had two hits in the game) and left for a pinch runner.

The Senators tied the score later in the inning, but relief pitcher Alex Carrasquel walked in the winning run in Chicago's half of the inning. Bill gave up eight hits, walked two, struck out one, and gave up four earned runs.

His third and final start of 1943 was the only poor outing of his six Washington appearances. Against the Browns at Sportsman's Park, he was greeted in the first inning with back-to-back home runs by Vern Stephens and Mark Christman, the former a three-run shot. Washington tied the score, and Bill managed to hold St. Louis scoreless for the next three innings. He was relieved by Carrasquel in the fifth. The Browns scored late in the game and won 7–4.

He pitched relief in three games before the close of the season. On September 12, in relief of Dutch Leonard, he worked four innings against the Athletics, giving up just one run. Washington rallied from behind late in the game, and Bill got his second win. He finished his call-up with a 2–0 record and a 4.45 ERA. He had had only one poor performance, and more importantly, he demonstrated his versatility as both a starter and reliever. After a strong spring, Bill joined the Senators for his first full season in the big leagues in 1944.

The pitching staff of the 1944 Washington Senators was something of a big-league anomaly. Four of the five starting pitchers—Leonard, Mickey Haefner, Johnny Niggeling and Roger Wolff—were knuckleballers. Rick Ferrell and backup Mike Guerra had the dubious task of catching them. Early Wynn was the fifth starter, with Carrasquel and Milo Candini making occasional starts.

Bill didn't see action until mid–May and was used only twice as a relief pitcher before June 1. On May 27 in Cleveland, he relieved starter Roger Wolff in the fifth inning with the Senators trailing 4–0. Washington tied the score at four in the eighth inning, and Bill held the Indians scoreless through the eleventh. After giving up a walk and a double with one out in the twelfth, he gave way to reliever Carrasquel, who promptly gave up the game-winning hit.

On the afternoon, Bill worked seven innings of four-hit ball. He was charged with the winning run and therefore the loss, but the outing

Lefty Lefebvre with the Senators in 1943. ©Brace Photograph.

got the attention of manager Ossie Bluege, who started Bill the following week against the first-place St. Louis Browns.

The Browns had started out like gangbusters, winning their first nine contests. By the first of June, they held a slim lead over the Yankees. Brownie starter Jack Kramer lasted only into the fifth, giving up ten hits and five runs. Stan Spence, Bill's old teammate with the Millers and now the Senators' center fielder, went a superb six for six on the afternoon, with a home run and five RBIs. Washington hitters gave Bill four runs over the first two innings and twenty hits on the day. He gave up a run in each of the last three innings, but the Senators added three in the seventh and two in the eighth for and 11–5 triumph.

Bill went all nine innings, allowing thirteen hits and five runs. It wasn't a pretty victory—he also gave up five walks—but he had succeeded in showing Bluege, not to mention the American League pennant winners, that he could hold his own.

Bluege used him more frequently in June, though mostly in mop-up roles. He pitched in both games of a doubleheader versus Boston on June 25. After pitching two scoreless innings in the seventh and eighth, he was credited with the victory in the Senators' 5–4 win. He worked a scoreless ninth in relief of Milo Candini to finish out the second game.

Unable to crack the starting rotation, Bill soon found that he could contribute in other ways. The Senators had lost their two best pinch hitters in the off season. Outfielder Gene Moore went to the Browns in the trade that brought Ferrell to the Senators. Infielder Sherry Robertson went into the service. Together, Moore and Robertson had combined for 17 pinch hits and a .294 batting average off the bench. In addition, both men were left-handed hitters.

Bluege suspected that he had more than a left-handed relief pitcher in Bill Lefebvre. The first-pitch homer notwithstanding, Bill had batted over .300 (eight for 25) in his brief major league trial. In addition to relief work, Bluege began to use Bill as a left-handed bat off the bench.

The experiment worked. Besides working 25 games as a pitcher, Bill appeared in an additional 36 games for Washington, mostly as a pinch hitter. He was a particular thorn in the side of the Detroit Tigers' Dizzy Trout, winner of 27 games in 1944. Bill managed two pinch hits off Trout, one of them a triple that drove in a run. No doubt chastened by their first two meetings, Trout walked Bill in their third and final encounter.

His *coup de grace* came in a doubleheader against the Yankees in August. New York was chasing the Browns and Tigers in a tight pennant race. A sweep of the Senators would have brought them to within two games of the league lead. The Yankees won the opener, 4–2, behind the pitching of starter Monk Dubiel. Batting for Senators pitcher Mickey Haefner in the ninth inning, Bill singled off Dubiel and was pulled for a pinch runner.

Going into the eighth inning of the nightcap, Washington led, 4–1. The Yankees scored three runs off Carrasquel in the top of the inning and seemed poised to leave town with their sweep. But with two outs in the ninth inning and the bases full of Senators, Bluege called second baseman Fred Vaughn back to the bench. Earlier in the game, Vaughn, a right-handed hitter, had driven in a run with a single. Right-hander Jim Turner, the Yankees' relief ace, was on the mound for New York. Bluege wanted a left-handed bat, and he called on Bill to pinch hit for the second time that day. The following day's *New York Times* described what happened next:

"...the McCarthymen saw Wilfrid Lefebvre, a relief pitcher by trade, belt Jim Turner for a pinch single with the bases loaded and the score tied in the ninth of the afterpiece and that surprise shot won this one for Oscar Bluege's tailenders, 5 to 4, to the cheers of 19,009."[16]

On the season, Bill batted .345 as a pinch hitter, better than the combined efforts of Moore and Robertson a year earlier. Remarkably, his ten pinch hits were tops in the American League. Prior to 1944, several pitchers led their leagues in pinch hits. Red Lucas made something of a career of it. From 1929 to 1937, Lucas led the National League in pinch hits on four separate occasions. But since 1944, no other regular pitcher has done it. Bill Lefebvre was the last.[17]

Bluege even used Bill at first base on two occasions to spell regular first baseman Joe Kuhel. He went hitless in both games, but played errorless ball.

"When I was at Holy Cross, we were playing Fordham. Hank Borowy was pitching for Fordham. I pitched against him, and I beat him. I got a couple of hits off him. It was an off day for the Yankees. Joe McCarthy was at the game. He was interested in Borowy.

"He came over to see me after the ballgame was over. McCarthy asked me what I was going to do [after college], and I think I told him I already committed myself to the Red Sox. I don't think he liked my pitching too much, but he said, 'You ought to be a first baseman.' I did play first base for two games with Washington. I couldn't run very fast, but I could hit."[18]

Apart from pinch hitting, there were other good performances on the mound. A week after beating the Yankees with his hit off Turner, Bill started against New York at Yankee Stadium. After giving up two runs in the first inning, he settled down and gave up only one run over the next seven. He singled off Yankees starter Ernie Bonham, but Washington could only muster one run in the sixth. The Senators lost, 3–1. Bill went the distance, scattering nine hits with two strikeouts and no walks.

He was scheduled to make another start a few days after the loss to the Yankees, but the game was rained out. Prior to the end of the season, he pitched relief in three ballgames. He worked a scoreless ninth inning on September 17 to earn his third save of the year, one of two against the Red Sox. He finished the season with a 2–4 record, and a 4.52 ERA.

The war caught up with Bill Lefebvre before spring training in 1945. He was drafted into the army and did his basic training at Camp Croft, South Carolina. He was assigned to a demolition unit in charge of mine sweeping. When basic training ended, portions of Bill's unit were to be sent off to France and Japan.

Bill's greatest challenges during the war came not from the European and Pacific theaters, but on the home front. Before he completed basic training, he returned home to Pawtucket for two weeks after his wife miscarried. Not long after returning to Camp Croft, he received word that his five-year-old son was involved in bus accident. Again he returned to Pawtucket while the boy recovered from his injuries.

By the time he returned to Camp Croft, his unit was gone. His hardship leaves had prevented him first from going to Japan, then from serving as an interpreter in France. He would serve out the remainder of his tour in the States.

Naturally, Camp Croft had a baseball team. Numbered among the players on the squad were Red Sox third baseman Jim Tabor and an unknown, eighteen-year-old catcher by the name of Smoky Burgess. Bill spent the summer of 1945 as Camp Croft's primary pitcher.

"The manager of the team was regular army. He thought he was Warren Spahn himself. He imitated him and everything. I think I pitched too much in the army. He pitched me every Monday, Wednesday, and Friday, which was all right with me. I still felt pretty good. But I think he ruined me."[19]

Bill returned to the Senators in 1946 after his discharge. Halfway through spring training, he was sent back to Minneapolis, where he was faced with a familiar dilemma. Zeke Bonura had started the '46 season as the Millers' manager. After Minneapolis began to wallow in the second division, Bonura was fired, and Tom Sheehan was brought back.

"I started the season in 1946, and I was doing OK. I had won eight and lost two by the first of June. I thought I was going to win 20 to 25 ballgames.

Sheehan wanted to win real bad. I would pitch a full game — the whole nine innings. The next day, he would come up to me and say, 'Bill, I want you to pitch to one hitter.' But it was never one hitter. I think that's how I hurt my arm.

"Some guys can pitch every day. I didn't have that type of arm. If I pitched one day, Christ, I couldn't wipe my ass the next day. All I'd do was play a pepper game and do my sprints in the outfield. I'd probably pitch batting practice on the second day, and on the third or fourth day I'd be ready to start a game.

"I had a rotator cuff [injury], but they didn't know what the hell that was back then. They'd get that hot stuff and rub your arm with it. 'You'll be all right, you'll be all right.'"[20]

But he wasn't. After his 8–2 start, Bill finished the season 11–12, with a whopping 6.41 ERA. He finished the season with the Millers, but it was clear that his arm wasn't getting better.

"I had a chance to manage Pawtucket in the New England League. That's where I was from. Meanwhile, the Minneapolis ball club was sold to the Giants. Carl Hubbell was the farm director, and he wouldn't give me my release. If a guy has a chance to go manage a team somewhere else, they usually give them their release. I didn't even pitch an inning for them. My arm was dead."[21]

Like many former ballplayers of his time, baseball figured prominently in Bill Lefebvre's life after his professional career ended. He went on to become the baseball coach at Brown University, a position he held for sixteen years.

After Brown, he returned to Pawtucket, where he spent 25 years teaching physical education for fifth and sixth graders.

He kept his ties to major league baseball, too, working as a scout for his first team, the Red Sox. It was his recommendation that brought Joe Sambito, a supposedly washed-up relief pitcher, to Boston. The left-handed Sambito was a strong presence in the Boston bullpen for the '86 pennant winners. He appeared in 53 games that year and earned 12 saves.

The son who was involved in the bus accident — the bus didn't hit him, *he* hit the bus—made a full recovery. Named Bill after his dad, he went on to catch for several years in the St. Louis Cardinals organization and lost an opportunity to play in the big leagues when Tim McCarver got called up to the parent club.

Bill retired to Florida and at this writing is recovering from knee replacement surgery, hoping to return to the golf course soon.

Throughout the history of the game, only a handful of players can rightly claim that they started off their careers with the same bang as Bill Lefebvre. Record books might forever pigeonhole him for that first-pitch home run off Stratton in June of 1938. But few players would ever have the good sense to put such a moment behind them and just play ball. Bill Lefebvre was able to do that. Some home runs are flukes, but the same cannot be said of one's character.

"I was never a great pitcher. Hell, I was never a great *ballplayer*. I don't brag about it, but I got my shot up there."[22]

8
Eddie Basinski

"Inside, I had the same competitive fire that Michael Jordan, Lou Gehrig, Joe DiMaggio and Tiger Woods had. I just don't look the part, and people don't like it."

—Eddie Basinski[1]

By his own admission, Eddie Basinski never really looked like a major leaguer. Players, fans, and managers eyed his slender frame and thick, wire-rimmed glasses with great skepticism. Out of uniform, he could have been a professor or a preacher. Dodgers president and general manager Branch Rickey referred to him as "the escaped divinity student."

Public underestimation aside, the things Eddie Basinski accomplished *in* uniform gave more than a few folks reason for pause. He was a slick-fielding infielder with remarkably quick reflexes who could turn a double play faster than anyone in the league.

His talents did not come naturally. More than any other quality, it was his competitive drive that separated him from the herd. He practiced tirelessly, approaching the game and how it was played in ways that his contemporaries never considered.

In a professional career that spanned 16 seasons he would earn accolades from some of the biggest names in baseball and even land himself in *Ripley's Believe It or Not!* He was, in point of fact, a true baseball iconoclast, but only in the best of ways.

Experience had prepared Eddie Basinski for the fate awaiting him as he walked into the baseball tryouts for East High School in Buffalo, New York. Throughout most of his young life, he had been on the receiving end of a peculiar brand of prejudice—the belief that an athlete must be "athletic-looking." In an age of robust sports heroes like Jimmie Foxx, Red Grange and Joe Louis, the frame Eddie cut with his slight build, scholarly appearance, and Coke-bottle glasses did little to bolster his chances for making the team, much less pierce the thick veneer of public opinion.

Here was a kid who looked like the "before" picture in the old Charles Atlas ads. What nerve, to think that he could make a team that had won nine consecutive baseball championships! What did this guy know about winning?

Most players encounter a few obstacles on their journey to the big leagues. Eddie Basinski encountered brick walls. He was born into a large, working-class, Polish family in Buffalo. His father was a former navy man who ran his house like a battleship, believing that in order to make it in life, his son needed an honest trade—carpenter, machinist, or tool and die maker, like his old man. Baseball was a frivolous pursuit and had no place in his son's development. Eddie had to sneak out of the house just to play and risked a beating at his father's hand if he was found out.

When it came to practicing baseball, Eddie was picky about the company he kept. He surrounded himself with like-minded ballplayers who shared his dedication to the game. One of them happened to be Buffalo native Warren Spahn.

"The city park was next to the street I lived on. There were five aspiring baseball hopefuls who practiced every day there.

"We rotated our practices so that each player got 30 swings of batting practice, each played the outfield and infield, and each of us pitched batting practice. We were able to make the complete rotation three times before it got dark."[2]

If no one else showed at the park, he still had his own training regimen to follow. He practiced base running and sliding. He stood a bat on end in front of the backstop, then went into the outfield to practice making throws to the plate.

"I had something going for me in baseball. I was quick on my feet. I could leap. I had long arms. I thought, 'This is it for me. There isn't any other way.' For me, it was trying to find some way to gain some sort of recognition, so I wasn't just one of those Polish punks over there from Kaiser Town in Buffalo. None of us were going anywhere. Sports was the only avenue I had at that time."[3]

There were other interests besides baseball. Music played a critical role in young Eddie's life. He studied classical violin from the age of five. By the time he reached East High School, he had joined its eighty-member symphony orchestra—a staple at East, as famous as its baseball team. Eddie began playing in the last chair of the second violins during his freshman year. By the time he was a junior, he was the concertmaster, having challenged and outplayed forty other violinists to get there. His determination was well known at East High School.

It was surely some measure of that determination that drove him onto East's baseball field, hoping to demonstrate his talents as an athlete. The coach, however, would not be moved.

"Pop Yerke never even looked at me. I went to try out for the team. He saw me with the glasses, knowing that I was very important to the principal with the orchestra. He said, 'My God, my boy! What in the hell are you doing out here?!' Like I was a freak, or something.

"I said, 'Mr. Yerke, I'd liked to make the baseball team!'

"He looked at me for a while and said, 'Is there anything else that you like to do?' I told him that I liked tennis. 'Good!' he said. 'I'll talk to the tennis coach!' That's how I made my letters—in tennis and cross-country."[4]

To his great credit, Eddie didn't allow the incident with Yerke to deter his drive to succeed at baseball. If anything, the coach's slight only served to fuel his determination. He continued to practice in earnest, hoping to someday play for the semipro AA leagues in Buffalo.

But he was careful not to let baseball interfere with his other pursuits—particularly academics and music. After graduating high school, he attended the University of Buffalo, which had a top-notch engineering program, but no baseball team. He continued to study the violin and even occupied a seat with the Buffalo Symphony Orchestra. In 1943, he earned a degree in mechanical engineering and went to work for the Curtiss-Wright Company in Buffalo.

Curtiss-Wright was one of the largest aircraft manufacturers in the country. By 1943, they were the primary producer of several U.S. warplanes, including the P-40 Warhawk, the P-47 Thunderbolt and the C-46 cargo plane.

Eddie's job as engineer was to perform time and motion studies on the assembly floor. He observed assembly line workers performing their specialized tasks—mounting propellers, riveting sheets of aluminum to the fuselage. He noted the physical movements required for each job. Using a stopwatch, he timed workers as they repeatedly performed each task. In doing so, he helped workers find more time-efficient means of performing even the smallest pieces of assembly and helped expedite the production of the planes.

As he spent long hours watching the workers on the line, he couldn't help but wonder if the same principles of time and motion could be applied to certain aspects of baseball. He thought about the mechanics necessary to field a batted ball, or make the pivot at second base on a double play. Could he also find the most time-efficient way to make those plays?

He found a forum in which to showcase the baseball skills he had been perfecting with his training. The city of Buffalo had an impressive system of summer leagues offered at every level of age and competition. The most competitive were the AA leagues—a network of three mutually exclusive semipro associations. Scheduling was designed so ingeniously that a player could join a team in each league and never have to worry about a conflict. Naturally, Eddie joined teams in all three leagues.

"Two of my teams played all their games during the week—two or three a week sometimes. All evening games. The top AA teams played all their games on weekends, sometimes doubleheaders."[5]

Eddie played shortstop and batted cleanup on each of his three teams. He began to apply his engineering skills to his work as an infielder, asking teammates to use a stopwatch to help him log how much time it took him to get rid of a ball once he fielded it or received it from another fielder on a double play. His offense began to turn heads as well. He immediately set about dismantling the competition, leading each league in several offensive categories. He led all three leagues in home runs and RBIs while batting .475, .575, and .609. For the latter team, he hit 18 home runs in 22 games, while stealing 34 bases in as many attempts.

It was the summer of 1943, and a number of key individuals began to take notice of the 20-year-old phenom. The first was Dick Fisher, who owned a sporting goods store in Buffalo and acted as a sometime bird dog scout for major league teams. The other was Johnny Mokan, a former major league outfielder with the Pirates and Phillies, who managed the park where Eddie did his training. Using their connections, both men began to lobby major league teams to take notice of the as yet unknown infielder.

At season's end, an All-Star team composed of the top Buffalo players from all three leagues met to play similar teams in New York and Pennsylvania. One such team from Oil City, Pennsylvania, boasted a 19-game winning streak. Fisher and Mokan had managed to convince Branch Rickey to send a scout to the Oil City game. Eddie did not disappoint.

"My team, the Buffalo All-Stars, hammered them 9–1. [They were] so bitter, we had to escape out of town without changing out of our uniforms."[6]

On the game, Eddie had a two-run triple, and two, three-run home runs. He accounted for eight of his teams nine runs. It was the perfect performance under perfect circumstances. The Dodger scout returned to Brooklyn and convinced Rickey to give Eddie serious consideration.

"The war was on at the time. I got eight deferments for the work I was doing [at Curtiss-Wright]. The draft board called me on three different occasions, and I had to go through these exams. I thought I was gone. Everybody was going. All my buddies I'd played with—they'd gone. There I was, a pretty good athlete, and I'm still around."[7]

Through their various sources, Mokan and Fisher felt certain that the Dodgers would be willing to offer Eddie a $5,000 signing bonus in addition to a regular contract. It was a great deal of money, but Eddie was cautious. He understood that signing with the Dodgers and reporting to one of their clubs meant forfeiting the deferments he earned with Curtiss-Wright. If the armed forces wanted him, he'd be there for the taking. But the money was important for other reasons.

"My folks moved from Buffalo to Lancaster, which is east of Buffalo. They bought a 60-acre farm and went into a heavy mortgage. There was a $7,500 mortgage on that farm. I said, 'Well, hell. If the army's going to get me anyways, I might as well grab the money.' I gave it to my folks and they paid off that mortgage."[8]

The army classified Eddie as "Limited Service," but never called him up. Although they never gave a reason why, one likely explanation was his eyesight, which in 1943 was 20–800.

Later that spring, Rickey flew to Buffalo. At the Buffalo Athletic Club, he met with Eddie, his father, and Mokan, who was acting as Eddie's agent. The major league season was already several weeks old, and the Dodger ranks were sorely depleted. Rickey didn't mince words.

"My boy, where do you think you can play?" he asked.

Eddie told him he was certain he could play at the Triple-A level and suggested that Rickey send him to the Montreal Royals of the International League. There was an ulterior motive to playing for the Royals, as Buffalo was one of their opponents. Eddie wanted to play in front of his friends.

"So Rickey said, 'Hmm, I'll tell you what, my boy. You'll join the [big-league] club in St. Louis where they are, and you will practice with them for two weeks. At the end of the two weeks, with Durocher and Dressen looking at you, we will decide where you will play.'

"And that's what happened. Those two weeks were the most exciting, wonderful, unpretentious, relaxed weeks. I had no responsibilities. I figured I wasn't going to play. I'm out there practicing. I come in and take a shower, while all these other guys have to go out and play. I said, 'God, this is wonderful!'"[9]

Reality set in two weeks later in the clubhouse at Crosley Field. Prior to a game against the Cincinnati Reds, Durocher pulled out his lineup card and read aloud the names of Brooklyn's starting nine. In the eight slot, he called out "Basinski, second base!"

"And, oh my God! The silence in that clubhouse. Durocher said, 'All right, you guys, I know what you're thinking. But we're in seventh place. Hell, we've got to do *something*. Give the kid a break!' I looked like a freak! I didn't even know how to wear the cap right!"[10]

When Eddie Basinski took the field for the Brooklyn Dodgers in Cincinnati on May 20, 1944, it's likely that neither he nor his teammates had any notion that an interesting bit of history was being made. There had been several ballplayers who made it to the major leagues without having played minor league ball. But in the history of the game, no other ballplayer had followed the same path to the majors as Eddie had: He attended and graduated from both high school and college, but did not play baseball at either institution. In addition, he went straight from Buffalo's semipro AA leagues to the Dodgers. *Ripley's Believe it or Not!* called it a ten million-to-one shot, and it's unlikely it will ever be repeated. Even before the first pitch of his first game had been thrown, Eddie had made the record books.[11]

As if the historical footnote wasn't enough, he added an exclamation point to the day. In his first big-league at-bat, Eddie stood in against Reds left-hander Clyde Shoun. One week earlier, Shoun had thrown a no-hitter against the Boston Braves. Eddie took Shoun's first offering, then lined the next pitch off the left field wall for a triple.

"Man, I'm telling you. In semipro there are no fences. You hit a ball to leftcenter—that's a home run. Durocher had to tackle me as I ran around third! I fell down and just barely got back to third. They would have thrown me out by thirty feet.

"I got back to third base and Durocher said, 'Where in the hell did you learn how to play ball? Christ almighty! Didn't you see the sign?' I said, 'What sign?'

"Anyway, I was ready to go back to Buffalo. I had done it—the impossible! I wanted to go back and bask in the glory of that one game for the rest of my life! That's the way I really felt."[12]

Although praised for his offense in the *Times* the next day, his defense also caused a stir:

"Eddie was the pivot man on a double play that came after [Hal] Gregg had issued his first pass to Eddie Miller, and his relay was so so swift that he nailed Chuck Aleno by at least ten feet after snaring Bill Hart's toss."[13]

Violinist, engineer, and one heck of a second baseman: Eddie Basinski with the Dodgers in 1944. ©Brace Photograph.

It was the first of many praises for Eddie's defense, on which he concentrated with characteristic fervor. In particular, he worked hard on his quick release on the pivot.

"There are four steps in making the pivot: the catch, the tag, the plant and the throw. Instead of four separate motions, each demanding more time, I wanted to combine all these movements—as close as possible—into one explosive action. This would require perfect anticipation and timing."[14]

Durocher taught him how to receive a throw from another infielder. Instead of catching the ball in the webbing or pocket of his glove, he saved time by ricocheting the ball off his glove and into his bare hand, ready to make the throw in an instant. His long, rangy build was perfectly suited to combining each component part into one fluid motion. In a split second, he could make the pivot and fire accurately to first base. Durocher began calling him "The Bazooka," referring to his powerful throwing arm. The engineer had made the art of playing second base a little more efficient.

By the first of June, he was hitting over .300, making both Durocher and Rickey look like geniuses. The sportswriters didn't quite know what to make of him, with his looks, college education (still a rarity in 1944), and the fact that he played the violin. At least they always had an angle when they wrote about him. Writers used words like "bespectacled" and "scholarly" to describe him. And they couldn't resist mentioning his musicianship at almost every turn:

"For while Ed numbers among his accomplishments the ability to play a violin, the Brooklyn horde in the stands will vow it never heard better music than that which master Basinski produced with his bat when he exploded first a single and later a double."[15]

Even Dodgers radio announcer Red Barber got in on the act. When Eddie made a fine play in the field, Barber was heard to quip, "The violin is playing sweetly today!"[16]

In reality, few if any people in Brooklyn had actually heard him play. Not wanting to risk damaging or losing his precious violin, he left it with his parents in Lancaster. As the press continued to mention his musical virtuosity in the same sentence as his fielding ability, a few Dodgers found it difficult to contain their curiosity.

The whole issue came to a head on a western roadtrip. Brooklyn had just swept the Cardinals in a Sunday doubleheader in St. Louis. Aboard the team train heading for Chicago, Durocher held court before the reporters in the club car. Spying Basinski across the aisle, he decided to have some fun at his rookie's expense.

"Leo challenged me about all the publicity I was getting about being a concert violinist. He said I was a fake. I studied for sixteen years! That really offended me."[17]

If Durocher's plan had been to get a rise out of his young ballplayer, he got more than he bargained for. With a small crowd gathering in the car, Eddie offered a challenge to Durocher. He would play his violin in front of Leo and any other music critics he wanted to bring with him. If they liked what they heard, Leo would pay him $1,000.

Durocher blinked. The kid had sand after all. Realizing that he had painted himself into a corner, he countered with a wager of his own: Eddie would play in the Brooklyn clubhouse before a home game. If he liked what he heard, Durocher would buy him the best suit of clothes that *Eddie* could afford. (This was an important stipulation, since Durocher often spared no expense on his own wardrobe.)

Eddie arranged to have his mother and older brother travel down from Lancaster to Brooklyn. They brought his violin along and took in a Dodgers game at Ebbets Field. "I practiced for several days, as baseball is not kind to finger dexterity and fluid performance."[18]

He picked the day and told Durocher to be ready. Arriving early before a night game against the Giants, he dressed in his Dodgers uniform and strolled through the clubhouse playing his violin as his surprised teammates arrived. He decided that Bach, Brahms and Tchaikovsky would not be appropriate, so he stuck to the "light classics"—Cole Porter, Irving Berlin, Victor Herbert—taking requests as they were hollered out.

As he played "Three O'clock in the Morning," requested by coach Charlie Dressen, Durocher appeared in the clubhouse doorway. He paused and proclaimed in a loud voice, "Well, I'll be a son of a bitch! The kid can play!" Eddie continued to play while Durocher shaved in his office.

"He lost the bet—something he rarely did. [He was] a shark gambler, especially at cards. I purchased an $85 suit in Cincinnati. Leo approved and paid for it."[19]

By mid-July, Eddie's hitting had fallen off. His average had dipped to .250, and he was beginning to learn that consistency was the most important part of being a major leaguer.

"The pressure got to me because I wasn't getting any support from any of the guys on the team. Of course, the first two weeks I was drilling the ball, but the guys were real quiet. Nobody was very friendly. I don't know what it was, but they didn't warm up to me. Anyway, they switched me with Barney Koch, who was with Montreal."[20]

The 20-year-old Koch proved to be a disappointment. He had hit .250 with Montreal, but with Brooklyn he batted just .219 and drove in a single run in 96 at-bats. Eddie finished the International League season with Montreal, batting .244 and thoroughly enjoying the chance to play in front of the home folks in Buffalo. When rosters expanded in mid-September, he was back in Brooklyn, replacing Koch.

Fifty-three different players wore Dodger blue in 1944, the highest total for any team during the war.[21] As players went off to the service, Branch Rickey did his best to plug the holes. Eddie finished his two stints at Brooklyn with a .257 batting average—better than his two months in Montreal. Even so, his future with the team was uncertain.

The Dodgers picked up Eddie Stanky from the Cubs in a mid-season trade. Stanky finished the season as Brooklyn's regular second baseman. When they lost shortstop Bobby Bragan to the draft after September, they added infielder Mike Sandlock from the Braves. Sandlock began his professional career as a catcher. He went on to become a promising shortstop in the Boston Braves organization, but a knee injury had begun to limit his range. Eddie went into the 1945 season with very little clue as to how he would be used, if at all.

"The next year, it didn't look like I was going to go with the team. Mike Sandlock, who I played against, was a big guy, a catcher. It looked like he was going to be the opening day shortstop for the Dodgers. I was working out at second base with Stanky, and it looked like Stanky had control of that. I didn't know where I was going to end up.

"But opening day in the Polo Grounds, without any warning, Leo reads the lineup, and he's got me down at shortstop. God, I almost fell off the damn chair!"[22]

The first two months of the '45 season were something of a rude awakening for Eddie. Although he sparkled defensively at shortstop, his hitting was subpar. He learned that unlike pitchers in semipro, *major league* pitchers throw curveballs. Once word spread throughout the league that Eddie struggled with the curve, he began to receive a steady diet of them wherever he played. His frustrations at the plate began to effect his play in the field.

"I was hitting around .200, playing good shortstop. I was showing a lot of my disgust when I ran out to the shortstop position, you know, kicking dirt and all. Durocher saw it. He called me into the clubhouse, and we had a private conversation.

"He told me, 'Look, kid, you're my shortstop. That's all I care about. You play shortstop and you don't have to hit *zero!* We'll be all right.'

"I said, 'Damn it, Leo, I can't accept that! I killed everybody [at Buffalo]. Eighteen home runs in 22 games!'

"He said, 'Well, listen, you gotta forget that, because it's starting to bother you at shortstop. You don't have to hit anything.'

"Well, I was insulted by that. After that happened, I decided the hell with it. I'm just going to stand up there, crowd the plate and force those damn pitchers to get the ball over before I swung at the ball. They were throwing these waste pitches, and pretty soon I was 2–0,

8. *Eddie Basinski*

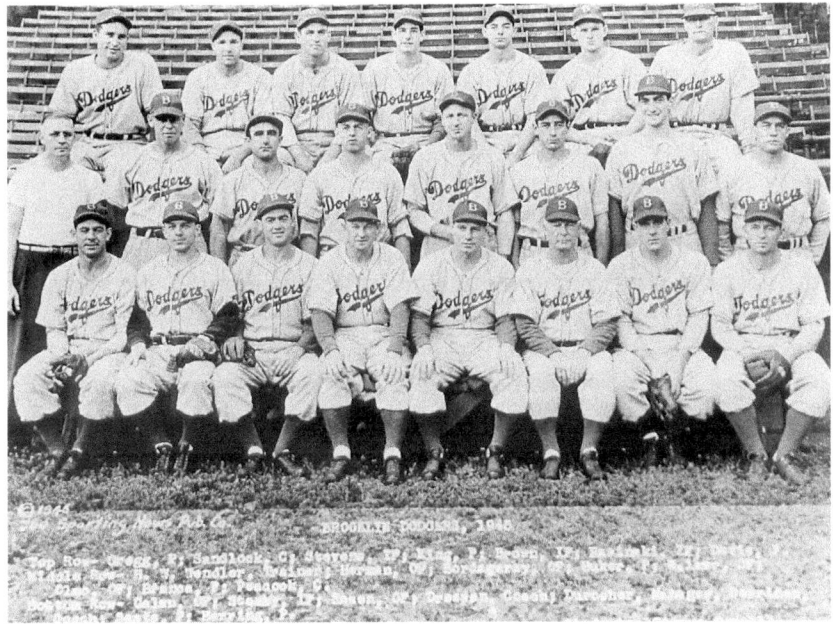

The 1945 Brooklyn Dodgers. Top row: Hal Gregg, Mike Sandlock, Eddie Stevens, Clyde King, Tommy Brown, Eddie Basinski, Curt Davis. Middle row: Doc Wendler (trainer), Babe Herman, Frenchy Bordagaray, Cy Buker, Dixie Walker, Luis Olmo, Ralph Branca, Johnny Peacock. Bottom row: Augie Galan, Eddie Stanky, Goody Rosen, Charlie Dressen, Leo Durocher, Red Corriden, Tom Seats, Art Herring. Lee Pfund was injured at the time of the photograph and is not pictured. Courtesy *The Sporting News*.

3–1, 3–0. I was getting those guys to come inside, and I was just murdering them.

"It was an insult by Durocher that made me so furious that I said, 'I'm not gonna move. If they want to hit me—good, let them hit me! I'm going to stand there and show them I'm not afraid.' That's how I started on that hitting streak."[23]

A hitting streak is one of those rare, baseball catalysts that can jump-start a player's season while igniting the play of an entire team. By June 7, 1945, the Brooklyn Dodgers had won 23 games while losing 20—a dramatic improvement from their seventh-place finish a year earlier when they finished just two games ahead of the last-place Phillies. Their record notwithstanding, the Dodgers failed to win consistently. After a poor start, they put together a nine-game winning streak in early May, only to squander the ground they gained over the next several weeks. Although several Brooklyn players were having their finest seasons, the Dodgers languished in fourth place behind the Giants, Cardinals, and Pirates. With only three games separating the four teams, something had to give.

Eddie started the month of June hitting below .250, considerably below the goal he had set for himself in this, his second big league season. Since he had resolved to make the pitchers come to him, there had been some success. He had a five-hit afternoon on June 3 against the Reds, but by the end of the first week in June, his name appeared at the bottom of the *Major League Averages* graphic in the Sunday *Times*, an incomplete list of the league's top hitters.[24] There were more than 40 names above his own—a sobering fact. He felt more comfortable at the plate and, as a matter of personality, he was never lacking in confidence. All the same, the hits just weren't falling.

Although no one would realize it at the time, Brooklyn's luck was about to change. For the next several weeks, the Dodgers would play less like a group of talented but underachieving ballplayers and more like pennant contenders. Through it all, it was Eddie Basinski who served as Brooklyn's unlikely standard bearer.

On June 8, the Dodgers played the Philadelphia Blue Jays at Ebbets Field. Brooklyn scored early and often, chasing starting pitcher Oscar Judd from the mound with four runs in the second inning. Later in the game, Eddie singled off relief pitcher Lou Lucier. The Dodgers won the game, 9–1.

Eddie had hits in each of his next two ballgames, then went three for four versus the Giants on June 12. The following day, he drove in two runs against the Giants in a 3–2 victory that brought Brooklyn to within a half-game of the National League lead.

It was the fifth straight game in which he had hit safely, and the hits kept coming. Over the next several games, he faced some of the best pitching in the National League, collecting hits off the Giants' Bill Voiselle, along with Jim Tobin and Mort Cooper of the Boston Braves. He ran the streak to ten games in the second game of a doubleheader against Boston on June 17, with a base hit off starter Bob Logan.

During the first 10 games of Eddie's streak, Brooklyn averaged better than twelve hits and nearly seven runs per game. They leapfrogged over each of the top three teams and took a one-game lead in the National League. Brooklyn had a long list of contributors to its latest success.

Eddie Stanky had reached base in each of his last twenty games, and was becoming the league's best leadoff hitter. He was followed in the lineup by Goody Rosen, who was batting .360 and having the season of his life. All-Stars Augie Galan and Dixie Walker came next, and both were putting together fine seasons. Walker was en route to leading the National League with 124 RBIs. Luis Olmo batted fifth and surprised everyone by driving in 110 runs. In the sixth spot was 6'6" first baseman Howie Schultz, who had started slowly, but was beginning to find the stroke he had shown in 1944, when he drove in 83 runs.

Eddie usually batted seventh or eighth, alternating with catchers Fats Dantonio, Sandlock, and 44-year-old Clyde Sukeforth, who had been pressed into service over the first two months of the season.

The streak spread like a virus throughout the Brooklyn clubhouse. Both Galan and Stanky had four-hit games within a day of each other. Rosen had two or more hits in six separate games. Since June 11, pitcher Hal Gregg had won all three of his starts. Olmo had boosted his RBI total to a league-leading 49. But none of Eddie's teammates hit the ball with his consistency.

On June 18, he singled in the third inning off Harry Feldman of the Giants in a twelve-inning Brooklyn victory. On June 20, he had hits in both games of a doubleheader against Philadelphia, which Brooklyn swept.

A day later, he singled off the Phils' Isidoro Leon and added a triple off reliever Andy Karl. Brooklyn won all three contests against Philadelphia and now led the National League by three and a half games. Eddie's streak was at 14 games.

June 22 brought the Braves to Ebbets Field, creating an interesting juxtaposition of two red-hot hitters. Boston right fielder Tommy Holmes was in the middle of his own hitting streak, having hit safely in his last 17 games going into the three-game series with the Dodgers. He was batting close to .400 and experiencing an unusual surge in his power numbers (he would lead the National League with 28 home runs). But unlike Eddie, Holmes played for a second-division club. The Braves struggled all season to stay above .500. Holmes was under pressure, but it was different from the kind of pressure Eddie felt.

So sat the table prior to the first game of the series. In the first inning of the opener, Holmes touched Gregg for a single, extending his streak to 18 games. Eddie singled off Ewald Pyle to run his streak to 15. The Dodgers won again, 8–7. Both hitters extended their streaks early in the second contest and ended with two hits apiece. Brooklyn scored five runs in the second and seventh innings and four more runs in the eighth. They hung on to win, 14–12. Holmes's streak stood at 19 games. Eddie's was at 16.

Sunday's doubleheader very nearly saw the end of both streaks. Eddie singled off Tobin in the first game to run his total up to 17 games. Holmes went hitless in his first four trips to the plate. Brooklyn starter Vic Lombardi led 9–3 after eight innings. Durocher left him in to finish the ninth. Holmes singled as a part of a three-run rally, but the Dodgers and Lombardi hung on to win, 9–6.

In the nightcap, Holmes made it 21 with a single off Curt Davis. In the second inning, Boston left fielder Joe Medwick smashed a low line drive toward the hole between short and third. With no time to turn with his glove hand, Eddie instinctively reached out with his bare right hand and snared the ball on one hop. He set himself and fired to Schultz at first to erase an incredulous Medwick.

It wasn't until the ball was being thrown around the infield that Eddie realized he'd been injured on the play.

"As I prepared to throw the ball to Eddie Stanky, it squirted out of my hand like a piece of wet soap."[25]

The ball was covered with blood. The impact of Medwick's drive had split the webbing between Eddie's ring and little fingers. He left the field and went into the clubhouse, where Dodgers trainer Doc Wendler used three stitches to close the wound. He also taped the two fingers together to prevent reopening. Eddie would play with the tape on his fingers for the next several weeks.

Because he had left the game prior to making an official plate appearance, his early departure did not end his streak, which held steady at 17 games. However, without Eddie in the lineup, Brooklyn lost for the first time in its last eight games.

As luck would have it, the Dodgers were idle for the next two days. Eddie had a chance to rest his hand as the Dodgers prepared to meet the Cubs for a four-game series at Ebbets Field. His fingers were stiff, and he still felt a lingering throb from the cut. Even so, he was dressed and in the starting lineup on Wednesday afternoon to open the series.

It didn't take him long to realize that swinging a bat wasn't going to be easy. Since the bottom two fingers on his right hand were taped together, he could not use them to grip the bat as he normally would. Rather, he relied on his index and middle fingers curled around the handle, meeting the thumb on the other side. The taped fingers were merely along for the ride.

In the second inning of his first game back, he faced Cubs right-hander Paul Derringer, who would win 16 games for Chicago in what ended up being his last big-league season. All melodrama ended with that first confrontation, as Eddie singled sharply to center field. As if to demonstrate that he felt no lingering aftereffects from the injury, he added two doubles later in the game. With Eddie back in the lineup, Brooklyn won, 6–5. More importantly, they now led the National League by four games.

On June 29, Eddie and the Dodgers faced Cubs pitcher Claude Passeau. Passeau was one of the toughest right-handers in the league. A 20-game winner prior to the war, he averaged better than 225 innings pitched from 1942 through 1945 and never had an ERA higher than 2.91 during the same span. He would go on to win 17 games for the Cubs in '45 and would pitch a one-hit shutout against the Tigers in the World Series. Passeau had a clear game plan with respect to Eddie Basinski.

"Passeau didn't overpower me, but he did outsmart me. He [pitched] me high fastballs over the outside part of the plate. I lifted long, high fly balls to the deepest part of center and right field. I should have made him come down into my power zone."[26]

Although he drove in a run with a sacrifice fly, none of his fly balls fell in for a base hit. Eddie's streak ended at 18 games, and the Dodgers fell to the Cubs, 11–8.

It could be argued that the Dodgers of June, 1945, simply came together as a team and began to win ballgames. Each player contributed to the atmosphere of winning. But Eddie's contribution to the overall success of the Dodgers was a singular achievement.

Over the 18-game stretch, he batted .411 (30 for 73). His average rose 62 points, from .254 to .316. The Dodgers won 16 games during the streak, and lost only two times. Their record improved to 39–23, four games ahead of their nearest rival. Eddie even succeeded in earning the praise of Branch Rickey. At a meeting of Brooklyn Rotarians late in June, Rickey went up and down the Dodgers' lineup, praising each player in turn.

When he got to Eddie's name, he grew serious for a moment and harkened back to the inscription he had placed on his late wife's tombstone. "'She was more to me than I expected.' So it is with Eddie Basinski." Rickey laughed at his comparison, then added, "He has been more than we expected, or even dreamed. He has come fast, he makes those tough plays, and he keeps swishing that bat."[27]

Although they would ultimately finish third behind the Cubs and Cardinals, their record of 87–67 marked a 24-game turnaround from their previous season—the most one-sided reversal of fortune in a single season by any major league team during the war. Eddie Basinski may not have been the lone spark that started Brooklyn on its winning ways, but his consistent hitting over those eighteen games did much to sustain Brooklyn's drive.

Eddie finished the season batting .262, a considerable cut above Durocher's "zero" figure. Plays like the bare-handed stab of Medwick's one-hop shot had earned him a reputation around the league as a fine defensive player. Gradually, he began to earn the respect of both his teammates and opponents. Once, when things weren't going well, he got a boost from an unexpected source.

"Stan Musial was my great hero. When Durocher was on my butt, Musial came over one time at Ebbets Field while they were taking batting practice. He saw me on the side, and he called me over.

"'Ed,' he says, 'you're doing a fantastic job for this ball club. Don't let anyone tell you any different. Keep up the good work.'

"I thought that was superb."[28]

Eddie knew that his position with the Dodgers in the spring of 1946 was precarious, at best. Stanky was firmly ensconced at second base after his performance a year earlier. Of particular concern for Eddie was the return of Pee Wee Reese from the navy. Reese had been the Dodgers' regular shortstop prior to the war, and he had played a good deal at Norfolk and other venues in the Pacific. Although he had established himself as a regular major leaguer, it appeared likely that Eddie would lose his starting job with Brooklyn.

Any notions to the contrary were probably erased when he received his '46 contract in the mail. As he had done with Cy Buker, Rickey offered Eddie a paltry $500 raise on top of his $6,000 salary. He knew he could try and hold out for more money, but he also knew that in the eyes of Rickey, his value to the team was minimal. Rickey could easily pick up a decent utility infielder, and probably for a song. Plus, Rickey was death on holdouts, a fact that was well known throughout the league.

But Eddie had an ace in the hole. Shortly before the '45 season ended, he received a phone call from Philadelphia. Ben Chapman had been Eddie's teammate with the Dodgers in both '44 and '45. A fine outfielder who batted .302 over fifteen big-league seasons, Chapman had worked with some success as a pitcher with Brooklyn before being traded to the Phillies, where he succeeded Freddie Fitzsimmons as manager. He and Rickey had collided on various issues over the two seasons, and there was no love lost between them.

Chapman told Eddie that he was interested in using him as the Phillies' regular shortstop in 1946. Acting in conjunction with Phillies general manager Herb Pennock, Chapman offered Eddie a $10,000 contract to play for Philadelphia. Under Chapman and Pennock's plan, Eddie would hold out with Brooklyn. Knowing how Rickey hated holdouts, Chapman and Pennock would then swoop in and ask to buy Eddie's contract. For a certainty, Chapman and Pennock's offer violated baseball's reserve clause. It was blatant tampering, but not an uncommon practice in 1946. On paper, it looked like it just might work.

"I wanted to make the move, knowing that Pee Wee Reese was returning from the service. Rickey smelled a rat, and under no circumstances would he sell me to Chapman and Philadelphia."[29]

Although he had no evidence to substantiate that Chapman and Pennock had conspired to bring Eddie to the Phillies, Rickey shared his concerns with baseball commissioner Happy Chandler. Catching Eddie somewhat off guard, Rickey arranged an impromptu meeting between Eddie and the baseball commissioner. Chandler had only recently succeeded the late Judge Kenesaw Mountain Landis as commissioner. He asked the young ballplayer if the allegations of tampering levied by Rickey were true.

"I saved Herb Pennock and Ben Chapman by denying the entire

event before Happy Chandler. I was the one that lost out. I was forced to report to Daytona Beach spring training and soon learned that I was to be a backup for Reese."[30]

It was a frustrating spring. Reese started every game, and Eddie wound up finishing the last three or four innings. Reese may have been the better hitter at the time, but what frustrated Eddie most was the quality of Reese's defense.

"During workouts—and this is absolute—Reese was rusty and slow. He was no threat to me—not even close. I approached Durocher and asked him straight out what the story was going to be. He said, 'Look, kid. You're a proven major leaguer. I want you around if something happens to Pee Wee.'"[31]

In Eddie's mind, a backup role wasn't good enough. This was his third year, and sitting on the bench would cause him to lose many of the skills he had worked so hard to perfect. He asked to be sent to St. Paul, where he would at least have the opportunity to play every day.

Initially, the Dodgers refused to farm him out. Looking for some sort of escape, Eddie sent a telegram to St. Paul manager Ray Blades. In the telegram, he told Blades that he would relish the opportunity to play for him. Blades was well liked by his players and respected within the Dodgers organization. Hearing that Eddie was "available," he contacted Rickey and asked for Eddie's services. Rickey relented and sent him to St. Paul, where he batted .252 and enjoyed an All-Star season in the American Association. Even so, he remained in Rickey's doghouse. In December of 1946, the Dodgers traded him to the Pirates for pitcher Al Gearhauser.

There were few bright spots for the '47 Pirates, who finished 62–92, tied for last place in the National League with Chapman's Phillies. Ralph Kiner hit 51 home runs—the first of two seasons in which he would hit better than 50. Hank Greenberg managed 25 home runs in the final season of his great career. But pitching was the Pirates' downfall. Solid veterans like Ernie Bonham and Fritz Ostermueller were barely able to turn in winning seasons, while Preacher Roe, so dependable during the war, went just 4–15.

The Pittsburgh front office managed a few minor trades in May, adding pitchers Hank Behrman and Ken Heintzelman from the

Dodgers and Phillies, respectively. In June, they picked up Mel Queen from the Yankees and immediately put him in the starting rotation, where he went 3–7. As compensation for Queen, the Pirates sent Eddie to the Yanks, who promptly shipped him off to Newark.

There was no room for Eddie in New York. Phil Rizzuto was at short, and Snuffy Stirnweiss still held down second. As it turned out, there wasn't much opportunity to play at Newark, either. Within two weeks, he was shipped off again, this time to the Portland Beavers of the Coast League, with whom the Yankees had a working agreement.

At face value, it was just another transaction in a hundred transacted by the Yankee organization that season. But for Eddie, it was a decision that dramatically influenced the rest of his life. He would eventually settle in Portland and play the next ten years with the Beavers. During that time, he would approach the elusive perfection he sought as a youth in the parks of Buffalo. And he would be offered a rare chance to return to the major leagues—which he would politely decline.

Jim Turner couldn't believe that the Yankees had sent him such a sorry specimen. One look at Eddie, and the Portland skipper was convinced he had been given the leavings of the Yankee organization. It riled him, but he was a company man. He knew that Eddie had been in the big leagues, and he decided to see what the kid was made of.

On an off day before Eddie's first game in the PCL, Turner put him through a grueling workout at second base.

"I've even got pictures of Turner standing with his arms crossed while I'm taking infield practice. I can tell the way he's standing there that he was thinking, 'You better show me something, pal!'"[32]

Apparently, he did. Turner started him ahead of his regular second baseman—it happened to be Ford Mullen—who was hitting better than .300. Eddie was clearly the better defensive player, but he was beginning to show that he was no slouch at the plate. He batted .278 the rest of the way, his highest average in his four years of pro ball. When the 1948 season began, the second base job was his.

For all intents and purposes, 1948 was the season in which Eddie Basinski came into his own as a professional baseball player. He continued to hit well, batting .277, and his home run and RBI totals resumed their climb.

As a second baseman, Eddie had reached a level of performance that was untouched and unapproached by any of his contemporaries in the Coast League and perhaps in all of baseball. Before 1948, he had been referred to as a virtuoso of the violin. Now he applied his virtuosity to the infield. Coast League managers Joe Gordon, Lefty O'Doul and Casey Stengel each marveled at his artistry afield: lightning-quick hands and a remarkable talent for making plays where no plays should have been made. He made the players around him look better.

That included his double play partners, shortstop Frankie Zak and first baseman Fenton Mole. "Zak-to-Basinski-to-Mole" became a mantra of sorts for "Bevo" fans. Ironically, the trio only played together for one season. Mole played briefly with the Yankees in 1949 and spent most of the year in Newark. Zak started the '49 season with Portland before being sent to San Diego. As it turned out, Eddie almost found himself playing in a different venue in 1949.

Eddie seemed to save his best that year for the Oakland Oaks—Casey Stengel's team—who would go on to win the Coast League championship in 1948. In spite of the way he treated his ball club, Casey Stengel loved Eddie. "I always performed well against Oakland. Some of my greatest tributes as a second baseman came from Casey Stengel, who stated, 'Not only is Basinski the best second baseman in the Pacific Coast League, but he is the best second baseman in all of baseball.'"[33]

On one occasion, Eddie made a play that even Stengel had never seen before. In front of a capacity crowd in Portland, Oaks first baseman Nick Etten stood in to face Beavers pitcher Jack Salveson. Etten was a left-handed power hitter, and the right side of the infield was shifted for him to pull. First baseman Mickey Rocco guarded the line. Eddie shaded toward the hole in between first and second.

"Etten hit a hot grounder to Rocco's right. I'm playing Etten to pull [so] I break for the ball to my left, running at top speed. I gloved the ball and looked up for the throw to first base. Salveson never came off the mound!

"I kept running and realized nobody was at first for the putout. I continued in without hesitating and beat Etten to first by diving on the bag!"[34]

It was an unassisted putout at first base by a *second* baseman. Stengel, who had been coaching first base, retrieved a towel from the dugout. He laid the towel on the ground, kneeled upon it, and began bowing in Eddie's general direction. No one could remember having seen such a play before. It was that play and others like it that stayed on Stengel's mind even after his tenure with the Oaks had ended.

On the last day of the 1948 season, the Yankees fired their manager, Bucky Harris, in spite of a second-place finish that year and a world championship the year before. Yankees general manager George Weiss had long been a fan of Casey Stengel. He waited until October 10—the day the Oaks won the PCL championship—to offer the Yankees' helm to Stengel. The official announcement was made on October 12, the day after the Cleveland Indians beat the Boston Braves in the World Series.

Although Weiss waited until October 10 to offer Stengel the job, rumors had suggested Casey as the new Yankees manager from the moment Harris was dismissed. Sometime before the October 12 announcement, Stengel contacted Jim Turner. Since Portland had a working agreement with the Yankees, Stengel had his pick of players to join him in New York. He liked catcher Charlie Silvera, who would go on to back up Yogi Berra for the next eight seasons. And it was no secret that he coveted Eddie Basinski.

Turner took Eddie down to the Portland bullpen at the end of the season to relay Stengel's message. He felt a little sheepish, no doubt recalling the reservations he had felt upon first meeting his player. Now he was telling him that the new manager of baseball's greatest franchise wanted him to be his starting second baseman. Turner wasn't ready for Eddie's response.

"I told him, 'Jim, it's a great honor. Casey is a great manager and I love the guy. He's great for baseball. But I've seen the politics up there. You've treated me real good. I just love this place here—this city and this part of the country. You're gonna have to tell Casey that I'm gonna pass up on it. I may be making a mistake.'

"And, of course, they won nine pennants after that! Charlie Silvera and I—just the two of us—were gonna go. He worked the bullpen and collected all those World Series checks. I'm sure I could have been there. Jerry Coleman doesn't know it, but the only reason he got to be the second baseman was because I said no."[35]

To the average player or fan, it was an extraordinary decision. By turning down the Yankees, Eddie had, in effect, exiled himself to the Coast League. There were, however, worse fates in baseball. He had found a home in Portland, and the Coast League proved to be the perfect venue for showcasing his talents. He settled in for the long haul and proceeded to delight Portland fans for the next decade with his great glove work and ever-improving offense. He even serenaded them with his violin on at least one occasion, playing a concert at home plate in between games of a doubleheader.

He became an iron man, playing every inning of every game for 557 consecutive games over three seasons. An injury sustained during a questionable play involving Sacramento first baseman Walt Dropo prevented him from pursuing the PCL's all-time consecutive-game streak for second basemen.

"I would have broken Hugh Luby's consecutive-game streak at second base — 886 games — had not Walt Dropo deliberately cut me down on a tag at second base. He was out by thirty feet — embarrassed, I guess — and he cut me down with a three-inch gash on my left shin.

"I wanted that record. I had 557 games at that time. When I returned to the lineup, I went another 343 consecutive games."[36]

As it turned out, there would be plenty of other records along the way. In his ten seasons with Portland, he played in more games than any other player in the history of the club. He set a Coast League record of 66 consecutive games without an error at second base — a record that still stands today. In 1950, in the middle of his consecutive-game streak, he became the only player in the history of professional baseball to play every inning of 202 regular-season games.

That year, L.H. Gregory, dean of Oregon sportswriters, named Eddie his most valuable Portland player. Eddie sent him a letter of thanks, and Gregory responded with a letter of his own.

"I don't deserve a bit of credit for naming you as my most valuable Bevo player choice, for how could I help it? You always have been my favorite violin-playing second baseman, anyway. How in the heck did you do it — stay in all those games with your slim build? I know — you're *rawhide* at heart. As a baseball manager of the old school I used to know very well, the late Walter McCredie, used to say, 'Give me those *rawhide* fellows; they don't look as if they could do it, but there's something about 'em that outlasts the big huskies.'"[37]

The Portland fans loved him. Asked to select the outstanding player for the first fifty years of the franchise, they chose Eddie. He would play two seasons with Seattle and one with Vancouver, retiring in 1959. He finished his career with a .271 lifetime batting average with over 100 home runs. In his sixteen professional seasons, he never played below the Triple-A level.

After baseball, he became an accounts manager in sales and marketing for Consolidated Freightways, Inc., of Portland, where he worked for 31 years, retiring in 1991. Over the years, he was inducted into various halls of fame, including the Oregon Sports Hall of Fame in 1987, and the Brooklyn Dodger Hall of Fame in 1996. In 1984, he was named to the all-time Coast League All-Star Team at second base for the years spanning 1903 to 1957.

He had managed to become living testimony to a simple adage that looks can be deceiving. He never allowed the doubts and prejudices of others to deter him, and he succeeded in changing a few minds along the way. As he would learn later on, he even had an influence on Pop Yerke, the high school baseball coach who had refused to let him try out for the East High School team.

"Back when I was going great guns for Brooklyn in 1945 I was warming up with Stanky in the infield, and the usher called me over.

"'Hey, Basinski! Some old, bald-headed guy wants to see you at Gate 15!'

"I had no idea who it was, and I told him to tell him I'd be there in a little while.

"I walked up and said, 'Mr. Yerke?'

"He said, 'Eddie, I'm here for one reason only. You taught me a great lesson. I've been a very successful baseball coach, but I will never, ever turn away from anyone who wants to try out. No matter how they look, whether they wear glasses or play the violin.'

"There were tears in his eyes."[38]

9
Nick Strincevich

In 1906, U.S. Steel began its first great capital project—a large, modern plant built to meet the burgeoning steel needs of the Midwest. U.S. Steel chairman Judge Elbert H. Gary chose a site about 30 miles southeast of Chicago hard against the southern shore of Lake Michigan, where ore could be received and steel could be shipped via the Great Lakes. The foundation for the Gary Works was laid that year, and with it grew the town of Gary, Indiana. By the end of the decade, both mill and metropolis were prospering.

Baseball and the steel industry have enjoyed a fruitful partnership since before the days of Andrew Carnegie and J. Pierpont Morgan. Wherever the industry decided to roost, company baseball teams sprang up in droves. Blast furnace workers played rivals in the electrical shop. Sheet mill workers played laborers in the coke plant, and so on. After creating U.S. Steel in 1901, Carnegie himself weighed in on the benefits derived from company sports teams, allowing that they promoted "American values, taught workers new virtues, and developed higher standards of character for workers."[1]

Nick Strincevich was born in Gary on March 1, 1915. His father, Luka, was born in present-day Bosnia and arrived in Gary the year both the mill and town came into being. Luka Strincevich was a tall, powerfully built Serb, who went by the nickname "Jumbo." He made his living working in the gashouse of the sheet mill. His oldest son, Nick, followed him into the mill by the time he was a teenager.

"My dad was a big guy. When I was a kid and they'd see me walking with him, they'd say, 'Hey, there's Big Jumbo and Little Jumbo.'"[2]

As he grew older and taller, 'Little Jumbo' was shortened to just 'Jumbo'—a nickname that would follow Nick for the rest of his life.

He went to work in the mill after his sophomore year in high school. The Depression was on, and the immediate benefits of another income in the household outweighed those of an education down the road. Nick worked as part of a labor gang in the sheet mill, shoveling slag for 33⅓ cents per hour, ten hours a day.

He had always played baseball in park leagues, sandlots, and American Legion teams. Now he spent his evenings playing alongside grown men in the mill league.

"We had a twilight league in the mill. All the mills had teams. I used to pitch for the Gary Sheet Mill team. There were other ones—tin mill, American Bridge Company. I pitched also for Barne's Ice. Those were Sunday teams."[3]

By the time he was nineteen, his pitching began to draw interest. Nick was a natural sidearmer. The horizontal delivery caused the ball to sink and baffled hitters in the mill league.

"It's like a half-assed screwball. You got to keep it low. You throw it around the knees, and it dips. You get a lot of ground balls."[4]

In the summer of 1934, Nick pitched in a ballgame umpired by a sheet mill worker named Bob Prysock. Prysock had played professional baseball years before and had managed a Yankees farm team in southern Illinois. In addition to working in the mill, he also bird-dogged for the Yankees.

Nick faced a team from Elkhart, Indiana, during the game. His sidearm delivery and sinker proved overwhelming to the Elkhart hitters. He struck out 18 batters and aroused the curiosity of the scout.

Prysock asked him if he had ever considered playing pro ball. He used his connections in the Yankees organization to arrange for Nick to pitch batting practice to the Yankees during a trip to Chicago. Later that summer, Prysock drove Nick to Comiskey Park, where the Yankees were playing the White Sox. Nick threw batting practice to the likes of Ruth, Gehrig, Crosetti, and Lazzeri.

"When I got done, Joe McCarthy asked me if I was interested in playing professional ball. I said, 'Yeah!'"[5]

Prysock drove Nick back home through the mills of southeast Chicago and northwest Indiana. They arrived at Nick's home in the Glen Park neighborhood of Gary.

"When I came home, my dad was sitting on a swing on the porch. He had a telegram that was sent to him. He just kept waving the telegram. The guy let me out of the car. My dad handed me the telegram, and on it said, 'Nick Strincevich, you are now the property of the New York Yankees.'"[6]

Nick's Yankee odyssey began in 1935 when he joined the Akron Yankees in the Class C Mid-Atlantic League. He started out well enough with a 1–2 record and a respectable earned run average. It was at Akron that Nick first made the acquaintance of Johnny Neun, a former big-league first baseman with aspirations to manage in the majors. Neun's playing days were nearing an ended. In addition to holding down first base, he also managed Akron.

"He was the one that done the most for me. He had a lot of patience with me. I was more or less a hothead. I'd get mad. It's just nature, I guess. He would talk to me and say, 'Just do your pitching, and don't worry about anything else.'"[7]

There were other things besides baseball on Nick's mind. Life away from home proved a daunting challenge for him. He got homesick after just a month and returned home to Gary. He went back to work in the mills for a time, made plans to marry his sweetheart the following year, and decided to return to pro ball for the 1936 season.

He ended up at Butler in the Penn State Association and managed to stick around for the entire season. He went 10–8 with Butler with a 3.94 ERA, good enough for a promotion to the Class B Norfolk Tars the following season. Here he was reunited with Neun, who had been named Norfolk's manager and was rising steadily through the Yankee ranks.

Nick went 11–8 with Norfolk, which finished with the second best record in the Piedmont League. Nick was unable to pitch in the playoffs because his father fell ill. The Tars advanced in the playoffs and won the league championship. Neun earned yet another promotion—this time to the Newark Bears of the International League. Newark was the Yankees' top farm club, and it began to appear that Neun just might realize his dream of managing in the big leagues. He brought one position player with him—second baseman Mickey Witek. He also brought along five pitchers: Hiram Bithorn, Norm Branch, John Haley, Xavier Rescigno, and Nick Strincevich.

The 1937 Newark Bears are still considered by many to be the greatest minor league team of all time. They led the International

League with a phenomenal 109–43 record—27 more victories than the second-place team. Their roster read like a Who's Who of major league lineups for the next decade: Joe Gordon, Tommy Henrich, Babe Dahlgren, George McQuinn, Buddy Rosar, Charlie "King Kong" Keller, Spud Chandler, Atley Donald, Steve Sundra, Joe Beggs, Marius Russo.

The Bears swept through the International League playoffs that fall, then came back from three games down to beat the Columbus Redbirds in the best-of-seven contest known as the Little World Series.

As a consequence, most of the key personnel went to the majors. Joe Gordon became the Yankees' regular second baseman. Tommy Henrich found a home in New York's outfield. Dahlgren spent a year on the Yankees' bench, then became their regular first baseman when ALS ended Gehrig's career. McQuinn became the starting first baseman for the St. Louis Browns. Beggs, Chandler, and Sundra also went to the Yankees.

When Newark's manager, Oscar Vitt, took over as the new manager of the Cleveland Indians, the Yankees chose Neun to replace him. The '38 Bears fared almost as well as their predecessors, winning 104 regular-season games and advancing to the Little World Series. This time, they lost in seven games to Kansas City—another Yankee farm club. Russo and Haley were the big winners on the club, each with 17 victories. Donald had 16. Nick pitched well, notching an 11–4 record against some of the finest competition in the minors.

As far as pitching was concerned, the Yankees were well armed for the next several years. Nick had a winning record with Newark, but his work was overshadowed in the organization by that of Donald, Russo, and Kansas City's Ernie Bonham. He went to spring training with the Bears in 1939 and started the regular season on their roster.

But he struggled early with Newark, posting a 1–2 record with a whopping 7.20 ERA. That spring, he was traded to the Sacramento Solons of the Pacific Coast League. He pitched sparingly for the Solons, finishing with a 2–6 record and a 3.86 ERA. Sacramento finished the year with a .500 record, but they upset the Seattle Rainiers and Los Angeles Angels in the playoffs, winning the Coast League championship.

In October of 1939, after the Coast League season ended, the Boston Bees drafted Nick in the annual minor league draft. The Bees had been impressed by his performance against them in a spring training game earlier that year. He joined the team in Florida in the spring of 1940 and quickly became an "iron man" in the starting rotation. In all, he worked 27 innings in spring exhibition games—most on the staff.

As they made their way north to their respective summer homes, major league clubs would often play three-game series with a geographic rival. Chicago, St. Louis, Philadelphia, New York, and Boston—all the cities with two or more major league clubs—would each play a "city series" with the National and American League clubs facing off against each other. In Boston, the Bees played the Red Sox. Bees manager Casey Stengel saved Nick for the third and final game of the series.

Playing at Fenway Park, the visiting Bees took an early 3–0 lead. Nick held the Red Sox scoreless for the first four innings. Then, in the fifth inning, he walked his mound opponent, Mickey Harris. Dominic DiMaggio followed with a single, moving Harris to third. Doc Cramer followed with another single, and Harris scored the Sox' first run.

That brought Ted Williams to the plate as the potential lead run. Williams was patient with Nick's offerings, hoping for a sinker that didn't quite sink. He wasn't prepared for Nick's last pitch.

"I struck him out. [There was] an article in the paper that said I threw a curveball to him that 'exploded.' The manager, Joe Cronin, said, 'I wish I had that kid.'"[8]

Nick wasn't out of the woods just yet. Jimmie Foxx followed Williams and stroked a double to the deepest part of center field. DiMaggio and Cramer scored to tie the game at three. Nick finished the inning, but was lifted in the sixth for a pinch hitter. The Bees scored four runs in the frame, and Nick ended up winning the game, 7–3.

For his part, Stengel was glad to have Nick, and he showed it by starting him in the Bees' second game of the season. It would be 63 years before another Bees/Braves manager would show such confidence as to allow a rookie to make his major league debut in just the second game of the season.[9]

He made his major league debut on April 23, 1940, lasting only into the second inning against the Brooklyn Dodgers at Ebbets Field. He surrendered a double to Dolph Camilli and home runs to rookies Charlie Gilbert and Herman Franks. Brooklyn won the game, 8–3.

He fared better just three days later on April 26, when Stengel started him against the Giants. His mound opponent that day was the great Carl Hubbell. Nick carried a 3–1 lead into the sixth inning. With two outs, he gave up three successive singles and was pulled from the game. His replacement gave up a two-run double and the Boston lead. New York won the game, 5–3.

His first major league win came on May 5 against the Pirates. As in the Giants' game, Nick allowed only one run—a homer by Pirate first baseman Elbie Fletcher—in the first five innings. But he ran into trouble again in the sixth. He had five walks in the game, and Stengel gave him the hook once more. Dick Coffman relieved him, and the Bees held on to win, 5–4.

Perhaps his most impressive start in the early going came against the Cubs on May 15. Nick and Cub starter Larry French traded scoreless innings through seven.

"Strincevich, a former Yankee farm hand, was so tough on the Cubs for seven innings that they could accumulate only two hits and a pair of passes. During this period, his mates made a couple of errors, but nevertheless he held the Chicagoans away from the plate."[10]

A third error in the eighth led to two unearned runs, giving the Cubs and French a 2–0 victory. It was a tough loss for Nick, whose record as a starter was just 1–6 by the end of May. Although the performance against the Cubs went a long way with Casey, he moved Nick to the bullpen in June.

"Casey liked me. He used to kid me all the time. We were in St. Louis, and Johnny Mize was up. I was in the bullpen, and I came into the game. There were a couple of guys on.

"I said to Casey, 'What do you want me to do with him?' I thought maybe Casey wanted me to walk him.

"He said, 'Naw, let's experiment with him. Throw him that low sinker.'

"Well, I went through my motion and threw that low sinker. He hit it over the roof. Home run!

"When, you're going good, you sit next to the manager. When you're going bad, you sit on the end of the dugout. When I got the side out, I went back on the end of the dugout. I could hear Casey. He had a voice like a frog.

"He asked, 'Hey Nick! Hey Nick! What was that?'

"They'd all ask you that when a guy hit a home run.

"So Casey said, 'Hey Nick! What'd he hit?'

"I said, 'A Spalding!'

"He jumped up and bumped his head!"[11]

It had been a season of bad luck and hard lessons. When August began, the Bees were 29–59. On August 2, Stengel decided to give Nick a start against the Cincinnati Reds. As he had done against the Cubs three months earlier, Nick held Cincinnati scoreless for seven innings. This time, he was treated to a 10-run lead. He gave up three runs in the eighth inning, including a Frank McCormick home run, but he finished the game—his first complete-game victory.

Stengel started him again on August 16 against the Dodgers, who had given him a baptism by fire in his first big-league game. Both Nick and Brooklyn starter Vito Tamulis lasted through nine innings with the score tied, 1–1. In the twelfth, with both starters still in the game, Boston first baseman Buddy Hassett singled home Eddie Miller with the winning run. Nick surrendered just five hits during the marathon and posted his second complete-game victory in as many weeks.

Stengel left him in the rotation, and he did not disappoint. He went the distance again on August 22 against the Reds, losing a bid for his third straight victory on a homer to Billy Werber in the ninth, which gave Cincinnati a 3–2 victory. Undeterred, he threw another complete-game victory just four days later against the Cardinals. A ninth-inning home run off the bat of Don Gutteridge ruined his bid for his first big-league shutout, but he won the game, 3–1.

Over the month of August, Nick was the Bees' best pitcher, posting a 3–1 record and salvaging what could have been a disastrous season. He added another tough loss on September 11, losing 3–1 to Paul Derringer and the Reds when have gave up two runs in the ninth.

His last outing of the year was noteworthy—not for the fact that the Cubs knocked him out in the second inning, but because it was the last victory in the Hall of Fame career of Dizzy Dean.

Overall, Nick pitched in 32 ballgames and finished with a record of four wins and eight losses. He pitched far better than his 5.53 ERA indicated, and his second-half turnaround gave him hope for the next season.

He returned to the Bees in 1941, pitching just three games early in the season. A freak accident that spring almost cost Nick the rest of his season. During a practice session, Nick was hit in the face by a ball thrown by a cutoff man from the outfield. Nick hadn't seen the ball coming, and he turned directly into the throw. The ball fractured his skull and broke his nose. He had severe headaches throughout the season and did not pitch for about three weeks. He felt the lingering effects of the injury for the next two seasons.

Midway through the spring, a front office decision led to the most important move of Nick's career. On May 7, Nick was traded to the

Pittsburgh Pirates in exchange for Hall of Famer Lloyd "Little Poison" Waner. The trade briefly united the younger Waner with his older brother, Paul "Big Poison" Waner. The Waner brothers had played 14 seasons together with the Pirates. Within a month, Lloyd was playing outfield for the Reds. Nick didn't know it yet, but he would spend the next seven seasons in the Pittsburgh organization.

The Pirates weren't immediately sure what to do with Nick. After leaving the Bees, he made two poor starts in May for Pittsburgh. Not impressed by his performance, the Pirates sent him to the Milwaukee Brewers of the American Association. He pitched in 12 games for the Brewers, winning four games while losing two. In September, the Pirates called him back up, and he made another lackluster start.

In 1942, they sent him to the Toronto Maple Leafs of the International League. Nick's fortune turned at Toronto. The Leafs were managed by Hall of Famer Burleigh Grimes, the last legal spitballer in the major leagues. Like Johnny Neun, Grimes challenged Nick on the mound.

"He was tough, [and] he taught you to be tough. I used to like him because he used to pitch a lot of batting practice and throw spitballs to the young guys. He enjoyed that very much!"[12]

Although he had enjoyed winning seasons throughout his minor league career, the International League was the first place where Nick truly dominated the competition. Working almost exclusively as a starter, he started more games (27) and pitched more innings (199) than he had in any previous season. He won 12 and lost 10 for a losing ballclub, and he posted a magnificent 2.40 ERA.

The Pirates were impressed enough with his numbers to bring him up for a September look-see. He pitched in seven games with Pittsburgh, including a start on September 20 against Cincinnati.

Pittsburgh had won just 66 games during the 1942 season, but they made a 14-game turnaround in 1943. The Pirates finished the season in the first division, winning 80 games. Although they had good run production from third baseman Bob Elliott and outfielder Vince DiMaggio, good pitching kept the Pirates afloat. They were led by Rip Sewell, purveyor of the "epheus" pitch—a tantalizing blooper that few batters had the discipline to let pass. Sewell tied for the National League lead with 21 victories. Bob Klinger finished with 11 wins. Max Butcher and left-hander Wally Hebert each had ten. Hank Gornicki won nine.

Nick had perhaps his finest season in professional baseball with Toronto in 1943, but there was no room for him on the Pirates' staff. He won 15 games for the Leafs, losing just seven times. He logged a career-high 233 innings and 113 strikeouts. He walked only 47 batters and had an ERA of 2.47.

Offensively, Toronto was even weaker than they had been in 1942. But their pitching staff was strong, and they finished the season with the best record in the International League, ten games ahead of Newark. They lost in the playoffs, however, to the Syracuse Chiefs.

The Pirates finished 25 games behind the first-place Cardinals in 1943, but Pittsburgh management declined to promote any of their Toronto starters to the parent club. That included 39-year-old major league veteran Luke Hamlin, who won 21 games for the Leafs and ended up pitching the 1944 season with the Philadelphia A's.

By spring, the Pirates were no longer so impressive. Bob Klinger was inducted into the navy. Hank Gornicki went into the army. Wally Hebert decided that his solid 1943 season was a good note on which to end his career. He retired to his home in Louisiana. All that remained of the '43 staff were Sewell, Butcher, and a lot of question marks. The Pirates invited Nick to spring training.

Prior to the war, the Pirates traveled south to Florida for their spring training. Under Judge Landis's restrictions, they chose Muncie, Indiana, as their springtime base of operations. When weather permitted, they worked out on the grounds of Ball State University. When the weather proved too inclement for baseball drills, manager Frankie Frisch sent them on long hikes.

Travel to exhibition games proved difficult. Train travel was restricted due to the massive number of troops being shuttled across the country. Desperate to make an exhibition game in Indianapolis, Frisch once ordered his own troops into the baggage car of a troop train.

"We traveled to the opening

Nick Strincevich followed a 14-win season in 1944 with 16 wins in 1945. ©Brace Photograph.

games in Cincinnati in an army train car. We rode that to Cincinnati from Muncie. We rode on [troop trains] all the time. We'd travel on them trains, and we seen some good fights. They'd get off a train and starting fighting."[13]

In the spring of 1944, Nick registered to take his army physical in Pittsburgh. He still spent the off season working in the sheet mill. The steel industry was considered an essential wartime industry. As long as Nick worked full-time in the mill, he earned a wartime deferment. Playing baseball for six months out of the year erased that exemption.

He passed his physical and was classified as 1-A, despite having a wife and child. A few weeks passed after the physical. The season had begun, and Nick was in Pittsburgh. Concerned that he hadn't yet been called, he asked the Pirates' management for advice.

"I asked the owner of Pittsburgh, 'How come they ain't calling me? They put me 1-A.'"

"He said, 'Just hang in there. They'll call you.'"[14]

But they never did. In spite of having no physical deficiencies or permanent deferments, Nick never was called to active military duty either during the war or after.

Nick began the 1944 season with a bang. Starting on April 30 at Crosley Field, he beat the Reds and their ace, Elmer Riddle. The Pirates scored seven runs against Riddle and won, 7–1. Nick went the distance, allowing just six hits. Beginning a unique pattern that would follow him over the next several seasons, he pitched all nine innings without striking out a single batter.

"I've heard many a manager say, 'I don't care what you do. Let 'em hit the ball!' I always figured I had eight guys behind me. I'm beating myself if I don't throw a strike so the guy can swing at something."[15]

Nick's sinker sank quite a bit in 1944. Twice that season, he notched a complete-game victory without a strikeout. All 27 outs came from batted balls. In 190 innings, he struck out just 47 batters and walked only 37. Ironically, the Pirates were one of the National League's poorest-fielding teams in 1944, but they saved their best glovework for whenever Nick was on the mound.

He won his first four decisions in '44—three of which were complete games. Frisch used him primarily as a starter, but he also made 14 relief appearances. He made several starts on just two days rest.

"In those days they used us both ways. I mean, even when I was a starter, I relieved, too. If you went six or seven innings, you had the next day off. Then the following day you were in the bullpen. We only carried about seven pitchers."[16]

Nick finished the season with 14 wins—12 as a starter and two more in relief. He completed 11 of his starts, and he saved two games. The Pirates won ten games more than they had in 1943, finishing in second place with 90 wins. Even that improvement was not enough to catch the Cardinals, whose 105 wins landed them in the World Series for the third straight season.

Nick answered the bell to the 1945 season almost as quickly as he had the year before. He won three of his first four starts. His third victory of the season on May 17 came against the Dodgers at Ebbets Field. The victory stopped an 11-game win streak for the Dodgers. Nick also ended a 14-game hitting streak belonging to Brooklyn outfielder Luis Olmo. He went the distance and was aided by twelve Pirate runs.

On May 31, he locked horns with the Dodgers once again in an epic battle at Forbes Field. Both teams were tied at four runs apiece through nine innings. Dodger starter Vic Lombardi left for a pinch hitter in the eighth inning. Clyde King pitched the next six innings for Brooklyn. In the top of the thirteenth, Nick allowed two runs on a triple by Goody Rosen. The Pirates failed to score in their half of the inning and lost, 6–4. The game marked a personal endurance record for Nick, eclipsing the twelve-inning game he pitched for the Bees in 1940.

The Dodger marathon started Nick on another endurance record. From May 31 through July 3, he pitched seven consecutive complete games, winning five of them. Twice during the 1945 season—and for the third time in two seasons—he threw complete-game victories against the Reds without striking out a batter. The latter win came in his final start of the season—a 2–1 Pirate win and Nick's 16th of the year.

He finished 1945 with a 16–10 record and a 3.31 ERA. His 16 victories were the most on the Pirates' staff. He logged 228 innings—most in his big-league career. He walked just 49 batters. On July 12, he threw his first complete-game shutout against the Phillies at Forbes Field.

He was Frankie Frisch's workhorse, and it seemed likely that he would have a prominent role in the Pirates' rotation in baseball's first postwar season.

Perhaps more than any other season, 1946 was a year of experimentation in and around major league baseball. The war was over, and dozens of prewar major leaguers returned to their teams seeking their old jobs. It was the time of the G.I. Bill and the start of a long period of economic prosperity. The war had changed people's minds about subjects that seem unquestionable only a few years before.

Jackie Robinson played his first game for the Montreal Royals of the International League. Entrepreneur Jorge Pasquel and his brothers offered wads of cash to major leaguers in an attempt to staff their revamped Mexican League. And in Boston, a 35-year-old Harvard-educated attorney decided that the climate might be right—among players and owners alike—to challenge baseball's reserve clause and unionize the majors.

Robert Murphy had practiced law in New York and Washington, D.C. He had investigated labor disputes as an examiner for the National Labor Relations Board. He was a baseball fan, and although he had never represented the side of organized labor as an attorney, he began a fact-finding mission that would eventually lead to an experiment known as the American Baseball Guild.

Murphy interviewed former major leaguers, asking them their opinions on business practices in baseball. The more he listened, he became convinced that players ought to organize. Major League Baseball had no minimum salary. A first-year player could earn as much as $5,000 or less than $3,500 depending on which team he played for. Players signed on for six-month seasons and were only compensated for the regular season. They received no compensation for travel, food, or other accommodations during spring training. Not since the short-lived Federal League had there been a serious challenge to the baseball establishment and the venerable reserve clause.

The reserve clause was created in the 19th century by the very magnates who controlled the game. To protect against inflated player salaries and bidding wars among owners, players signed one-year contracts that "reserved" their services for the following season. Although players could negotiate with their own club for contracts each season, they could not shop themselves to other ball clubs, seeking an even higher wage from a competitor. The agreement among the owners ensured that no such offers existed.

Unless traded or released, players remained members of the team with whom they signed their original contracts. In effect, they were bound indefinitely to a team but could be released at any time if given a ten-day notice. If traded for cash or purchased for a waiver price, players received no percentage of the transaction. If dissatisfied with the club's offer for the coming season, they could hold out for more money. But lacking the leverage of a strong union or offers from other clubs, holding out was often a futile endeavor.

Murphy sent letters to every major league player. He attended spring training camps in Florida, recommending that current players talk to former players about their financial situations during and after their careers. Eventually, he hoped to find a former major leaguer who could lead players into the world of organize labor. Murphy himself would have been content to serve as the Guild's legal advisor. He began looking for the right ball club whose players were open to the possibility of allowing the American Baseball Guild to bargain collectively for their contracts. Not surprisingly, Murphy looked to Pittsburgh—a city long associated with strong unions—to test his infant idea.

He lobbied the Pirates' players throughout the early spring of 1946, finding an ally in Pirates catcher and captain Al Lopez. In mid-April, he registered the American Baseball Guild as a formal labor organization. At a press conference, he detailed the goals of the Guild—among them, the creation of a minimum salary of $6,500 a year and the elimination of the ten-day clause. By the end of May, Murphy felt confident that an overwhelming majority of the Pirates were supportive of the Guild. He wrote to Pirates management, requesting that players be allowed to vote on whether or not the Guild should operate as their collective bargaining agent.

Murphy set a June 5 deadline for management to decide on the election. Management stalled. He was told that the regular season was not the appropriate time to discuss the issue. Murphy knew that to discuss the subject during the off season—when the issue was no longer so hot, and players were scattered across the country—was management's attempt to defuse the situation. When the June 5 deadline arrived, management refused to decide, asking for more time to consider the issues.

Here Murphy committed a critical error. No action on the part of the Pirates' management infuriated a number of the players, many of whom wanted to strike immediately. Murphy was not one to make decisions while tempers were hot. He announced a new deadline of June 7. If Pirates management could not decide the matter by game time on that date, the Pirates' players would definitely strike.

The two extra days gave the Pirates' front office the opportunity to devise and implement a plan to thwart a strike. Two Pirate players,— Rip Sewell and infielder Jimmy Brown—had been outspoken in their anti–Guild views. That Sewell was the highest-paid Pirate at $15,000 and Brown made in excess of $10,000 did not seem to deter other players from hearing their views.

June 7 arrived without a decision from management. Murphy arrived at Forbes Field convinced that 90 percent of the players favored a strike. This was an important figure, as players had agreed that no simple majority was enough to strike. Rather, they decided that only a two-thirds majority—at least 24 votes in all—would be required to carry the motion. By Murphy's count, he had well in excess of that figure.

But Murphy and the Pirates were greeted by a surprise visitor in the clubhouse. Pirates owner Bill Benswanger asked if he could address the players in private prior to their vote. Although the players wanted Murphy to stay, manager Frankie Frisch ordered him from the clubhouse.

Owners traditionally shied away from the players' clubhouse, but this was an extraordinary case. Benswanger told his team that he had never deliberately tried to hurt a player. He told them that his door was always open to them when they had issues to discuss *individually*. Although he reportedly did not recommend to the players which way they should vote, his words pulled a number of fence-sitting Pirates over to management's side.

The Pirates privately discussed the strike issue for the next two hours—all without Murphy, who had to buy a general admission ticket just to enter the ballpark. Finally, just one half-hour before game time, a vote was cast. The players voted 20–16 in favor of a strike, but fell just four votes shy of their two-thirds majority. Benswanger won, and the strike was averted. After the game—a 10–5 victory over the Giants— the Pirates' owner returned to the clubhouse and praised his players for their sound decision.

Although Murphy put on a brave face before the press and claimed that the Guild had only suffered a setback, it was clear that his momentum was lost. By choosing not to strike on June 5, he had allowed management time to regroup. The decision was costly. Only when the Guild no longer appeared to be a strong threat did management allow its players to vote on the Guild. On August 20, 1946, the players voted 15–3 *against* accepting the Guild as its collective bargaining agent. A dozen Pirates abstained from voting.

The American Baseball Guild did arouse concern among baseball owners. A strike had been averted in the eleventh hour—and by only *four* votes. The owners formed a committee in the summer of 1946 to discuss some of the planks in the Guild's platform. They invited players to share their points of view and allowed each league to elect their own representatives to serve on the committee. The National League chose Dodger outfielder Dixie Walker as its representative. American League players went with Yankee relief specialist Johnny Murphy.

After meeting several times and in several different cities, the committee recommended that Major League Baseball make several changes: establish a minimum salary of $5,500; provide a $25 per week stipend to be paid players during spring training; establish a player pension to be funded by owners through player contributions.

The Guild had failed because the players had failed to unite at a critical moment. The committee's concessions, though welcome, were paltry offerings at best. In effect, they made any future opposition to management even more difficult. As far as management was concerned, they had magnanimously listened to the players and dealt with their concerns.

Major League Baseball would not see another serious threat to its reserve clause for another quarter-century.

Nick Strincevich began the 1946 season in the Pirates' bullpen. Though Nick had anchored Pittsburgh's starting rotation the previous season, Pirates manager Frankie Frisch inexplicably relegated Nick to relief work in April and May. He had been the Pirates' top winner in 1945. In addition to Rip Sewell, Frisch gave starting assignments to Fritz Ostermueller and Ken Gables, both of whom made starts late in the '45 campaign. By the end of April, Ken Heintzelman had become a regular starter, too. Also making starts early in the year were Jack Hallett, Jim Hopper, Ed Albosta, and Ed Bahr.

Frisch's experiment with the latter four hurlers ended with May and the Pirates in sixth place. On June 8—the day after the thwarted strike vote—Nick made his first start in six weeks. He lost that game and each of his next two starts. By the last week in June, his record was 0–7. He had been the good soldier, weathering his stay in the bullpen per Frisch's request. He had kept the Pirates in the game for two of his three June starts, and in spite of his abysmal record, Frisch stuck with his sidearmer.

Nick's luck began to change on June 25. He faced the Giants at the Polo Grounds, both teams trying to stay out of last place.

"It was not Frank Frisch's sense of humor that led him to name Nick Strincevich, baseball's losingest pitcher with an 0–7 record for the season, as Pittsburgh's starter. It was just Strincevich's regular turn. Anyway, those close to the situation insist that Nick, despite his unpretentious form chart, is far from being the poorest member of Pittsburgh's mound patrol.

"Such a thought was farthest from the minds of the 20,317 spectators who saw Strincevich take charge at the outset and never stop cracking the whip, until he had the Giants tied in knots with a masterful four-hit shut-out..."[17]

Nearly half the season was gone, and he had earned just his first victory. Rather than rue what was lost, he concentrated on what remained of the season.

Beating the last-place Giants was one thing. Facing the second-place Cardinals was another. Five days after his gem against the Giants, Nick faced St. Louis at Forbes Field. The Pirates took an early 1–0 lead in the second when a Bill Baker single scored Al Gionfriddo from second. Nick traded goose eggs with Cardinals starter Harry Brecheen for the rest of the game. The one-run lead held up, and Nick had his second shutout in as many starts. He allowed the Cards just three hits, while striking out three.

Next came the Reds on July 4. The Pirates gave Nick more run support, scoring six times. Nick scattered nine Cincinnati hits and allowed just one run. He had his third complete-game victory in a row. The Pirates weren't going anywhere as a team, but Nick was beginning to develop a reputation around the league as a force to be reckoned with.

From June 25 through the end of August, Nick won nine games and lost four. Two of the losses were against the Phillies and Schoolboy Rowe, who beat the Pirates by scores of 4–1 and 2–0. Nick was a particular thorn in the side of the Brooklyn Dodgers who were trying desperately to fend off the advancing Cardinals.

On July 28, with the Cardinals just two and a half games behind Brooklyn, Nick took on the Dodgers at Ebbets Field. Brooklyn fans likely viewed the Pirates as easy prey, but things didn't work out as planned.

"Somebody is always tossing a monkey wrench into the Flatbush pennant machine just when it appears to have started rolling in high gear. Yesterday at Ebbets Field the wrench-thrower was Nick Strincevich, a one-time Yankee farm hand, who held the Brooks to six fairly well scattered hits as the Pirates bounced back to beat them, 7 to 3."[18]

On August 14, Nick continued his mistreatment of the Cincinnati Reds, beating them 3–2 at Forbes Field. It marked the fifth time in three seasons—and *fourth* time against the Reds—that he pitched a complete-game victory without a strikeout.

And on August 20—the day they voted not to recognize the Guild—the Pirates handed the Dodgers their worst defeat of the season. Nick pitched his third shutout of the year, allowing just four singles. He helped his own cause by driving in three runs with a single and a triple.

He was no less merciful with the Cardinals. In addition to the 1–0 shutout on June 30, he beat them 6–1 on August 31 in Pittsburgh, preventing them from adding to their lead on the now second-place Dodgers.

After winning nine of his last thirteen decisions, Nick struggled in September. For their part, the Pirates didn't give him much help. In his final four starts of the season, they scored a total of three runs. Nick lost all four games and won once more in relief, giving him a 10–15 record on the season. He had started the season 0–7, but went 10–8 to finish out—easily the best comeback of the year in the National League. Once given the opportunity to prove himself, he had turned his season completely around. He proved to everyone that his wartime success had been no fluke.

At the time, Nick was the only Serbian player in the major leagues. Not surprisingly, he was immensely popular among the large Serbian population in northwest Indiana and western Pennsylvania.

"They were all gung-ho about me. At Aliquippa, the Serbs over there had a day for me. It's only about forty miles from Pittsburgh. I

Nick Strincevich showcases his sidearm delivery with the Boston Bees in 1940. ©Brace Photograph.

took about four Pirates with me. They laid a big lamb on the table for us. They gave me some sweaters with the colors of the Serbian flag. The boys danced with the girls, and we had a good time. Every week when we were playing in Pittsburgh, those guys were all saying, 'Hey, Jumbo! Let's go back to Aliquippa!' We had a ball over there!"[19]

In August of 1947, the city of Gary held "Nick Strincevich Day" at Wrigley Field. As the city's first big-leaguer, Nick was presented with a brand-new Pontiac. Nick won the hearts of the citizens of Gary, but he lost the ballgame that followed.

Big things were expected of him during the 1947 season. *Baseball Magazine* ran a feature article on him in January under the heading "Big Nick Starts to Click."

"If it is true that the percentage evens things up in the end, Strincevich is heading for some rosy campaigning. The law of averages gave him a thorough kicking around last season."[20]

In spite of growing confidence and expectations of baseball fans, 1947 was a hard year for Nick. He pitched in 32 ballgames that year—the same total as the previous season. But he had trouble with his arm all season and made just seven starts. He finished the year with a disappointing 1–6 record. When he started poorly in 1948, the Pirates traded him to the Phillies.

"I was having problems then with my arm. I think that's what hurt me more than anything. They sent me to the Phillies, and the Phillies sent me to Toronto."[21]

He managed to right the ship in the International League, posting a 9–7 record the rest of the way with a 3.39 ERA. He followed that effort with an 11–15 performance in 1949, again with a 3.39 ERA. The Phillies managed to eclipse the .500 mark for the first time in seventeen seasons. They were a season away from the National League pennant. But when it came time to seek help from the minors, Nick's name was overlooked.

"One day, I was called into the office. The manager called me, Chet Laabs, and a pitcher by the name of Ed Wright. He said all three of us were there to develop the younger Phillies. I guess it didn't go over too good with me. I was kind of hot-headed all the time. I just packed my suitcase and came home."[22]

He returned to Gary and found work as a die setter in the Budd Plant, which specialized in producing automotive parts. He joined the United Auto Workers and became the plant's first union steward. He was promoted to the position of plant safety inspector and worked at the plant for the next thirty years, retiring in 1980.

"We didn't make the money that the guys make now. My biggest thing was when I came to play at Wrigley Field and seen my mother and father, my wife and kids, my brother and sisters—all sitting in a box seat behind the dugout. I felt better than even if I'd pitched a no-hitter or hit a home run. I loved that."[23]

10

More Wartime Players

Dave "Boo" Ferriss
BOSTON RED SOX, 1945–1950

Boo Ferriss came into the American League like a house on fire. He won each of his first eight starts—four of them shutouts. He went on to win 21 games in his rookie season. In an excerpt from a letter to the author, Ferriss describes his first game in the major leagues, on April 29, 1945.

"I served two and a half years in the Army Air Corps in World War II before being discharged in March, 1945. I had a short stay at the Red Sox' top farm club [Class AA] in Louisville. The Red Sox called me up the second day of the American Association season, so I never saw action there. I joined the Red Sox in late April, going by train from Toledo. Manager Joe Cronin had just suffered a broken leg, so he was not with the team. The injury ended Cronin's playing career.

"My first game was against Connie Mack's A's in Shibe Park on a Sunday afternoon, the final game of the series.

> First hitter, Charlie Metro, walked on four straight balls; Second hitter, four balls, no strikes. [Coach] Baker came out. Bob Garbark, catcher, told him I was just missing; Third hitter, Bobby Estalella: two balls, popped up third pitch; Fourth hitter, Frank Hayes: four balls, no strikes; Fifth hitter, Dick Siebert: On a three-two pitch, he hit a bouncer over my head. Shortstop Skeeter Newsome fielded it near second base, stepped on second, and threw to first for the greatest double play I ever saw!
>
> Walked the first two batters to start the second inning, but retired the side and went on to win—a 2–0 shutout.

"At bat, I got three singles (three for three) off the great Bobo Newsom, all solid hits to the outfield. After the third hit, he came over to first base and cussed me out. Scared me to death. You can see why I'll never forget my first game."

Ferriss's 21 wins were no wartime fluke. He followed up his dazzling rookie year with a 25–6 record for the Red Sox in their pennant-winning season of 1946. The Sox faced the St. Louis Cardinals in the World Series.

"It was a real thrill to have the opportunity to pitch in a World Series, particularly in my home park where I was fortunate to win thirteen consecutive games. (Believe it's still a record.) Rudy York hit a three-run homer off Murry Dickson in the first inning, a great lift. Several great fielding plays were most helpful. [I] picked Stan Musial off second in the first inning. Struck out "Country" Slaughter to end the game. I was most fortunate to get the shutout—the 50th in World Series history, one of three Red Sox pitchers to have a World Series shutout—Babe Ruth and Bill Dineen being the others."[1]

Chris Haughey
BROOKLYN DODGERS 1943

October 3, 1943, is a date Chris Haughey will remember as long as he lives. It was the last day of the regular major league baseball season. It was also Haughey's 18th birthday. Days earlier, Haughey had signed a contract with the Brooklyn Dodgers. Brooklyn skipper Leo Durocher promised the young man that he would see action before the season's end. But Durocher was in a pickle, and he did his best to deliver on his promise. In an interview with the author, Haughey talks about his route to the big leagues and the birthday present he got from his manager.

"I was born in New York. In CYO ball, I had three no-hitters and two one-hitters in a row. I was averaging 2.5 strikeouts an inning. I didn't want to sign when I got out of high school. I didn't want to play major league ball. I had eight major league clubs that I could have signed with. I had an athletic scholarship to Fordham. While there, I decided I was going to be drafted anyway, so I might just as well have some fun and play major league ball. So I signed with the Dodgers."

It was late in the baseball season. The Dodgers were more than 20 games behind the Cardinals in the National League, but they still had a chance to finish third. A third-place finish meant a higher "share" or cash reward for each player at season's end. Brooklyn began the last day of the season a half-game ahead of the Pittsburgh Pirates. Pittsburgh played earlier in the day. The Dodgers played the Reds that afternoon.

"It was at Cincinnati. I was against Johnny Vander Meer. Whitlow Wyatt started for the Dodgers and went one inning. It was a situation where the Pirates had to win. They were tied for third place [sic]. They had to win in order to put Brooklyn into fourth place. That's why [Durocher] started Wyatt. During the first inning, the Pirates had lost. We were hopefully in third place. If the Pirates won, we would have had to win.

"At third base, we had Gil Hodges. He was my roommate. That was the first game that Gil ever played in organized ball, as well as I. He played third base, and it was the only time he played third in his whole career. We had Mickey Owen, Bobby Bragan, Billy Herman, Pee Wee Reese.

"I went seven innings. They got a total of five hits. It was quite an experience. I gave up one double, two bunts, and two singles. Up until the seventh inning, it should have been a one-run game. We gave up six runs, but we had two or three errors involved in it. My roomie, Hodges, let a double play ball go right through. I'm not going to talk about that, but I didn't let him forget about it!

"[Joe] Nuxhall was 15. He never finished an inning. I'm the youngest pitcher that the Dodgers ever had in a game. And I'm the youngest pitcher that went from the second, right to the end of the game. I don't know if that's good or bad, but that's what happened."[2]

Jim Castiglia
PHILADELPHIA A'S, 1942

Jim Castiglia was a talented athlete who was sought after by professional teams in two different sports. He is one of a handful of men who played in both the major leagues and the National Football League. While with the A's, he was approached by the normally reticent Joe DiMaggio, who asked him what it was like to get hit as a running back in the NFL. Jim's major league career lasted just 16 games, but he hit .389 and made the most of his brief stay. In a letter to the author, he discusses his career in two professional sports.

"I played baseball during my college years in 'outlaw' leagues in Quebec—the Provincial League—which was made up of many ex–major leaguers. [They] were paid more money there than they received with their former major league teams. My experience was there. I was always a good, solid hitter batting left and right. As a catcher [I] had a great arm, and my knowledge of handling pitchers was welcomed by all the managers.

"At Georgetown University, I was elected to the Hall of Fame in football and baseball. I played pro football with the Philadelphia Eagles in 1941. George Marshall, owner of the Washington Redskins, told Connie Mack that I was one of the best prospects in the U.S. So while with the Eagles in the fall of 1941, I got the opportunity to meet Connie Mack.

"I was signed as a batting practice catcher. But the further we went into spring training, I started to play more and more against the Pacific Coast ball clubs, plus the Chicago Cubs, White Sox, and Pittsburgh Pirates. I was one of three catchers retained on the roster. This was early 1942. All the major league ballplayers were still active. It wasn't until after 1942 that ballplayers started to leave for the service in World War II.

"I played 16 games [and] was the main pinch hitter in April and May. [My] first time in the major leagues was at Fenway Park. I pinch hit in the seventh inning. First time up, first hit—a line drive over second base, hitting left-handed.

"Mr. Mack told me that I was his first catcher starting in July, 1942. However, World War II intervened. I enlisted in the service later in June and served almost four years as a captain in the air force. Many of us served. We were all soldiers serving our country. [Although] it took me away from the love of baseball, serving my country was my duty and my pleasure.

"Mr. Mack signed me to a $5,000 contract in 1946, but I opted to play pro football for the Eagles.

"I have no regrets and did everything to prove that I could star in the major leagues."[3]

Mike Sandlock
BOSTON BRAVES, 1942, 1944
BROOKLYN DODGERS, 1945–1946
PITTSBURGH PIRATES, 1953

Sandlock was a shortstop and catcher during the war. He was one of a handful of wartime players who returned to the big leagues in 1946. Had he remained active in the major leagues in 1947, he would have been eligible to receive a big-league pension. In an interview with the author, he discusses those players overlooked by Major League Baseball.

"Yeah, we're the guys that don't get any pension. Pete Coscarart is fighting and fighting for this. In fact, the last note I got from somewhere's in San Diego, he says, 'I don't know, but I'm going to keep fighting this. I think I'm going to lose my house and everything else.' I guess it's on hold now, and he's still gonna fight it."

Coscarart was a nine-year major league veteran known for his fine defensive play. He experienced a resurgence in playing time during the war and finished the 1945 season poised to serve as a good glove man for any major league club. But Coscarart was also involved in the battle for players' rights. When a strike vote failed early in the 1946 season, he was sold to the Hollywood Stars in the Coast League. Had he been on a major league roster at the end of the season, he would have been eligible for the pension.

"There's only a few of us left that's looking for the pension. There's only about ten of them, I would say. There was quite a few. I remember always talking to Buddy Hassett. Never got a cent. There's a guy, put in nine years. I only put in a few years there. But damn it, he ought to get something. Geez, it's a shame. Dolph Camilli's another one that didn't get anything, and there's a few others that I kept track of. They all passed away now.

"You know, all they had to do was take one or two percent of these big salaries and just make a little pot. That's all they'd need. But that was turned down, too, I think. Oh, well. It's over now, so no use crying. You gotta hang in there, now!"

Coscarart and 75 other players filed a suit against Major League Baseball to be included in the pension plan in 1996. An Appeals Court in California ruled against them in December, 2001. Coscarart passed away on July 24, 2002, without ever having received a significant amount from Major League Baseball.

"I started out as a catcher in 1938, but I came up as a shortstop. Brooklyn bought me, and I opened the [1945] season with them. By midseason, Durocher had trouble finding a good catcher. They went and bought Johnny Peacock I guess [Fats] Dantonio was another one who was with us. Durocher and Peacock didn't get along too well.

"All of a sudden Durocher says, 'Would you do any batting practice catching for me?' We were in Washington playing an exhibition game against the Senators. Peacock was supposed to catch that damn game, and I'd been working behind the plate previously. During the intermission, or the show that was supposed to be going on, we were sitting in the clubhouse. Peacock and Durocher got into some kind of rhubarb. Durocher didn't like what he had to say. [He] scratched him out, put my name down, and I've been catching ever since. It's the craziest game, isn't it?!

"Durocher didn't like me. If I got hit or rapped, I took it. [Enos] Slaughter hit me, boy—the one that ruined my knees. He really gave me a couple. Well, when you're in a one-run or tie game, you expect it. You're supposed to knock him down next time he comes up, and all that stuff. Didn't bother me. Durocher thought I wasn't nasty enough."

Sandlock hit two home runs in his five seasons. Both came in 1945, and both were hit off the same pitcher.

"There was a relief pitcher with the Giants—Rube Fischer. First one I hit was in the Polo Grounds, up where it said *Chesterfield*. That was my best shot. Upper deck. And then he relieves in Brooklyn, and I go and hit the clock over there. Off the same guy. Same pitch, too. He never learned, did he?"[4]

Mike Kosman
CINCINNATI REDS, 1943

Like Chris Haughey, Mike Kosman's big-league career lasted just a single day. In a letter to the author, he describes how he got there, as well as the circumstances surrounding his only appearance.

"I was discharged from the marines in February of 1943 and

decided to play ball somewhere. Being single, I had no obligations. I saw an ad in the *Sporting News* where a scout for the Yankees was looking for ballplayers. Before I answered the ad, I called my baseball coach at Indiana University and told him what I was planning to do.

"He told me not to do anything until he talked to the Cincinnati Reds, who were in spring training at the university. There was no spring training in Florida. Cleveland was at Purdue University and the Cubs were at West Baden, Indiana, near French Lick.

"Coach called me to tell me that Cincy wanted me at spring training. I was there a few days, and they signed me to a contract—$450 per month and a $400 bonus. I was in spring training for about four weeks until the season began.

"My big-league experience was nothing. We're playing the Cubs at Crosley Field in Cincinnati, and it's raining. Bill McKechnie, manager for Cincinnati, called my name and put me at third as a pinch runner. I was told that if the ball was hit to short or second, to go on home. It was hit to short. I took off, and the catcher was waiting for me as I slid and [I] was called [out].

"The next morning I was optioned to the Reds' club in Birmingham, Alabama, in the Southern Association. I played two years there and left when the good players were coming back from the war.

"The Cincy manager was good to me when he put me in, since he knew I was going to the minors. Now I could say I played in the big leagues."[5]

Charlie Metro
DETROIT TIGERS, 1943–1944
PHILADELPHIA A'S, 1944–1945

Charlie Metro was a true baseball "lifer," having spent parts of six decades in professional baseball. He was a prolific minor league manager who twice managed in the big leagues. He rose from the coal mines of Pennsylvania to play three years in the majors and profoundly influenced the careers of dozens of players. Six of his charges went to the Hall of Fame, and eleven others went on to become big-league managers themselves. In an interview with the author, Metro talks about his rough road to the major leagues.

"I was classified 4-F. I came from the coal and steel country [of] western Pennsylvania. Nanty-Glo, near Johnstown. After my senior year, I was still working in the coal mines. I was in a gas explosion that killed several men. I was burned up, and my father had a skull fracture and a broken arm. I came out with burns and trauma and everything else. I tried to enlist in every phase of the service, but never did go. I did have three brothers and a sister that went.

"I was signed by Jack Fournier, Browns scout, for 60 bucks a month. I worked my way up with the Browns. Then I was released and signed by Texarkana, and I was a player selected by the Detroit Tigers. I went to Beaumont, Texas, in '42 with Steve O'Neill.

"I always played center field, but I ran into a pretty good stumbling block at Beaumont. The center fielder was Hoot Evers. The right fielder was Dick Wakefield, and the left fielder was Anse Moore. I could outplay all of them in the field, [but] they hit one, two, and four in the league! I relieved the guys defensively in the outfield.

"Steve liked me. I was kind of his fair-haired boy. He saw me make one of the greatest plays he ever saw an outfielder make. I was playing center field when Hoot Evers was injured. There was a man on second with one out. A guy hit a fly ball to deep center. I went back and caught it right at the wall. I turned around and threw a strike to third base. The runner had thought it was going to be off the wall. He was halfway to third and came back. He tagged up, and the ball beat him."

Steve O'Neill became the Detroit Tigers' manager in 1943.

"He told me he was going to take me up. We went up, and I played a little bit there. I didn't hit much because I didn't play much the year before. The first game I played in was against the Browns. Al Hollingsworth, a left-hander, was pitching. Steve had me in center field, and I was leading off. I took three pitches. I was expecting blinding speed from this big-league pitcher. All he was doing was goosing the ball up there, and I kept looking for a fastball.

"I took the third strike. I came back, and Steve said to me, 'Charlie, were you nervous?' I said, 'Yeaaah.' So the next time up, I doubled. The next time up, I singled. I got over that fright."

Charlie batted .200 in his inaugural year, during which he played in just 44 games. He was batting just .192 in August of 1944 when he was traded to Connie Mack's Philadelphia A's.

"I was a student of the game because I didn't play an awful lot. When I went over to Philadelphia, I didn't get a change to play too much either. I played some center field and some third and second base for

Mr. Mack. When I wasn't playing, I got a scorecard, and I would keep score in this manner: I'd put down a hitter, and I'd put a mark for fastball or curveball. Then I'd total the pitches out at the end of the inning.

"Long about the third inning, Mr. Mack said, 'Son, come over here.' You know, he sat in the center of the dugout in his suit and starched collar and everything. You've seen the pictures.

"He said, 'What are you doing? Let me see that.'

"I showed it to him.

"He said, 'Why are you doing this?'

"I said, 'Well, Mr. Mack, I watch every pitch that our pitcher makes, and every pitch that the other pitcher makes.'

"He asked, 'Where did you learn it from?'

"I said, 'Nobody taught me. I just thought it up myself.'

"He said, 'That's fine, son. You keep it up.'

"Now, I'm managing Montgomery in 1950 in the Southeastern League. We're playing this exhibition game against the A's, and Mr. Mack was there. He was sitting there in the box seats, kinda by home plate, and he called me over prior to the game.

"He said, 'Son, I want to ask you a question.'

"I said, 'Yes sir, Mr. Mack?'

"He said, 'Are you still keeping that scorecard I saw you with?'"

"The most outstanding game that comes to mind was in Philadelphia. We played a 24-inning, 1–1 ballgame against the Tigers. It was called on account of darkness. I was sent in to pinch hit for a pinch hitter in the 24th. The reason for that was that Mr. Mack and the umpires didn't want another inning to start because it would be to the advantage of the visiting club. We'd be hitting in the dark.

"Well, they agreed to call it at the end of that inning. Les Mueller pitched 19⅔ innings, I believe, and Dizzy Trout came in and finished the game—the last four innings, or so. He was pitching, and he threw me a fastball inside. I missed a home run by about ten feet in left field. Then I singled sharply. You remember those great events. It was a real pleasure playing in a game like that."

"I went out to Oakland and played for Casey Stengel. When I was at Oakland, I used to throw batting practice to Billy Martin. He was a guy who worked around the clubhouse shining shoes and stuff like that. He used to call me "Big Leaguer."

"He'd say, 'Hey, Big Leaguer! Throw me some batting practice!'

"I'd say, 'I can't get any baseballs!'

"He'd go into the clubhouse and talk to the clubhouse guy, Red Adams, who was a great benefactor of those kids in California. He'd take them off the streets and get them started in baseball. Billy was one of those kids.

"I'd throw batting practice to him for half an hour. Then I'd say, 'Now you throw some to me!'

"'Oh, no,' he'd say, 'I got to go in and do the work!'

"We became friends, and he gave me a job as a coach for the Oakland A's—way back there in my last year in uniform."

Charlie was more than just a student of the game. He was also a baseball innovator, of sorts.

"I hit off a hollow reed in Pennsylvania. I had an old, taped baseball and set it on that hollow reed. I hit into an old, discarded mattress that I'd prop up with a bat. I was playing on the town team in high school. That's where I got the original idea.

"I invented the 'tee' they use for 'tee-ball'—the *Metro Batting Tee*—in 1947. I made that thing in Bisbee, Arizona. I got pictures and everything to prove it. I made some for commercial type and sold quite a few of them. Billy Martin bought the first one from me. I taught hitting with it. I became a pretty good hitting instructor."[6]

Val Heim
Chicago White Sox, 1942

"I was signed to a minor league team—Jonesboro, Arkansas—by former White Sox outfielder Johnny Mostil in 1940. I was in my third year of professional baseball in 1942. I worked my way up, and when Taffy Wright left for military service, I was brought up from Waterloo, Iowa and joined the Chicago team in Boston.

"At the time I joined the Chicago club, I was also very close to being drafted. However, my draft board gave me time to finish the season with Chicago.

"My first game was against the Philadelphia team. Connie Mack was the manager. Mr. Mack wore a business suit, along with a felt hat. I was used as a pinch hitter. The Philadelphia pitcher was [Russ] Christopher. My first at-bat was a base hit to center field. The ball was given to me and signed by the Chicago players.

"My last game was in St. Louis. At that time, I was contacted to play service ball at the St. Louis Air Base as a Seaman First Class. With the St. Louis Navy team, I played outfield with ballplayers who had been drafted from major league teams: Johnny Berardino, Dick Sisler, Bob Scheffing, Hal Schumacher, Emil Kush, Bob Blattner, and others. I played baseball there two years and was then sent to the South Pacific."

"Luke Appling was very nice to me, driving me to the ballpark in his car. The fans looked for Mr. Appling and would cheer and yell as we drove by. When I came up, many of the great players were still playing with their major league teams. My short stay was just short of the war year teams. The service teams were the 'big league' teams during the war years."[7]

Arnold "Jug" Thesenga
WASHINGTON SENATORS, 1944

"I signed up to play Class A ball in Sioux City, Iowa [Western League], in 1935. I finished the season with Philadelphia—Connie Mack's team. I didn't sign a contract, but pitched batting practice for a couple of weeks. Connie Mack said I needed more experience. I went back to Class A baseball. Got traded and sold a couple times. I decided to stay in semipro ball and quit traveling so much.

"That's how I ended up in Wichita, Kansas, working in the defense industry and managing a baseball team. I was on a deferment as a tool and die worker.

"In 1944, I had won two games in the National Baseball Congress World Series against a good Army and Navy team. I won fifteen games that year. Washington made me an offer—$2,500—to finish the season, which lasted six or seven more weeks.

"I joined the Washington Senators in New York City and started a game the next day. I flew to New York and was sick on the plane all the way. I pitched against Emerson Roser. I shut them out five innings. I didn't get credit for the win because they came back and tied the score. We ended up winning the game."

Jug walked eight Yankee hitters and struck out one. Alex Carrasquel relieved him when he got into trouble in the sixth inning. Washington manager Ossie Bluege sent him to the bullpen, where he pitched in four more ballgames.

Jug was named to the National Sandlot Hall of Fame for his performance in 1943. He won more games at the National Baseball Congress (NBC) World Series than any other pitcher in the tournament's 60-year history. He was inducted into the Kansas Baseball Hall of Fame in 1982 and the NBC Hall of Fame in 1994.[8]

Appendix
Statistics

Frank Mancuso

BORN: May 23; YEAR: 1918; BIRTHPLACE: Houston; HEIGHT: 6'; WEIGHT: 195; THROW: R; STATE: TX; POSITION: C

Year	Team	League	G	AB	R	H	2B	3B	HR	RBI	BB	SO	SB	HBP	BA	OBA	SA
1937	Blytheville	N.E. Ark.	97	344	75	102	18	12	13	88	73	59	6	0	.297	.420	.532
1938	Cedar Rapids	I.I.I.	39	114	16	27	3	2	2	16	17	38	0	0	.237	.336	.351
1938	Fort Smith	West. Assoc.	23	74	16	31	9	1	1	17	11	15	0	1	.419	.500	.608
1939	(Inactive)																
1940	St. Joseph	West. Assoc.	130	480	92	149	24	16	7	103	69	59	4	8	.310	.406	.471
1941	Carthage	West. Assoc.	134	468	92	142	33	8	18	97	85	65	4		.303	.410	.524
1942	San Antonio	Texas	131	435	52	109	12	3	11	49	37	71	2	2	.251	.312	.368
1943	(Military Service)																
1944	St. Louis	AL	88	244	19	50	11	0	1	24	20	32	1	2	.205	.271	.262
1945	St. Louis	AL	119	365	39	98	13	3	1	38	46	44	0	2	.268	.354	.329
1946	St. Louis	AL	87	262	22	63	8	3	3	23	30	31	1	2	.240	.323	.328
1947	Washington	AL	43	131	5	30	5	1	0	13	5	11	0	0	.229	.257	.282
1948	Toledo	AA	111	337	41	92	14	4	13	61	38	40	0	0	.273	.347	.454
1949	Baltimore	IL	122	364	45	94	10	5	17	48	41	55	1	2	.258	.337	.453
1950	San Antonio	Texas	111	303	23	72	16	0	9	42	35	38	1	2	.238	.321	.380
1951	San Antonio -Beaumont	Texas	108	358	41	95	22	1	11	62	44	41	2	1	.265	.347	.425
1952	Wichita Falls	Big State	101	286	52	83	19	0	14	55	66	32	3	1	.290	.425	.503
1953	Houston	Texas	63	166	8	39	8	0	2	13	19	23	0	0	.235	.314	.319
1953	Omaha	Western	40	102	7	20	4	0	2	13	23	17	0	0	.196	.344	.294
1954	Ardmore	Sooner St.	32	72	19	24	4	0	7	22	20	10	3	1	.333	.484	.681
1955	Ardmore	Sooner St.	25	33	6	8	3	0	1	7	17	10	0	0	.242	.500	.424
	Minor League Totals		1267	3936	585	1087	199	52	128	693	595	573	26	18	.276	.374	.451
	Major League Totals		337	1002	85	241	37	7	5	98	101	118	2	6	.241	.314	.306

Mullen, Ford

BORN: Feb. 9; YEAR: 1917; BIRTHPLACE: Olympia; STATE: WA; HEIGHT: 5'9"; WEIGHT: 165; BAT: L; THROW: R; POSITION: 2B-3B

Year	Team	League	G	AB	R	H	2B	3B	HR	RBI	BB	SO	SB	HB	BA	OBA	SA
1939	Alexandria	Evangeline															
1939	Jacksonville	East Texas	61	257	46	84	10	1	0	20	24	15	5	0	.327	.384	.374
1940	Henderson	East Texas	104	429	84	146	23	5	0	46	46	31	15	2	.340	.407	.417
1941	Winston-Salem	Piedmont	118	433	55	120	15	3	2	24	40	46	10	3	.277	.342	.339
1942	Vancouver	West. Int.	139	559	94	164	19	4	5	51	53	39	19	0	.293	.355	.369
1942	Seattle	PCL	3	4		2									.500		
1943	Seattle	PCL	110	426	57	116	17	0	0	30	29	31	17	1	.272	.320	.312
1944	Philadelphia	NL	118	464	51	124	9	4	0	31	28	32	4	4	.267	.315	.304
1945	(inactive)																
1946	(inactive)																
1947	Kansas City	AA	14	45	2	8	2	0	0	9	2	3	0	0	.178	.213	.222
1947	Portland	PCL	73	223	30	72	6	3	0	17	20	19	8	1	.323	.381	.377
1948	Portland	PCL	102	240	28	72	10	2	1	9	15	21	2	1	.300	.344	.371
1949	Portland	PCL	86	208	25	47	9	0	1	27	28	15	2	0	.226	.318	.284
1950	Boise	Pioneer	121	434	75	115	25	6	0	39	112	36	26	1	.265	.417	.350
Minor League Totals			931	3258	496	946	136	24	9	272	369	256	104	9	.290	.364	.355
Major League Totals			118	464	51	124	9	4	0	31	28	32	4	4	.267	.315	.304

Ed Carnett

BORN: Oct. 21, 1916, at Springfield, MO; HEIGHT: 6'; WEIGHT: 185; BATTED LEFT; THREW LEFT; MANAGER: Vancouver W Int 1946; Borger WTNM 1948-49. 51: Ponca City West A 1954; Gainesville/Ponca City Sooner St. 1955

Year	Club	League	POS	G	AB	R	H	2B	3B	HR	RBI	SB	BA
1935	Ponca City	WestA	P-OF	57	170	15	46	9	2	0	19	0	.271
1936	Ponca City	WestA	P-OF	77	244	41	63	14	6	2	33	5	.258
	Los Angeles	PC	P	7	4	0	1	0	0	0	0	0	.250
1937	Tulsa	Texas	P-1B	66	168	28	51	11	4	0	26	2	.304
1938	Los Angeles	PC	P	21	31	4	8	1	0	0	1	0	.258
1939	Milwaukee	AA	P	53	106	11	29	3	2	1	11	1	.274
1940	Kansas City	AA	P	8	11	3	5	0	1	0	5	0	.455
	Newark	Int	P	5	4	1	1	0	0	0	0	0	.250
	Binghamton	Eastern	P	22	34	4	7	2	0	0	3	0	.206
1941	Boston	National	P	2	0	0	0	0	0	0	0	0	.000
	Kansas City	AA	P	49	48	15	16	4	0	0	11	0	.333
1942	Binghamton	Eastern	1B	14	53	5	9	0	2	1	3	0	.170
	Seattle	PC	P	42	62	6	16	1	0	0	4	1	.258
1943	Seattle	PC	OF-P	121	403	44	121	12	4	2	28	21	.300
1944	Chicago	American	O-1-P	126	457	51	126	18	8	1	60	5	.276
1945	Cleveland	American	OF-P	30	73	5	16	7	0	0	7	0	.219
1946	Seattle	PC	OF-1B	52	181	17	37	2	3	1	13	1	.204
	Vancouver	West Int	1B	36	141	25	39	7	2	3	18	3	.277
1947	Tulsa	Texas	1B16	29	4	7	1	1	0	4	0		.241
	W. Falls/Paris	Big St	OF-1B	105	389	89	132	23	4	9	69	17	.339
1948	Borger	WTNM	OF-1B	135	563	158	230	59	10	33	161	9	.409
1949	Borger	WTNM	OF-1B	96	338	81	112	21	6	13	79	5	.331

Year	Club	League	POS	G	AB	R	H	2B	3B	HR	RBI	SB	BA
1950	Borger	WTNM	OF-1B	144	538	126	194	47	6	24	135	13	.361
1951	Borger/Albuq.	WTNM	OF-1B	111	366	44	115	22	5	1	60	4	.314
1952	Borger	WTNM	1B-OF	125	475	83	151	36	1	16	107	0	.318
1953	Abilene	WTNM	OF-1B	63	247	23	84	22	0	0	37	0	.340
1954	Ponca City	West A	OF	100	304	38	86	20	6	4	64	1	.283
1955	Gaines/P. City	Sooner St	OF	93	282	39	68	11	0	4	41	7	.241
	Majors										67	5	.268
	Minors			158	530	56	142	25	8	1	67	5	.268
				1618	5191	904	1628	328	65	114	932	90	.314

Pitching Record

Year	Club	League	G	IP	W	L	H	R	ER	BB	SO	ERA
1935	Ponca City	WestA	34	256	19	11	264	124	91	94	160	3.20
1936	Ponca City	WestA	31	215	16	10	217	127	91	84	155	3.81
	Los Angeles	PC	6	17	0	3	25	15	15	6	3	7.94
1937	Tulsa	Texas	33	177	15	6	196	105	81	53	110	4.12
1938	Los Angeles	PC	21	91	3	6	110	63	42	30	54	4.15
1939	Milwaukee	AA	26	138	4	11	158	81	67	58	76	4.37
1940	Kansas City	AA	8	28	2	2	24	14	12	15	7	3.86
	Newark	Int	4	7	1	1	9	8	8	4	1	10.29
	Binghamton	Eastern	13	65	6	3	59	24	20	30	17	2.77
1941	Boston	National	2	1	0	0	4	3	3	3	2	27.00
	Kansas City	AA	26	77	4	2	88	53	42	32	26	4.91
1942	Seattle	PC	22	84	4	6	85	37	33	37	26	3.54
1943	Seattle	PC	11	63	4	4	62	33	22	22	18	3.14
1944	Chicago	American	2	2	0	0	3	2	2	0	1	9.00
1945	Cleveland	American	2	2	0	0	0	0	0	0	1	0.00
1946	Vancouver	West Int	2	9	0	1	15	8	8	3	6	8.00
	Tulsa	Texas	2	3	0	0	5	7	6	4	1	18.00
1947	WF-Paris	Big St	7	36	3	2	-	-	-	-	-	4.75

(Ed Carnett Pitching Record, continued)

Year	Club	League	G	IP	W	L	H	R	ER	BB	SO	ERA
1948	Borger	WTNM	27	86	5	2	118	63	54	25	71	5.65
1949	Borger	WTNM	18	67	0	2	121	68	61	30	38	8.19
1950	Borger	WTNM	25	137	13	6	148	69	48	38	81	3.15
1951	Borger/Albuq.	WTNM	23	121	9	7	177	87	63	42	47	4.69
1952	Borger	WTNM	19	135	10	6	150	90	60	45	42	4.00
1953	Abilene	WTNM	12	104	4	7	110	58	47	34	41	4.07
1954	Ponca City	West A	14	80	7	3	82	44	36	37	51	4.05
1955	Gaines/P. City	Sooner St.	7	–	0	1	–	–	–	–	–	–
	Majors		6	5	0	0	7	5	5	3	4	9.00
	Minors		391	1996	129	102	2223	1178	907	723	1031	4.16

Lee Pfund

BORN: Oct. 18; YEAR: 1918; BIRTHPLACE: Oak Park; STATE: IL; HEIGHT: 6'1"; WEIGHT: 185; BAT: R; THROW: R; POSITION: P

Year	Team	League		IP		R	ER	SO	BB	SAVES	W	L	ERA
1941	Albany	Geo.-Fla.	27	157	186	120	90	84	94		10	10	5.16
1942	Decatur	I.I.I.	28	163	176	112	88	70	64		6	10	4.86
1943	(Inactive)												
1944	Mobile	SA	10	53	66	27	18	21	22		6	2	3.06
1944	Columbus	AA	19	70	96	49	46	25	36		4	4	5.91
1945	Brooklyn	NL	15	62	69	51	36	35	27	0	3	2	5.2
1946	Mobile	SA	38	202	239	118	87	64	52		7	16	3.88
1947	St. Paul	AA	18	123	132	68	59	28	42		5	7	4.31
1947	Montreal	IL	6	16	19		9	4	9		1	0	5.06
1948	St. Paul	AA	6	24	25		17	7	16		0	1	6.38
1948	Elmira	Eastern	20	139	143	80	54	48	69		6	13	3.5
1949	(Inactive)												
1950	Pueblo	Western	9	59	67	46	41	15	39		3	4	6.25
Minor League Totals			181	1006	1149	620	509	366	443		48	67	4.55
Major League Totals			15	62	69	51	36	35	27	0	3	2	5.2

George Hausmann

BORN: Feb. 11; YEAR: 1916; BIRTHPLACE: St. Louis; STATE: MO; HEIGHT: 5'5"; WEIGHT: 145; BAT: R; THROW: R; POSITION: 2B

Year	Team	League	G	AB	R	H	2B	3B	HR	RBI	BB	SO	SB	HBP	BA	OB	SA
1938	Corpus Christi	Texas Valley	121	557	157	198	38	14	14	120	74	31	33	3	.355	.434	.549
1939	Springfield	I.I.I.	160	475	96	150	24	13	5	57	62	34	13	2	.316	.397	.453
1940	San Antonio	Texas	160	608	66	153	22	12	2	56	38	42	7	3	.252	.299	.337
1941	Springfield	I.I.I.	84	336	61	95	17	7	9	33	37	18	4	1	.283	.356	.455
1941	San Antonio	Texas	42	114	28	2	0	0	5	20	8	1	0		.246	.358	.263
1942	San Antonio	Texas	153	550	87	166	20	7	0	53	47	50	9	2	.302	.359	.364
1943	New Orleans	SA	136	517	101	154	15	12	1	54	70	27	15	1	.298	.383	.379
1944	New York	NL	131	466	70	124	20	4	1	30	40	25	3	0	.266	.324	.333
1945	New York	NL	154	623	98	174	15	8	2	45	73	46	7	1	.279	.356	.339
1946	Torreon	Mexican	90	372	75	114	14	15	1	41	46	20	12		.306	.306	.433
1947	Monterrey	Mexican	116	453	76	126	17	9	0	39	52	27	13		.278	.278	.355
1948	(Inactive)																
1949	Nuevo Laredo	Mexican	27	103	10	23	4	3	1	20	12	5	1	0	.223	.304	.350
1949	New York	NL	16	47	5	6	0	1	0	3	7	6	0	0	.128	.241	.170
1950	Dallas–Houston	Texas	95	289	35	63	8	1	1	17	34	15	3	2	.218	.305	.263
1951	San Antonio	Texas	138	439	42	105	16	1	0	36	50	29	4	2	.239	.320	.280
1952	Anderson	Tri-St.	120	441	98	145	18	7	6	58	69	25	15		.329	.420	.442
1953	York	Piedmont	16	20	4	5	1	0	0	0	1	3	0	0	.250	.286	.300
1954	Austin	Big State	77	320	45	84	16	2	2	25	33	15	2	0	.263	.331	.344
1955	Austin	Big State	97	332	57	99	15	8	1	35	40	15	3	4	.298	.380	.401
1956	Winston-Salem	Carolina	2	2	0	0	0	0	0						.000		
	Mexican League Totals		233	928	161	263	35	27	2	100	110	52	26		.283	.359	.386
	Minor League Totals			5928	1020	1708	247	111	43	649	685	364	135	20	.288	.364	.389
	Major League Totals		301	1136	173	304	35	13	3	78	120	77	10	1	.268	.338	.329

Cy Buker

BORN: Feb. 5; YEAR: 1919; BIRTHPLACE: Greenwood; STATE: WI; HEIGHT: 5'11"; WEIGHT: 190; BAT: L; THROW: R; POSITION: P

Year	Team	League	G	GS	IP	H	R	ER	SO	BB	SV	W	L	ERA
1940	Wausau	Northern*										0	0	
1940	Clinton	I.I.I.*												
1941	(Inactive)													
1942	Wisconsin Rapids	Wisconsin St.	12		68	83	59	52	36	37		5	5	6.88
1943	(Inactive)													
1944	St. Paul	AA	25		128	125	54	46	62	49		11	3	3.23
1945	Brooklyn	NL	42	4	87	90	41	32	48	45	5	7	2	3.31
1946	Montreal	IL	29	22	163	148	83	69	85	77		12	7	3.81
1947	St. Paul-Milwaukee	AA	34		139	178	103	82	52	71		8	8	5.31
1948	Milwaukee-Kansas City	AA	32		73	99	81	69	35	45		4	4	8.51
1949	(Inactive)													
1950	(Inactive)													
1951	Colorado Springs-Sioux City-Lincoln	Western	30		75	88	48	38	37	28		2	6	4.56
1952	Lincoln	Western*												
	Minor League Totals		162		646	721	428	356	307	307		42	33	4.96
	Major League Totals		42	4	87	90	41	32	48	45	5	7	2	3.31

*Less than 45 innings—limited data

Bill Lefebvre

BORN: Nov. 11; YEAR: 1915; BIRTHPLACE: Natick; STATE: RI; HEIGHT: 5'11"; BAT: L; THROW: L; POSITION: P

Year	Team	League	G	GS	IP	H	R	ER	SO	BB	SV	W	L	ERA
1938	Minneapolis	AA	23	14	127	156	66	60	45	35		8	8	4.25
1938	Boston	AL	1	0	4	8	6	6	0	0	0	0	0	13.50
1939	Boston	AL	5	3	26	35	17	17	8	14	0	1	1	5.81
1939	Louisville	AA	30	18	116	142	78	71	42	43		6	10	5.51
1940	San Francisco	PCL	5	27										
1940	Little Rock	SA	26	21	159	170	75	64	30	46		6	13	3.62
1940	Scranton	Eastern												
1941	Louisville	AA	33	21	169	192	80	66	51	52		12	7	3.51
1942	Minneapolis	AA	47	15	162	186	91	74	64	63		9	11	4.11
1943	Minneapolis	AA	24	18	162	145	51	40	53	38		12	8	2.22
1943	Washington	AL	6	3	32	33	18	16	10	16	0	2	0	4.45
1944	Washington	AL	24	4	70	86	48	35	18	21	3	2	4	4.52
1945	(Inactive)													
1946	Minneapolis	AA	35	24	167	221	133	119	58	49		11	12	6.41
1947	Providence-Pawtucket	New England	12	4	47	53	42	39	23	39		3	3	7.47
Minor League Totals			235	162	1109	1265	616	533	366	365	3	68	76	4.33
Major League Totals			36	10	132	162	89	74	36	51	3	5	5	5.03

Year	Team	League	G	AB	R	H	2B	3B	HR	RBI	BB	SO	SB	HP	BA	OBA	SA
1938	Minneapolis	AA	27	57	8	16	2	0	1	5	3	12	0	0	.281	.317	.368
1938	Boston	AL	1	1	1	1	0	0	1	1	0	0	0	0	1.000	1.000	4.000
1939	Boston	AL	7	10	3	3	0	0	0	1	2	2	0	0	.300	.417	.300
1939	Louisville	AA	31	38	2	8	2	0	0	1	2	7	0	0	.211	.250	.263
1940	San Francisco	PCL	7	14		2									.143		
1940	Little Rock	SA	32	63	10	15	3	1	1	7	6	11	0	0	.238	.304	.365
1941	Louisville	Aa	34	57	7	11	0	0	0	1	5	6	0	0	.193	.258	.193
1942	Minneapolis	AA	48	52	6	8	1	1	0	5	4	12	2	0	.154	.214	.212
1943	Minneapolis	AA	39	73	5	18	4	0	0	5	7	9	1	0	.247	.313	.301
1943	Washington	AL	7	14	0	4	3	0	0	1	0	1	0	0	.286	.286	.500
1944	Washington	AL	60	62	4	16	2	2	0	8	9	12	0	0	.258	.352	.355
1946	Minneapolis	AA	41	58	5	7	2	0	2	3	11	24	0	2	.121	.282	.259
1947	Providence–Pawtucket	New England	29	34	4	4	1	1	0	6	12	7	0	0	.118	.348	.206
Minor League Totals			288	446	47	89	15	3	4	33	50	88	3	2	.200	.283	.274
Major League Totals			75	87	8	24	5	2	1	11	11	15	0	0	.276	.357	.414

Eddie Basinski

BORN: Nov. 4; YEAR: 1922; BIRTHPLACE: Buffalo; STATE: NY; HEIGHT: 6'1"; WEIGHT: 172; BAT: R; THROW: R; POSITION: 2B

Year	Team	League	G	AB	R	H	2B	3B	H	RB	BB	SO	SB	HBP	BA	OBA	SA
1944	Montreal	IL	68	270	32	66	10	1	2	20	22	24	5	2	.244	.306	.311
1944	Brooklyn	NL	39	105	13	27	4	1	0	9	6	10	1	2	.257	.310	.314
1945	Brooklyn	NL	108	336	30	88	9	4	0	33	11	33	0	4	.262	.293	.313
1946	St. Paul	AA	136	515	66	130	17	5	5	46	85	44	9	6	.252	.365	.334
1947	Pittsburgh	NL	56	161	15	32	6	2	4	17	18	27	0	0	.199	.279	.335
1947	Newark	IL	12	35	2	7	1	0	0	2	3	7	0	0	.200	.263	.229
1947	Portland	PCL	59	209	22	58	9	2	2	30	15	31	5	1	.278	.329	.368
1948	Portland	PCL	175	632	83	175	24	3	4	50	35	83	8	5	.277	.320	.343
1949	Portland	PCL	164	592	74	158	32	7	12	79	76	76	4	2	.267	.352	.405
1950	Portland	PCL	202	722	80	173	39	1	15	75	69	97	1	7	.240	.312	.359
1951	Portland	PCL	169	687	109	183	32	6	16	73	65	77	3	2	.266	.332	.400
1952	Portland	PCL	166	552	60	136	25	1	10	58	64	62	4	4	.246	.329	.350
1953	Portland	PCL	156	529	49	127	18	1	6	61	56	63	2	4	.240	.317	.312
1954	Portland	PCL	157	551	73	142	34	2	14	54	55	62	4	6	.258	.332	.403
1955	Portland	PCL	98	280	31	76	16	0	5	32	26	39	1	0	.271	.333	.382
1956	Portland	PCL	114	309	32	80	11	3	5	25	28	43	2	1	.259	.322	.362
1957	Portland-Seattle	PCL	136	436	53	118	22	1	10	42	29	47	3	2	.271	.319	.394
1958	Seattle	PCL	107	349	42	105	28	1	8	47	33	22	1	4	.301	.368	.456
1959	Vancouver	PCL	43	94	12	13	2	0	2	8	4	8	0	3	.138	.198	.223
Minor League Totals			1962	6762	820	1747	320	34	116	702	665	785	52	49	.258	.329	.367
Major League Totals			203	602	58	147	19	7	4	59	35	70	1	6	.244	.292	.319

Year	Team	League	G	GS	IP	H	R	ER	SO	BB	SV	W	L	ERA
1955	Portland	PCL	2								0	0		

Nick Strincevich

BORN: Mar. 1; YEAR: 1915; BIRTHPLACE: Gary; STATE: IN; HEIGHT: 6'1"; WEIGHT: 180; BAT: R; THROW: R; POSITION: P

Year	Team	League	G	GS	IP	H	R	ER	SO	BB	SV	W	L	ERA
1935	Akron	Mid-Atl.	4		18	17	9	7	13	20		1	2	3.50
1936	Butler	Penn. St.	22		153	146	67	58	92	58		10	8	3.41
1937	Norfolk	Piedmont	34		177	170	100		90	92		11	8	
1938	Newark	IL	30	9	102	102	60	49	44	46		11	4	4.32
1939	Newark	IL	20	2	40	62	35	32	16	28		1	2	7.20
1939	Sacramento	PCL	12		56	60	29	24	19	27		2	6	3.86
1940	Boston	NL	32	14	129	142	89	79	54	63	1	4	8	5.53
1941	Boston–Pittsburgh	NL	15	3	34	42	28	22	13	19	0	1	2	5.77
1941	Milwaukee	AA	12		63	72	35	32	31	21		4	2	4.57
1942	Pittsburgh	NL	7	1	22	19	7	7	10	9	0	0	0	2.82
1942	Toronto	IL	34	27	199	191	75	53	86	59		12	10	2.40
1943	Toronto	IL	35	29	233	203	90	64	113	47		15	7	2.47
1944	Pittsburgh	NL	40	26	190	190	86	65	47	37	2	14	7	3.08
1945	Pittsburgh	NL	36	29	228	235	94	84	74	49	2	16	10	3.31
1946	Pittsburgh	NL	32	22	176	185	77	70	49	44	1	10	15	3.58
1947	Pittsburgh	NL	32	7	89	111	59	52	22	37	0	1	6	5.26
1948	Pittsburgh–Philadelphia	NL	9	1	21	34	22	21	5	12	0	0	1	9.00
1948	Toronto	IL	24	16	109	110	52	41	47	26		9	7	3.39
1949	Toronto	IL	41	26	202	215	95	76	63	62		11	15	3.39
1950	Toronto	IL	14	3	33	38		17	6	13		0	3	4.64
Minor League Totals			282		1385	1386		462	620	499		87	74	4.05
Major League Totals			203	103	889	958		400	274	270	6	46	49	

Notes

1.—Frank Mancuso

1. Frank Mancuso, interview by author, October 15, 2000.
2. *Ibid.*
3. Frank Mancuso, interview by author, January 21, 2000.
4. *Ibid.*
5. *Ibid.*
6. Mancuso, October 15, 2000.
7. *Ibid.*
8. *Ibid.*
9. *Ibid.*
10. *Ibid.*
11. Frank Mancuso, interview by author, February 11, 2001.
12. *Ibid.*
13. *Ibid.*
14. McGoogan, William J. "Paratrooper Mancuso Lands with Brownies," *The Sporting News*, March 30, 1944, p. 1.
15. Mancuso, October 15, 2000.
16. Frank Mancuso, letter, October 12, 2000.
17. Mancuso, October 15, 2000.
18. *Ibid.*
19. *Ibid.*
20. Aaron Robinson of the Yankees batted .281 in just 160 at-bats. Ironically, next to Frank's .268 average, the next highest batting average among all American League catchers belonged to Rick Ferrell, who batted .266.
21. Mancuso, October 15, 2000.
22. *Ibid.*
23. Mancuso, January 21, 2001.
24. *Ibid.*
25. Mancuso, January 21, 2001.
26. *Ibid.*
27. Mancuso, February 11, 2001.
28. Mancuso, January 21, 2001.
29. Mancuso, October 15, 2000.

2.—Ford Mullen

1. Ford Mullen, letter, July 26, 2000.
2. Ford Mullen, interview by author, January 26, 2002.
3. McGowen, Roscoe. "Brooklyn Subdued by Barrett, 4 to 1," *The New York Times*, April 19, 1944, p. 17.
4. Ford Mullen, interview by author, September 1, 2001.
5. *Ibid.*
6. On June 22, Tobin exacted revenge on the Phils, throwing a five-inning no-hitter. The Braves won, 7 to 0. Ford went 0 for two in the game, the second leg of a doubleheader. The first game had been delayed by rain, and the second was called on account of darkness. Over time, even this honor would elude Tobin as major league baseball changed the rules governing the criteria for no-hitters. To qualify for immortality today, a pitcher must go at least nine innings and allow no hits or runs. Ford's hit prevented Tobin from temporarily laying claim as the only

pitcher to ever hurl *three* no-hitters in the same season.
  7. Mullen, January 26, 2002.
  8. *Ibid.*
  9. Mullen, July 26, 2000.
  10. *Ibid.*
  11. Mullen, September 1, 2001.
  12. In fact, the 1947 season would be Tabor's last in the big leagues. He managed to hit just .235 in 75 games.
  13. Newspaper reports speculated that the deal, announced on April 14, 1947, sent Etten to the Phils for the waiver price of $10,000. In reality, Ford was offered as partial compensation. *The New York Times,* April 15, 1947, p. 25.
  14. Mullen, July 26, 2000.
  15. Mullen, September 1, 2001.

3.—Ed Carnett

  1. Ed Carnett, interview by author, January 29, 2001.
  2. Ed Carnett, interview by author, March 2, 2001.
  3. *Ibid.*
  4. *Ibid.*
  5. In the 1937 All-Star Game, Dean was struck on the toe by a line drive off the bat of Earl Averill. Dean came back too soon from the injury and, favoring the foot, altered his delivery. The adjustment led to a more serious arm injury, which brought his career to a premature end.
  6. Carnett, January 29, 2001.
  7. *Ibid.*
  8. Ed Carnett, interview by author, March 21, 2001.
  9. In spite of the return of all of their '38 pitching staff, the Cubs finished 84–70, in fourth place. Larry French had one of his finest seasons, finishing at 15–8.
  10. Carnett, March 2, 2001.
  11. "Brewers Rally for 5 Runs to Whip Cubs, 7–6," *The Chicago Tribune,* June 27, 1939, p. 19.

  12. Carnett, March 2, 2001.
  13. Five of Ed's teammates with the Kansas City Blues made it to the Yankees in 1940. They were Frenchy Bordagaray, Gerry Priddy, Phil Rizzuto, Johnny Lindell, and Ernie Bonham. Billy Hitchcock and Aaron Robinson would follow within two years. The Newark Bears boasted the likes of Hank Borowy, Snuffy Stirnweiss, Hank Majeski, Tommy Holmes, Bud Metheny, Buster Mills, and Alex Kampouris,—all of whom were in the big leagues by 1943.
  14. Carnett, March 2, 2001.
  15. *Ibid.*
  16. *Ibid.*
  17. *Ibid.*
  18. In the last century, only 13 players made their debuts as pitchers and went on to play at least one full season as a position player. With Ed Carnett, they are: Butch Schmidt, Babe Ruth, Rube Bressler, Smoky Joe Wood, Lefty O'Doul, Reb Russell, Max Macon, Gil Torres, Johnny Cooney, Willie Smith, and Bobby Darwin.
  19. Carnett, March 2, 2001.
  20. Though he led the White Sox with 70 RBIs, Trosky's migraines caused him to sit out the entire 1945 season. He returned to Chicago for 88 games in 1946 before leaving the game for good.
  21. Carnett, January 29, 2001.
  22. Ryan, Jack. "Hill Sit-Down Lifted Carnett to White Sox as Handyman," *The Sporting News,* June 22, 1944.
  23. Carnett, March 2, 2001.
  24. *Ibid.*
  25. *Ibid.*
  26. "Senators Shut Out White Sox in Field Meet," *The Chicago Tribune,* July 27, 1944.
  27. Carnett, January 29, 2001.
  28. Feller, Bob, and Gilbert, Bill. *Now Pitching, Bob Feller* (New York: HarperCollins Publisher, 1990), p. 132.
  Feller admits to tinkering with a slider as early as 1941 and "perfecting"

it while at Great Lakes. He did not add it to his repertoire until 1946. It is likely that many people contributed to the development of Feller's slider, including Ed Carnett.
    29. Carnett, March 2, 2001.
    30. Carnett, March 21, 2001.
    31. Carnett, January 29, 2001.
    32. *Ibid.*
    33. Carnett, March 21, 2001.
    34. Carnett, January 29, 2001.
    35. Gilstrap, Harry. "Carnett, One-Man Team, Also Stars in Front Office," *The Sporting News,* October, 1951.
    36. Carnett, November 2, 2000.

4.—Lee Pfund

    1. Lee Pfund, interview by author, October 21, 2000.
    2. *Ibid.*
    3. *Ibid.*
    4. *Ibid.*
    5. *Ibid.*
    6. *Ibid.*
    7. *Ibid.*
    8. *Ibid.*
    9. *Ibid.*
    10. From *Flag Chasers*—a 1945 film sent to servicemen which featured all three New York managers—Mel Ott, Joe McCarthy, and Leo Durocher—talking about their club's chances.
    11. Pfund, October 21, 2000.
    12. *Ibid.*
    13. McGowan, Roscoe. "Dodgers Run Streak to 9 Straight As Pfund Halts Pirates, 4 to 1," *The New York Times,* May 15, 1945, p. 15.
    14. Pfund, October 21, 2000.
    15. *Ibid.*
    16. *Ibid.*
    17. *Ibid.*
    18. *Ibid.*
    19. *Ibid.*
    20. *Ibid.*
    21. *Ibid.*
    22. Lee Pfund, letter, August 7, 2000.
    23. Pfund, October 21, 2000.
    24. *Ibid.*
    25. *Ibid.*
    26. *Ibid.*
    27. *Ibid.*
    28. *Ibid.*
    29. *Ibid.*
    30. *Ibid.*
    31. Pfund, August 7, 2000.

5.—George Hausmann

    1. George Hausmann, interview by author, December 16, 2000.
    2. *Ibid.*
    3. Drebinger, John. "Giants Down Phils, 7–6 and 5–1, Climbing Back to Fourth Place," *The New York Times,* June 25, 1945, p. 11.
    4. Effrat, Louis. *The New York Times,* June 28, 1945, p. 14.
    5. Hausmann, December 16, 2000.
    6. *Ibid.*
    7. *Ibid.*
    8. George Hausmann, interview by author, July 28, 2001.
    9. *Ibid.*
    10. Goldstein, Richard. *Spartan Seasons.* New York: MacMillan Publishing Co., Inc., 1980, p. 280.
    11. Phillips, John. *The Mexican Jumping Beans.* Perry, GA: Capital Publishing Company, 1997.
    12. Hausmann, December 16, 2000.
    13. Hausmann, July 28, 2001.
    14. *Ibid.*
    15. Lowenfish, Lee. *The Imperfect Diamond.* New York: Da Capo Press, Inc. 1980, p. 161.
    16. Hausmann, December 16, 2000.
    17. *Ibid.*
    18. *Ibid.*
    19. George Hausmann, letter, August 22, 2000.

6.—Cy Buker

    1. With eight teams in each league and 25 men to a team, the majors could boast no more than 400 players at any given time. Understandably, no other

period in major league history has seen such a remarkable turnover in personnel.
2. Karl was 9–8 with 15 saves and a 2.99 ERA with the Phillies. With the Giants, Adams went 11–9, also had fifteen saves, and posted a 3.42 ERA.
3. Cy Buker, interview by author, January 30, 2001.
4. *Ibid.*
5. *Ibid.*
6. *Ibid.*
7. *Ibid.*
8. *Ibid.*
9. *Ibid.*
10. Cy Buker, interview by author, April 17, 2001.
11. Buker, January 30, 2001.
12. Buker, April 17, 2001.
13. *Ibid.*
14. Buker, January 30, 2001.
15. Buker, April 17, 2001.
16. Box scores for the second game of a doubleheader played against the Giants at the Polo Grounds on September 2 show a *third* home run off Buker by Hall of Famer Mel Ott, a claim that Buker flatly denies. "If Mel Ott hit a home run off me, I'd brag about it!"
17. Buker, January 30, 2001.
18. *Ibid.*
19. *Ibid.*
20. *Ibid.*
21. *Ibid.*
22. Buker, April 17, 2001.
23. Buker, January 30, 2001. 24. Rickey also had the option of sending Robinson to the St. Paul Saints of the American Association. He chose Montreal in the International League because its southernmost city was Baltimore, Maryland.
25. Buker, January 30, 2001.
26. *Ibid.*
27. For all intents and purposes, Herring took over Cy Buker's job, with eerily similar results. Herring won seven ballgames (two as a starter), lost two, and saved five games—the identical numbers Buker had posted a year earlier. Moreover, Herring pitched 86 innings (one less than Buker) and finished with a 3.35 ERA (compared with Buker's 3.30 ERA).
28. Buker, April 17, 2001.
29. Buker, January 30. 2001.
30. *Ibid.*
31. *Ibid.*
32. *Ibid.*
33. *Ibid.*
34. Buker, April 17, 2001.
35. Buker, January 30, 2001.
36. *Ibid.*
37. *Ibid.*

7.—Bill Lefebvre

1. Bill Lefebvre, interview by author, June 16, 2001.
2. *Ibid.*
3. Bill Lefebvre, interview by author, January 17, 2002.
4. *Ibid.*
5. Lefebvre, June 16, 2001.
6. Besides Dudley and Morgan, National Leaguers with first-pitch, first at-bat homers include Clyde Vollmer, Chuck Tanner, Jim Bullinger, Jay Gainer, Chris Richard, and Gene Stechschulte. In addition to Bill Lefebvre, American Leaguers who accomplished the feat include George Vico, Bert Campaneris, Brant Alyea, Don Rose, Jay Bell, Junior Felix, Esteban Yan, and Marcus Thames.
7. Lefebvre, June 16, 2001.
8. Lefebvre, January 17, 2002.
9. Lefebvre, June 16, 2001.
10. *Ibid.*
11. American Association Press Release. "Newcomers Worth Watching," July 5, 1939.
12. Lefebvre, June 16, 2001.
13. *Ibid.*
14. Hall, Halsey. "Fine Grind on Hill for Millers Lifts Lefty Lefebvre to Majors," *The Sporting News*, July 5, 1943, p.4.

15. Bill Lefebvre, interview by author, November 14, 2001.
16. Drebinger, John. "Pinch Single in 9th Beats Yanks After Dubiel Tops Senators, 4–2," *The New York Times,* August 28, 1944, p. 14.
17. Rene Monteagudo led the National League with eighteen pinch hits in 1945. Although he began his career as a pitcher and was still working as a reliever in 1945, he was used more frequently as an outfielder (35 games) than as a pitcher (14 games).
18. Lefebvre, November 14, 2001.
19. *Ibid.*
20. Lefebvre, June 16, 2001.
21. *Ibid.*
22. *Ibid.*

8.—Eddie Basinski

1. Eddie Basinski, letter, June 17, 2002.
2. Eddie Basinski, letter, January 23, 2001.
3. Eddie Basinski, interview by author, June 25, 2002.
4. *Ibid.*
5. Eddie Basinski, letter, April 5, 2002.
6. Eddie Basinski, letter, January 19, 2002.
7. Basinski, June 25, 2002.
8. Basinski, April 5, 2002.
9. Basinski, June 25, 2002.
10. *Ibid.*
11. *Ripley's: Believe It or Not!* King Features Syndicate, 1961.
12. Basinski, June 25, 2002.
13. McGowan, Roscoe. "Gregg of Dodgers Defeats Reds, 6–1," *The New York Times,* May 21, 1944, p. 15.
14. Eddie Basinski, letter, February 6, 2002.
15. Drebinger, John. "35,428 See Dodgers Subdue Giants, 3–2," *The New York Times,* June 14, 1945, p.22.
16. *Line Drives from the Dodgers* (newsletter), July, 1945, p. 4.
17. Basinski, April 5, 2002.
18. *Ibid.*
19. *Ibid.*
20. Basinski, June 25, 2002.
21. Of the 53 players who played for Brooklyn in 1944, 20 were making their major league debuts. Connie Mack's A's had 22 newcomers in 1943—the highest total of the war. 1944 saw 100 debuts in the National League alone. The National League had the highest number of major league debuts between 1943 and 1945. NL newcomers outnumbered those in the AL by 244 to 187.
22. Basinski, June 25, 2002.
23. *Ibid.*
24. *New York Times,* June 10, 1945, p. S3.
25. Basinski, April 5, 2002.
26. *Ibid.*
27. Flynn, Art. "Rickey and Dodgers Tell Rotarians of Their Power," *The Sporting News,* June 28, 1945, p. 3.
28. Basinski, June 25, 2002.
29. Basinski, April 5, 2002.
30. *Ibid.*
31. Eddie Basinski, letter, February 21, 2002.
32. Basinski, June 25, 2002.
33. Basinski, January 19, 2002.
34. Basinski, April 5, 2002.
35. Basinski, June 25, 2002.
36. Basinski, February 6, 2002.
It is interesting and amazing to note the list of players who occupied the other infield positions during Basinski's streak. Hank Arft, Joe Laffata, Ed Mikelson, Fenton Mole, Mickey Rocco, Vince Shupe, and George Vico all played first base during the streak. Frankie Austin, Jack Littrel, Buddy Peterson, Lenny Ratto, and Frankie Zak each played shortstop. Mike Baxes, Eddie Bockman, Don Eggert, Rickey Krisnich, Hillis Layne, Harvey Storey, and Leo Thomas were at third base at various times. Basinski was never removed for a pinch hitter or runner or for defensive purposes. Only *his* name appears at second base for all 557 games.

37. L.H. Gregory, letter to Eddie Basinski, November 12, 1950.
38. Basinski, June 25, 2002.

9.—Nick Strincevich

1. Pesavento, Wilma J. "Sport and Recreation in the Pullman Experiment: 1880–1900," *Journal of Sport History,* 9 (1982), p. 38–62.
2. Nick Strincevich, interview by author, September 5, 2003.
3. Nick Strincevich, interview by author, August 25, 2003.
4. *Ibid.*
5. *Ibid.*
6. *Ibid.*
7. *Ibid.*
8. *Ibid.*
9. On April 2, 2003, Atlanta Braves manager Bobby Cox allowed left-hander Horacio Ramirez to make his major league debut in just the second game of the season.
10. Vaughan, Irving. "Cub Southpaw Limits Enemy to Two Singles," *Chicago Tribune,* May 16, 1940, p. S 1.
11. Strincevich, August 25, 2003.
12. Strincevich, September 5, 2003.
13. *Ibid.*
14. *Ibid.*
15. *Ibid.*
16. *Ibid.*
17. Effrat, Louis. "Pirates Force Giants into Cellar as Strincevich Wins 4-Hitter, 3–0," *New York Times,* June 26, 1946, p. 28.
18. McGowen, Roscoe. "Dodgers Defeated by Strincevich, 7–3," *New York Times,* July 29, 1946, p. 15.
19. Strincevich, September 5, 2003.
20. Miller, Hub. "Big Nick Starts to Click," *Baseball Magazine,* January, 1947, p. 263.
21. Strincevich, September 5, 2003.
22. *Ibid.*
23. *Ibid.*

10.—More Wartime Players

1. Boo Ferris, letter to author, August 30, 2000.
2. Chris Haughey, interview by author, January 18, 2001.
3. Jim Castiglia, letter to author, August 23, 2000.
4. Mike Sandlock, interview by author, January 7, 2001.
5. Mike Kosman, letter to author, September 7, 2000.
6. Charlie Metro, interview by author, October 6, 2000.
7. Val Heim, letter to author, September 2, 2000.
8. Arnold Thesenga, letter to author, August 19, 2000.

Selected Bibliography

The Baseball Encyclopedia: The Complete and Definitive Record of Major League Baseball, 10th ed. New York: Macmillan, 1996.
Creamer, Robert W. *Stengel: His Life and Times*. New York: Simon and Schuster, 1984.
Crissey, Harrington E. *Teenagers, Graybeards, and 4-F's*, Volumes 1–2. Published by the author, 1982.
Durocher, Leo, and Linn, Ed. *Nice Guys Finish Last*. New York: Simon & Schuster, 1975.
Feller, Bob, and Gilbert, Bill. *Now Pitching, Bob Feller*. New York: HarperCollins, 1990.
Gilbert, Bill. *They Also Served: Baseball and the Home Front, 1941–1945*. New York: Crown, 1992.
Goldstein, Richard. *Spartan Seasons: How Baseball Survived the Second World War*. New York: Macmillan, 1980.
Gonzalez Echevarria, Roberto. *The Pride of Havana: A History of Cuban Baseball*. New York: Oxford University Press, 1999.
Lowenfish, Lee. *The Imperfect Diamond*. New York: Da Capo, 1980.
Mead, William B. *Baseball Goes to War*. Washington, D.C.: Broadway Interview Source, 1998.
Phillips, John. *The Mexican Jumping Beans*. Perry, GA: Capital Pub. Co., 1997.
Sullivan, Neil J. *The Minors*. New York: St. Martin's, 1990.
Sumner, Benjamin B. *Minor League Baseball Standings*. Jefferson, N.C.: McFarland, 2000.
Van Lindt, Carson. *One Championship Season*. New York: Marabou Publishing, 1994.

Index

Numbers in *italics* indicate photographs.

Adams, Ace 77, 82, 90
Adams, Buster 63
Adams, Red 170
Akron Yankees (Mid-Atlantic League) 144
Albany, GA 54
Albosta, Ed 156
Aleno, Chuck 125
Aliquippa, PA 158–159
Allied invasion of Normandy 7, 47
All-Star Game: *1933* 55; *1937* 65; no game in 1945 75
Almendares 85
Alton, IL 57
Amarillo (WT-NM) 51
American Association 41, 57, 102–103, 107–108, 136, 149, 161
American Baseball Guild 153–156, 158
American Legion 70, 89, 143
American Red Cross 65
Anderson (Tri-State League) 88
Ankenmann, Pat 72
Appling, Luke 171
Ardmore Cardinals (Sooner State League) 21
Army Air Corps 161
Atlas, Charles 120
Austin (Big State League) 89
Averill, Earl 65

Bagby, Jim 111
Bahr, Ed 156
Baker, Bill 157
Ball State University 150

Baltimore Orioles (IL) 21, 100
Banta, Jack 98
Barber, Red 126
Barney, Rex 101
Barnicle, George 43
Barrett, Dick "Kewpie" 28, 45
Barrett, Johnny 61, 109
Barrett, Red 58
Barry, Jack 105
The Baseball Encyclopedia 24
Baseball Magazine 160
Basinski, Eddie 3, 119–141, *125, 129*; "The Bazooka" 125; *Ripley's Believe It or Not!* 119, 124
Bean, Belve 107
Beaumont (Texas League) 168
Beggs, Joe 145
Behrman, Hank 100–101, 136
Bell, Fern 41
Benswanger, Bill 155
Berardino, Johnny 171
Berg, Moe 107
Berra, Yogi 100, 139
Betzel, Bruno 43
Big State League 89
Binghamton (NY State League) 42–43, 45
Birmingham (SA) 167
Bisbee (Arizona-Texas League) 170
Bithorn, Hiram 144
Blades, Ray 72, 136
Blattner, Bob "Buddy" 79, 171
Bluege, Oscar "Ossie" 113–115, 172
Blytheville Giants 9
Boise Braves (Pioneer League) 34

Bonewitz, Paul 53
Bonham, Ernie "Tiny" 42, 115, 136, 145
Bonura, Zeke 116
Borger Gassers (WT-NM) 50, 52–53
Borowy, Hank 42, 115
Boston Bees/Braves (NL) 3, 21, 29, 36, 43, 49, 77, 94, 100, 124, 128, 130–131, 139, 145–149, 152, 165; Braves Field 43
Boston Red Sox (AL) 3, 33, 104–109, 116, 117, 146, 161; Fenway Park 104, 106, 108, 146, 164
Bowman, Joe 44
Bragan, Bobby 128, 163
Branca, Ralph 59, 95, 101, *129*
Branch, Norm 144
Brannick, Eddie 80
Brecheen, Harry "The Cat" 17–18, 157
Bressler, Rube 46
Bridges, Tommy 94
Brooklyn Dodgers 3, 28–29, 43, 59, 63–68, 72, 77, 82, 90–98, 100–101, 119, 123–137, *129*, 141, 146, 148, 152, 156–158, 162–163, 165–166; Bear Mountain Resort 59, 92–93; Daytona Beach, FL 97, 136; Ebbets Field 60, 63–64, 68, 94, 96, 127, 130, 132, 146, 152, 158
Brooklyn Dodgers Hall of Fame 141
Brooklyn Eagle 97
Brown, Jimmy 155
Brown University 117
Brubaker, Bill 41
Bryant, Clay 40
Budd Plant 160
Buffalo, NY 119–128; AA Leagues 121–123; All-Stars 123; Athletic Club 123; East High School 119, 121, 141; Kaiser Town 120; Symphony Orchestra 121; University of 121
Buker, Cy 3, 59, 90–103, *93, 129*, 135
Burge, Les 98
Burgess, Smoky 116
Burlington Flints (III) 53
Bush, Donie 107–108
Bush, George Herbert Walker 22
Butcher, Max 29, 149–150
Butler (Penn-State Association) 144

Byrne, Tommy 42
Byrnes, Milt 15

C-46 cargo plane 121
C-47 transport plane 12
Camelli, Hank 32
Camilli, Dolf 43, 146, 165
Camp Croft, SC 116
Campanis, Al 98, 100
Candini, Milo 33, 112, 114
Cape Cod League 105
Cape Girardeau, MO 14
Carlton, Bob 91–92
Carnegie, Andrew 142
Carnett, Ed 3, 36–53, *37*; and "pepper" games 38
Carolina League 89
Carrasquel, Alex 83, 112, 114, 172
Carthage (Western Association) 11
Case, George 47
Casey, Hugh 100
Caster, George 15–16
Castiglia, Jim 163–164
Cavarretta, Phil 103
Cedar Rapids Raiders (III) 9
Chandler, Albert "Happy" 82, 85–86, 135–136
Chandler, Spud 145
Chapman, Ben 33, 59, 109, 135–136
Chicago Cubs (NL) 9, 10, 25, 38, 40–42, 58, 63, 65, 68, 82, 94, 132–134, 147, 164, 167; Catalina Island 40; West Baden, IN 167 Wrigley family 40; Wrigley Field 65, 160
Chicago White Sox (AL) 3, 36, 46, 65, 104, 106, 109, 111, 143, 164, 170–171; "Black Sox" scandal 70; Comiskey Park 143
Chozen, Harry 58
Christman, Mark 15–16, 18, 112
Christopher, Russ 171
Cieslak, Ted 28
Cincinnati Reds 29–30, 62, 73, 95, 124, 130, 148–149, 151–152, 157–158, 166–167; Crosley Field 65, 82, 95, 124, 151, 163, 167
Cleveland Indians 2, 36, 46, 48, 65, 109, 111–112, 139, 145, 167; League Park 111

Index

Clinton (Ill) 90
Cochrane, Mickey 57
Coffman, Dick 76, 147
Coffman, Slick 56
Cohen, Andy 108
Coleman, Jerry 139
Collins, Eddie 105–106
Colman, Frank 62
Colorado Springs (Western League) 103
Columbus Redbirds (AA) 57–58, 145
Cooney, Johnny 46
Cooper, Mort 17, 130
Cooper, Walker 48
Corpus Christi Spudders (Texas Valley League) 71
Coscarart, Pete 165–166
Cramer, Doc 146
Cronin, Joe 106–107, 109, 146, 161
Crooks, Elizabeth 28
Crosetti, Frank 143
Crues, Bob 50, 52
Cuba 67, 78–79, 85
Cuccinello, Tony 111
Curtiss-Wright Co. 121, 123
Curtright, Guy 46
Cusick, Joe 105

Dahlgren, Babe 44, 62, 145
Dallesandro, Dom 32
Danning, Harry 9–10
Dantonio, John "Fats" 131, 166
Darwin, Bobby 46
Dasso, Frank 109
Davis, Curt 59, 98, 101, *129*, 132
Dean, Dizzy 40–41, 65–66, 148
DeBerry, Hank 10
Decatur Commodores (Ill) 56–57
de la Cruz, Tommie 83
Derringer, Paul 133, 148
Detroit Tigers (AL) 2, 15–16, 18, 25, 57, 65, 94, 114, 133, 167–168
DeWitt, Bill 71
DeWitt, Charlie 71
Dickson, Murry 162
Dihigo, Martin 84
DiMaggio, Dominic 109, 146
DiMaggio, Joe 23, 26, 40, 78, 119, 163
DiMaggio, Vince 149
DiMaggio brothers 38

Dineen, Bill 162
Doerr, Bobby 109
Donald, Atley 145
Donnelly, Blix 18
Dressen, Charlie 63, 69, 94–95, 124, 127, *129*
Dropo, Walt 140
Dubiel, Walter "Monk" 47, 114
Dudley, Clise 107
Durocher, Leo 59–62 69, 87, 94–97, 124–129, *129*, 132, 134, 136, 162, 166
Durret, Red 99
Dykes, Jimmy 46

Earley, Tom 43
Early, Jake 20–21
East Texas League 25, 106, 168
Eastern Shore League 9
Eau Claire, WI 91–92, 97, 102
Edwards, Bruce 67
Eisenhower, Gen. Dwight D. 77
Elliott, Bob 41, 149
Errickson, Dick 43
Estalella, Bobby 83, 161
Etten, Nick 33, 138
Eugene, OR 26; Eugene High School 26, 27
Evangeline League 9
Evers, Hoot 168

Federal League 153
Feldman, Harry 29, 64, 77, 82, 131
Feller, Bob 2, 48, 57, 78
Ferrell, Rick 11, 13, 15, 112, 114
Ferriss, Dave "Boo" 161–162
Filipowicz, Steve 59, 73
Fischer, Rube 77, 166
Fisher, Dick 122–123
Fitzsimmons, "Fat" Freddie 28, 135
Fleming, Bill 32
Fletcher, Elbie 147
Fordham University 115, 162
Ft. Lewis, WA 32
Ft. Smith Giants (Western Assn.) 9, 10
Fournier, Jack 168
Foxx, Jimmie 109, 120, 146
Franks, Herman 98–100, 102, 146
French, Larry 40, 147
Frisch, Frankie 62, 150, 152–153, 155–157

Gabbard, John 99
Gables, Ken 156
Galan, Augie *129*, 131
Galehouse, Denny 15, 48, 57
Galveston, TX 8; Great Flood of 1906 8
Garbark, Bob 161
Garber, Jan 40
Gardella, Danny 77, 77–83, 85–86, 88
Gary, IN 3, 142, 144; Glen Park neighborhood 143; Nick Strincevich Day 159
Gary, Judge Elbert H. 142
Gary Works, U.S. Steel 142
Gazella, Mike 39
Gearhauser, Al 136
Gehrig, Lou 40, 119, 143
Georgetown University 164
Georgia-Florida League 56
Gilbert, Charlie 146
Gionfriddo, Al 157
Gordon, Joe 138, 145
Gornicki, Hank 149–150
Gorsica, John 57
Governor's Island, NY 93
Grange, Red 120
Gray, Pete 4, 18–20
Great Lakes Naval Base 48, 51
Greenberg, Hank 2, 136
Greenville (East Texas League) 106
Gregg, Hal 28, 59, 95, 101, 125, 131, *129*
Gregory, L.H. 140
Grimes, Burleigh 149
Groh, Heinie 90
Groth, Johnny 48
Grove, Lefty 109
Guerra, Mike 112
Gutteridge, Don 15, 148

Hack, Stan 103
Haefner, Mickey 112, 114
Haley, John 144
Hallett, Jack 156
Hamlin, Luke 150
Handley, Lee 76
Harris, Bucky 139
Harris, Mickey 146
Hart, Bill 125

Hartnett, Gabby 9, 41–42
Hassett, Buddy 148, 165
Hatten, Joe 100
Haughey, Chris 162–163, 166
Hauser, Joe 52
Hausmann, George 3, 70–89, *74*, *77*
Hayes, Frankie 11, 13, 161
Hayworth, Myron "Red" 13–14, 16–18, 20
Hayworth, Ray 13
Head, Ed 101
Hebert, Wally 149–150
Heim, Val 170–171
Heintzelman, Ken 136, 156
Henderson Oilers (East Texas League) 25
Henrich, Tommy 145
Herman, Babe 27, 45, *129*
Herman, Billy 57, 58, 163
Herring, Art 94–95, 101, *129*
Higbe, Kirby 100
Hobson, Howard 25
Hockett, Oris 48
Hodges, Gil 163
Hollingsworth, Al 168
Hollywood Stars (PCL) 165
Holmes, Tommy 103, 131–132
Holy Cross College 104, 115
Hopper, Clay 99
Hopper, Jim 156
Hotel St. Catherine 40
Houston Buffaloes (Texas League) 9
Houston Cardinals (Texas League) 88
Houston, TX 7, 11, 21
Howell, Dixie 98, 103
Hubbell, Carl 8, 37, 46, 117, 146

Illinois, University of 56
Illinois-Indiana-Iowa League (Three-I, III) 9, 72, 90
Indiana University 167
Indianapolis (AA) 111
International League (IL) 21, 27, 42, 67, 98–99, 102, 123, 127, 144–145, 149–150, 153, 160

Jacksonville Jax (East Texas League) 25
Jackuki, Sig 15–16

Index

Javery, Al 44, 73
Jersey City, NJ 9, 72
Johnson, Billy 33
Johnson, Roy "Hardrock" 38
Jorgensen, Spider 98
Judd, Oscar 130
Jurges, Billy 44, 76

Kampouris, Alex 43
Kansas Baseball Hall of Fame 172
Kansas City Royals (AA) 33, 42, 44, 58, 92, 103, 111, 145
Karl, Andy 90, 131
Kehn, Chet 99
Keller, Charlie "King Kong" 145
Keltner, Ken 57
Kentucky Wesleyan University 68
Kerr, Johnny 59
Kiner, Ralph 136
King, Clyde 64, 152
Klein, Chuck 28, 31
Klein, Lou 83, 85
Klinger, Bob 149–150
Koch, Barney 127
Konstanty, Jim 30
Kosman, Mike 166–167
Kramer, Jack 15–16, 113
Kreevich, Mike 15, 18
Kress, Red 87
Kuhel, Joe 115
Kurowski, Whitey 63, 96
Kush, Emil 171

Laabs, Chet 15, 160
Lamesa (WT-NM) 51
Lancaster, NY 123, 126–127
Landis, Judge Kenesaw Mountain 2, 27, 72, 135, 150
Lang, Don 38
Lanier, Max 17, 83, 85–86; Max Lanier All-Stars 85
Laredo, TX 71
Lavagetto, Cookie 43
Lazzeri, Tony 143
Lebanon, MO 36, 50
Lee, "Big" Bill 40–41
Lefebvre, Bill "Lefty" 3, 104–118, *105*, *113*; pinch-hitting 114–115
Leon, Isidoro 94, 131
Leonard, Dutch 112

Letchas, Charlie 27, 29
Lewis, Bill "Buddy" 58
Libke, Al 95
Lincoln (Western League) 103
Lindell, Johnny 41
Little Rock (SA) 110
Little Rock (Western League) 103
Little World Series: 1937 145; 1938 145; 1946 102
Litwhiler, Danny 32
Lockman, Whitey 2
Logan, Bob 130
Lombardi, Ernie "Schnozz" 31, 59, 76–77, *77*, 103
Lombardi, Vic 59, 101, *129*, 132, 152
Lombardo, Guy 40
Lopat, Eddie 41
Lopez, Al 154
Los Angeles Angels (PCL) 38, 40, 145
Los Angeles Lakers 68
Louis, Joe 120
Louisville Colonels (AA) 92, 102, 108, 110–111, 161
Luby, Hugh 72–73, 75, 140
Lucas, Red 115
Lucier, Lou 130
Luque, Adolfo 77, 82

Mack, Connie 105, 161, 164, 168–169, 171
Maglie, Sal 2, 77, 79–83, 85, 87
Magualo, Lou 70–71, 89
Majeski, Hank 42
Mallory, Jim 76
Mancuso, Frank 1–2, 7–23, *8*, *19*, 74; Houston City Council 21–22; mayor pro tem 22; Naval Air Corps 11; Officer Candidacy School (OCS) 11; 101st Airborne Battallion 7, 12; paratroops 11–14; pop fouls 14, 16; U.S. Army 11; U.S. Marine Corps 11; wife, Marian 23
Mancuso, Gus 8–10, 74
Maris, Roger 4
Marshall, George 164
Martin, Billy 170
Martin, Fred 83
Martin, Hersh 50
Mayfield, KY 71

McCarthy, Joe 115, 143
McCarver, Tim 118
McCormick, Frank 148
McCredie, Walter 140
McCullough, Clyde 42
McKechnie, Bill 63, 167
McQuinn, George 15–16, 18, 47, 145
Medford, WI 91
Medwick, Joe 43, 132
Melton, Rube 101
Memphis Chicks (SA) 18, 33
Metro, Charlie 161, 167–170; Metro Batting Tee 170
Mexican League 78–85, 87–88, 153
Mexico City Reds (Mexican League) 81–82
Miami Heat 68
Mid-Atlantic League 144
Miller, Eddie 125, 148
Milwaukee Brewers (AA) 41–42, 103, 111, 149
Minneapolis Millers (AA) 107–108, 110–111, 113, 116–117
Minner, Paul 101
Mize, Johnny 57, 147
Mobile Bears (SA) 58, 66, 101
Mokan, Johnny 122–123
Mole, Fenton 138
Monteagudo, Rene 83
Monterrey (Mexican League) 85
Montgomery (SA) 169
Montreal Royals (IL) 67–68, 98–99, 123, 127–128, 153
Moon Mullins 24
Moore, Anse 168
Moore, Gene 15, 114–115
Morgan, Eddie 107
Morgan, J. Pierpont 142
Moses, Wally 46
Mostil, Johnny 170
Moulder, Glen 99, 101
Mueller, Les 169
Mueller, Ray 45
Mullen, Ford "Moon" 3, 24–35, *26*, *30*, 137
Muncrief, Bob 15–16
Murphy, Johnny 156
Murphy, Robert 153–156
Murtaugh, Danny 27
Musial, Stan 2, 4, 18, 32, 83, 134, 162

Nagy, Steve 99
Nanty-Glo, PA 168
National Association of Professional Baseball Leagues 103
National Baseball Congress Hall of Fame 172
National Baseball Congress World Series 172
National Football League 163–164
National Labor Relations Board 153
National Sandlot Hall of Fame 172
Naylor, Earl 99
NCAA Basketball Championship 25
Nemiec, Al 26
Neun, Johnny 144–145, 149
New England League 117
New Orleans (SA) 72
New York Giants (NL) 3, 8–10, 29, 31, 59, 64–65, 72–80, 77, 82–83, 85–88, 90, 117, 127, 130–131, 146–147, 155, 157; Polo Grounds 10, 59, 73, 84, 128, 157, 166
New York State Appellate Court 86
New York State League 42
The New York Times 28, 61, 115, 125, 130
New York Yankees (AL) 9, 15–16, 22, 33, 39–40, 42–45, 50, 65, 70, 77, 89, 108–109, 113–115, 137–139, 143–144, 156, 158, 167, 172; Yankee Stadium 115
Newark Bears (IL) 42, 100, 137–138, 144–145, 150
Newsom, Bobo 18, 161
Newsome, Skeeter 161
Nicholson, Bill 103
Niggeling, Johnny 112
Norfolk Tars (Piedmont League) 144
Norman, OK 48
Northey, Ron 31–32
Notre Dame, University of 105
Nuevo Laredo (Mexican League) 81, 87
Nuxhall, Joe 163

Oakland A's (AL) 170
Oakland Oaks (PCL) 45, 49, 72, 138–139, 170
O'Dea, Ken 9–10, 18
O'Doul, Lefty 36, 138

Ohio State University Buckeyes 25
Oil City, PA 122–123
Olmo, Luis 63, 82, *129*, 131, 152
Olympia, WA 25, 27, 34
Omaha Cardinals (Western League) 21
O'Neill, Steve 168
Oregon, University of 25
Oregon Ducks 25
Oregon Sports Hall of Fame 141
Orengo, Joe 44
Ostermueller, Fritz 109, 136, 156
Ott, Mel 73, 75, *77*, 79–80, 82–83, 87
Owen, Mickey 43, 59, 62, 82, 163

P-40 Warhawk 121
P-47 Thunderbolt 121
Pacific Coast League (PCL) 3, 25–27, 32–33, 38–39, 45, 48, 59, 72, 75, 79, 88, 107, 109–110, 137–141, 164
Pafko, Andy 2, 27, 96,
Paige, Satchel 110
Paris (Big State League) 50
Parmalee, Roy 107
Pasquel, Alfonso 78
Pasquel, Bernardo 83
Pasquel, Jorge 77–86, 153
Passeau, Claude 133
Pawtucket (New England League) 117
Peacock, Johnny *129*, 166
Pennock, Herb 135
Pfund, Lee 3, 54–69, *61*, 95
Pfund, Randy 68
Philadelphia Athletics (AL) 11, 28, 105, 112, 161, 163, 171; Shibe Park 161
Philadelphia Blue Jays/Phillies (NL) 24–28, 31–34, 76, 83, 90, 94, 122, 130–131, 135–137, 152, 157, 160; Shibe Park 28
Philadelphia Eagles 164
Piedmont League 25, 89, 144
Pierce, Billy 2
Pinelli, Babe 73–74
Pioneer League 34
Pittsburgh Pirates (NL) 29, 40–41, 60–61, 63–65, 76, 87, 122, 130, 136, 147, 149–160, 164–165; Forbes Field 65, 152, 155, 157–158, 163; Muncie, IN 150

Ponca City Angels (Western Association) 37–40
Ponca City Cubs (Sooner State League) 53
Portland Beavers (PCL) 34, 137–141
Potter, Nelson 15, 17
Priddy, Gerry 42
Providence College 105
Provincial League 88
Prysock, Bob 143
Puebla (Mexican League) 81–82
Purdue University 167
Pyle, Ewald 132

Quebec (Provincial League) 164
Queen, Mel 137

Reese, Harold "Pee Wee" 43, 100, 108, 134–136, 163
Reiser, Pete 43, 100
"replacement" players 68–69
Rescigno, Xavier 144
"Reserve Clause" 86, 153–154, 156
Reyes, Napoleon 59, *77*, 83
Reynolds, Allie 41
Rhode Island 105
Rickey, Branch 3, 55–56, 58–60, 62, 64–67, 69, 72, 92, 97–100, 102, 119, 123, 126–127, 134–135
Riddle, Elmer 151
Rizzuto, Phil 41–42, 137
Robertson, Sherry 114–115
Robinson, Jackie 67–68, 70, 99, 153
Rocco, Mickey 138
Roe, Preacher 60, 76, 136
Roosevelt, Franklin D. 1, 2
Root, Charlie 27
Rosar, Buddy 145
Rosen, Goody *129*, 131, 152
Roser, Emerson 172
Rowe, Schoolboy 57, 157
Roy, Jean-Pierre 101
Ruffing, Red 9, 18
Russo, Marius 145
Ruth, Babe 36, 55, 143, 162

Sacramento Solons (PCL) 45, 140, 145
St. George Hotel, Brooklyn, NY 64
St. Joseph Saints (Western Association) 10

St. Louis Browns (AL) 2, 4, 7, 10–11, 13–18, 20–21, 31, 70–71, 88–89, 168, 171; Sportsman's Park 16–17, 65, 70, 112
St. Louis Cardinals (AL) 9, 16–18, 21, 31–32, 50, 54, 56–59, 63–65, 83, 95, 100–101, 105, 118, 126, 130, 132, 147–148, 150, 152, 157–158, 162, 163; Sportsman's Park 16–17
St. Paul Saints (AA) 66–68, 91, 101–102, 111, 136
Salkeld, Bill 76
Saltzgaver, Jack 61
Salveson, Jack 138
Sambito, Joe 117
San Antonio Missions (Texas League) 11, 21, 72, 74
San Diego Padres (PCL) 138
San Francisco Seals (PCL) 75, 109–110
Sandlock, Mike 128, *129*, 131, 165–166
Sauer, Hank 103
Scheffing, Bob 171
Schoendienst, Red 2
Schultz, Howie 131–132
Schumacher, Hal 171
Seats, Tom 59, *129*
Seattle Mariners (AL) 23, 34
Seattle Rainiers (PCL) 25–27, 45–46, 48–49, 145
Seminick, Andy 28
Sewell, Luke 14, 17–18, 23
Sewell, Joe 14
Sewell, Rip 149–150, 155–156
Shaw, Artie 40
Shea, Merv 31
Sheehan, Tom 110, 116–117
Shoun, Clyde 48, 73, 124
Siebert, Dick 161
Silvera, Charlie 139
Sioux City (Western League) 103, 171
Sipek, Dick 95
Sisler, Dick 171
Slaughter, Enos "Country" 162, 166
Smith, Willie 46
Sooner State League 21
Southern Association (SA) 4, 18, 33, 58, 72, 110
Spahn, Warren 41, 116, 120
Spence, Stan 108, 113

Spokane Indians (WIL) 48
The Sporting News 14, 47, 53, 111, 167
Springfield (III) 72
Springfield, MO 39
Stanky, Eddie 62, 95–97, 128, 131–132, 134, 141, *129*
Stengel, Casey 3, 29, 36, 43, 49, 138, 146–148, 170
Stephens, Vern "Junior" 15, 82, 112
Stirnweiss, Snuffy 33, 42, 137
Stoneham, Horace 80
Stratton, Monty 104, 106–107, 118
Strincevich, Luka 142
Strincevich, Nick "Jumbo" 3, 29, 142–152, *150*, 156–160, *159*
Sukeforth, Clyde 131
Sundra, Steve 15, 145
Suzuki, Ichiro 34
Syracuse Chiefs (IL) 150

Tabor, Jim 33, 116
Tamulis, Vito 148
Tatum, Tom 99
Tauscher, Walter 107–108
Taylor, Harry 101
Terry, Bill 10
Texarkana (East Texas League) 168
Texas League 9, 11, 21, 39, 49, 72, 88, 103, 168
Texas Valley League 71
Thesenga, Arnold "Jug" 171–172
Tobin, Jim 29, 76–77, 130, 132
Toledo Mud Hens (AA) 14, 21, 92, 111
Torgeson, Earl 49
Toronto Maple Leafs (IL) 27, 149–150, 160
Torreon Lagunas (Mexican League) 81–84
Trautman, George 103
Trosky, Hal 46–47
Trout, Paul "Dizzy" 15, 114, 169
Trucks, Virgil 57
Tucker, Thurman 46
Tulsa Oilers (Texas League) 39–41, 49
Turner, Jim 115, 137, 139

United Auto Workers 160
U.S. Coast Guard 72

U.S. Steel 142
USS *Alabama* 48

Valley Forge Hospital, Philadelphia, PA 47
Vance, Joe 37
Vancouver Capilanos (WIL) 25, 49
Vander Meer, Johnny 29, 163
Vaughan, Arky 41
Vaughn, Fred 115
Veracruz Blues (Mexican League) 82
Verban, Emil 32
Veteran's Act 78
Vitt, Oscar 145
Voiselle, Bill 59, *77*, 130

Wahl, Kermit 95
Wakefield, Dick 57, 168
Walker, Dixie 59–60, 94, 103, *129*, 131, 156
Waner, Lloyd "Little Poison" 149
Waner, Paul "Big Poison" 43, 149
Washington Redskins 164
Washington Senators (AL) 3, 15–16, 18, 20–21, 31, 33, 47, 65, 83, 104, 109–116, 166, 171–172; Griffith Stadium 37; knuckleballers 112
Waterloo (III) 170
Webber, Les 28
Weintraub, Phil 59
Weiss, George 139
Welch, Louie 22
Wendler, Doc *129*, 132
Werber, Billy 148
West Texas-New Mexico League (WT-NM) 50, 52
Western Association 9, 10
Western International League (WIL) 25–26, 48–49
Western League 21
Western Union 81

Wheaton, IL 57
Wheaton College 68
White, Jo Jo 49
Whitney, Rod 71
Wichita Falls Spudders (Big State League) 21, 49–50
Williams, Ted 26, 38, 78, 107–108, 146
Winston-Salem (Carolina League) 89
Winston-Salem Twins (Piedmont League) 25
Wisconsin Football Coaches Association Hall of Fame 103
Wisconsin Rapids (Wisconsin State League) 91
Wisconsin State League 91, 96
Witek, Mickey 72, 79, 144
Wolff, Roger 112
Wood, "Smoky" Joe 36
Woodling, Gene 57
Woods, Tiger 119
Worcester, MA 105
World Series: *1933* 9, 14, 37; *1938* 9, 40; *1944* 16–19; *1945* 133; *1946* 162
Wright, Ed 160
Wright, Taffy 170
Wyatt, Whit(low) 108, 163
Wynn, Early 2, 4, 112

Yerke, Pop 121, 141
York (Piedmont League) 89
York, Rudy 162

Zabala, Adrian 77, 87
Zak, Frankie 138
Zardon, Jose 65
Zarilla, Al 15
Zimmerman, Roy 77, 79–83, 85, 87
Zuber, Bill 107

www.ingramcontent.com/pod-product-compliance
Ingram Content Group UK Ltd.
Pitfield, Milton Keynes, MK11 3LW, UK
UKHW042004140426
5217IPUK00015B/969

Keeping the Faith

Keeping the Faith

Religious Belief in an Age of Science

THOMAS J. SCHOENBAUM

McFarland & Company, Inc., Publishers
Jefferson, North Carolina, and London

ALSO BY THOMAS J. SCHOENBAUM

The New River Controversy, A New Edition
(McFarland, 2007)

Frontispiece: Plate with Relief Decoration, artist unknown, 83.AM.342 (reprinted by permission of the J. Paul Getty Museum, Villa Collection, Malibu, California). In this fifth century silver plate found in the Mediterranean Sea off the coast of Gaza is depicted the triumph of religion over science. On the left is Ptolemy of Alexandria, a leading exponent of science and the author of the geocentric conception of the universe that was accepted as true until the sixteenth century. He is debating a religious man labeled as Hermes. Ptolemy is clearly puzzled and the loser in this exchange, as Hermes gazes and points to a heavenly apparition floating above them, probably Jesus Christ. Behind each man stands a woman: on the left is a figure labeled "Skepsis," expressing doubt, while on the right is a confident figure pointing to the heavenly apparition above. This book explores the age-old problem depicted in this silver plate.

LIBRARY OF CONGRESS CATALOGUING-IN-PUBLICATION DATA

Schoenbaum, Thomas J.
    Keeping the faith : religious belief in an age of science / Thomas J. Schoenbaum.
      p.   cm.
    Includes bibliographical references and index.

    ISBN-13: 978-0-7864-3173-1
    softcover : 50# alkaline paper ∞

    1. Religion and science. I. Title.
BL240.3.S345   2008
201'.65—dc22   2007041487

British Library cataloguing data are available

©2008 Thomas J. Schoenbaum. All rights reserved

No part of this book may be reproduced or transmitted in any form or by any means, electronic or mechanical, including photocopying or recording, or by any information storage and retrieval system, without permission in writing from the publisher.

Cover art ©2007 Shutterstock

Manufactured in the United States of America

McFarland & Company, Inc., Publishers
  Box 611, Jefferson, North Carolina 28640
    www.mcfarlandpub.com

To Naomi

"Matto è chi spera che nostra ragione
possa trascorrer la infinita via...."
Dante Aligheri
Purgatorio III. 34–35
Divine Comedy

Table of Contents

Preface	1
1 — The Controversy Between Science and Religion	7
2 — Creationism and the Constitution	12
The Cultural Wars of Religion	12
The Scopes Case	13
Evolution Eclipsed	14
Science Makes a Comeback	14
Equal Time for Creation Science	15
Enter Intelligent Design	18
A Fundamental Flaw	20
3 — The World of Science	23
Categories of Reality	23
The Scientific Method	26
Classical Physics	28
Energy and Force	31
1. HEAT	31
2. ELECTRICITY AND MAGNETISM	32
3. LIGHT	33
4. SCIENTIFIC MATERIALISM	35
A New Frame of Reference: Relativity	35
1. SPECIAL RELATIVITY	36
2. GENERAL RELATIVITY	37
Another Frame of Reference: The Very Small	38
1. ATOMS AND MOLECULES	38
2. CHEMISTRY COMES OF AGE	40
3. ATOMIC PHYSICS	42
The Quantum Revolution	43
1. QUANTUM MECHANICS	43

2. Quantum Electrodynamics	45
3. Quantum Chromodynamics	46
Astronomy	50
1. Stars	50
2. Galaxies	51
3. Cosmology	52
Theories of the Earth	53
The Life Sciences	55
1. The Birth of Biology	55
2. Darwinism	58
3. The Descent of Man	62
Scientific Truth: An Evaluation	64

4 — The World of Religion   71

What Is Religion?	71
Religious Knowledge	72
Homo Religiosus	73
Mythic Discourse	73
Ritual, Community and Culture	74
Sacred Places	75
Science and Religion: Independence or Conflict?	75
How Science Influences Religion: Four Paradigms	77
1. Dante's Medieval Synthesis	78
2. Deism	79
3. Design and the World Soul	80
4. The Triumph of Randomness and Chance	81
Lessons from Science about Religion	85
Mysterium Tremendum: Our A Priori *Knowledge of the Holy*	88
The Necessity to Choose	90
1. Nietzsche	91
2. Kierkegaard	92
Religion and Faith: Is There a Difference?	92
Mystical Experiences	93
The Quest for God: The Content of Religious Belief	94
1. Hinduism	95
2. Judaism	98
3. Zoroastrianism	101
4. Jainism	103
5. Buddhism	104
6. Religions of China	107
7. Religions of Japan	110
8. Christianity	115
9. Islam	119
10. Sikhism	122

Table of Contents ix

    Some Problems of Religious Pluralism   123
    Religious Freedom   126
        1. FREE EXERCISE OF RELIGION   126
        2. ESTABLISHMENT OF RELIGION   128
    Summing Up: Final Thoughts about Religious Knowledge   130

5 — The World of Philosophy   135
    The Importance of Philosophy   135
    The Limits of Knowledge   136
    Intelligent Design: Rational Arguments for the Existence of God   138
        1. COSMOLOGICAL PROOFS   138
        2. TELEOLOGICAL PROOFS   139
        3. THE ONTOLOGICAL ARGUMENT   141
    A New Idea of God   141
    Expressing the Transcendent   144
        1. MYTH   145
        2. ANALOGY   146
        3. SYMBOLISM   146
        4. HERMENEUTICS   147
    The Genesis Creation Story   148
    The Mystery of Existence   150
    Ethics: How We Should Live   151
    Ethics and Religion   151
    Systems of Ethics   153
    A Better Alternative: Virtue Ethics   156
    Practical Reason and Objective Goods   160
    Existentialism   161
    Summing Up   162

6 — Faith and Reason   167
    Setting the Stage   167
    Pope Benedict XVI and Islam   167
    Critical Evaluation of Religion   170
    Religion and Values   172
    Theories of Right Action   175
    Religion and Violence   177
    Suppression of Minorities   179
    The Status of Women   179
    Religion and Law   181
    The Concept of Law   183
    Three Conceptions of Law   184
    Which Is Best?   186
    The Function of Law   187

The Constraint of Natural Law   187
Enter Positivism   188
A New Concept of Natural Law   190
Summing Up   193

Concluding Remarks   197
Bibliography   203
Index   205

Preface

A paradox of modern life is that billions of people are profoundly affected in their daily lives by religious ideas that were developed fifteen hundred to almost three thousand years ago; yet human life has been transformed by a series of scientific revolutions beginning in the sixteenth century and continuing apace today. This book explores this paradox.

The leading edge of the culture controversies over science, at least in the United States, is the theory of evolution, originally formulated by Charles Darwin and Alfred Russel Wallace. In the eighteenth century, long before anyone dreamed of the science of genetics, people began to realize that living organisms, indeed the whole world, change — they did not use the term evolve — over time. Actually this insight is very old: in the sixth century BCE, the Greek philosopher Heraclitus wrote, "*pánta chórei kai oúden ménei*": "everything changes; nothing remains the same."

Darwin, in his book *On the Origin of Species* (1859), put together several ideas to explain how and why this is so with respect to living things. First, small variations arise over time even within individuals that are members of the same species. Second, these variations are heritable; they can be passed to subsequent generations. Third, animal and plant populations tend to grow faster than their food supply, producing competition even within the same species. From this he concluded that the mechanism driving "descent with modification" — now called evolution — is "natural selection," the principle that a natural organism's survival is determined by how well the characteristics it is born with respond to the demands of its environment.

One would think that, considering Darwin's book was published almost 150 years ago and that his essential ideas have been confirmed many times over by subsequent discoveries in genetics and biotechnology, the theory of evolution would be beyond question. Yet the teaching of evolution is still controversial, and according to a Pew Research Center Poll in 2005, 42 percent of Americans believe that "living things have existed in their present form since the beginning of time."

What can explain this?

The controversy over evolution is important in itself; but we must also realize that this debate is part of a larger clash between secular values and religious values — between science and religion. This debate is not new; it began in earnest in the sixteenth century if not before. Moreover, the clash between science and religion during the last four hundred years is part of an even older debate between reason and faith, which has been ongoing for thousands of years.

This book addresses the controversy over evolution in the broader context of the clash between science and religion and between reason and faith. One of the great divides in the world today is between the secular and the religious; between people who live secular lives and seldom think about religion, on the one hand, and people who regard religion as the center of their lives and the principal part of their identity.

Media reports highlight two polar positions with respect to the culture wars between religion and science. On the one hand, atheistic humanists regard religious belief as little more than superstition. For such people science depicts a world devoid of God run by impersonal natural laws and chance. Darwin's ideas on evolution as well as science in general tell us that we are nothing more than the result of random processes. As a result, the world in which we find ourselves has little meaning, and cultural values accepted for thousands of years are problematical.

Typical of this view are the best selling books by Sam Harris, *The End of Faith* (2005) and *Letter to a Christian Nation* (2006). Promoted as "full-throttle attacks" on religious belief, these books contain arguments based on reason and science to promote atheism and "secularized values world-wide." The Bible and the Qur'an are said to contain nothing more than "mountains of life-destroying gibberish." A second recent attack on religion is *Breaking the Spell* (2006) by Daniel C. Dennett, who advocates that the spell of religion "must be broken and broken now." A third book extolling atheism is *The God Delusion* (2006) by Richard Dawkins, who maintains that belief in God is not only a delusion but a pernicious one. He presents three familiar arguments in favor of atheism: (1) religious phenomena can be explained by science and purely natural causes; (2) we can live happy and moral lives without religion; and (3) religion causes more evil than good in the world.

A second polar view is that of religious fundamentalists or evangelicals. These people accept the literal truth of their religion as revealed by God. With scriptural certainty as their guide, they reject anything that conflicts with their faith; their views begin and end with how their religion views the world, and they are hostile to reason and to science itself. Such people comprise vocal minorities in the three Western monotheistic religions, Judaism, Christianity and Islam.

Religious objections to science and evolution are supplemented by pseudo-scientific and philosophical arguments purporting either to undermine Darwin's theories or to achieve consistency with them. Perhaps the leading example of this is Michael J. Behe, the author of *Darwin's Black Box: The Biochemical Challenge to Evolution* (1996), which attempts to prove that the natural world and life itself exhibit intelligent design, implying the necessary existence of a "Designer" God.

This book explores the middle ground between these two extremes, maintaining that we can accept both the marvels of modern science and the religious ideas of pre-modern times. Both, however, must be examined with a critical eye. We must learn as much about science as possible to really appreciate both the magnificence and the limits of scientific knowledge. We must study carefully not only our own religious traditions but also the role religion plays in the globalized world of the twenty-first century. We now routinely come into contact with and are profoundly affected by people who hold religious views different from our own. We must not let our religion become a crutch, an excuse not to think for ourselves. We can appreciate our religious traditions only through examining them through the prism of reason and philosophy.

We must reject fundamentalist religion that attempts to equate religious truth with science and history. Religious doctrines and values operate on a different epistemological plane from science and factual truth. We cannot apply scientific criteria to religion any more than we can use religion as the basis for science. The Establishment Clause of the First Amendment to the U.S. Constitution rightly prohibits the attempt by fundamentalists to equate religion with scientific and historical truth. However, the First Amendment should not be interpreted so the state is hostile to religious belief.

But science does not oust religion. When we closely examine scientific knowledge, we find elaborate myths, suppositions and fictions; it is simply untrue that every scientific truth can be rigorously linked to empirical certainty. Contrary to popular belief, scientific truth is based fundamentally on pragmatic considerations as well as on the coherence of the data involved.

Religious belief is the attempt we make to attain the transcendental — reality that is fundamentally inconceivable and unknowable. We can do this only through passionate commitment and mythological discourse. The fact that not every religious proposition can be supported by empirical findings need not disturb us. Religious truth in the last analysis rests upon faith, coherence of beliefs as well as pragmatic considerations.

Humans have a universal *a priori* faculty — more intuitive than rational — to apprehend the sacred and the holy. Our expression of the holy is very much influenced by our culture, our language and our religious traditions. As a result our religions are closely connected with and conditioned by cultural differences. This helps to explain the multiplicity of religious traditions — a fact to be celebrated rather than to be denigrated. Religion also plays an important role in *creating* human culture, so participating in our religious traditions is necessary if we are to live an authentic human life that is fully engaged with the world in which we find ourselves.

The key to reconciling religion and science is the realization that both are essentially *human* creations that rest upon similar foundations: faith, pragmatism and a coherent idea of truth. In both cases the beliefs involved may be considered successful if they allow us to make correct predictions and judgments about reality and our personal and social lives.

We must also have the intellectual humility to admit that the search for absolute certainty is a will-of-the-wisp. As the late Pope John Paul II said in 1997, speaking about scientific discoveries: "The search for truth, even when it concerns a finite reality of the world or of man, is never-ending, but always points to something higher than the immediate object of study, to the questions which give access to mystery."*

To sum up: in both science and religion, uncertainty and mystery pervade the world in which we find ourselves.

On a purely personal note, I wrote this book after being diagnosed with cancer and during my painful recovery from major surgery and medical treatment. There is nothing like serious disease to concentrate the mind, although the body is another matter.

We all face mortality and the question of how we should give meaning to our lives. I hope this book shows that there are no facile or final answers

---

*John Paul II, *Address to the University of Krakow for the 600th Anniversary of the Jagiellonian University* (June 8, 1997).

and that, in the end, the meaning of our lives depends on us, what we choose to do with the brief span we have, and the impact of our existence on other people and the world around us.

> Thomas J. Schoenbaum
> *Washington, D.C., and Tokyo, Japan*
> *October 2007*

CHAPTER 1

The Controversy Between Science and Religion

The controversy over teaching evolution in public schools has raged in the United States for almost a century. Why is this so? Scientists tell us that the theory of evolution, which was originally formulated in the mid–nineteenth century by Charles Darwin and Alfred Russel Wallace, is as well established as any law of natural science. Yet opposition to evolution runs very deep, and many people have (and still are) devoting tireless effort to overturning its tenets. Many thought (as did I growing up in the 1950s) that the anti-evolutionists got their definitive comeuppance with the famous Scopes trial in Dayton, Tennessee, in 1925. Not only was John Scopes' conviction for teaching evolution overturned (the story went), his lawyer, Clarence Darrow, bested his opponent, the so-called "Great Commoner," William Jennings Bryan, who promptly suffered a fatal heart attack, as if by divine intervention in reverse.

But opposition to evolution on religious grounds is far from dead. A CBS News survey in October 2005 showed that 51 percent of Americans believe that God created human beings in their present form; only 15 percent believe that God had no part in human creation. And two-thirds of Americans believe that religious creationism (or intelligent design) should be taught alongside the theory of evolution. What is going on here?

What gets lost in the debate over evolution is just what this term means. Evolution is usually equated with Darwinism, but in fact theories of evolution preceded Darwinism by almost one hundred years.[1] Darwinism is — properly speaking — an explanation of how evolution (or "descent with modification" as Darwin puts it) takes place: natural selection. Similarly, creationism and intelligent design are widely misunderstood. Creationism is a vague concept with many possible meanings. For example, one can believe in creationism at the level of the Big Bang, or at the level of the creation of each individual human soul, as well as every level in between. Intelligent design, which is now often equated with creationism, is actually quite distinct. Intelligent design is a philosophical concept going back to the ancient Greeks.

In spite of the fact that a mountain of evidence gathered in the last century and a half confirms Darwin's theory of evolution, and that we now understand how evolution works at the molecular level of DNA and RNA, substantial numbers of people find this very troubling, even threatening. People of religious conviction, as a result, have waged an unending campaign against evolution, first to suppress its teaching, and then to undermine it and to supplant it with alternative ideas that go by the names of "creation science" and "intelligent design."

There is a temptation to dismiss the intelligent design creationists as religious fundamentalists or worse, and to label their enormous efforts as bunkum, not to be taken seriously. But this tactic was tried without success after the *Scopes* case in the 1920s. Yet litigation over evolution and controversy over teaching its tenets continues to the present day. In December 2005 a U.S. Federal District Court declared the teaching of intelligent design in the Dover, Pennsylvania, public schools was contrary to the Establishment Clause of the First Amendment to the U.S. Constitution, which forbids government endorsement or sponsorship of religion.[2]

Perhaps the 2005 court case over intelligent design will be the end, but I doubt it. The religious campaign against evolution began shortly after Darwin's book, *On the Origin of Species* (1859), was published and has continued unabated to the present day. Despite losing a string of court decisions that uphold the teaching of evolution, the creationists have partially succeeded in their efforts: their campaign has obviously convinced many Americans, as shown by the public opinion polls. And despite adverse court rulings, creationists have greatly influenced how biology is taught in U.S. schools. A 2002 survey of nearly 800 biology teachers in Indiana showed that 19 percent rejected evolution and more than 40 percent stated their approach to evolution was "avoidance" or "briefly mention." A similar survey of teachers in Minnesota virtually replicated the Indiana results. Clearly teachers of science all across the country are facing pressures to marginalize or eliminate teaching evolution.*

In the United Kingdom as well, many teachers of science now present creationism as a legitimate alternative to evolution. See "Revealed: rise of creationism in UK schools," The Guardian, November 29, 2006, p. 1.

1— The Controversy Between Science and Religion

This book is an examination of the controversy between evolution and different forms of creationism from the point of view of the law, science, and philosophy. But I also wish to address a larger issue: whether there is an inherent conflict between science and religion. This, it seems to me, is the real concern of most people. Darwinism seems to many to be the most damaging of the tenets of a tradition of scientific materialism that began with Galileo and Newton. Darwinism hits a raw nerve because it concerns not only nature but also the origin and destiny of human beings. The triumph of Darwinism thus threatens the very heart of religious concerns about the meaning of life, ethical values, and spiritual realities.

Religious people who espouse a version of creationism as an alternative to Darwinism are further disturbed by the fact that many — perhaps most — practicing scientists and academics, including some of the most prominent experts on evolution, are avowed atheists. However, two prominent exceptions stand out. The late Stephen Jay Gould, a scientist who made significant contributions to evolutionary theory and was also a gifted writer, maintained that there is no conflict between science and religion because these two ways of thinking represent what he called NOMA — "Non-Overlapping Magisteria."[3] This is a principle of "respectful noninterference" between science and religion whereby each reigns supreme and unchallenged in its own sphere. As Gould put it:

> I ... do not understand why the two enterprises should experience any conflict. Science tries to document the factual character of the natural world, and to develop theories that coordinate and explain these facts. Religion, on the other hand, operates in the equally important, but utterly different, realm of human purposes, meanings and values — subjects that the factual domain of science might illuminate, but can never resolve.

Gould defends in beautiful detail his thesis that science and religion are separate and should not be entwined. But probably most in both camps still disagree: most scientists are agnostic, and religious people seek (and often find) support in scientific doctrines. Furthermore, while I believe Gould is fundamentally correct, his NOMA does not offer any positive reasoning why we should pay any attention to the magisterium of religion.

The philosopher Michael Ruse offers a second important reconciliation of science and religion and even evolution and intelligent design. Ruse makes a key distinction between what he calls "methodological naturalism" and "ontological naturalism." The former is employed by the scientist who seeks to explain the natural world in purely naturalistic and materialistic fashion. The scientist is restricted to observable and provable facts. Ruse believes this is a valid method of proceeding that validates evolution as a scientific doctrine. But Ruse rejects extending this method to the ontological, the realm of metaphysics and belief. As he puts it, "scientific theories cannot be metaphysically consequential." This is a doctrine of compatibility between science and religion. In this view one can fully accept evolution and yet believe in the existence of supernatural realties, actions and concerns. And contrary to Gould, Ruse would permit some overlap between science and religion: for example, the human soul (or consciousness) may be a product of evolution that is in fact part of God's grand design.[4] Ruse's compatibility thesis is an elegant one that makes science a true but incomplete description of reality. This seems to require further explanation: why should science be so limited? Why should one add unscientific and unverifiable spiritual realities? What need do they fulfill?

This book seeks to build upon the ideas of Gould and Ruse and to examine the larger questions of the potential conflicts between science and religious and ethical values. I will argue that the creationists are off-base in opposing the teaching of evolution and the scientific method, and their strategy of turning creationism into quasi-science and trying to get it accepted as a scientific alternative is utterly wrong and counterproductive to their own position. But I will demonstrate that it is essential to study and to teach religious and ethical values in the public schools in addition to the scientific method. The way this can be done to comply with the First Amendment to the U.S. Constitution is through the study of comparative culture, philosophy and comparative religion.

Accordingly, the second chapter of this book discusses the First Amendment of the U.S. Constitution in the context of the evolution debate and recent court decisions concerning religion.

Although contemporary debate between science and religion in the United States concerns chiefly the matter of evolution, we should realize that this particular issue is important only for literal adherents to the sacred writings — Holy Scriptures — of the three monotheistic Western religions — Judaism, Christianity and Islam — because they essentially spring from the same roots and have in common the idea that God created the universe and man out of nothing. Other world religions do not feel this conflict. Nevertheless, non–Western religions also must come to terms with science and the challenges it presents. For this reason it is necessary to treat the debate over evolution in the context of the larger debate between science and religion.

Accordingly, Chapter 3 sketches a brief history of science, including the theory of evolution, and offers a critique of the scientific view of the world. Chapter 4 analyzes religious belief and the great variety of world religions. Chapter 5 examines the place of philosophy in the debate between religion and science. Chapter 6 demonstrates that reason is an essential complement to religious faith. The final chapter summarizes the argument and concludes that religion and belief are essential to a full and complete human life.

Along the way, this work addresses the famous four questions posed long ago by Immanuel Kant in his lectures on philosophy: (1) "What can I know? (2) What may I hope? (3) What ought I to do? (4) What does it mean to be a human being?" The first question concerns the important issue of what are the criteria for truth; the second with the religious view of reality; the third concerns ethics and morality; and the fourth the meaning of life.

Notes

1. See Robert J. Richards, *The Meaning of Evolution* (1993) for a survey of the development of the concept of evolution from the eighteenth century to Darwin's time.
2. *Tammy Kitzmiller v. Dover Area School District*, 400 F. Supp. 3d 707 (M. D. Pa. 2005).
3. Stephen Jay Gould, *Rocks of Ages* (1999).
4. Michael Ruse, *Darwin and Design: Does Evolution Have a Purpose?* (2003).

Chapter 2

Creationism and the Constitution

The Cultural Wars of Religion

Religion is the very first subject addressed in the Bill of Rights, the first ten Amendments to the U.S. Constitution done in 1791. The First Amendment provides that "Congress shall make no law respecting an establishment of a religion, or prohibiting the free exercise thereof." This injunction is also binding on the states and local governments through the Fourteenth Amendment. Obviously there is a tension in this formulation: the Constitution both recognizes and protects the practice of religion and religious values, but the government is forbidden to foster or sponsor religion — this must be left to the private sector.

The cultural wars between the evolutionists and creationists have been waged against the background of this constitutional provision.

The roots of the controversy go back to nineteenth century and the concern over the so-called "higher criticism" of the Bible, a movement begun in Germany that advocated naturalistic and symbolic readings of the text, and interpretations drawn from its historical and cultural context. Conservative Christians regarded this movement as a source of negative social and religious trends. In the 1920s several southern states passed laws forbidding the teaching of evolution — even making it a crime to teach that "man had descended from a lower order of animals," as the Butler Act in Tennessee stated.

The American Civil Liberties Union decided to test these laws and placed newspaper advertisements soliciting teachers willing to volunteer to be a plaintiff in such a legal challenge. The town leaders of Dayton, Tennessee, many of whom were fundamentalist Christians, saw a chance to put their town on the map, and beat the ACLU to the punch. A local teacher, John T. Scopes, was called aside from playing tennis and talked into agreeing to be served with a warrant charging him with the crime of violating the Butler Act. Scopes was a science teacher (as well as track coach) at the Dayton High School. He had assigned his students to read the chapters on evolution in a biology class. Scopes then returned to his tennis game.

The Scopes *Case*

So began one of the most famous trials in American history. Scopes was an amiable young man of 24, gifted intellectually, but shy and well mannered. He would later become a successful oil company geologist. But then he was but a pawn in the high-stakes game of what was billed as the "trial of the century." The ACLU recruited the most famous defense lawyer in the country, Clarence Darrow, to contest the prosecution. This persuaded William Jennings Bryan, former secretary of state and a three-time Democratic candidate for president, to serve as special counsel for the prosecution. The national media descended on Dayton, and the trial was carried live on radio. Incredibly, Bryan was sworn as a witness as well, but when he took the stand, Darrow made him look foolish: he stumbled over whether Noah's flood also killed fish; where Cain found his wife; and how the snake that tempted Eve moved before God made it crawl on its belly. Bryan confessed that he knew little about either religion or science.

The no-nonsense Tennessee judge John T. Raulston, however, cut to the chase and concluded such testimony about the merits or demerits of the biblical account and evolution was irrelevant. He struck the entire testimony from the record and refused to allow pro-evolution experts to testify. The only issue was (correctly) whether Scopes had in fact taught evolution. Thus the verdict was a foregone conclusion: guilty as charged. Scopes was fined one hundred dollars, the penalty prescribed by law.

On appeal, the verdict was overturned, but not because teaching evolution was not a crime. The judge had made one small error: Tennessee law required that all fines over fifty dollars had to be set by a jury. Darrow and his New York legal team had failed to notice this problem and did not bring it to the judge's attention. Although the Tennessee Supreme Court reversed Scopes' conviction, the court specifically upheld the law in question:

> We are not able to see how the prohibition of teaching the theory that man has descended from a lower order of animals gives preference

to any religious establishment or mode of worship. So far as we know, there is no religious establishment or organized body that has in its creed or confession of faith any article denying or affirming such a theory.[1]

The ACLU's grand plan to challenge the anti-evolution statute in the U.S. Supreme Court was dead.

Evolution Eclipsed

Following the *Scopes* trial came two divergent ripple effects. On the one hand, the influential national media berated antievolutionists as pre-modern religious fundamentalists and bible-thumping know-nothings. This was personified by the acerbic wit of the *Baltimore Sun* reporter H. L. Mencken, who wrote about "forlorn pastors who belabor halfwits in the galvanized iron tabernacles behind the railroad yards." Another contribution to this image was the successful Broadway play *Inherit the Wind* by Jerome Lawrence and Robert E. Lee in 1955, about a young teacher tried and imprisoned for teaching evolution by backward religious bigots in a small town. Although the play was not intended by its authors to be faithful to history and was aimed more at 1950s style McCarthyism and suppression of free speech, many took the play to be an accurate portrayal of the events in Dayton in 1925.

On the other hand, the anti-evolution movement gained momentum particularly in rural America and in the South. School boards imposed restrictions on teaching evolution, and anti-evolution laws increased at the state level. Evolution largely disappeared from American classrooms. By 1930 an estimated 70 percent of schools omitted it entirely,[2] and biology textbooks decreased or omitted coverage.[3] So despite the idea conveyed in the national media that only a few uneducated bible-belt fundamentalists did not accept evolution, in reality generations of Americans grew up entirely ignorant of the subject. For most people, evolution and Darwinism were either deemphasized or omitted entirely from their educations.

Science Makes a Comeback

In 1957 the Soviet Union launched Sputnik, the world's first artificial satellite, beating the United States into the new frontier of space exploration.

This caused an agonizing reappraisal of science education in America, and a new emphasis on teaching evolution. Darwinism reappeared, much to the chagrin of many religious people. This sparked the new movement of "creation science,"[4] the idea that creationism could be given a scientific foundation.

But the laws in some states prohibiting the teaching of evolution altogether were still on the books, and they collided with the renewed emphasis on teaching evolution. In Arkansas, for example, teaching the theory or doctrine that mankind "ascended or descended from a lower order of animals" was a misdemeanor and a reason for dismissal from employment. A young teacher, Susan Epperson, challenged the constitutionality of the law with the backing of the Arkansas Education Association. This time the case reached the United States Supreme Court, which ruled in her favor.

In the *Epperson* case the Supreme Court ruled that the Arkansas law was in conflict with the First Amendment to the Constitution's injunction against the establishment of religion.[5] The court said that the "law selects from the body of knowledge a particular segment which it proscribes for the sole reason that it is deemed to conflict with a particular religious doctrine; that is, with a particular interpretation of the Book of Genesis by a particular religious group." The court pointed out that the First Amendment mandates government neutrality toward religion and between religion and non-religion. Thus, a state may not "aid or oppose" any religion. Arkansas' law was not neutral; rather it attempted to "blot out" a particular theory because of its "supposed conflict" with the biblical account. This led the court to strike the law down because of its constitutional infirmity.

Equal Time for Creation Science

The *Epperson* case was a defeat, but the religious right now saw an opening for a new strategy. Creation science was advanced as an alternative scientific theory to evolution, and the vaunted government neutrality of the First Amendment should mean that creation science must be given equal time. This idea was spearheaded by an organization founded in 1972, the Institute for Creation Research (ICR). Soon the ICR was promoting creation science through books, pamphlets, lectures and movies. Workshops were offered on how to combat evolutionists.

As originally formulated creation science was just a misnomer. Its central published work, a book called *The Genesis Flood* (1961), simply contends that there is scientific evidence that the earth is less than 10,000 years old and that, therefore, evolution is impossible. The book relies on what is termed "flood geology," evidence from rocks of a worldwide catastrophe, such as a flood that shaped the earth's surface in relatively recent times. But the flood geology concept together with what was termed "abrupt appearance theory" was presented as science without overt reliance on biblical sources. Creation science lawyers argued that it was unconstitutional to teach evolution "without any alternative theory of origins because it undermines [students'] religious convictions and hinders religious training by parents."[6]

The creation science movement grew during the 1970s: equal time bills were introduced in at least 27 states, and were enacted into law in Arkansas and Louisiana. This set the stage for the next court battles. The Arkansas law, Act 590, was challenged immediately by the Arkansas American Civil Liberties Union (AACLU), which procured the pro-bono legal services of an excellent New York law firm, Skadden, Arps, Slate, Meagher and Flom. A Methodist clergyman, William McLean, was persuaded to be the lead plaintiff, and many religious organizations and churches joined him, including the resident Arkansas bishops of the Episcopal, Roman Catholic, Methodist, and African American Methodist churches, several clergy of various denominations, and the American Jewish Congress. This made it difficult to argue that the case was hostile to religious views.

This case produced a landmark case — *McLean v. Arkansas Board of Education*[7] — graced by a powerful and intelligent opinion authored by Judge William R. Overton of Little Rock in May 1981. The judge interpreted the Establishment Clause of the First Amendment using the test laid down by the U.S. Supreme Court in the 1971 case of *Lemon v. Kurtzman*.[8] The *Lemon* test sets out three criteria (in legalese these are called "prongs") which a law must meet under the Establishment Clause: (1) it must have a secular rather than religious purpose; (2) it must not have the effect of promoting or inhibiting religion; and (3) it must not create "entanglement" between government and religion.

Act 590 was determined to fail all three prongs of the *Lemon* test: both its purpose and effect were the advancement of religion with a resulting government entanglement with religion. The equal time law was "simply and purely an effort to introduce the Biblical version of creation into the public school curricula." Therefore the only purpose was to advance religion. Most importantly, the *McLean* opinion found that creation science is in fact not science. The court stated that "the essential characteristics of science are":

2 — Creationism and the Constitution

It is guided by natural laws;
It has to be explanatory by reference to natural laws;
It is testable against the empirical world;
Its conclusions are tentative, i.e., are not necessarily the final word; and
It is falsifiable.
Creation Science fails to meet these essential characteristics ... it depends upon a supernatural intervention which is not guided by natural law. It ... is not testable and is not falsifiable.
The two-model approach of the creationists ... has no factual basis or legitimate educational purpose. It assumes only two explanations for the origins of life and existence of man, plants and animals: it was either the work of a creator or it was not. Application of these two models, according to creationists ... dictates that all scientific evidence which fails to support the theory of evolution is necessarily scientific evidence in support of creationism, and is, therefore, creation science "evidence."
The methodology employed by creationists is another factor which is indicative that their work is not science. A scientific theory must be tentative and always subject to revision or abandonment in light of facts that are inconsistent with or falsify the theory. A theory that is by its own terms dogmatic, absolute, and never subject to revision is not a scientific theory.

This point is crucial: creationism is not science because the assertion of its propositions is not supported by scientific evidence. Furthermore, the arguments it musters against evolution, such as the gaps in the fossil record, are not enough either to falsify the theory of evolution or to prove the existence of a creator.

The *McLean* case was not appealed, so there was no higher court test of the Arkansas law. However, a similar Louisiana law was winding its way through the courts, and it reached the United States Supreme Court in 1987. The Louisiana law carried a long and clumsy title: "The Balanced Treatment for Creation-Science and Evolution-Science in Public School Instruction Act." This law did not require the teaching of either evolution or creation science; but if one was taught the other must also be taught. Neither the law nor its defenders cited any religious purpose; affidavits filed in the case defined creation science as "origin through abrupt appearance in complex form." The law's defenders argued that this viewpoint constitutes a true scientific theory.

In *Edwards v. Aguillard*[9] the Supreme Court struck down the Louisiana Balanced Treatment Law. The opinion written for the court by Justice Brennan was straightforward and broke no new ground. Again the ground for invalidating the law was the purpose prong of the *Lemon* test under the Establishment Clause of the First Amendment. In applying this test the court looked past the stated purpose of the law — the protection of academic freedom and fairness — and found, to the contrary, that academic freedom and fairness would be curtailed. The court cited the fact that even before the law, any scientific concept could be included in the curriculum in Louisiana public schools so the act provided no new authority. Next the court found that it was "not happenstance" that the legislature required the teaching of a theory that coincided with a religious view. Thus, the court had no trouble finding that "the primary purpose of the ... Act is to advance a particular religious belief" which meant that the law was contrary to the standard of the First Amendment.[10] This forbidden purpose was either to promote a particular religious view or to inhibit a theory not favored by certain religions.

The *Edwards* opinion is considerably different from the opinion in *McLean*. First, *McLean* was decided after a full trial with testimony by witnesses on both sides; the *Edwards* case was decided on summary judgment without live testimony and cross-examination. Thus, for example, the Supreme Court made no findings whether creation science was in fact science. The Supreme Court's opinion is drawn more narrowly too on the legal point: *Edwards* found that the Louisiana law violated only the first prong — religious purpose — of the *Lemon* test, while the *McLean* court found a violation of all three of the *Lemon* criteria.

Enter Intelligent Design

The *Edwards* result did not end the creationist crusade but merely signaled the opening of a new phase in the battle: intelligent design. With the failure of creationism dressed up as a science, it was clear the case for young earth creationism, flood geology, and abrupt appearance was going nowhere. Thus, intelligent design (known as ID) was conceived as a working compromise. The first important proponent of ID was retired University of California–Berkeley law professor Phillip Johnson who authored the leading book of the movement, *Darwin on Trial*,[11] in 1991. The main tenet of ID is that an "intelligent designer" created the physical universe and the living world, which he or she or it continues to control in furtherance of a purpose. Thus ID is vague about the age of the earth and even the identity of the designer. ID is itself designed, however, to be a big tent — to include even young earth creationists as well as creationists who believe that the designer acts largely through natural processes.[12] ID proponents are united, however, in their opposition to Darwinism, which they usually equate with evolution. Darwinism, ID asserts, is only a theory for which the evidence is extremely weak or non-existent. Darwinism-evolution persists basically because it is supportive of scientific materialism, which dominates today's world.

Thus, intelligent design's primary thrust is to negate Darwinism, which for them is an epithet for materialism and the exclusion of God and the supernatural. This is done in four primary ways:

1. Darwinism-evolution is derided as "only a theory," which is equated with "guess" or "hunch"; thus, it is without foundation in "fact."[13]
2. There are gaps and even instances of fraud in the fossil record that is relied upon as evidence for evolution.[14]
3. Many living and non-living systems in nature show "irreducible complexity" so that it is impossible that they evolved and were not created.[15]
4. Mathematical probability theory shows the impossibility that many of the complex organisms and structures in the natural world evolved; instead they must have been specially created.[16]

Intelligent design's day in court came in 2005. In 2004 the Dover, Pennsylvania, School Board passed a resolution: "Students will be made aware of gaps/problems in Darwin's theory and of other theories of evolution, including, but not limited to, intelligent design."

This statement was supplemented by a press release explaining that, while Pennsylvania's academic standards require students to study "Darwin's Theory of Evolution" in preparation for a standardized test on science, "Gaps in the Theory exist for which there is no evidence.... Intelligent Design is an explanation of the origin of life that differs from Darwin's view. The reference book, *Of Pandas and People*, is available for students who might be interested in gaining an understanding of what Intelligent Design actually involves."

This policy — known as the ID Policy — was challenged in federal court by Tammy Kitzmiller, the mother of two students attending Dover High School, as well as several other interested parties. A full trial of the constitutional issues was carried out for almost two months before Judge John E. Jones III of the United States District Court for the Middle District of Pennsylvania. The witnesses included many of the leading experts on Intelligent Design, including Dr. Michael Behe, author of *Darwin's Black Box*.

On December 20, 2005, Judge Jones rendered his decision,[17] which was a resounding defeat for the proponents of intelligent design. His 139-page opinion is an exhaustive review of the history of the intelligent design movement and its tenets. The key to the case in Judge Jones view was his finding that intelligent design is not science and is specifically not biology. Citing the testimony of ID advocates, he found that "the intelligent designer works outside the laws of nature and science." Furthermore, "this intelligent designer everyone understands to be God." These findings led to the inescapable conclusions that ID is a religious explanation of the origin of life that depends upon belief in the existence of God. In effect, ID is but another version of creationism masquerading as science. Thus, both the purpose and effect of the ID movement was the advancement of religion. In fact, citing the so-called "Wedge Document" developed by the Discovery Institute's Center for Renewal of Science and Culture, Judge Jones found that the goal of the ID movement is "to replace science as currently practiced with theistic and Christian science." Thus, the Dover Area School Board's ID Policy was unconstitutional because it violated the *Lemon* test criteria and the injunction against public advancement of religion in the First Amendment. In 2006 a new school board was elected in Dover County, and one of their first actions was to announce that the *Kitzmiller* case would not be appealed. So the decision stands as a resounding defeat for fundamentalists and creationists.

A Fundamental Flaw

The futile history of creationism and the courts clashing over the Establishment Clause of the First Amendment is very revealing. First, whatever one's sympathy in this matter, the passion and determination of religious partisans is remarkable. No one can doubt the genuineness of their commitment. Second, it is worthy to note that of all the scientific advances in the last century and a half—special and general relativity and quantum mechanics in physics, plate tectonics in geology, the "big bang" and black holes in astronomy, genetics in biology, and the atom and the periodic table of the elements in chemistry—adherents of religion—at least many convinced Christians and other religious people—focus exclusively on Darwinism in their campaign against what is termed scientific materialism. The citadel of Darwinism is their nemesis; it must be overrun and defeated.

Why is this so? The answer appears to be that many religious people have the idea that Darwinism, if it is true, means that belief in God is impossible. Darwinism explains the variety of living things and mankind itself as simply the products of chance through natural selection. This randomness means there is no higher purpose overseeing the world and no creator God.

The religious adherents who equate Darwin and natural selection with atheism are mistaken. Their fundamental error lies in their idea of truth and knowledge. Such people find irreconcilable conflict only because they believe there is only one kind of truth in the world. In fact, there are many different kinds of truth and varieties of human knowledge. Darwinist theories of evolution and natural selection are founded on but one kind of knowledge and truth, that which we call science. The fundamental flaw behind almost a century of trying to replace Darwinism with creationism is that as an affirmative and operational explanation of the creation of the universe, the origin of life, or the genesis of mankind, no version of creationism or intelligent design is within the bounds of the method of knowledge we call science. Science has developed over many centuries of effort a methodological approach based on empirical evidence, independent objective verifiability, and reproducible and predictive results. Science deals only in tangible, physical phenomena, but this is not materialism properly speaking. Science can and should take no position as to matters that are not within its methodological ken. Science has adopted a materialistic approach to knowledge for only one reason: it is an immensely useful approach that has proven value. There can be no claim that science attains a God's eye view of reality or that other approaches to knowledge and truth are meaningless. The implications of these ideas are developed further in the next chapter.

Notes

1. *Scopes v. State*, 289 S. W. 363, 367 (Tenn. 1927).
2. Edward J. Larson, *Trial and Error: The American Controversy over Creation and Evolution*, 85 (3d ed. 2003).
3. Gerald Skoog, "The Topic of Evolution in Secondary School Biology Textbooks: 1900–1979," *Science Education* 63:621–640 (1979).
4. The major tenets of creation science were set out in Henry M. Morris and John Whitcomb, *The Genesis Flood* (1961). See also Henry M. Morris (ed.), *Scientific Creationism* (1974).
5. *Epperson v. Arkansas*, 393 US 97 (1968).
6. Wendell R. Bird, Resolution for Balanced Presentation of Evolution and Science, ICR Impact, May: 4, ii (1979).
7. 529 F. Supp. 1255 (E. D. Ark.1982).
8. 403 US 602 (1971).
9. 482 US 578 (1987).

10. Justice Scalia filed a long and emotional dissenting opinion which was joined by Chief Justice Rehnquist. Scalia's main point was that the court should accept the law's recitation of a secular purpose, and it is not wrongful for individual legislators to sponsor or vote for a bill out of religious conviction.

11. Phillip E. Johnson, *Darwin on Trial* (1991).

12. The first book contending for ID was Charles Thaxton, Walter L. Bradley and Roger L. Olsen, *The Mystery of Life's Origins* (1984).

13. Phillip E. Johnson, *Evolution as Dogma: The Establishment of Naturalism* (1990); Percival W. Davis and Dean H. Kenyon, *Of Pandas and People* (2d ed. 1993).

14. Jonathan Wells, *Icons of Evolution: Science or Myth?* (2000).

15. Michael Behe, *Darwin's Black Box* (1996).

16. William Dembski, *No Free Lunch: Why Specified Complexity Cannot Be Purchased Without Intelligence* (2001).

17. *Tammy Kitzmiller v. Dover Area School Board*, 400 F. Supp. 3d 707 (M. D. Pa. 2005).

Chapter 3

The World of Science

What is science? What is the nature of scientific knowledge? What does it mean to posit a scientific law or theory or hypothesis? Answering such questions is very difficult but important, for the conflict between religion and science as exemplified by Darwinism versus creationism (or intelligent design) cannot be understood without exploring these questions.

Categories of Reality

We must start, however, at a more fundamental level, by asking what are the categories of reality — that is to say, what kinds of things do we as human beings know? The most cogent answer to this question comes from a distinguished philosopher of science, Karl Popper (1902–1994), the author of the classic text *The Logic of Scientific Discovery* (*Die Logik der Forschung*, originally published in Vienna in 1934). Popper famously maintained that there are three "Worlds" of reality for human beings:

- World One is the world of objective reality with which we interact, everything from buildings, grass and birds to the stars and planets. Of course, although we perceive World One as containing these objects, our scientific instruments and theories tell us that this world is really composed of tiny particles and waves moving at incredible speeds; and what looks solid is mostly empty space. Furthermore, what we know of this reality is limited by what we can perceive through our senses, aided at times by sophisticated scientific instruments. Therefore our vision of World One is limited both in what we can find there and how we find it. The intriguing

question about World One is what is there that our senses are unable to perceive; there may be nothing more, but that is highly unlikely.
- World Two is the psychological world of consciousness, mental states and mental operations, which are traditionally categorized as either reasoning or desire, intellect and will. We also understand this world to contain sub-conscious states and desires. The objects we perceive in World One have their counterparts as mental phenomena in World Two.
- World Three is the product of human minds, the many bodies of knowledge skills we construct and produce through the interaction of Worlds One and Two. World Three is made possible by the invention of human language that allows us to communicate with each other in extremely sophisticated ways. World Three is a vast edifice of human-created physical objects like sculpture, music, art and architecture as well as the many fields of human knowledge, such as philosophy, mathematics, history, law, medicine, and — yes — both science and religion.

These three worlds of course are interrelated in a dynamic way; Worlds One and Two together produce World Three, and World Three in turn affects World Two. For example, music exists as sound vibrations in World One, as mental ideas in World Two, and becomes an objective body of work in World Three. When I listen to Mozart, it is because I can access World Three in some way, which engages my World Two (most pleasantly, I might add); but all this is possible only because of the existence and the physical reality of the wave vibrations of World One.

Popper points out that Plato was the first to discover World Three, but he made the mistake of assuming that this world must have physical reality in some transcendent realm. Plato thus confused World Three with World One. Plato invented the idea of a world of Forms or Ideas that have some mystical existence: most famously the True, the Beautiful and the Good. For Plato these abstract Forms constituted authentic reality and the world of physical objects are only "shadows" of True Being. Not many people today are convinced by Plato's theory of Forms, but it still fascinates. Plato was right, however, in positing the objective existence of World Three. This objective existence is elusive, however, for much of World Three has a kind of virtual reality. The world of science exists, for example, even though we cannot point to any physical place where it may be found, and no single human being has or ever will possess perfect and complete knowledge of this world. This is also true of the many other fields of World Three. Of course, some of World Three overlaps somewhat with the other two Worlds, for example, the case of man-made physical objects like buildings and books.

In many respects, World Three is the most important world for human beings. Our introduction to this world of the products of human mind and work begins at birth. We spend many long years in school learning aspects of World Three. After we graduate we spend our lives engaged along with other people in World Three. This has two major impacts on all of us. World Three is the source of our relationships with reality and also with society. Our contact with World Three shapes what we refer to as our culture, whether it be Western, Christian, Hindu, Buddhist or whatever. Our contact with World Three, then, is partly our own choice and partly an accident of the time and place of our birth.

Knowledge refers to how we come in contact with reality and how we shape reality. Knowledge is not the search for certainty; it is the search for truth. The nature of the three worlds of reality limits certain knowledge to a few tautologies. I can be certain that all bachelors are unmarried, but beyond that there is little I can know for certain. But in spite of this we have developed a vast body of knowledge. Yet, we must admit that most of it is not certain and is subject to revision. This leads to a general theory of truth in knowledge, what Popper calls "critical rationalism."[1] This idea should be applied in every field of knowledge. This is the view that the search for truth must proceed through a process of rational thought subjected to criticism. This means every proposition even including one's own must be subjected to criticism and rational debate. This testing is absolutely crucial to the search for truth.

Nevertheless, each field of human knowledge in World Three has developed its own specific criteria for the search for truth. History, for example, relies for sources on both written documents of various kinds as well as what historians call "material culture," physical artifacts. But no historian will accept such evidence uncritically. Thus, when a cremated skeleton was found in an apparent royal grave at Vergina, Greece, in 1977, a vigorous debate ensued over whether the bones were those of Philip II, the father of Alexander the Great. A consensus has developed that they are indeed Philip's, but this will ever be subject to further critical review. We could examine many different fields and their criteria, but we must not lose sight of our real inquiry: the meaning of scientific knowledge. This purpose of this chapter is to examine the range of World Three and our current state of scientific knowledge, including evolution and Darwinism.

The Scientific Method

Science is both a body of knowledge and a practice or set of methods for gaining that knowledge. Only beginning in the sixteenth and seventeenth centuries were the steps taken that were necessary to create the methods that led to the scientific body of knowledge we have today. Three fundamental new ideas were fundamental to this process: first, *observation* that emphasized inductive reasoning and building a body of data had to be valued over *theory* and deduction. And when the two came into conflict, theory had to be rejected or modified. This new method moves from the particular to the general instead of emphasizing deductions from theory.

Second, new mathematical tools had to be invented in order to facilitate complex measurements and calculations. To this end, about 1600 Francois Viete rationalized the system of algebraic symbols; in 1614 John Napier invented logarithms; René Descartes developed a system of analytic geometry in 1637; and later in the century Isaac Newton and Gottfried Leibniz independently developed calculus, making possible the measurement of continuous change. New mathematical tools of course continue to be developed right up to the present.

Third, new scientific instruments had to be invented to allow better observations. This process began in 1650 when Christian Huygens invented the pendulum clock, a great advance for measuring exact intervals of time; and in the seventeenth century telescopes and microscopes came into common use. This process also continues today; in 2007 a great new tool, the CERN, the world's leading laboratory for particle physics, began operations in Switzerland in 2006.

The roots of modern science go back to Aristotle, but for many centuries what we now call science was indistinguishable from philosophy and religion. In fact, the English word "science" came into common use only in the nineteenth century.[2] At the beginning of what we now call the scientific revolution in the sixteenth century, the men involved believed they were engaged in "natural philosophy." Their devout religious faith led them to believe that God, who was all-good and all-knowing, had created a rationally ordered universe, and that this divine plan could be discovered by mankind to the greater glory of God. For example, Johannes Kepler (1571–1630), who confirmed Nicolas Copernicus' hypothesis that the sun must be at the center of what we now call the solar system,[3] stated in the Preface to his masterwork, *The Harmony of the World* (1619), which sets forth his celebrated three laws of planetary motion,[4] "I have stolen the golden vessels of the Egyptians to create a sacred place for my God.... God himself has waited 6000 years for someone to gaze upon his creation with understanding."

The origin of what we now regard as scientific method arose only in the sixteenth century in the exhortations of Francis Bacon (1561–1626). In Bacon's view, natural philosophers were guilty of mixing what we now call science (in Bacon's term, natural philosophy) and religion "to the detriment of both."[5] Bacon called for the study of "things themselves," and the method of induction, which he described as proceeding from particulars to general propositions that are then subjected to testing by experiment. He distinguished his proposed method from empiricism, by which he meant the idea that by merely observing nature truth will be revealed. Rather, Bacon advocated a "marriage of the empirical and the rational," whereby creative experiments are used to subject hypotheses to rigorous testing and revision. Perhaps most importantly, Bacon said that the purpose of what we now call scientific knowledge was usefulness, to acquire knowledge that works "to reduce our suffering and enhance our well-being."

Bacon was taking issue with the prevailing natural philosophy of the time, medieval scholasticism, which mixed observations of the natural world with arguments from various types of authority, including scripture, as interpreted by religious orthodoxy, and ancient authors and texts that have stood the test of time and were compatible with Christian beliefs. Scholasticism jumbled the natural world and the supernatural together under various doctrines, such as Aristotle's idea that all natural phenomena can be explained in terms of their four causes: material cause, which is the matter of which they are composed; formal cause, which is their essence or substance; efficient cause, which is God, the creator of all things; and final cause, which is their purpose or reason for being. The latter cause was particularly important for the scholastics who believed that by analyzing the purposes of created things we can discern God's design for the world. For example, it was believed that the purpose of rainfall was to allow crops to grow and rivers flow to meet their final destiny in the sea. The doctrine of the four causes also allows us to rank and distinguish things in terms of their "perfections," their different values in what was termed the "great Chain of Being."

Bacon's new method for analyzing the natural world was a radical departure from this scheme. His emphasis on induction and on testability meant that the metaphysical and supernatural could no longer be considered part of the natural world since in principle they could not be tested. Thus, Bacon's scheme called for a strictly materialist methodology that disregarded supernatural causes.

This idea that the natural world can be understood through induction and testing of objectively provable facts and laws was given a boost by the French philosopher and mathematician René Descartes (1596–1650), whose ideas achieved great appeal in the seventeenth century. In his quest for perfect knowledge, Descartes formulated his famous "Cogito ergo sum" (I think, therefore I am), which implied a complete separation between the material and spiritual worlds of being. Cartesians (followers of Descartes) henceforth followed the dictum that, while the essence of mind (soul) is thinking, the essence of body and all matter is "extension." For Cartesians this meant that the material world could be analyzed separately from and leaving aside the spiritual and supernatural. And since the essence of matter is extension, the natural world can be studied in terms of precise measurements, i.e. by means of mathematics and geometry. This also meant that we no longer had to worry about Aristotle's four causes; instead, causation could be analyzed in terms of matter coming into physical contact with other matter — bodies in motion.

Classical Physics

Classical physics is the edifice erected in the sixteenth and seventeenth centuries that finally supplanted Aristotelian and Ptolemaic physics and astronomy, which had dominated for almost two thousand years. Aristotle held the Earth to be at the center of the universe, and the moon and other heavenly bodies were governed by circular motions that were changeless and timeless. Below the level of the moon the four terrestrial elements had natural motions with respect to the center of the Earth: air and fire tended to rise; and water and earth tended to fall. Motion contrary to this natural motion — which Aristotle termed violent motion — was possible only through contact between a mover and the moved. In the second century CE, Ptolemy of Alexandria invented a geocentric cosmology based upon the Aristotelian conception of the universe that became the definitive conception of the universe. The Polish monk and amateur astronomer Nicolas Copernicus (1473–1543) proposed a better model — a heliocentric universe[6] — that he believed avoided the anomalies of Ptolemy's system, but he retained the idea that all the stars were contained in the outermost sphere and that heavenly bodies moved only in perfect circles. So great was Aristotle's and Ptolemy's authority that Copernicus did not even dare to publish his ideas until the year of his death.

3 — The World of Science

Not until Johannes Kepler (1571–1630) did Copernicus' heliocentric model draw much attention. Kepler, relying on data compiled by Copernicus and the Danish astronomer Tycho Brahe, proposed three new laws of planetary motion that governed the working of the heliocentric universe. He calculated that (1) the planets move not in circles but in ellipses with the sun at one focus; (2) the speed of the motions of the planets is not constant but sweeps out equal areas in equal times (decreasing as the planet moves away from the sun); and (3) the square of a planet's orbital period (its year) is proportional to the cube of its mean distance from the sun. For Earth, for example, this calculation is the square of one (the earth's year) over the cube of one (the Earth's distance from the sun is one astronomical unit) = 1. Kepler also rejected the Aristotelian idea that motions on Earth were fundamentally different from motions in the heavens.

Galileo Galilei (1564–1642) not only accepted the Copernican system but also conducted numerous experiments on velocity and motion. He discovered that the horizontal motion of a falling object is independent of its vertical motion, and that the commonsense idea that heavier objects fall faster than lighter objects is untrue; both fall at the same rate of speed, which he calculated to be proportional to the square of the time of the fall. Galileo also formulated the principle of inertia: that an object in motion tends to stay in motion until acted upon by an outside force. He also maintained that a uniform state of motion was just as natural as a uniform state of rest, contradicting Aristotle's idea that motion requires contact between the mover and the moved.

This set the stage for the central figure of classical physics, Isaac Newton (1643–1727). Although Newton still considered himself a natural philosopher, he sought to explain the physical motions of the world of everyday experience. In doing so he not only changed the history of science, he effected a lasting change in human culture. In order to explain changing motion, he invented a new mathematical tool, infinitesimal calculus. He was able to confirm Kepler's laws of planetary motion using mathematical proofs.

Newton also formulated three laws of motion taking his cue from Descartes: (1) the law of inertia (originally formulated by Galileo) that every body continues in its state of rest or in uniform motion unless it is acted upon by an outside force; (2) a force exerted upon a body is equal to its mass times acceleration; and (3) every action produces an equal and opposite reaction.

Newton employed Kepler's insight that these laws applied not only to terrestrial bodies but also to larger planetary ones. This was revolutionary because everyone had always assumed that supernatural laws different from anything of earthly origin ruled the heavens. Newton's law of universal gravitation[7] explained the motions of the moon and the planets in terms of the same force that operates in our daily experience on the earth's surface. Nevertheless, Newton's formulation was not without its puzzling aspects — how could gravity exercise force over a distance? Newton replied that he was content with a secondary explanation of this force; why and how gravity operates was not his concern. In the tradition of Bacon, his law of universal gravitation was useful and true; for Newton that was sufficient.

Newton's accomplishment gave rise to the idea that the physical world was an ordered place running according to preordained natural laws that could be discovered by human reason. Newton's method was the key to further progress as well. Careful observation, induction, and the formulation of a hypothesis that is testable mathematically or experimentally would allow us to discover all of nature's laws. For Newton and his contemporaries, this did not present any problems with respect to religious belief. In fact Newton thought his work offered objective proof of the existence and nature of God, who "created everything by number, weight and measure." His contemporary, the philosopher John Locke (1632–1704), greatly influenced by the new philosophy, published a tract he called *The Reasonableness of Christianity* (1695) to show exactly how the Christian God can be deduced from the wondrous workings of the natural world — intelligent design.

Another famous figure of the seventeenth century in England was Robert Boyle (1627–1691), one of the fathers of chemistry, who published *The Sceptical Chemist* (1661), which not only repudiated Aristotle's four elements theory (that all matter is composed of earth, air, fire and water), but also disputed as nonsense the practice of alchemy, then much in vogue. Boyle also promulgated what is still known as Boyle's Law: the pressure and volume of a gas in a closed container are inversely proportional.[8] This means that at a constant temperature, reducing the volume of a gas increases the pressure, and if the volume is increased, the pressure will decrease proportionately.

Like Newton and Locke, Boyle was a devout Christian, who in his will famously endowed lectures at Oxford with the purpose of "proving the Christian religion against notorious infidels."[9]

Nevertheless, in the eighteenth century fissures opened between the new confidence in the power of human reason to solve all problems and religious faith. By emphasizing the rational structure and workings of the universe, the natural philosophers reduced God to a remote and impersonal force. There was no need for revelation or religious doctrines if we know God as the author of the natural world.

The idea that natural laws operate the universe was also used to negate the idea of miracles and other supernatural events. Christian clergy are also not necessary since we can know God through his works. A new religious view developed we call deism, the idea that God created the world and the natural laws for its operation, but has no further involvement with mankind or the world. Soon influential voices were raised in favor of outright atheistic naturalism. Dennis Diderot (1713–1784) argued there is no need for God if mechanistic processes can explain the motions of bodies and the physiology of living things. David Hume (1711–1776) in his *Dialogues Concerning Natural Religion* (1776) challenged the idea of the Christian God as inconsistent with the observed evil, pain and suffering of the world. This vision of an impersonal, deterministic, mechanical universe operating according to eternal, mathematical laws — matter in motion — culminated with the publication of *Exposition du systeme du monde* (1796) by the French mathematician Pierre Laplace (1749–1827). One day Napoleon, who was very interested in astronomy, is said to have asked LaPlace what part God plays in the motions of the stars and planets. Laplace's replied haughtily: "I have no need of that hypothesis."[10]

Energy and Force

1. Heat

The eighteenth century view of the universe as a perpetual motion machine was overturned by developments in the nineteenth and early twentieth centuries concerning the role of energy. Descartes' idea that motion can be imparted to matter only by contact with other matter was contradicted by Newton's principle of gravity that acts at a distance. Soon other sources of energy — defined as the ability to do work (force acting on an object so as to cause a displacement) — were discovered: first, the kinetic theory of heat — that heat is caused by atoms (or molecules) in motion — replaced the earlier caloric theory that heat was a massless fluid that flowed in and out of objects. Soon it was understood that various forms of energy, such as heat and mechanical energy, are interchangeable, and the total amount of energy in a closed system is constant. An English brewer, James Prescott Joule (1818–1889),[11] demonstrated that compression of air produces heat, and then deigned to show that falling water (or any liquid) converts gravitational energy to heat. (Thus the water at the bottom of a waterfall is warmer than at the top.)

This discovery led to the formulation of a general law, the First Law of Thermodynamics, which holds that energy (like matter) cannot be created or destroyed, but it can be transformed.[12] Soon a second more disturbing law was understood: the Second Law of Thermodynamics, which holds that heat moves (by convection, conduction or radiation) only in one direction — from warm to cold. A depressing conclusion follows: in any open system the degree of disorder or heat loss (also called entropy) will inexorably increase over time. In contrast to Newton's steady-state universe, therefore, the Second Law of Thermodynamics reveals that the Sun, Earth, stars and the universe itself are headed for inevitable "heat death." William Thomson (1824–1907), later Lord Kelvin, calculated his absolute scale of temperature based on this law, for which absolute zero — the total absence of heat — is -273.15 C. This undesirable state, it seems, is our own ultimate destiny, absent supernatural intervention.

2. Electricity and Magnetism

The nature of electricity was first intensively investigated in the eighteenth and nineteenth centuries. Experiments with static electricity as well as lightning (Benjamin Franklin famously experimented by flying a kite in a thunderstorm) demonstrated that some substances have the capacity to become electrically charged and that charged substances can do work — repel or attract. Franklin and his contemporaries believed that an electric charge was a fluid, but we now know that a negative charge reflects an excess of electron while a positive charge reflects a deficit. Charles Coulomb (1736–1806) conducted experiments to prove that the force between two charged objects equals the product of the two charges divided by the distance between them. (This is analogous to gravity except that gravity is always attractive.[13]) The Italian physicist Alessandro Volta (1745–1827) determined that alternating plates of metals placed in a saltwater solution produced an electric current, and the electric battery was born.

The next advances came through investigation of the nature of magnetism, a strange force known since antiquity.[14] The Danish scientist Hans Christian Oersted (1777–1851) noticed in 1820 that when a magnetic compass needle is held over a wire carrying an electric current, the needle deflects at right angles to the wire. This suggested that a magnetic force operates in a circle or even a series of circles around the wire, an utterly strange idea since classical physics excluded circular motion without a corresponding force. But the English scientist Michael Faraday (1791–1867) demonstrated that passing an electric current through a coil of wire wound around a steel rod produces a magnet, and conversely, a magnetized iron rod creates a current flowing in a wire. This discovery not only led to the invention of the first electric motors, but also to the realization that electricity and magnetism are aspects of the same phenomenon; they are the force we now call *electromagnetism*.

Later in the nineteenth century James Clerk Maxwell (1831–1879) devised four famous equations to show the exact relationship between electricity and magnetism. In order to do so he postulated that these forces interact through the medium of an aethereal substance. This aether must contain both rotating vortices that penetrated the wire as well as tiny spheres like ball bearings to which were imparted the electric charge. He believed that this aethereal substance was everywhere and functioned as the carrier of electromagnetic waves. Using Faraday's findings, Maxwell comprehensively calculated mathematically the relationship between the two forces of electricity and magnetism. Maxwell's equations expressed in words are as follows:

1. Between any two electrically charged objects a force exists that is proportional to the two charges and inversely proportional to the square of the distance between them.
2. Magnetic poles always occur in pairs.
3. A changing electric field always produces a magnetic field.
4. A changing magnetic field always produces an electric field.[15]

These four equations unified two of the most fundamental forces in nature. By manipulating these equations, Maxwell found that electromagnetism functioned as a wave that was transmitted through a supposed aethereal substance at a speed of 186,000 miles per second, which was known to be the speed of light. Thus, he surmised, light too might be an electromagnetic wave.

3. Light

None other than Isaac Newton began the study of optics in the seventeenth century. He performed various experiments, most notably passing light through a prism and finding the familiar spectrum of red, orange, yellow, green, blue, indigo, and violet. Although the colors of the rainbow were known in antiquity, Newton showed that this spectrum is an intrinsic property of light itself. Newton also worked out a theory that light was a stream of "corpuscles," particles whose velocity depended on the medium through which it traveled. He observed that light can interact with matter in three distinct ways: by transmission (as with glass); by absorption (with conversion into heat); and by scattering (reflection).

In 1676 the Danish astronomer Ole Roemer (1644–1710) actually measured the raw speed of light by careful observation of the eclipses of Jupiter's inner moon, which has a regular period when it disappears into Jupiter's shadow of 42 hours, 28 minutes and 35 seconds. Roemer found that over a six month period there was a 15 minute time difference in his measurements, which he posited must be the time necessary for light to travel a distance equal to the length of the diameter of the earth's orbit around the sun.[16] Since he thought he knew this distance (he did not), he was able to give what he thought was a precise speed for light of 192,500 miles per second. Although his conclusion was wrong, he is rightly credited for an ingenious experiment and for establishing that light travels at a finite speed. Not until the end of the nineteenth century was the speed of light measured with accuracy and precision.

In 1804 the English physician Thomas Young (1773–1829) passed light through a two-screen apparatus with the first having a single slit and the second a double slit, projecting a ray of light onto a third screen. He noted an interference pattern — bright and dark regions — the unmistakable sign that light is a wave. Further testing by Augustin Fresnel (1788–1827) established that light was in fact a transverse wave, like a vibrating string. This had a profound impact: Maxwell's equations proved that light is in fact an electromagnetic wave.

The wave theory of light led to further research into the electromagnetic spectrum and the investigation of wavelengths and frequencies.[17] It was found that the electromagnetic spectrum is actually a continuum of all possible wavelengths. We see only a small part of this spectrum as visible light,[18] and within this spectrum we also see colors because of the color receptors in our eyes. This realization opened a wonderful (and sometimes fearful) new world of invisible radiation including x-rays, microwaves, radio waves, gamma rays, infrared and ultraviolet rays. These discoveries have revolutionized our technology and the way we think of the world.

At the end of the nineteenth century nothing seemed more certain than the wave theory of light, which had been confirmed in hundreds of experiments. Of course, in the twentieth century we discovered that the wave theory of light is not the final answer. Quantum theory, as we shall see, established that light after all is quantized — it comes in discrete bits we call photons. But the quantum revolution did not overthrow the wave theory completely. Rather quantized light has the characteristic of a wave. But scientists cannot explain how photons, which should be moving straight ahead, know how to spread and assemble into a wave. This wave-particle dual feature of light is one of the famous self-contradictions of modern physics.

4. Scientific Materialism

As a result of these scientific discoveries, the mid–nineteenth century was the heyday of scientific materialism. Advances in physics, chemistry and, as we shall see, geology, seemed to confirm a Newtonian idea of the world as matter in motion acted upon by impersonal forces operating according to impersonal, predictable laws. In English and French the word science came into common use; in German, Wissenschaft. People working in this field were no longer philosophers but scientists and Naturwissenschlaftlern. In Germany Ludwig Feuerbach published *Essence of Christianity* (1841), which argued that belief in the Christian God was simply a projection of human needs. Karl Marx of course echoed this view, famously holding that religion is the "opium of the masses." The Dutch physiologist Jacob Moleschott published *The Cycle of Life* (1852), declaring that even life can be explained in purely materialistic terms as the forces of heat, light, electricity acting on matter. Ludwig Büchner, a German physician, advocated the elimination of supernaturalism as simply superstition in his book, *Force and Matter* (1855). This was part of the broader social and literary movement sweeping the European world called Realism, which permeated the arts and letters of the time. In politics too, Realpolitik was the watchword of the age.

A New Frame of Reference: Relativity

We live our lives in a particular frame of reference — the surface of the Earth — that we take to be the most important in the universe. Of course, it is, as far as our daily lives are concerned. Unless we stop to think about it, we are not particularly aware that the Earth is moving in an elliptical orbit around the sun as well as turning on its axis approximately every twenty-four hours. In our everyday lives we still operate as if we are at the center of things even if we know that the earth is not at the center of the universe. But our ordinary experience of the world does not correspond at all with reality. Not only is our experience of centrality mistaken, but there is no privileged frame of reference in the universe at all. In fact, absolute space and time are simply figments of our imagination. Space and time are the products of the relative motions of matter in the universe in which we find ourselves.

The story of what led to this astonishing insight begins in the late nineteenth century with experiments involving the speed of light. The discovery that light is an electromagnetic wave that travels at a speed of about 300,000 km/second (186,000 miles/second) led to efforts to discover the nature of the supposed medium that carried the wave, a presumed substance that was termed the ether. Albert Michelson and E. W. Morley, two Americans, devised an ingenious experiment for this purpose. Two beams of light starting from the same point were sent to two mirrors both placed equidistant from the light source, one in the direction of the Earth's motion through space, and the other perpendicular to this motion. After reflecting off their respective mirrors, the two beams were reflected back to the point of their inception and allowed to interfere. Michelson and Morley hypothesized that, although both had covered the same distance, the light beam traveling perpendicular to the Earth's motion would travel at a faster speed because the other light beam traveling in the direction of the Earth's motion would be heading into the ether wind. Yet to everyone's surprise when the two light beams converged after their respective journeys, no interference pattern was produced. This could mean only one thing: their velocity was exactly the same. The experiment was taken to disprove the idea of the ether, and led to further investigation of the speed of light.

1. Special Relativity

Thinking about the speed of light in different settings led Albert Einstein (1879–1955) to formulate his revolutionary Special Theory of Relativity in 1905. Einstein made the assumption that the speed of light had to be what is called a cosmological constant, a constant of nature exactly the same for every observer, so that even someone one running toward or away from a light beam at 99 percent the speed of light will experience light as traveling 300,000 km/second. This in turn leads the idea that there is no special frame of reference in the universe, no absolute space against which motion can be measured. Rather, the laws of physics are the same for every observer at rest or in uniform motion (which are the same thing). Every observer in uniform motion is entitled to say, "I am at rest," and all motion (except the speed of light) can be measured relative to this state.

Special relativity has incredible implications. Time and space are flexible entities relative to the position of every observer. Each of us has our own unique experience of space-time; of course they are so much the same that we do not notice the differences. But at very high speeds the differences would be very apparent. At speeds approaching the speed of light time and space undergo dramatic changes: time slows and space shrinks so that objects become smaller and gain in mass, and at the speed of light their mass approaches infinity.[19] Thus, if I could travel by spaceship at 90 percent of the speed of light to a distant star, I might be away for 20 years by my calculation, but when I returned I would find that a thousand years had passed on planet Earth. Moreover, while I was underway my spaceship and everything in it would undergo dramatic length contraction only to return to their at rest size when I arrived back on earth.

Three additional astounding scientific findings drop out of Einstein's theory: (1) since the mass of any object is infinite at the speed of light, it is physically impossible for any material object to exceed the speed of light because an infinite force would have to be applied for that to happen; (2) since mass varies with velocity, mass must be in fact a form of energy according to the famous equation $E = mc^2$ — mass and velocity are interchangeable; and (3) time and space are not separate phenomena but rather one and the same entity: thus, we live in a world of space-time, and each of us experiences this world a little differently.

2. General Relativity

Einstein's next step was to formulate his relativity idea into a general theory, one that was not restricted to states of uniform motion. In 1916 he published his General Theory of Relativity extending relativity to accelerating states of motion. His key insight was that gravity and accelerated motion are equivalent. This idea has been verified experimentally to a high degree of accuracy. Thus, although we think of ourselves as at rest on the surface of the Earth, we are actually in a state of constant acceleration because of gravity. This also means that matter—all matter—has the capacity to bend space-time, to create large and small dimples in space-time so that all objects and even light move under the influence of this curved space-time. In the words of John Wheeler of Princeton University, "matter tells space-time how to curve, and space-time tells matter how to move." Thus, the force we call gravity is space-time bent into curves by matter. Although we experience the world in terms of straight lines, the real geometry of the universe is non–Euclidean—a geometry of curved surfaces.

Through his general relativity theory Einstein gave us a new picture of reality very different from the mechanical world — bodies in motion in absolute space and time — of classical physics. In Einstein's world there is no absolute space and no absolute time. Both are relative to the observer, and no frame of reference is central or privileged. Space and time are not separate but are aspects of the same thing, which is the relationship of matter to energy in the universe. Gravity is the way energy in the form of matter shapes space-time. Because the top speed of matter and energy is 300,000 km/second, gravity cannot act instantaneously as Newton believed. The speed limit of gravity is the speed of light. But incredibly, Einstein's theory holds that from the point of view of the photon, a particle of light, travel is in fact instantaneous because at the speed of light there is no space and no time.

Einstein proposed his theories of relativity on the basis of thought experiments and mathematical calculations. However, they have been empirically confirmed as well many times. For example, astronomers can observe the bending of light by large objects such as the sun, confirming general relativity. Special relativity was also proved by experiments, such as observing the slowing of atomic clocks on airplane flights. GPS satellite systems must be corrected for special relativity to work properly. Length contraction and the increased mass of fast moving objects are taken into account in scientific research involving particle physics. Thus, relativity is an everyday scientific phenomenon. But is it settled? General relativity is a classical theory that does not take into account the quantum world of particle physics. Scientists are searching for conditions of relativity violations which might point the way toward a new theory which would combine general relativity (gravity) with principles of quantum mechanics. We might find, for example, that both space and time, which appear to be continuous, are really quantized and come in little bits of volume and area too small for us to notice.[20]

Another Frame of Reference: The Very Small

Atoms and Molecules

Just as the world looks very different to an observer in a high-speed frame of reference, so too is the world of the very small totally foreign to ordinary human experience and understanding. The idea of the atom as the smallest unit of matter was first proposed by the Greek philosopher Democritus (or perhaps by his teacher Leucippus) in the fifth century BCE. Most likely he had two reasons for doing so. In the first place, if reality was divisible into finite particles, it would answer the philosophical puzzles posed by Zeno, another Greek who put forth a series of paradoxes proving that motion and other commonplace things of the world were logically impossible because if there is an infinity of matter or space between two points, it is not possible to bridge the gap in finite time; but the existence of atoms means that the distance between reality is not infinite.[21] Second, the idea of the atom was proposed to reconcile the views of the philosopher Parmenides, who made convincing arguments that there can only be one unchanging Being in the world, and his rival Heraclitus who believed, on the contrary, that change and variety is the salient characteristic of the world. If the world is made up of atoms — tiny uniform particles — there is one reality, but change can be explained by their constant motion and realignment.

Most of the ancients were not convinced, however, most notably Aristotle, who rejected the idea in favor of substance or essence. For Aristotle all things had their own substance, their formal cause or essence, and change could be explained by the fact that each substance is accompanied by attached "accidents" not essential to their being. Thus, a human being has the essence of a human being, but her red hair and green eyes are accidents that may vary from person to person.

The idea of the atom was revived in the seventeenth century by Pierre Gassendi (1592–1655), a French cleric who was a professor of mathematics at the College Royale in Paris. Isaac Newton also accepted the idea that matter was fundamentally indivisible particles of some sort. But the first person to carry this idea forward was John Dalton (1766–1844) in England who was interested in meteorology and the behavior of gases. From his observations that different gases combined in definite ratios — known as the law of definite proportions — he came up with the idea that different substances must have different kinds of atoms. Dalton published a three volume treatise, *A New System of Chemical Philosophy* (1808–27), based on the idea that matter is composed of elements that differ in their weights and sizes. He envisioned atoms as tiny, hard spheres. The Italian Amadeo Avogadro (1776–1856) carried this forward by hypothesizing that at a given temperature the same volume of any gas must contain the same number (known as Avogadro's number) of elements, but Avogadro did not distinguish between atoms and molecules.

Stanislao Cannizzaro (1826–1910), a professor of chemistry in Palermo, realized Avogadro's confusion and composed a table of atomic and molecular weights relative to one atom of hydrogen. Cannizzaro thus distinguished atoms from molecules and derived atomics weights using Avogadro's number. (Cannizzaro led an exciting life: in 1860 he took time off from his professorial post to fight for Italian unification — the Risorgimento — under Giuseppi Garibaldi.) About this time the new technique of spectroscopy[22] was developed which facilitated the identification of many new elements.

2. Chemistry Comes of Age

The science of chemistry did not fully emerge until the nineteenth century. Only then came the general realization that there are fundamental bits of matter called elements that cannot be transformed into anything else by ordinary physical or chemical means. Very few elements exist in nature in pure form; most are found in compounds. As a result, distinguishing the different elements proceeded slowly. Ancient peoples like the Greeks identified and used (without any conception of element in the modern scientific sense) precious metals like copper, silver, gold, and platinum; they also used the metals tin, iron, mercury, lead, and antimony; and they were familiar with carbon from fire and sulfur from volcanoes. The later alchemists identified additional elements including arsenic, zinc, bismuth and phosphorus. But only in the nineteenth century did techniques such as electrolysis and spectroscopy allow a systematic search for new elements.

Cannizzaro's work inspired several chemists to look for patterns in the known elemental substances — by the 1860s over 60 elemental substances had been identified.[23] Dmitri Mendeleev (1834–1907), professor at the University of St. Petersburg in Russia and the author of a two volume text, *Principles of Chemistry* (1868–1870), developed what we now call the Periodic Table of the Elements. Mendeleev arranged the elements according to their chemical properties and atomic weights,[24] and came up with a chart-like grid that clearly showed there were missing pieces — elements yet to be discovered. Mendeleev's vision revolutionized chemistry and provided the incentive for other researchers to fill in the blanks, which was done over the succeeding decades. The science of chemistry had come of age.

A fuller understanding of the Periodic Table of the Elements and the reason for chemical reactions had to await further developments in atomic physics. According to the so-called Bohr Model (named for its discoverer, the Danish physicist Niels Bohr), an atom consists of a positively charged nucleus surrounded by a cloud of negatively charged electrons that are arranged in shells. If the number of electrons in orbit is the same as the protons in the nucleus, the atom is electrically neutral; any difference will produce an electrically charged atom (known as an ion). The Periodic Table works because elements with similar chemical properties have similar arrangements of outer electrons. The most stable elements are those in which the outer shell has a full component of electrons — outer shells with the numbers 2, 10, 18, 36, 54, or 86 electrons. Atoms bond to one another because of their tendency to rearrange their electrons to achieve a low-energy stability state[25] — one of these magic numbers of electrons that represent a filled outer shell. The science of chemistry in fact assumes that every atom or group of atoms will tend to achieve the stability of a filled outer electron shell. Atoms of elements with less than a completely filled outer shell have high chemical potential energy and will be to some degree unstable and reactive.

Atoms with potential chemical energy have a tendency to combine with other atoms through a strategy called bonding. Chemistry is the science that essentially studies and takes advantage of these bonding tendencies; chemical reactions occur when the atoms of elements combine or separate into different substances by the process of either breaking or reforming chemical bonds. There are three types of chemical bonds: (1) ionic bonding where two atoms exchange one or more electrons forming two oppositely charged ions; (2) metallic bonding where atoms release electrons to create a mass of unbound electrons that can be shared as a group by positively charged ions; and (3) covalent bonding which is localized sharing of electrons. Ionic bonding creates natural substances such as sand and various rock-forming minerals as well as glass and ceramics. Metallic bonding produces common alloys such as brass, steel, and many metallic ores. Covalent bonding is the most versatile of all, producing common liquids and gases, including water. Covalent bonding is also the basis of organic chemistry because of the versatility of carbon, which requires four additional electrons to complete its outer shell. Carbon can also bond with itself so that it has the ability to form tens of thousands of compounds: over 90 percent of all known compounds contain carbon. Carbon is also the key element in the chemistry of life.

Our world and the universe itself are the result of the bonding interactions of about 100 chemical elements. Atoms of these elements in combination display distinctive physical and chemical qualities. Differences of temperature and pressure produce different states of matter — solid, liquid and gaseous and plasma. Change occurs — chemical reactions, changes of states of matter and phase transformations — through the rearrangement of the submicroscopic structure of molecules and atoms.

3. Atomic Physics

Toward the end of the nineteenth century, there was confidence that the physical and chemical sciences had reached a plateau and there was little left to discover. In 1894 Michelson suggested that we now understood the laws of nature, and only a period of consolidation remained; no far-reaching discoveries were possible.

This comfortable consensus was overturned with the discovery of the electron by J.J. Thomson in 1899. Thomson succeeded in measuring the mass of mysterious rays that were observed being emitted from the cathodes (negative electrodes) in vacuum tubes. Because these "corpuscles," as he called them, had only about one two-thousandth of the mass of a hydrogen atom, he concluded they must be "part of the original atom getting free ... from the original atom."[26] Soon these corpuscles were dubbed electrons, the Greek word for amber. The atom was after all *not* the smallest unit in nature; there were smaller particles still! Indeed, the term atom, which in Greek means "indivisible," is a misnomer.

Thomson constructed a picture of what he thought the atom looked like, a tiny round ball in which electrons were embedded. This was soon termed the "plum pudding" model of the atom.

Many scientists still refused to believe atoms really existed, however. They had never been actually seen; perhaps they were simply convenient constructs of reality. These doubts were quelled by Einstein's 1905 paper on Brownian motion in which he refined Avogadro's number and provided "evidence of the existence of atoms of finite size."[27] Atoms were first viewed by electron microscopes only beginning in the 1980s.

In 1886 the French scientist Henri Becquerel had accidentally discovered what we now call radioactivity when he left some uranium salts lying about. Later scientists led by Marie Curie (nee Sklodowska, 1867–1934) and her husband, Pierre Curie (1859–1906), investigated and found an unsuspected new source of energy emitted spontaneously from the interior of certain atoms that were radioactive.[28] In 1913 Ernest Rutherford (1871–1937) used one of the products of radioactive decay — alpha particles emitted from radium, one of the radioactive elements found in nature — as tiny bullets aimed at a piece of gold foil. To his astonishment, about 1 in 1000 of the alpha particles bounced back instead of passing through the foil. This led to the idea that the interior of the atom must contain a nucleus. Accordingly Rutherford posited a solar system model for the structure of the atom with a nucleus in the center surrounded by circling, planetary electrons. Further development of this model led to the discovery that the atomic nucleus contains a positively charged particle, the proton, which balances the negatively charged electron, and a particle with neutral charge, the neutron.[29] Surprisingly, however, these particles have very little mass; over 97 percent of the atom is empty space.

The discovery of the nucleus of the atom and its constituents led in turn to the development of nuclear physics and nuclear chemistry, what is commonly called nuclear fission and fusion. Einstein's Theory of Special Relativity proved that matter and energy are aspects of a single reality, and that in accordance with the equation $E = mc^2$, mass converts into energy so that matter is a practical source of great quantities of energy. Nuclear fission is the basis of technologies that have great danger and destructive power, but also constructive uses that range from generating electricity to medical treatments. Nuclear fusion may one day provide a new and important source of energy to power daily human life.

The true idea of the atom was not confirmed, however, until after the bizarre concept of the quantum was uncovered. This is the idea that all energy and matter — perhaps space and time itself — exist not as the continuities we experience but rather as tiny quanta.

The Quantum Revolution

1. Quantum Mechanics

The insight that light takes the form of a wave of electromagnetic energy led to studies of the way light interacts with matter. As we have seen, a material object can absorb light, and a "black body" (such as asphalt) has the most capacity for absorption. Beginning in 1895, Max Planck (1858–1947), professor of theoretical physics at the University of Berlin, experimented with black bodies in order to determine mathematically the frequencies of radiated energy and entropy. He found that in order to match his calculations with the experimental data he had to include a certain "fudge factor," that was the ratio of a certain quantum of energy to its frequency.[30] This was puzzling since it was assumed that energy was continuous and indivisible. Albert Einstein took this up in describing the photoelectric effect,[31] one of his famous 1905 papers, and made Planck's constant a property of nature, h, which he factored into his calculations. This was the beginning of the so-called quantum revolution. Planck's constant means that energy, like matter, comes in small, discrete packets. Einstein calculated that when an atom absorbed or emitted electromagnetic energy, it would be in discrete units that were multiples of v (frequency) × h, Planck's constant. Incredibly, light and all electromagnetic energy had properties of both waves and particles *at the same time.*

It was not long before the concept of the quantum changed the way physicists viewed the atom. A fundamental flaw in the Rutherford solar system atomic model was the question, what prevented the orbiting electrons with their negative charges, from plummeting instantaneously into the nucleus with its positive charge? Applying the quantum approach, the Danish scientist Neils Bohr (1882–1962) suggested that orbital electrons occupy stable and specific orbital shells within the atom and radiate energy only when they change orbits. Wolfgang Pauli (1900–1955) added an exclusion principle: there are a maximum number of free electrons that can be in orbit in any of the atomic shells. This was the Bohr Model of the atom, which was confirmed by spectrographic analysis. The Bohr atomic model is based on the idea that electron orbits are energy states and so electrons must be found only in certain of these orbits by the application of quantum rules. In 1924 Louis de Broglie (1892–1987) proposed that electrons themselves — indeed all matter — has wave as well as particle properties in accordance with Planck's constant.[32] In 1926 mathematical models of the behavior of electrons in atoms were worked out independently by both Erwin Schrödinger (1887–1961) and Werner Heisenberg (1901–1976). All matter and energy is quantized according to the equation $E = h$ (Planck's constant) × f(frequency); thus, there is a proportionality between frequency and energy. Wave-particle duality is expressed by the formula h divided by m (mass) × v (velocity).

Schrödinger and Heisenberg's models predict how electrons can randomly change orbits, emitting particles of energy called photons when going into a lower orbit and absorbing a photon when changing to a higher orbit. Both frequencies and energy levels of photons emitted by transiting electrons can be measured. This is known as quantum mechanics. Nevertheless, these models presented puzzles. The action of electrons was random; no cause could be identified. In addition, we cannot know the both the position of a particle and its momentum. This was termed Heisenberg's Uncertainty Principle. This principle arises because of the wave-particle duality of energy and matter at the quantum level. In 1929 Bohr and Heisenberg collaborated to produce what is still called the Copenhagen Interpretation of Quantum Mechanics, the idea that nature operates probabilistically, and we can never picture ultimate reality because our everyday concepts are not adequate to the task. This was profoundly disturbing to Einstein[33] who believed that reality was subject to conceptualization even at the smallest levels. This controversy is still unresolved, and continues to haunt us. In any case, the quantum revolution along with radioactivity and relativity shattered the deterministic, mechanistic universe of nineteenth century science.

2. Quantum Electrodynamics (QED)

In 1929 the English physicist Paul A.M. Dirac incorporated special relativity into quantum mechanics to accommodate interactions between light and atomic structures, especially the electron. Dirac's model immediately raised eyebrows. First, Dirac's equations for the energy states of electrons posited negative as well as positive solutions. This set off a search for an electron with a positive charge, and this was discovered in 1932 by two teams of researchers. This was the first indication of the existence of antimatter in the form of counterparts to subatomic particles. We now know that all particles have opposites of this kind with quantum properties.

Dirac's work confirmed that electrons are energy particles that have the ability spontaneously to emit or absorb photons as they change energy states. Wave-particle duality coupled with relativity theory led Dirac to depict the electron as a mathematical probability curve, whose position and velocity simultaneously involves many possibilities. Rather than a point, an electron is best described as a cloud-like wave of possibilities. The precise position of an electron can be determined by bombarding it with photons; however, this act of measurement will collapse the wave function. In other words, an electron can be pinned down to a particular location, but this destroys the wave. Einstein called this "spooky" because the reason for the collapse cannot be explained.

Even stranger is the concept of entanglement of electrons. QED predicts that if two electrons are produced by the same event and fly off in different directions, they remain somehow connected, so if the property of one is fixed by measurement, this same property would instantaneously be found in the other. This entanglement phenomenon has been demonstrated experimentally with both electrons and photons,[34] but why this occurs is not understood. Either the law of special relativity (excluding instantaneous interaction at a distance) does not hold in this case, or the concept of locality does not apply to these particles, despite the fact that to our eyes they are separated by space and time.

Dirac's work provided the foundation of a new sub-science known as quantum electrodynamics (QED), which was developed by Tomonaga Shinichiro (1906–1979), Julian Schwinger (1918–1994) and Richard Feynman (1918–1988). QED is a comprehensive theory of the interactions of electrons with one another, with the nucleus of the atom and with electromagnetic radiation. QED thus explains at the quantum level almost every kind of happening. QED has proved its worth. Applications of QED principles produced advances in semiconductor technology, and led directly to the invention of the laser and the transistor. QED also enabled scientists to create the chain reactions necessary for nuclear fission and the science of nuclear physics. As for the strangeness of QED operation, most scientists (although not Einstein) argue that it makes no difference that we do not understand how it works or that we cannot reconcile it with the picture idea of reality; what is important is that it works and provides coherent knowledge. This pragmatic view of quantum science still dominates today.

QED was instrumental in identifying two new forces of nature,[35] both associated with the nucleus of the atom. Experiments established that the nucleus, which is made up of bundles of protons and neutrons, is held together by nature's strongest force, about one hundred times as strong as the electromagnetic force. The force that holds the nucleus of atoms together is called the strong force. It is very strong indeed — but only over very short distances. When the atomic nucleus contains too many particles, the strong force is not strong enough to prevent the emissions of particles we call radioactivity.

Observing beta decay in atoms led to the discovery of what is called the weak force, which is the force that holds the neutron within the atomic nucleus. The weak force takes its name from the fact that neutrons are inherently unstable; they tend to transform into a proton, an electron and a third small, uncharged particle called a neutrino. When this happens so-called beta radiation occurs, which is a variant of the electromagnetic force. This weak force succeeds in keeping neutrons stable, at least most of the time. But this weak force is overcome when the atomic nucleus is very large; this explains the beta radiation given off by certain larger atoms such as radium.

3. Quantum Chromodynamics (QCD)

The next step in the quantum revolution was to investigate a new series of subatomic particles that were showing up in what are called atom smashers, ever-larger facilities that have the ability to focus high energy particles onto target atoms to dissolve the atoms into their subatomic constituencies.

One such machine, CERN (the European Center for Nuclear Research), with a track measuring 27 kilometers, is located in Switzerland. A new facility, the Large Hadron Collider (LHC), located on the Franco-Swiss border near Geneva, is currently being built as a factory for the production and study of subatomic particles.

The identification and analysis of these subatomic particles is known as quantum chromodynamics (QCD). Due to efforts by thousands of scientists in many countries (perhaps most famous is the American Murray Gell-Mann), the so-called Standard Model is a comprehensive theory that identifies the basic subatomic particles in nature and specifies how they interact. This Standard Model, which has been called "the most successful theory of nature in history,"[36] was developed over the last three decades of the twentieth century. The two categories of particles in the Standard Model are called fermions and bosons. Fermions include quarks (also called hadrons), the main particles in the atomic nucleus, and leptons, very light particles such as the electron, and the three kinds of neutrinos (mu, tau, and the electron neutrino). Bosons are force-carrying particles: the photon, the carrier of the electromagnetic force; the gluon, the carrier of the strong force; W and Z particles, which carry the weak force; and the mysterious Higgs boson, which is postulated but not yet discovered. On the subatomic level these particles interact with one another, change, are created and destroyed. These interactions occur primarily between fermions and bosons — the force-carrying particles are either emitted or absorbed upon contact with various fermions.

Intensive research has established that all the reality we observe — trees and birds to stars and galaxies — consists of atoms whose nucleus consists of varying triplets of quarks — protons are two up quarks and a down quark; neutrons are one up quark, two down quarks and the electron-neutrino bound together by gluons and W and Z particles. Outside the nucleus, electrons (a kind of lepton) complete the structure of the atom; the number of electrons also varies with the element involved.

Mass is imparted to the universe we observe through constant interactions between fermions and the Higgs field that are thought to permeate the universe. This Higgs field consists of bosons that interact with the other particles, imparting mass like a person walking through high grass. Mass also arises from the at-rest value of quarks as well as the motion of quarks and gluons within the atomic nucleus.

The matter we discern with our eyes and scientific instruments is apparently only about one-sixth of the matter in the universe and only about 5 percent of the total mass-energy of the universe. Most (70 percent) of the mass-energy of the universe is so-called dark energy, a mysterious force that scientists surmise must be powering the rapid cosmological expansion our instruments observe. One-half of 1 percent of the universe consists of neutrinos, particles with a tiny mass that are by-products of ongoing atomic reactions — mainly in stars such as our sun, the waste energy from radioactive (beta) decay. About a quarter of the mass-energy of the universe is a mysterious dark matter we cannot see but we identify from its gravitational effects.

Although the Standard Model is regarded as tested and true, most physicists believe it to be only a special case of an even more elaborate theory of reality known as the Supersymmetric Standard Model (SSM). The principal reason for believing the Standard Model is incomplete is the fact that, while there are 17 subatomic particles, only six plus the Higgs boson are necessary to generate all the reality of the world we observe. The SSM accounts for the seemingly missing particles by positing that every known particle must have a superpartner particle related to it by supersymmetry — every fermion has a boson superpartner and vice versa. The Standard Model also identifies what is called a second generation of four fermions that mirror the fermions of our world — these are the charm quark, the strange quark, the muon and the mu-neutrino. There is also a third generation of fermions: the top quark, the bottom quark, the tau and the tau-neutrino. These two additional families of particles must have the capacity to interact with the massless bosons — photons and gluons — and may also encounter slightly different Higgs fields as well, just like the first generation of particles.

Supersymmetry is based on the idea that if the universe began as a Big Bang, there should have evolved equal parts matter and antimatter. Supersymmetry seeks to explain where the antimatter is hiding. Supersymmetry may also disclose that at high enough energy levels the three quantum forces — the strong force, weak force and electromagnetism — all coincide. At a somewhat higher energy level gravity may also assume an identical value with these quantum forces. Thus, what appears to be different forces in nature may really be just one force that manifests itself in different values.

Supersymmetry may also explain the mysterious dark matter of the universe. A prevailing idea is that superpartner particles are unstable and decay into the lowest mass possible, a phantom substance which is called the Lightest Superpartner or LSP. This instability and decay may be the reason we cannot readily detect this type of mass-energy.

LSP and Supersymmetry may complete the standard model, but they do not tell us why there are three families of particles in the first place. What is still to be discovered is a theory that explains the reasons for all of the particles of the Standard Model (as well as the SSM) and also gives us a quantum theory of all of the forces in nature including gravity. One promising candidate for this task is called string theory, which holds that all the subatomic particles we observe are really tiny one-dimensional vibrating loops or strings. We cannot see these strings because they are unimaginably tiny — about Planck length, 10^{-33} centimeters or less than a billionth of a billionth of the size of an atomic nucleus.

The mathematics of string theory requires that each string must vibrate in ten space-time dimensions, which means there must be six more dimensions to reality than the four of the space-time that we experience. This idea is attractive because, according to mathematical calculations put forward many years ago by Theodor Kaluza and Oskar Klein, gravity and electromagnetism, which appear to be related because both fall off inversely proportional to the distance from their source, turn out identical equations in a five dimensional universe. If these extra dimensions exist, where are they hiding? Physicists speculate that they are too small to have come to our attention. But if string theory is correct — and no one knows if it is — the existence of these hidden dimensions and its associated energy leads to the fanciful idea that there must be hundreds of independent directions, not just the four — north, south, east and west — that we experience. These hundreds of directions lead some physicists to posit that there must be a whole landscape of universes, each coexisting side by side with the others, each unaware of the others' existence. Our universe, which is about 20 billion light-years in diameter, may well be just one small region in this larger landscape of countless universes.

The holy grail of QCD is to achieve a Theory of Everything (TOE), a set of equations that will show how all the forces of nature are really one, and all matter and energy are aspects of that single force. One of the most eminent physicists of our time, Stephen Hawking (born 1942), has famously said that if we succeed in our quest for a theory of everything, "we will know the mind of God." But is this correct? It seems disingenuous to say that resolving any of the current mysteries of theoretical physics will bring us any closer to God. Indeed, wrapping everything up into one simple TOE would seem to have the opposite effect — we could then declare the end of science as well as the end of mystery in the world. But the end of science has been predicted many times and has always been terribly wrong. Instead, we find that every new scientific discovery, each new scientific theory merely multiplies our questions and the mystery of reality. This is consistent with the idea that the divine is the inconceivable and the indefinable. What brings us into contact with the divine is the unfathomable and continuing mystery of the universe, not the dissipation or disappearance of mystery.

Astronomy

1. Stars

In the view of medieval natural philosophy the stars we see in the nighttime sky were all contained in the same plane of one of the highest heavens, and this entire plane was believed to rotate in a perfect circle around the Earth. What a different conception of the stars we have today! People in the nineteenth century believed that, because of their distance from Earth, we could never know much about the stars, but in the twentieth century this view was disproved, and we now know more than ever could be imagined one hundred years ago. We are now able to (1) measure the distances of the stars from Earth with reasonable accuracy; (2) measure their motion from the so-called Doppler shift of the spectrum of light they emit; (3) know their temperature and composition from mass spectroscopy; (4) establish measures of brightness giving an idea of their total energy output; and (5) estimate the mass of a star from its motion in relation to other celestial bodies. New kinds of telescopes and measuring tools make close observation of distant stars possible as never before.

Stars, which are mainly composed of hydrogen, are powered by atomic fusion reactions deep within their cores. Hydrogen fusion produces first deuterium, an ion of hydrogen, and then helium plus a tremendous amount of energy. Astronomers categorize the great variety of stars on the basis of their surface temperatures (brightness) and their output of energy.[37] Our sun is one of a common type known as a main sequence star. Based on its rate of hydrogen burning, astronomers predict that in several billion years, the sun will build up helium in its core, and hydrogen reactions will take place farther and farther toward its surface. At some point this will cause the sun to greatly expand to become what is called a red giant, engulfing Mercury and Venus and making the Earth uninhabitable. Then the helium within the sun's core will fuse to produce the element carbon-12, and the atomic fusion process will slow so the sun will contract into what is called a white dwarf, an old-age star that will slowly cool according to the Second Law of Thermodynamics.

Many stars are either much smaller or much larger than our sun. Much smaller stars burn hydrogen more slowly and simply burn on for perhaps one hundred billion years before heat-death occurs. Stars that are larger than the sun will have a much more eventful life span. Hydrogen and helium burning under tremendous pressures will produce elements heavier than carbon in the core: oxygen, magnesium, in fact all the elements up to iron-56, which is as far as it can go. At this point the nuclear fires will dramatically slow, causing the star first to collapse and then to explode to become what we call a supernova. The collapse of a supernova fuses atomic nuclei with such force that every element in the Periodic Table is formed and then is flung out in all directions into space. This material serves as raw material for future stars and solar systems, such as our own. It is believed that our own solar system (including, of course, planet Earth) was formed about 4.6 billion years ago through the consolidation of material from supernova explosions. So the material which now makes up the Earth, particularly the heavier elements, including, of course, the elements that make up the human body, were formed in the stars billions of years ago.

The remnants of an exploding supernova will also eventually collapse into an object of incredible density. Depending on the mass involved, this will either form a neutron star that will rotate very rapidly because of its strong magnetic field, emitting radio signals called pulsars, or the collapse will produce an object of such great gravitational force so as to form a black hole, a point from which no matter or energy, not even light, can escape.

2. Galaxies

Only in the twentieth century with improved technologies was it possible to solve the mystery of objects in the sky that appear as fuzzy masses. The American Edwin Hubble (1889–1953) was most responsible for establishing that these nebula are actually gravitationally bound collections of sometimes billions of stars. We now call these objects galaxies, and we now know that our own solar system is located in an arm of one of these galaxies we call the Milky Way. Even these huge galaxies seem to be arranged as part of a larger structure of galaxy groups. Ongoing work seeks to map the major galaxy structures. It is estimated that there are at least 50 billion galaxies in the universe, and each of these contains from tens to hundreds of billions of stars. The scale of the universe is clearly beyond all human imagining.

2. Cosmology

The discovery of galaxies and the application of quantum theory and general relativity have made possible new theories about the origin and fate of the universe, theories of which have been termed since ancient times cosmology. At present the dominant theory as to the origin of the universe is known as the Big Bang. This is the idea that the universe came into existence at one moment in time (before this moment there literally could be no time) in a burst of incredible energy and immediately underwent and is still undergoing expansion. This Big Bang was not an explosion into preexisting space, however, because prior to the Big Bang there was no space or time.

The Big Bang is a creation myth of our own time. Current models have it that the entire universe began as a tiny speck of some primal substance (or energy) the size — perhaps (no one really knows) — of an atom. For some unknown reason an unimaginable event occurred — we think of it as an explosion but this is inadequate to describe what occurred — that caused this primal substance to expand. In the beginning of this process the two elemental worlds of general relativity — the modern theory of gravity — and quantum mechanics, which today operate in totally different domains, must have been unified into one mysterious force. Their separation was responsible for an enormous release of energy that caused the universe to undergo sudden inflation to an enormous size in less than a trillionth of a second. The matter that was uniformly distributed during the first microseconds of the Big Bang now exhibited slight imperfections, a clumping together caused by the physics of quantum mechanics. The elemental particles of the Standard Model were formed as the universe began to cool — first the force particles and then quarks and leptons darted in and out of existence in a primal soup of matter and antimatter. Then for some unknown reason the matter-antimatter symmetry was broken, and matter as we know it began to appear. The forces that keep matter together — the strong force, the weak force and electromagnetism began their effect, and when the universe cooled to 3000 degrees (about 400,000 years after the Big Bang), the first atoms — hydrogen and helium — were formed and universe became transparent and filled with light as photons no longer scattered but took paths dictated by general relativity. The galaxies of our universe tend to be found at the points of the original primal clumps of material, now stretched to distances of up to 500 million light years apart.

Evidence for the Big Bang comes from three sources. First, Edwin

Hubble established in the 1920s that light from almost all galaxies is shifted towed the red end of the spectrum. This is called the Doppler Effect, and its meaning is that galaxies throughout the universe are receding from us and from one another. Hubble also found that the most distant galaxies are moving the fastest, according to a law (Hubble's Law) that states velocity = a constant H (Hubble's constant) times distance.

A second form of evidence is the universal background of microwave radiation found throughout the universe (we see this as static on our television screens). This radiation — photons which continue to cool — is thought to be a remnant of the Big Bang.

Third, measurements of the relative amounts of light elements in the universe are thought to confirm the Big Bang. Hydrogen and helium represent over 99 percent of all the matter in the universe. These are the elements formed in the Big Bang. Heavier elements are much rarer; these are formed in the centers of stars which release them into the universe during their death throes.

The current estimate for how long ago this event occurred is about 13.7 billion years ago. This is worked out by the application of Hubble's constant and the general theory of relativity. Such calculations reveal anomalies, however, that the total gravitational force operating in the universe is much greater than the amount of visible matter. Cosmologists posit therefore the existence of a strange dark matter that we have not yet discovered. This dark matter may make up over 90 percent of the mass of the universe.

The ultimate fate of the universe is also the subject of speculation. Current thinking based on the discovery of cosmic expansion is that the universe is theoretically infinite and accelerating expansion (beginning about 5 billion years ago) will continue so that everything will grow more and more apart — a lonely universe is this prospect. There could even occur what is called the Big Rip, a hyper speedup of the current expansion. Another scenario is a slowing or an ultimate collapse — the Big Crunch powered by gravity. Another unlikely case is a steady state universe that stabilizes at some point. In any case continued expansion will result in heat death some untold trillions of years from now. Of course, no one really knows.

Theories of the Earth

The Earth sciences have also experienced revolutionary changes during the past 300 years. The European and western worldview until the eighteenth century was to accept the biblical account of creation as literal truth. James Ussher (1581–1656), archbishop of Armagh (Ireland) and vice chancellor of Trinity College, Dublin, deduced specific dates for key biblical events: God created the world on Sunday, October 22, 4004 BC; Adam and Eve were driven from Paradise on November 10, 4004 BC; and Noah's ark touched Mount Ararat after the flood on May 5, 2348 BC.[38] While most natural philosophers hesitated to get this specific, the general idea was to look for support of the biblical creation account in the natural world.

Only in the eighteenth century were there conjectures that the Earth might be somewhat older than 5700 years or so. In France Benoit de Maillet, who served as ambassador to Egypt and knew Arab culture, published a posthumous work, *Telliamed* (1748), in which the main character, an "Indian" (so a non–Christian), speculated that originally the Earth was covered with waters that gradually diminished, and that fish developed the ability to use their fins as feet so they could live on dry land.[39] Another Frenchman, Georges-Louis Leclerc, known as the Comte de Buffon, published his book, *Epochs of Creation* (1778), speculating that the Earth was formed when a comet struck the sun, and that life appeared only some 33,000 years later; and humans only 70,000 years after the appearance of life on Earth. This was the first idea of different ages or epochs in prehistory and that the Earth was in fact quite ancient. In 1795 James Hutton reported to the Royal Society of Scotland his conclusions that the Earth in fact had undergone "equable and steady" changes due to its internal heat over a long period of time.

In the nineteenth century a consensus developed at least among scientists that the Earth was very old. The study of fossils and rock strata convinced scientists that the Earth had changed greatly over time. A debate developed between experts who thought the cause of the Earth's features such as mountains and rivers was primarily due to volcanic activity or was the effect of waters. This controversy between the Vulcanists and the Neptunists as the contending sides were called, was settled by Oxford don William Buckland (1784–1856), who established both volcanoes and waters changed the Earth's surface in different ways.[40]

Only in the mid–twentieth century was it established that the Earth is about 4.6 billion years old, as is the solar system itself, and the prehistory of the Earth can be divided into different characteristic periods of several hundred million years each. In the 1960s came the plate tectonics revolution, establishing that the Earth's surface is composed of about a dozen tectonic plates, relatively thin slabs of rock only tens of kilometers thick but thousands of kilometers wide. These plates, which were once joined into a super-continent called Pangea, have the capacity to drift thousands of kilometers on the geological time scale, opening oceans when they drift apart, and forming mountains when they crash together. Areas where different plates are now coming together are zones of earthquakes and volcanoes, such as the Pacific Rim's ring of fire. In some places the plate boundaries meet in mid-ocean. This is the case in the Atlantic where new crust is being formed at the Mid-Atlantic Ridge plate boundary. Evidence for the theory of plate tectonics comes from (1) the shapes of continents that face each other, particularly North and South America and Africa, which fit together like pieces of a puzzle: (2) matching deposits of fossils and rock types; (3) the distribution of earthquake and volcanic activity; and (4) matching sea floor magnetic data to plate movements.

The Life Sciences

1. The Birth of Biology

We finally come to the life sciences, Darwinism and evolution. There are three reasons for leaving this to last. First, the scientific study of living things was the last of our modern sciences to be incorporated into the corpus of what is now considered scientific knowledge. The term biology was not even invented until the nineteenth century. Second, the revolutionary nature of Darwin's theory of evolution cannot be fully appreciated except against the background of the many other revolutions and developments in the scientific world. Third, the impact of the life sciences on religious sensibilities has been more pronounced than in any other scientific field. This is no doubt because of the close relationship of biological evolution with the creation of mankind and what many see is a direct assault on religious doctrine; in the case of the other scientific fields the impact on religious views is less direct.

Biology was the last of the sciences to develop because it was settled doctrine that every kind of living thing, including man, had come into being as the result of a single act of divine creation. God had created a great chain of being that included the plants, animal, mankind and the angels of heaven and hell. Life was therefore fundamentally different from the rest of the natural world. While the heavens and bodies on earth could be subject to mechanical laws, life could be explained only as a mysterious, supernatural life-force.

At the turn of the eighteenth century the German philosopher Friedrich Schelling (1775–1854) asserted the idea that living things follow a different path of organic development, a process that originates from within, generated by a life-force, which oversees the orderly development of constituent parts into a coherent whole. In his *System of Transcendent Idealism* (1800) he extended this idea even to the physical world; he asserted the idea that the natural world and its processes are suffused with Mind, and that Nature is Mind in the process of becoming conscious as a World Soul. This view became the basis of German idealism and the movement known as romanticism, which flourished in Europe in the first three decades of the nineteenth century. The Romantic Movement in philosophy, art and literature reflected the idea of the unique qualities of living things that were somehow exempt from the mechanical, deterministic world depicted by classical physics.

The idea of what is now called evolution was first put forward in the eighteenth century by French natural philosophers, who espoused what they called the transformism of living things. This was preceded by four important new developments. First, close study of the classification of living things led the Swedish taxonomist Carl Linnaeus[41] to conclude that some species were the result of natural hybridization occurring in nature. The systematic classification of living things brought into question the Great Chain of Being idea of creation. Second, studies of embryos showed how organs and new living things could develop out of an undifferentiated mass of material. Embryos of different species went through a similar process of development in early stages.[42] Third, the new theories of the Earth discussed in the preceding section gave rise to the realization that if the Earth was millions of years old, life too must be much older than the biblical accounts of creation assumed. Fourth, the systematic study of rocks and rock formations led to the serious study of fossils and the realization that these are the remains of creatures that lived long ago. For the first time fossilized remains of large prehistoric creatures — dinosaurs as well as mammoths and mastodons — were discovered and studied. It was evident that animals and plants living in the past were in some cases at least, very different from those living today.

Georges Cuvier (1769–1832), a leading member of the French Academy of Sciences, a pioneer in the study of fossils, developed the theory of catastrophism to explain the fact that life forms that existed in earlier times are no longer with us. In Cuvier's view, although God had originally created all the species that had ever lived or would ever live, various catastrophes occurring before recorded history had destroyed certain life forms so they no longer exist today. Cuvier thus excluded transformism, the idea that new forms of life had evolved over time. But his theory posed difficult new questions: for example, why would God permit catastrophes to destroy part of His creation?

Opposed to Cuvier's ideas were the views of Jean-Baptiste Lamarck (1744–1829), who was the first to put forward a full-blown theory of transformism — evolution. Lamarck believed that the older species of living things Cuvier said were extinct still exist, but that they had changed over time. In his book, *Zoological Philosophy* (1809) he rejected catastrophism as "too convenient" an explanation. Instead, Lamarck claimed that life had emerged by "spontaneous generation" through the action of heat, water and electricity, and that living things possess an internal drive — a "power of life" — so that they become more complex over time. This means that living things spontaneously react to their environment by using certain organs or capabilities and neglecting others. Through use and disuse organisms change and adapt over time. For example, the long neck of the giraffe was an acquired characteristic developed from long periods of stretching to reach the leaves of trees for food. Lamarck assumed that the characteristics acquired through use could be inherited.

Lamarck's sensational ideas were extremely controversial, but they were perhaps decisive to a changed conception of living things. In the history of ideas a corner was turned and several new conceptions emerged. First, at this time the word biology was coined to denote a new field of study: the science of life and living things. Lamarck had showed that living things developed according to certain natural laws that could be studied systematically. Second, although Lamarck himself was not an atheist, his account of creation omits the direct intervention of a creator God. In fact, Lamarck's ideas imply that the deistic explanation of the natural forces of the universe can be carried over to living things. Life forms also can be explained by the operation of impersonal natural laws. Not much later appeared a best seller that made this explicit: *The Vestiges of the Natural History of Creation* (1844), published anonymously,[43] was read and discussed by virtually everybody by mid-century. Its controversial thesis was that the traditional religious ways of thinking were simply no longer adequate to understand the natural world. Rather, natural laws ruled in nature and with respect to living things as well. People should face up to the fact that life had originated through operation of natural laws and had developed naturalistically from primitive to ever more complex forms. God was not excluded,[44] but was reduced to the impersonal deistic creator who was not directly involved in the world.

The stage was now set for Charles Darwin and his controversial book, *On the Origin of Species* (1859).[45]

2. Darwinism

As is well-known, Charles Darwin (1809–1882) conceived his basic ideas about evolutionary change during his five-year voyage around the world (1831–1836) as naturalist aboard the H.M.S. *Beagle*. Although he disagreed fundamentally with Lamarck, Darwin hesitated to publish his ideas because he was well aware of the controversy they would provoke. Only after he received a letter in 1858 from Alfred Russel Wallace containing ideas similar to his own did Darwin decide to publish *On the Origin of Species* in 1859.[46]

The argument in *On the Origin of Species* is straightforward. Evolution, or as Darwin says, descent with modification, is a fact of the natural world; all living things are descended from common ancestors. What Darwin sets out is how this is possible — the mechanisms of evolution. First, taking his cue from Thomas Malthus, *Essay on the Principle of Population* (in several editions from 1798 to 1830), Darwin maintained that in all species more individuals are produced than can possibly survive given natural constraints of food and other conditions of life. Second, there are natural variations among individuals of the same species; Darwin uses the phrase "individual variability" for this idea. Third, such variations are inheritable; Darwin put this idea forward without understanding the exact mechanism of inheritance, but he observed that a second form of variation exists in this area: variation in reproductive success among individuals of a species.

Chapters 3 and 4 of *On the Origin* are devoted to Darwin's key idea: natural selection. He posits a struggle for survival, but this idea is widely misunderstood. There is a struggle for survival in the ecological sense: each individual will seek out the best possible ecological niche that is within its capabilities to exploit. This will be the niche with the fewest competitors. Natural selection, then, leads to adaptive evolution: the ecological struggle for survival will produce heritable variations in subsequent generations that are linked with reproductive success. What is more, this competition leads to divergence and a tree-like pattern of new species. "Survival of the fittest" (a phrase Darwin was reluctant to employ but favored by Wallace) will not lead necessarily to extinctions, but rather to heritable variations that are useful as far as reproductive success is concerned, and most likely such reproductive success will correlate with an ability to exploit new habitat niches where competition is lighter. Given the passage of long periods of time, which Darwin took from his study of Charles Lyell's *Principles of Geology* (1831–1833),[47] many new species will evolve from a common ancestor. The key event in species formation is the loss of the ability to interbreed.

Today, almost 150 years after the publication of *On the Origin*, Darwin's theory of evolution through natural selection is regarded as basically correct.[48] What is the evidence for evolution? First, the fossil record, while incomplete, shows many indisputable evolutionary sequences. In addition, fossils establish the appearance of life in the form of one-celled organisms some 3.8 billion years ago. It is believed that all life on Earth evolved from the earliest of these primitive life forms. Second, embryonic development shows that all life has the same basic development and exhibits the same basic structures (homology). Third, comparative anatomy shows that many vestigial organs exist such as the human appendix and tailbone. Fourth, we now understand the mechanisms of heredity and can observe evolution in process, for example in the case of bacteria that evolve immunity to drugs such as antibiotics.

One important aspect of his theory continued to puzzle Darwin until the end of his life — how are the traits and characteristics of parents passed on to their offspring? Darwin accurately observed that in inheritance, as a general rule, like begets like, but there are variations on which the mechanism of selection can operate. But what explains these variations? And if what passes from generation to generation was, as Darwin believed, fluids of inheritance, one from the male and another from the female, how when these combine can result variations of one parent rather than the other and, stranger still, traits not found in either parent? And why do these variations persist rather than being simply blended away in subsequent generations?

Subsequent to Darwin's work, the mechanisms of heredity were elucidated in three stages. First, the botanist and monk Gregor Mendel (1822–1884) developed descriptive laws of heredity through his experiments in the cross-breeding of pea plants. Mendel posited the existence of atoms of inheritance as carriers of heredity. Second, the discovery that every living thing is made of what we call cells led to observations of cell division through the process of mitosis, in which one cell becomes two identical daughter cells. Third, molecular biology established that the nucleus of every cell contains specialized molecules we call chromosomes, which are made of various proteins and deoxyribonucleic acid (DNA), Mendel's laws were correlated to the behavior of these chromosomes early in the twentieth century by the American biologist Walter Sutton (1877–1916), who discovered and named the gene as the fundamental unit of heredity. In 1953 James Watson and Francis Crick, working in the Cavendish Laboratory at the University of Cambridge, solved the riddle of the structure of DNA after viewing an x-ray diffraction pattern in a photo of DNA taken by Rosalind Franklin of King's College, London. The DNA molecule — shaped as a double helix — contains the genetic code for each form of life. And together with ribonucleic acid (RNA), DNA synthesizes the many proteins that are the building blocks of life.

Darwin's puzzlement about the mechanism of inheritance is now explained: inheritance is based not upon fluids but upon particles; and the genetic instructions contained in these particles are distinct from the traits they produce. Specific attributes are not passed from generation to generation; rather what passes are genes with their encoded instructions. Heredity is not mixing and blending of parental characteristics.

Moreover, all living things share the same basic genetic mechanism. Every human cell contains twenty-three pairs of chromosomes, each containing a sequence of many genes. Early in the twenty-first century the human genome was mapped, and genetic engineering is now commonplace. This advance has great potential to cure disease and to develop better varieties of plants and animals, but is also fraught with difficult and controversial moral questions.

Darwin's theory of evolution by natural selection has so far proved its worth. Attempts to undermine it are not convincing. Calling evolution a theory does not mean there is no scientific evidence that it is true. The reason we call evolution a theory is to distinguish it from a mathematical law. Unlike gravity or the second law of motion, natural selection cannot be reduced to a law of nature. So it is called a theory. Another argument against natural selection is that it cannot explain so-called irreducible complexity, the idea that some organisms and structures are simply too complex to have evolved. But this objection was anticipated by Darwin and answered in *On the Origin* itself. Taking the example of the eye, Darwin argued that by means of small changes over a great enough period of time, an organ of great complexity could evolve. Modern research on the origins of eyes has proved him right.[49] The eye, in fact, evolved in many different forms on different occasions.

Another objection to evolution is that the fossil record has gaps. Of course this is to be expected since only a tiny fraction of ancient life was preserved by chance in fossil forms. Yet, many fossil sequences have been identified as demonstrations of evolution.[50] Still another objection is made from a probabilistic standpoint — that the odds against natural selection producing a human being are infinitesimal. This shows a misunderstanding of Darwin's theory. The point of natural selection is that it operates randomly;

reproductive success is the basic driver. There is no aim to reach any final state or stage of progress or perfection. Traits do not even evolve for the good of the species. Thus concepts of progress, odds and probabilities are irrelevant.

Of course the randomness of evolution gives no comfort. Although Darwin was not arguing against God or religion, his theory implies the exclusion of intelligent design and creationism.[51] The randomness of natural selection is also contrary to the principles of classical physics and its picture of a deterministic, mechanical world. Evolution has more in common with modern physics, which posits the operation of chance as dominant in the atomic and quantum worlds. Ironically, Darwin himself did not accept the full implications of his randomness hypothesis. In the 1859 version of *Origin of Species* (p. 131) he says: "I have hitherto spoken as if the variations — so common and multiform in organic beings under domestication, and in a lesser degree in those in a state of nature — had been due to chance. This, of course, is a wholly incorrect expression, but it serves to acknowledge plainly our ignorance of the causes of each particular variation." This sentence shows that Darwin — like Pierre Laplace — was in fact a determinist in that he believed that nothing really happens by chance but is the necessary result of the operation of natural laws. Chance for Darwin was merely an illusion arising from the finitude of human reason.

But Darwin was acutely aware of the implications of his theory for religion. He knew that many people would regard evolution as a fatal injury to "the pretensions of religion."[52] Darwin himself gave up Christianity when he was forty and referred to himself as agnostic as far as the existence of God was concerned.[53] Two other implications of his theory are perhaps equally controversial. The social reformer Herbert Spencer applied the concept of evolution to social theory and in his book *First Principles*[54] published in 1862 used the term "survival of the fittest" to justify a hands-off approach to less fortunate members of society. Darwin was not comfortable with this extension of his ideas.[55] Another application of Darwinism is evolutionary psychology, much in vogue following the publication in 1975 of E. O. Wilson's book *Sociobiology: The New Synthesis*. Wilson's work raises the question whether evolution can explain human behavior. Although most will concede that evolution influences human behavior, few would make evolution the determining factor. The point was made by Darwin himself in his second most important book, *The Descent of Man*,[56] published in 1871. In the case of man, he maintained, individual decisions and cultural influences may override natural selection.

3. The Descent of Man

Darwin's book on *The Descent of Man* considers the evidence that human beings evolved from ape-like ancestors; he also discusses the possible evolution of mankind's moral, social, and mental faculties, including the development of altruistic behavior.

Modern scientific methods including scientific archaeology and sophisticated ways of dating the past, such as tree-ring dating (useful from the present to 8000 B.C.); radiocarbon dating (accurate from about A.D. 1500 to 40,000 years ago); and potassium argon dating (used from 250,000 years ago to the origin of life), have given us a picture of human evolution that largely confirms Darwin's basic thesis, but differs greatly in the details.

In the early twenty-first century scientists who study human prehistory[57] say there is evidence that humans and our closest living ape-like relatives, chimpanzees, shared a common ancestor but went their separate ways no later than 6.3 million years ago and probably less than 5.4 million years ago. By comparing the genetic codes of humans and chimpanzees it was determined that the split probably occurred after a prolonged period of hybridization (interbreeding) rather than through a quick break.[58] Before this time the details of human evolution are unclear. After this split there is evidence of many varieties of hominids (primates including the earlier human subspecies and their direct ancestors) living on African savannas, an ecological niche not normally occupied by the great apes, who were forest dwellers. Probably they found a home on the savannas because there was no choice — forest cover in Africa had decreased because of climate change. The most numerous of these we call by the name *Australopithicus* (Latin for "southern ape"), which includes the famous "Lucy" (*Australopithicus afarensis*), who lived in East Africa about 3.2 million years ago. About 2.5 million years ago there appeared a tool-making hominid in central Africa, to which paleontologists give the name *Homo hablilis* (Latin for tool-maker).

About 1.9 million years ago appeared modern mankind's direct ancestor, *Homo erectus,* an adventuresome type that left his African homeland and radiated out to settle in small groups over much of Eurasia. (Early forms of *Homo erectus* are also called *Homo ergaster.*) Over time *Homo erectus* split into many several anatomically distinct populations in various parts of the world.

Modern humans (*Homo sapiens sapiens*) apparently evolved in East Africa about 150,000 B.C. Why did this occur? Evolutionary theory posits that small, relatively isolated populations can accelerate change. This may have been the situation responsible for the breakthroughs that created modern humans. Of course, no one knows for sure. But evidence of the African origin of modern humans is derived from analysis of human mitochondrial DNA (MtDNA), a form of DNA that is inherited only through the female line and is passed from mother to offspring. Researchers trace the origins of anatomically modern humans by a regression analysis based on the known rates of MtDNA genetic changes. Evidence for an African origin comes from analysis of the different types of MtDNA found in contemporary human beings. From a sampling of more than 5000 people from all continents, it was found that the greatest diversity in MtDNA is in Africa, an indication that Africa was the earliest home of modern humans.[59] From this Africa homeland modern humans emerged beginning—it is most likely from the fossil evidence—between 85,000 to 60,000 years ago. This migration dispersed waves of *Homo sapiens sapiens* to virtually all areas of the world; the last area in the world to be settled by modern humans was apparently New Zealand, which was not reached until about A.D. 1000.

For almost all of prehistory *Homo sapiens sapiens* lived by hunting and gathering. As late as 10,000 B.C. virtually all humans lived this hunter-gatherer life style. But then occurred what is called the Neolithic Revolution: agriculture and the domestication of animals began somewhere in the Near East and rapidly spread to other areas. Agriculture was almost certainly independently invented as well in areas such as China and the Indus Valley (India and Pakistan). Gradually the entire pattern of human life was radically changed so that by the first century BC most human beings were farmers or pastoralists. In addition, about 5000 years ago (beginning about 3300 BC) relatively sophisticated urban cultures, the invention of writing and civilization appear in ancient Mesopotamia, and a little later in Egypt and Anatolia (Turkey). From this time on, as the saying goes, the rest is history.

Why the Neolithic Revolution took place after so many years of stability is unknown, but undoubtedly factors stimulating the changes included the warming climate after the end of the Ice Age (about 15,000 years ago); more sophisticated language development; and advances in population, culture and technology in certain areas of the world, such as the Near East, Egypt, the Indus Valley, China, and later, in the Americas. In any case, this stunning story of the development of humanity on this planet has only become apparent in the last fifty years with advances in science and archeology that enable us to discover our own species' history for the first time.

Scientific Truth: An Evaluation

From this overview of the state of scientific knowledge at the beginning of the twenty-first century we can see that, although Darwinism and evolution are the focus of one facet of the conflict between science and religion, in fact the conflict runs much deeper. Even before Darwin was born, before the concept of evolution was formulated, scientific thinking caused crisis for faith in God. For this reason, to explore the crisis, we must consider not evolution and its conflict with creationism but rather we must examine the character and meaning of scientific truth itself.

On the one hand, scientific truth is a powerful tool which has proved its worth to provide stunning insights into reality as well as eminently useful knowledge. All of our technology is based on the scientific truths uncovered since the sixteenth century. The scientific method, the primacy of induction and the rigorous testing of hypotheses by objective methods employs a strict criterion for truth — verifiability and falsifiablity. To be scientific a proposition must be capable of being tested in a way that will determine, not whether it is true, but whether it is in any way false. This criterion of truth promotes the idea of a scientific community. Science is a cooperative effort that must be carried on by a community of people all employing the same methods and criteria so that there will be a continual stream of testing and hypothesizing. This insight was expressed by Karl Popper as follows:

> What is important is to realize that in science we are always concerned with explanations, predictions, and tests, and that the method of testing hypotheses is always the same. From the hypothesis to be tested — for example, a universal law — together with some other statements which for this purpose are not considered a problematic — for example, some initial conditions — we deduce some prognosis. We then confront this prognosis, whenever possible, with the results of experiment or other observations. Agreement with them is taken as corroboration of the hypothesis, though not as final proof; clear disagreement is considered as refutation or falsification.[60]

There are many implications of this strict criterion for scientific truth. One pointed out by Popper himself is what he called a "demarcation problem" — that is, to be scientific, a proposition must in principle be testable and falsifiable. But this means that the scientific method excludes from investigation all propositions that are not amenable to measurement. This in turn creates an interesting question: what is the character of a proposition that is not testable and falsifiable?

The beguiling power of the scientific method is such that some have said that any such proposition is simply meaningless. This is the conclusion of scientific materialists and logical positivists.[61] But this cannot possibly be right; it carries the scientific method to the extreme. It is also involves a logical contradiction: the proposition that no scientifically non-testable hypothesis has any meaning is itself not objectively verifiable so it is also a meaningless statement from this point of view. In addition, recall the Three Worlds idea posed at the beginning of this chapter. Science is not objective reality; rather it is an aspect of World Three, a human creation, a body of knowledge based on certain criteria for truth. Science is only one aspect of this World Three; other aspects of World Three have different and equally valid criteria for truth. Even bodies of knowledge closely related to science — the social sciences and mathematics — have somewhat different truth requirements. Still different truth standards are employed in areas such as history, art, literature, philosophy, and — yes — religion. In other words, there are many different criteria for truth in World Three, and all are due respect. Reliance on scientific truth alone is not only wrong, it is disastrous and in the end, as we shall see, impossible. It leaves aside most of what we call human culture without which it is not possible to live a completely human life.

The scientific method also has distinct limitations as far as knowledge of World One, the world of objective reality, is concerned. First, our brief review of the history of science shows constant change and upheaval in our idea of the nature of reality and the laws and natural processes that govern the universe. Such revolutions have occurred in every aspect of science — physics, chemistry, the earth sciences, biology and astronomy. Thomas Kuhn,[62] taking notice of this, formulated the idea that science is a succession of "paradigms," hypothetical models of reality that serve as the basis of "normal science," scientific inquiry into the details of the accepted definition of how reality works. Normal science has always in the past uncovered discrepancies and anomalies, and this has frequently led to the overthrow of a previous paradigm or its relegation to being a special case of reality, and the elaboration of a new paradigm. The history of science demonstrates the constant formulation of new paradigms to explain the world. It would be the height of folly to believe that we have reached the point where the paradigms we now take as true will never be overthrown. Thus, we can never regard science as settled or finalized. Even according to its own criterion of truth, science does not deliver final truth. Every scientific proposition and paradigm must be regarded as tentative and subject to future revision in some presently unknowable way. Thus, the history of science teaches us that it is a mistake to take any particular law or theory of the natural world — World One — as final truth. We do not know what view of the world science will present to those who will be alive in the year 2107 — one hundred years from now, but one thing seems certain: what we take as truth today may be regarded as only a partial special case or even entirely wrong.[63]

Another evident characteristic of scientific truth is that it gives us only a descriptive, secondary knowledge of World One — reality. Scientific laws and theories tell us only how things work; they do not give us much insight into why the laws operate the way they do or the inherent character of either the living or the non-living worlds. For example, neither Newton nor Einstein were able to explain what characteristic of matter is responsible for the force we call gravity. They can only tell us how gravity works. Science gives us therefore a very limited knowledge only with regard to World One.

This leads to another problem: is science even capable of giving us a true picture of reality? In the twentieth century the so-called Copenhagen Interpretation of Quantum Mechanics answers this with an emphatic No! With respect to the ultimate structure of matter, energy, and the universe itself, modern physics tells us that our theories, while they seem to be confirmed through the application of the scientific method, simply tell us how reality works. Our theories are simply theoretical constructions; we labor in vain to create from them a picture or model of reality. For example, an understanding of the General Theory of Relativity does not give us a precise picture of space-time; and our precise understanding of the quantum world does not permit us to create an accurate working model of the atom. It is impossible to picture a Big Bang expansion that does not expand into any preexisting space. Yet too often we mistake our theories for models and give them more credit than they deserve.

Theoretical physics in the twenty-first century presents even greater challenges to anyone looking to science to provide a complete picture of reality. First, physicists must posit almost a score of so-called cosmological constants, mathematical fudge-factors that they do not really understand, but are necessary to make mathematical models work. The most famous of these, of course, is Planck's constant, but there are dozens more. In addition, new hypotheses as to the nature of reality and the universe are increasingly abstract and beyond human comprehension. For example, string theory posits ultimate reality as tiny vibrating strings; super-symmetry posits pairs of particles and anti-particles; there may be many more dimensions in the world than the four that are familiar to us; and the universe may in fact be nothing but a hologram — its seeming volume and even the flowing of time may be illusory.[64]

All this has profound implications with respect to our idea of truth and knowledge and our ability to understand the world. We do not have and will never have a God's eye view of reality. We are limited by our senses, the way we perceive reality, our language and our point of view; we cannot rise above these inherent limitations. We must give up what philosophers refer to as the "correspondence theory of truth," the idea that we can always formulate an accurate picture of reality, a correspondence between our ideas and what is real. Rather the most we can aim at is a coherence theory of truth: that our ideas are consistent and interrelate — cohere — one with another. The ultimate test of this is pragmatic — our ideas cohere if they work to our satisfaction, that is, if they enable us to solve human problems and to create the conditions for a better life. Thus, pragmatism is the ultimate test of truth in science, and, we shall see, in other areas as well.

In summary, scientific truth is derived from one method of knowing the world, a method that is very powerful but excludes by necessity investigation of non-material values. Furthermore, scientific truth is itself subject to inherent limitations, and even with respect to the phenomenon that are within its ken, science in many cases cannot provide a conceptual picture of reality, but can only give a pragmatic account of the world.

Notes

1. David Miller (ed.), *Popper Selections*, 33 (1985).
2. The credit for inventing the term is usually given to William Whewell, a mathematician and master of Trinity College Cambridge.
3. *De Revolutionibus Orbium Coelestium* (1543).
4. Kepler's first law was that the planets, including the earth, move in elliptic orbits around the sun; his second law held that the line joining a planet to the sun — the radial vector — sweeps out equal areas in equal times; his third law holds that the square of the revolution of a planet is proportional to the cube of its average distance from the sun.
5. Francis Bacon, *Novum Organum*, Introduction (1618). See also Bacon's *New Atlantis* (1621).
6. *De Revolutionibus Orbium Coelestium* (1543).
7. This is known as the "inverse square law": gravity diminishes according to the square of the distance between two objects. Newton developed these insights in the 1660s but did not publish them until he completed his work, *Philosophiae Naturalis Principia Mathematica* in 1687.
8. This assumes that the temperature is kept constant.

9. Another famous person of the time was Robert Hooke (1635–1703), still remembered for formulating Hooke's Law of elasticity of materials.

10. Thomas Crump, *A Brief History of Science*, 298 (2001).

11. In his honor the unit of energy is the joule. The rate of energy release, called power, is energy divided by time. The unit of power is the watt (after the Scottish inventor James Watt), which is equal to one joule per second.

12. The conversion inevitably involves some loss of useful energy, however, so an engine cannot be designed to convert heat energy 100 percent into useful work.

13. Electric force is also much greater than gravity.

14. Andre Ampere (1775–1836) in France was the first to propose relating these two forces. In his honor we name the flow of electrons the ampere.

15. "A Dynamic Theory of the Electromagnetic Field" (1864).

16. Because the diameter of the earth's orbit was not correctly known, however, the precise speed of light was established only in the nineteenth century. The meter was calibrated to be related to the speed of light now measured to be exactly 299,792.458 km/second, which means the length of one meter should be slightly adjusted so the speed of light is exactly 300,000 km/second.

17. Wavelength refers to the distance between alternate crests of a wave, and frequency is the number of crests that pass a point per unit of time, usually a second. Amplitude is the height of the crest of a wave. Frequency and wavelength are of course inversely proportional.

18. The wavelength of visible light ranges from about 15 to about 30 millionths of an inch.

19. It is not that the atoms they are comprised of get closer, rather space itself shrinks.

20. This is known as loop quantum gravity. See Lee Smolin, "Atoms of Space and Time," *Scientific American*, Special Edition 56 (Feb. 20, 2006).

21. Zeno's paradox with respect to motion was not completely disproved until the invention of calculus in the seventeenth century. One of the fundamental ideas of calculus is the differential, which quantifies the idea of instantaneous speed.

22. Spectroscopy produces a characteristic pattern of bright lines in a spectrum, and each element produces a characteristic pattern as distinctive as a barcode. Spectroscopy was developed primarily by the German physicist Josef von Fraunhofer (1787–1826).

23. This was a long, hard task beyond the scope of this book. Only about ten of what we now call elements were known to the ancient world: the easy ones—gold, silver, copper, iron, tin, antimony, mercury, lead, carbon (from charcoal), sulfur (from volcanoes) and in some cultures platinum.

24. Although Mendeleev used atomic weight as the basis for his Table of the Elements, the modern version arranges the elements in order of increasing atomic number, not increasing weight. Atomic number refers to the number of the protons in the nucleus of each atom; atomic weight includes protons and neutrons. The distinctive nature of an element is determined by the number of protons, which also determines the number of electrons, so atomic number is more exact than Mendeleev's Table.

25. This occurs when the outer shell of electrons contains 2, 10, 18, 36, 54, or 86 electrons. All chemical reactions occur because of the rearrangement of electrons in atoms. There are three kinds of chemical bonding between atoms to form mole-

cules: (1) ionic bonding involving an exchange of electrons; (2) metallic bonding involving comprehensive sharing of electrons; and (3) covalent bonding involving localized sharing of electrons.

26. J.J. Thomson, *Philosophical Magazine* 48: 547 (1899).

27. John Stachel (ed.), *Einstein's Miraculous Year* (1998)

28. There are three kinds of radioactive decay: alpha decay releases a fast moving particle composed of two protons and two neutrons (a helium atom stripped of electrons); beta decay causes a neutron to spontaneously become a proton (which remains in the nucleus), an electron, and a neutrino, which fly off at high speed; and gamma decay, which is electromagnetic radiation called gamma rays. This is ionizing radiation, which means that it has the capacity to strip electrons from atoms — particularly dangerous to living cells.

29. The neutron was discovered by James Chadwick (1891–1974) in 1931.

30. This value he calculated as 6.262176×10^{-34} joules.

31. The photoelectric effect refers to the fact that light shining on certain metals causes electrons to be ejected from the metals' surfaces. The greater the intensity of the light, the greater the number of electrons emitted. Experiments revealed that the energy of the emitted electron could be determined by observing the color — the frequency — of the light emitted. Einstein argued the explanation for this is that the light beam is composed of particles (photons) that hit the electrons. The more photons the more electrons are hit and with greater intensity.

32. Wave-particle duality is apparent, however, only at the quantum level because of the smallness of Planck's constant.

33. Einstein raised this issue in a series of papers and correspondence beginning with his famous 1935 EPR Paradox paper, composed with two colleagues, Boris Podolsky and Nathan Rosen (hence EPR).

34. See Brian Greene, *The Fabric of the Cosmos*, 114–115 (2004). This is the phenomenon also known as "Schrodinger's cat" because of a thought experiment put forward by Erwin Schrodinger showing that a cat whose life may depend on the particle may be statistically both dead and alive because of the probability cloud.

35. This was first proposed by the Japanese scientist Hideki Yukawa in 1937.

36. Gordon Kane, "The Dawn of Physics Beyond the Standard Model," *Scientific American* Special Issue, 5 (Feb. 20, 2006).

37. Using these measures stars are plotted on what is known as the Hertzsprung-Russell Diagram.

38. G. Y. Craig and E. J. Jones, *A Geological Miscellany* (1982).

39. This was the first idea that present day life had evolved from more primitive organisms.

40. Mott T. Greene, *Geology in the Nineteenth Century*, chapter 2 (1982).

41. *System of Nature* (1735).

42. This led the German zoologist Carl Kielmeyer (1765–1845) to conclude that living things are governed by unique forces that operate on parallel levels, and that the development of the individual recapitulates the development of the species.

43. Over ten years after its publication, the author was revealed to be a Scottish publisher, Robert Chambers.

44. The scientific materialists, however, did exclude God entirely. Typical was Ludwig Buchner's highly successful book, *Force and Matter* (1855) attacking religion and concepts such as the idea of an immaterial soul.

45. The full title is *On the Origin of Species by Means of Natural Selection, or the preservation of favoured races in the struggle for life* (1859).

46. For the reasons for Darwin's delay, see David Quammen, *The Reluctant Mr. Darwin: An Intimate Portrait of Charles Darwin and the Making of His Theory of Evolution* (2006).

47. Lyell believed that the processes shaping the Earth today are essentially the same as those of the past, and that gradual change is the hallmark of these processed. This view is called "uniformitarianism" in contrast to the "catastrophism" school of thought that believed in a series of catastrophic events in the past history of Earth. Of course now we believe that both of these ideas are correct and are not mutually exclusive.

48. The theory has been refined, for example, to add catastrophic changes as factors in evolution and to add the idea that change may arrive in small bursts after periods of relative stability (this is called punctuated equilibrium).

49. Stephen C. Stearns and Rolf F. Hoekstra, *Evolution: An Introduction*, 20 (2000).

50. John Dupre, *Darwin's Legacy: What Evolution Means Today*, 24 (2003).

51. Michael Shermer, *Why Darwin Matters: The Case Against Intelligent Design* (2006).

52. Ibid., 42.

53. Janet Browne, *Charles Darwin, The Power of Place*, Vol. 2, p. 484 (2002).

54. *System of Synthetic Philosophy: first principles* (London 1862).

55. Browne, op. cit. 263.

56. *The Descent of Man*, and selection in relation to sex (1871).

57. Brian Fagan, *World Prehistory* (6th ed. 2006).

58. Nick Patterson et al., *Nature* (2006). A carbon dated fossil known as Toumai with both human and ape-like features has been dated to between 6.5 to 7.4 million years ago.

59. Some molecular biologist have even proposed that all modern humans are descended from a single female, an African Eve who lived in tropical Africa about 200,000 years ago. Rebecca L. Kahn, "Our Recent African Past: New Mitochondrial Perspectives on Human Evolution," in Leonard Warren and Hilary Koprowski, *New Perspectives on Evolution* (1991), pp. 209–223.

60. Karl Popper, *The Poverty of Historicism*, 12 (1957).

61. A.J. Ayer, *Language, Truth and Logic* (Dover Press, 1952); Ludwig Wittgenstein, *Tractatus Logicus Philosophicus*.

62. Thomas S. Kuhn, *The Structure of Scientific Revolution* (1970).

63. As the Encyclical Letter of Pope John Paul II, Fides et Ratio (1998) puts it (para. 106): "Scientists are well aware that the search for truth, even when it concerns a finite reality of the world or of man, is never-ending, but always points to something higher than the immediate object of study, to the questions which give access to mystery."

64. For details on these ideas, see *Scientific American*, "The Frontiers of Science," Special Edition, February 20, 2006.

Chapter 4

The World of Religion

Surveys show that over 5 billion of the 6.5 billion people on the planet are religious adherents, and many say that religion is the most important facet of their lives. As our conception of the world has become smaller, people are more conscious than ever before of the many different religious conceptions in the world. We also are apt to come in contact with people holding very different religious views from our own.

As a category of knowledge religion is unique in many ways. First, almost the entire corpus of what we call religion dates from pre-modern times; the great religious traditions that dominate today stem from the period approximately from 2000 BCE to 650 CE. No other category of human knowledge is so firmly tied to the ancient past. Second, while in the present age of globalization all fields of knowledge have adopted universal or at least universally understood principles, religion is characterized by its bewildering variety, and many of these claim to have a monopoly on truth. Third, many religions claim not only a human but also a divine origin. No other field of human knowledge makes this claim.

These characteristics pose difficult problems. But before we explore the many interesting issues arising out of religion, we must dispose of some threshold matters: (1) What is religion? (2) What is the nature of religious knowledge? (3) What is the source of religious experience?

What Is Religion?

Religion is difficult to define because there are so many varieties of what people consider religion. The English word religion comes from the Latin word "ligare," which means to fasten, bind or tie. Thus the etymological root of the word religion refers to the existence of a bond between the individual and a set of propositions or beliefs. A common denominator of such propositions or beliefs is that they concern supernatural events or beings. Thus, one definition of religion might be the following: belief in supernatural beings or events. This definition is general enough to encompass all manner of religions; it is superior to more specific definitions such as, for example, "faith in God," which is too Western in orientation. Another possible definition is Paul Tillich's famous idea that religion is simply a person's "ultimate concern."[1] In both these formulations, however, the idea of God or a supreme being seems absent.

Is it possible to develop a definition of religion that is more comprehensive and revealing than either belief in the supernatural or ultimate concern? The French sociologist Emile Durkheim (1858–1917) defined religion as "a unified system of beliefs and practices relative to sacred things, that is to say, things set apart and forbidden — beliefs and practices which unite into one single moral community called a church, all those who adhere to them."[2] This definition has the advantage of more detail: not only belief, but also practices and community, are included in an idea of what we call religion. Yet Durkheim's definition seems flawed in several respects. First, the sacred is not restricted to things, and we cannot say that the sacred is always forbidden. So we might add that the sacred includes not only things but also events, places and beings that inspire reverence and awe. Second, religion does not always include the idea of a church — this is a Western concept. Thus it is better to emphasize community rather than church. So how can we define religion? Perhaps a good working definition is: a Religion is a unified system of beliefs and practices with respect to the "sacred," the ultimate purposes and meaning of human life — a Being (God) or beings, places, things and/or events — that unite believers into a moral community.

Religious Knowledge

Since religion is concerned with the supernatural, religious knowledge may be defined as doctrinal and historical propositions that are not subject to empirical verification. Of course, some religious propositions and events are verifiable, such as, for example, the dates of Martin Luther's birth and death, and how many people profess to be members of the Church of England. Such verifiable propositions are not, however, purely religious; they may also be considered and studied as history and sociology. There is undeniably a core of knowledge in every religion that is not subject to empirical verification: belief in God, in angels; in the Hindu doctrine of karma; in the reality of heaven and hell.

Religious knowledge should be distinguished from theology, which is primarily a Western conception derived initially from Judaism and the study of the Hebrew scriptures. In the Christian era theology was transformed into the systematic study of God, His nature and relationship to mankind and the universe.[3] The prototypical example of Christian theology is the work of Thomas Aquinas in the thirteenth century.[4] Contemporary theology is strongly tied to the various religions and has spread to Islam and Judaism as well as various Christian sects. There appear to be three basic types of theology: (1) Fundamentalist theologies parse the sacred texts of a religion in order to determine revealed truth (examples abound especially in Islam and Christianity); (2) Rational theologies incorporate concepts and findings from other disciplines, including history, archaeology, philosophy, anthropology, and even such subjects as economics[5]; This is perhaps the most fruitful type of theological investigation and leading recent examples include the work of Karl Barth (1896–1968)[6] and Karl Rahner (1904–1984)[7]; (3) Partisan theologies work out the nature of God in the context of some preconceived idea. Examples include feminist theology and the existentialist theology of Rudolph Bultmann (1884–1976).[8]

Homo Religiosus

Anthropologists and historians note that religion is a universal human phenomenon; religion appears to be as old as humankind. Prehistoric human societies were religious and evidence of religious practice characterizes Neanderthal and Cro-Magnon societies.[9] Acknowledgment of the supernatural seems to be so pervasive in human life that anthropologists and historians such as Mircea Eliade[10] term human beings *homo religiosus*, religious man, because religion is one of the essential characteristics of mankind and one of the distinctive ways we differ from all other animals.

Mythic Discourse

Religious beliefs and practices are often expressed in what we call myths or mythic discourse. A religious myth is a story about sacred beings and supernatural events that expresses how things are or came to be. Myth is distinguished from history in the sense that while history deals with people and events that at least in theory can be verified, myths deal in truths that are not subject to verification using historical methods. Yet mythic discourse should be distinguished from fairy tales, legends and fables. Myths in contrast are a means of interpreting the world and its relationship to human life. For example, the story of Job is an exploration of the problem of evil; Adam and Eve in the Garden is an explanation why human life is full of travail. Myth enables us to approach the problems, mysteries and contradictions that beset human lives. Myth is an approach to truth through metaphor and allegory. We must not take all mythic discourse at face value but neither should we dismiss it altogether.

Myth is one of the only ways we have of confronting the unfathomable. Mythmaking is therefore unavoidable; if we dismiss religious myths we will inevitably embrace secular myths: some famous examples are Karl Marx and his myth of the inevitability of class conflict, Friedrich Nietzsche and his master and slave morality, and Martin Heidegger and his embrace of Nazism.

What is crucial to realize and what is missed by religious fundamentalists is the distinction between myth and history. A mythic narrative is not intended to be factual or historical; it is intended to transcend time and place. The truth it expresses is not factual; it is intended to be therapeutic and to express meaning and value. The creation myths of Genesis 1 and 2, like similar creation myths in Egypt and Mesopotamia, are intended to demonstrate the struggle necessary to bring order out of chaos and to reassure us that the divine forces of order are in control. These creation accounts were designed to be living celebrations to renew our faith in the victory of order over chaos. For example, in the Enuma Elish, a creation story popular in the ancient Near East, the god Marduk defeats the monster Tiamat after a desperate struggle, then splits its corpse in half to create heaven and earth. Marduk then fashions the first man and establishes laws of cosmic order for the universe. This story, presumably accompanied by music, was chanted in public each year on the fourth day of the New Year festival. By this means the community renewed its faith in the value and meaning of human life for the coming year.

Ritual, Community and Culture

Religions are also characterized by ritualistic practices. Rituals are formalized patterns of meaningful ceremonies, actions and verbal expressions in order to celebrate or commemorate sacred beings or events. Examples range from the sacrifices offered in ancient Greece and Rome to the Catholic Mass to the Buddhist chant. Rituals are essential and universal in every religion. Rituals function to bind the religious community together; thus, religion is almost always and everywhere a community value. Religion also is an essential carrier of culture. Historically, religion has served as a central cultural value in such diverse places as India, Western Europe, China, Japan, Israel, and the Middle East. In pre-modern societies religion was essential as a force to bind the community together. Even in the modern world, religion plays a vital role even if certain individuals are not religious. Religion continues to play a vital role in creating both culture and community in all human societies.

Sacred Places

An essential characteristic of every religion, whether modern or ancient, is the recognition of sacred places as essential to religious practice. These can be shrines, churches or natural areas of beauty and contemplation. An essential human characteristic is to single out certain areas for common worship or to commemorate meaningful events or people. Such sacred places are recognized in every country in the world and are community and religious centers. Sacred places highlight the cultural relevance of religion.

Science and Religion: Independence or Conflict?

Especially over the last 200 years, science and religion have increasingly collided. Although many people, especially fundamentalist Christians and Muslims, focus on Darwinism and evolution as destroyers of religion, in fact, almost every scientific advance of the past two centuries can be considered to have undermined religious belief. Scientism — not just Darwinism — is now the principal reason for declining church membership in many countries.

Two polar positions may be identified with respect to prevalent attitudes on science and religion. First, is the warfare model that takes the view that science has eliminated religion, and that religious belief is simply superstition or psychological self-delusion.[11] Those who hold this view are avowed atheistic materialists. Their views are rooted in the application of the scientific method to religious propositions. For example, in his best selling book, *The End of Faith*, Sam Harris declares that faith and religion are simply irrational. He defines religion as "the acceptance of historical and metaphysical propositions without evidence."[12] A similar view is expressed by John Dupre in his book, *Darwin's Legacy: What Evolution Means Today*. Science, he states, "especially ... Darwinism, has undermined any plausible grounds for believing that there are any gods or other supernatural beings."[13]

The atheistic-materialist sees irreconcilable conflict between religion and science. Is this correct? Logically analysis makes clear this cannot be justified. Those who take this view are relying upon the methods of science to prove or disprove a non-scientific truth. In this case it does neither. Applying an evidence standard cannot prove or disprove any supernatural being or event; it merely results in a lack of evidence and so is inconclusive. An even more fundamental objection is that it is as inappropriate to apply scientific methods to religion as it would be to apply religious methodology to scientific questions. Science and religion are conceptually distinct and each has a long history as a World Three subject of human knowledge. Their separate worlds of knowledge must be respected and observed.

This conclusion leads to the second polar position advocated by many respected scientists and church leaders: the independence theory of science and religion. This view is that, as stated by the evolutionary biologist Stephen Jay Gould, "the *lack of conflict* between science and religion arises from a *lack of overlap* between their respective domains of professional expertise."[14] This idea of complete independence is attractive to many; in theory any religious proposition may be blithely accepted while at the same time all of the latest scientific findings as well.

The independence thesis is propounded most notably by the Catholic Church at the highest levels. In his 1950 Encyclical *Humani Generis*, Pope Pius XII while calling for "the greatest moderation and caution in this question" notably said the "Teaching Authority of the Church does not forbid ... the doctrine of evolution ... in as far as it inquires into the origin of the human body as coming from pre-existent and living matter." In 1996 Pope John Paul II added to this statement in an important address to the Pontifical Academy of Sciences that "new knowledge has led to the recognition that the theory of evolution is more than a hypothesis,"[15] presumably meaning that it may be considered scientific fact. Both Pius XII and John Paul II specified, however, that acceptance of evolution must be consistent with acceptance of the doctrine of the ongoing creation by God of human souls and their infusion into individual human bodies.

The independence thesis, however comforting, has many weaknesses. From the Judeo-Christian viewpoint the classic problem is, of course, how to square the creation accounts in the Book of Genesis with evolution. But additional and more serious issues arise as well. For example, both Jesus and Mary were assumed bodily into heaven; thus heaven must be a physical place — presumably somewhere in the sky — capable of sustaining physical life. In fact the Christian doctrine of the resurrection of the dead assumes that this place we call heaven is capable of sustaining billions of human beings (looking at things optimistically) at the end of time. And Jesus was not the first to be bodily taken into heaven. According to the Hebrew Bible (Old Testament) the prophet Elijah ascended in a whirlwind into heaven[16] and has not been seen since. Hell must also be a real, physical place where Jesus went briefly after his death on the cross. In addition, Christians believe that all humans are descended from one set of parents, Adam and Eve. The doctrine of original sin (not accepted by Judaism) makes this essential to Christian orthodoxy. This appears, however, to add a supernatural gloss to evolution that is hard to accept.

These difficulties cause people such as Richard Dawkins to posit a general objection to the independence thesis as follows:

> It is completely unrealistic to claim, as Gould and many others do, that religion keeps away from science's turf, restricting itself to morals and values. A universe with a supernatural presence would be a fundamentally and qualitatively different kind of universe from one without. The difference is, inescapably, a scientific difference. Religions make existence claims, and this means scientific claims.[17]

This leads to the idea that both the warfare model and the independence thesis are oversimplifications, and we must analyze the relationship between science and religion more carefully.

How Science Influences Religion: Four Paradigms

The independence thesis is further undermined by the history of the entanglement of science and religion. It is false to assume that the famous confrontation between the Catholic Church and Galileo over heliocentrism was the only significant conflict before the current brouhaha over evolution. In fact, science has exerted great influence and generated continued religious controversy throughout history. For example, in Athens in the fifth century

BCE, Anaxagoras of Clazomenae's claim that the sun was merely an incandescent rock, not a god, disturbed public opinion to such a degree that he was tried and convicted for impiety.

In the history of science four paradigms of influences may be discerned.

1. Dante's Medieval Synthesis

Dante Alighieri's magnificent poem, *The Divine Comedy*, written in the early years of the fourteenth century, exhibits a magisterial synthesis of over two thousand years of scientific and religious thought and experience. Over the course of 100 Cantos divided into three Books, *Inferno*, *Purgatorio* and *Paradiso*, Dante is led on a supernatural journey of discovery into the inner workings of the universe and God's relationship to His creation and to mankind. Dante is familiar with the science of Aristotle and Ptolemy as their works had been adapted to Christian doctrine by the medieval scholastics. Both scientific laws and natural phenomena are designed by God to exhibit His love, power, mercy and justice.

God himself is a supernatural being whose essence is beyond Dante's power to describe or comprehend, but whose outward manifestation is brilliant light:

> O luce etterna che sola in te sidi
> Sola t'intendi, e da te intelletta
> E intendente te ami e arridi!
> [Oh Eternal Light, Supreme Being
> Who is only by you, yourself, understood
> And your intellect, comprehending itself, smiles and generates Love!]
> Paradiso, Canto XXXIII, lines 124–126

Dante's God is assimilated to Aristotle's First Mover and First Cause. His domain is the Empyrean, a region of heaven above the outer reaches of the material world. From the Empyrean emanates "the love that moves the sun and the other stars."[18]

For Dante, God is the creator of the universe as well as of Adam, the first man, who was created in 5198 BCE and who lived 930 years. The Earth is at the center of this universe, but this does not reflect any privileged status—quite the opposite: the Earth is the farthest removed from God and His love, which explains, along with Adam and Eve's original sin, the existence of evil. Hell is a real, physical place in the interior of the Earth, formed when God hurled the rebel angel Satan and his fellows out of heaven. Satan came to rest in the place in the universe at the maximum distance away from God: the center of the Earth. This point is also the deepest pit of hell itself. Purgatory, a halfway house where souls are purified so they can enter heaven, is a mountain rising out of the ocean waters of the southern hemisphere that was formed out of the earth displaced by the formation of hell.

Dante's heaven is the region beyond the Earth and its associated spheres of air and of fire. He posits ascending heavenly spheres or domains: the Moon, Mercury, Venus, the Sun, Mars, Jupiter, Saturn, the Fixed Stars and the Primam Mobile, the abode of the Angelic Orders, and beyond all is the Empyrean, the abode of God and the saints. Each of Dante's heavens is a sphere of increasing perfection as each is nearer to God. Physical and moral differences in this universe are explained by the differing intensities of God's love, which shines like a beacon down upon His creation. Even in a single sphere there can be differences: for example, the dark and light spots on the moon reflect different intensities of God's grace and love.

The laws of physical motion to Dante reflect the purposes God built into His creation. Earthly things, with the exception of fire, fall downwards because of their base condition. Human beings, however, once they are purified of sin, naturally rise into the heavenly spheres. Dante, after his tour of hell and the rigors of the mountain of purgatory, discovers, to his delight that, being purified, he naturally rises through each sphere of heaven until he is found worthy to enter the Empyrean itself.

Every living and non-living thing in Dante's universe is arranged in a great Chain of Being that reflects its relative state of perfection. Even the angels assemble according to a celestial hierarchy of nine varieties from the seraphim at the highest to the angels at the lowest. This celestial host constitutes secondary causes whose job is the implementation of divine providence.

In Dante's universe, science is fully in the service of religion.

2. Deism

The early modern scientific revolution of the seventeenth and eighteenth centuries in Europe was begun for the most part by men with strong religious faith, Christian believers who believed their investigations would deepen that faith and lead to a greater understanding of God's plan. Galileo did not think that heliocentrism was inconsistent with his Christian faith. Kepler and Newton looked upon their work as demonstrations of the goodness of God. Increasingly, however, Newton's laws of motion and the disappearance of the idea that the motions of the moon, stars and planets were fundamentally different from earthly motion led to the view of the universe as bodies in motion, all governed by impersonal and unvarying physical laws. Galileo and Newton's formulation of the First Law of Motion — the law of inertia that a body will remain in motion or at rest until acted upon by an outside force — undermined the Aristotelian idea of First Mover and First Cause.

In the eighteenth century many associated with the so-called Enlightenment took the view that the universe was simply matter in motion governed by mechanical laws. God's role could therefore be logically reduced to setting out a few governing principles; there was no need or even room for continuing divine intervention or sustenance. Voltaire and Denis Diderot posited a God who was far removed from creation and from human affairs. This idea, known as deism, held wide appeal. Religion was now being shaped by science instead of the other way around as had been true for so long. In some respects deism was a throwback to ancient times when the Roman poet Lucretius (99–55 BCE), under the influence of atomism, held the view that the gods were far removed from the events of the universe:

Nature is seen to be free and rid of her proud masters, doing all by herself of her own accord without the help of the gods.[19]

3. Design and the World Soul

A third very important influence of science upon religion began toward the end of the eighteenth century. This was the time when theories of the Earth and the earth sciences were first being formulated. As we have seen in Chapter 3, for the first time, at least since antiquity, was it realized that the Earth itself was older than had hitherto been supposed, and that it had changed dramatically over time. Controversies raged among scientists as to the cause of such changes. One group, the Vulcanists, maintained that volcanic activity was the chief agent of change, while another, the Neptunists, posited flooding and water as the cause. A second debate occurred between those such as Georges Cuvier, who speculated that the Earth and living things had been shaped over time by a series of catastrophic events, and those such as James Hutton and Charles Lyell, who found evidence of slow, gradual change over time, known as uniformitarianism.

Even more important was the birth of what we now call biology. By the turn of the eighteenth century there was a new fascination with living organisms as distinct from the mechanical operation of the "bodies in motion" so beloved by classical physicists. Living things seemed to be totally different in the way that they grow and behave. The study of fossils revealed for the first time that extinctions of species had occurred in the distant past and the idea of an unchanging fixity of species was challenged by evidence that species may change over time, the doctrine known as transformism (now called evolution).

This new emphasis on geological and biological processes coupled with a general reaction against the excesses of rationalism ushered in the movement known as romanticism, particularly in Germany and England. In both science and religion new thinking emerged. One strand, dubbed *Naturphilosophie*, argued in favor of a holistic view of the natural world. Newtonian mechanics alone cannot explain the material world. Johann Wolfgang von Goethe, a literary giant who also dabbled in science,[20] maintained that "the world is the living visible garment of God."[21] He shared Spinoza's idea that God reveals himself in the material world.

This *Naturphilosophie* bore fruit in the fields of both philosophy and religion. In philosophy Friedrich Schelling, as we have seen in Chapter 3, asserted that Nature itself is an organism in the process of growing and becoming. Thus, a Mind or World Soul of some sort must be intrinsic to this organic development. This idea of a transcendental World Soul was developed by the philosopher G. W. F. Hegel into a system of transcendental idealism that amounts to a kind of pantheism.

In religion new thinking emerged in what was termed Natural Theology. The most important representative of this movement was William Paley, an Anglican clergyman who published *Natural Theology, Evidences of the Existence and Attributes of the Deity Collected from the Appearances of Nature* in 1802. This work presents the famous argument from design in its modern form. This idea, which is central to Natural Theology, is that, just as the finding of a watch on a desert island implies the necessary existence of a watchmaker, so too does the intricate design of nature, particularly the complexities of living organisms, imply the existence of God. Paley's book was immensely successful and quickly became required reading in academic and school circles in England and America.

4. The Triumph of Randomness and Chance

In the nineteenth century, although there were doubters, a broad consensus was possible that science and religion were compatible partners. If the World Soul remained the God of the philosophers, orthodox Christians could take comfort in the argument from design and the manifest and complementary idea that nothing in science could explain human origins or the human condition.

Enter Charles Darwin. More than anyone else, Darwin was responsible for ending this comfortable consensus. After much soul-searching and only upon receipt of an essay by fellow naturalist Alfred Russel Wallace, who had arrived at similar conclusions, Darwin published his landmark *On the Origin of Species* (1859). What was revolutionary and upsetting about Darwinism was not so much the idea of evolution but rather his theory as to the mechanism driving evolution — natural selection. *On the Origin of Species*, which sold out on the day it was published and became a runaway best seller, is a highly readable argument that evolution, not creationism, explains the origin of the tremendous variety of living things and that the driving force behind evolution was chance or what he termed natural selection. The process of natural selection was based on five key ideas: 1. Thomas Malthus's idea[22] — extended to all living things — that species commonly produce many more offspring than can easily survive into adulthood; 2. That individuals in a species commonly vary in some of their characteristics; 3. That these variations are essentially random — governed by chance; 4. That these random characteristics are heritable; and 5. That because of the inherent struggle to survive and reproduce successfully, certain of these random characteristics will spread to many individuals over the course of time.

Darwin could not offer absolute experimental proof of evolution by natural selection, but he compiled an extensive body of circumstantial evidence based on the following:

- Progressions in the fossil record of plants and animals
- The widespread existence of rudimentary and vestigial organs
- The geographic distribution of species
- The geographic proximity of similar species
- The existence of natural groupings or families of species.

The bitter pill to be swallowed coming out of the theory of natural selection is the idea of chance. Natural selection is a totally random process driven by chance. Where then is the idea of design, of progress, of perfection? Natural selection is inconsistent with any higher purpose or idea of progress. This is an idea that is not well understood even today. For example, in an article on evolution published on March 7, 2006, the *New York Times* stated the following definition of natural selection: "Under natural selection beneficial genes become more common in a population as their owners have more progeny."[23] This definition is deficient because it masks the randomness point and by using the word "beneficial" implies some higher purpose. Even Darwin had a hard time accepting his own idea that the selection process is guided only by chance and the survival struggle.[24] Natural selection eliminated any idea that there was some internal force driving adaptive changes in specific directions. Contingency alone was the basis of evolution. Darwin's theory was the final death knell for Aristotelian teleology in nature.

In 1871 Darwin published his sequel, *The Descent of Man*, which applied his key ideas to human evolution. He minced no words, opening with the proposition that "there is no fundamental difference between man and the higher animals in their mental facilities." He then discusses the animal origins of all of the faculties that we consider uniquely human — language, reasoning, imagination, morality, and even the sense of religion. Although he could not trace the actual biological ancestry of humans, he traced the human species back to the Old World Monkeys and advanced the argument that humans and the still existing species of apes had descended from a common ancestor.

Darwin's views obviously engendered controversy. Cartoonists had a field day drawing Darwin with the head of an ape. When Darwin received an honorary degree at Cambridge, someone dressed a stuffed monkey in an academic gown to preside over the ceremony. Many churchmen also made fun of Darwin and his ideas — most famously Samuel Wilberforce, the bishop of Oxford. Darwin's facts, he proclaimed, did not support his findings. "Is it credible that a turnip strives to become a man?" he asked. At the famous Oxford debate in 1860 Wilberforce confidently made fun of his opponent, Thomas Huxley, asking whether it was on his grandmother's or his grandfather's side that he was related to an ape. Huxley replied:

> If I would rather have a miserable ape for a grandfather or grandmother or a man highly endowed by nature and possessed of great means and influence, and yet who employs those faculties for the mere purpose of introducing ridicule into a grave scientific discussion — I unhesitatingly affirm my preference for the ape.

Huxley ever after was paraphrased that he would rather be a monkey than a bishop.

Huxley, a distinguished scientist in his own right, is best known today for his defenses of Darwinism. At a dinner in Edinburgh in 1875 Huxley was seated next to Thomas Carlyle, the eminent Victorian literary giant, when Carlyle turned to him and said, "If my progenitor was an ape I will thank you, Mr. Huxley, to be polite enough not to mention it." Carlyle also asked Darwin if he thought there was a possibility of men turning back into apes again.[25]

But it was not only public figures and churchmen who were skeptical of Darwinism; scientists found problems not so much with evolution as with natural selection. The physicist William Thomson (the future Lord Kelvin) maintained that the Earth could be at most only 100 million years old, not enough time for the massive changes Darwinism presupposed to have happened by the slow process of natural selection. Biologists who were experts on inheritance also disputed Darwin on the ground that any variation that would pass the survival test of natural selection would soon be swamped out of existence as organisms with this trait would have no choice but to mate with others lacking the trait so that even an advantageous variation could not survive in the long run. Critics also pointed to gaps and missing links in the fossil record and argued that natural selection alone could not produce the complexity exhibited by natural systems. As a result of these objections, by the turn of the nineteenth century, Darwinism was in eclipse, and scientists searched for new ideas to explain evolution.

In the twentieth century, however, Darwinian natural selection came roaring back to the point where it is now not seriously disputed. Further research has cleared away virtually all the objections to natural selection and chance variation as the essential mechanism, although refinements have been added such as that on occasion evolution is more by punctuated equilibrium rather than a continual process that always proceeds at the same pace. The following discoveries[26] solidified the triumph of natural selection:

- Lord Kelvin's ideas as to the age of the Earth were discredited and the currently accepted age of approximately 4.6 billion years provides ample time for natural selection.
- Gaps in the fossil record were cleared and massive fossil evidence was (and still is) accumulated for variations in species over time. For example, in 2006 scientists reported the discovery of an evolutionary "missing link" between fish and land animals in the form of an ancient river dwelling predator with arm joints in its fins, an alligator like head and ribs heavy enough to support its body on dry land.
- Gregor Mendel's experiments in the 1860s with heredity mechanisms, which were carried out in isolation from Darwinism and remained

largely unknown until the twentieth century, produced a picture of heredity that corroborated natural selection. Mendelian genetics disproved the blending theory of inheritance in favor of an inheritance pattern that retained traits in full in a discontinuous pattern that sometimes skipped over generations. For example, when Mendel crossed tall and short pea plants the next generation was completely tall; but short types would reappear in subsequent generations depending on the parent plants. This pattern of inheritance was further confirmed by the discovery of the gene and the science of genetics and molecular biology.
- Fossil hominids now give us a relatively complete picture of human evolution itself, which has confirmed the Darwinian pattern and the African origin of modern humans.

Confirmation of Darwin's theory of natural selection raised the specter of randomness against partisans of Natural Theology, the idea that the existence and character of the creator is displayed in the natural world and that design in nature provides a basis for theological understanding. If chance variations determine the variety and characteristics of living things, there is no room for design.

Modern physics in the twentieth century seems to confirm the idea that at the most fundamental levels of reality, randomness and chance prevail. At the quantum level nature operates probabilistically; the action of atomic particles is random, and the atom is a nucleus of particles surrounded by a cloud of electrons, whose position and momentum can be described only in statistical terms. Neither time, nor space nor extension is absolute. Chance and randomness seem to characterize reality and its most fundamental processes; design and the natural laws we observe appear to be only the outward manifestations of a deeper reality that remains outside ordinary human experience.

Lessons from Science About Religion

What can we learn from science about our religious beliefs? Several important lessons are apparent.

First, science and scientific findings are open and tentative by their very nature. The history of science reveals not only astounding discoveries and facts and processes we now take for granted, but also an endless progression of paradigms, theories and laws. Some of these paradigms are overthrown, such as the phlogiston theory of combustion, but more often theories and laws become relegated to special cases of more fundamental theories and laws. For example, Newton's second law of motion is a special case of the theory of special relativity in that the equation acceleration equals force divided by mass must be adjusted for frames of reference moving at very high velocities. Science is an open project, and the only certainty seems to be that scientific truths of any given time — even those of our own time — cannot be regarded as final truths. Therefore, while we cannot return to taking Dante's synthesis of science and religion literally,[27] it would appear to be folly to base our religious beliefs (or non-belief) on the scientific paradigms that happen to be accepted dogma in whatever time we live.

Second, we must be aware that, for all of its undoubted power to reveal truth, scientific methods have inherent limits.

- Science provides information only on how things work in the natural world, not why they have the properties that they do. Science tells us about what are called secondary causes. For example, gravity is associated with mass, but we do not understand and science does not tell us what about mass gives the property of gravity.
- Many advances in science rely on black box figures known as cosmological constants, which describe reality but do not provide any reason for their existence. All we can do is accept them and work with them. A primary example of this is Planck's constant h, which is the basis of quantum physics. This is used to describe the size of a packet of energy: $e = hv$; but science cannot tell us why this or other cosmological constants are necessary features of reality.
- Science provides us with glimpses into a world the human brain simply cannot fully comprehend. We cannot draw a picture of the world of the quantum; even an atom with its cloud of electrons in probabilistic modes surpasses our understanding. We who live in absolute time and space cannot picture the universe of special and general relativity. The universe of the Big Bang and the unimaginable time frames we know exist only serve to tell us that reality is a dream and a phantasm we can know only through mathematical abstractions.
- Karl Popper's insight that scientific truths can only be disproved; they can never be proved, induces humility. No theory is final; we must always be prepared to be wrong. Therefore we should be prepared

to take risks when it comes to seeking truth. Risk-taking is the only way forward in the search for truth.
- While the scientific method is primarily inductive, it is not true that science relies only on experimentation in its search for truth. Many important advances of science have occurred not because of successful experiments, but because of flashes of insight or even flights of fancy that were later confirmed by observation or experiment, sometimes many years later. For example, Newton's insight that the force holding the moon in its orbit was the same force that causes an apple to fall was intuitive, not an experimental result. Einstein also worked out his theories in his mind; others confirmed them experimentally.
- Although scientific knowledge is gathered by observation and experiment, in fact, most scientific observations are theory dependent in the sense that the observations are the result of reliance on theory. For example, in the early twenty-first century the search for the Higgs boson is totally dependent on acceptance of quantum theory. All of what Thomas Kuhn calls "normal science" fits into this framework.
- Science limits itself to material reality, by definition excluding all else. But the history of science confirms the usefulness of non-inductive reasoning in those cases where experiments can later be devised. Religion and philosophy employ non-deductive methodologies, but in many cases no experiment can be devised to subject their propositions to the test of falsification. Yet it is totally inappropriate to restrict these religious and philosophical truths to the falsification methodologies of science, and if they are not falsifiable, to declare them untrue or meaningless. Science cannot be considered to have a monopoly on truth.
- A lesson of scientific knowledge is that knowledge is not certainty; knowledge is the quest for truth, a never ending process. The test for truth in this case must be pragmatic; a proposition is true if it works, if it is useful. This does not deny the reality of absolute truth or say that all truth is subjective or relative; it merely recognizes the inherent limitations of the human condition.

In summary, what science can tell us about religion is that our knowledge of reality is limited. Physics, chemistry and biology give us remarkable insights into the working of nature and reality. Our knowledge of the origin of the cosmos, the history of life on Earth and how the material world works is nothing short of astounding. Yet the more we know the greater are the mysteries that we encounter. The complexities and the laws that govern the natural world are beyond the wildest imagination of any writer of fiction. Nevertheless, what we know is limited. We know how to manipulate reality to produce an array of useful (and also deadly) technologies. Yet there is a sense that science cannot give us complete knowledge of reality; we are limited to knowledge and the manipulation of secondary causes. Every advance in scientific knowledge brings new questions and problems. For example, modern physics tells us that our vast knowledge of the cosmos may leave out as much as 90 percent of reality; there seem to be mysterious substances we call dark matter and dark energy that elude our normal scientific instruments. Theories known as super-symmetry hypothesize the existence of many more dimensions of reality than the four we know. There is a sense that if these mysteries are solved, others will be revealed. Science is an endless frontier.

Therefore, the criterion of truth of the logical positivists — sense verification — is not even strictly applied in science and cannot be carried over to non-scientific fields of inquiry.[28]

Mysterium Tremendum: Our A Priori Knowledge of the Holy

Although not a formal proof, our experience of reality through the world of science leads directly to religious knowledge as we have defined it. The first step is psychological, the effect of World Three on World Two in Popper's categories. Our contemplation of the world produces a religious experience noted by many perceptive observers. Rudolph Otto[29] has termed this *mysterium tremendum*, employing a Latin phrase because our ordinary language seems inadequate to express what we mean. The essence of this *mysterium tremendum* is feelings of awe, reverence, mystery, dependence and wonder. William James alludes to this psychological state as a "feeling of objective presence, a perception of what we may call 'something there.'" Otto[30] quotes lines from Goethe's *Faust*:

> Das Schaudern ist der Menschheit bestes Teil
> Wie auch die Welt ihm das Gefuhl verteure
> Ergriffen fuhlt er tief das Ungeheuere

[Awe is the best part of man/ How for him the world sharpens the feelings/ Plunging us deep into an immense and terrifying dread.]

What is this *mysterium tremendum?* Otto says it is much more than a mere feeling; rather it is a significant category of human knowledge. Otto alludes to Immanuel Kant and the famous opening lines of his *Critique of Pure Reason*:

> That all our knowledge begins with experience there can be no doubt. For how is it possible that the faculty of cognition should be awakened into exercise otherwise than by means of objects that affect our senses? But, though all our knowledge begins with experience, it by no means follows that all arises out of experience.

Kant's point is that the human mind, in interpreting the world, processes it in terms of certain structures. These structures are not *a priori* ideas from a previous existence or truths implanted by God; they are rather fundamental categories of the human mind that are used to interpret the objective world. He calls them *a priori,* by which he means that they are in advance of or independent of experience. Thus, we process the information of the senses into such categories as cause, effect and substance. These are what are known as synthetic *a priori* processes; we have a natural facility or intuition of spiritual reality through our sense of wonder at the mystery of existence. Knowledge therefore always involves a fusion of experience and psychology. The psychological part is not Platonic style forms, but rather patterns that pre-exist in our minds. Religious experience — the *mysterium tremendum* — what Otto calls the numinous, is such a category of the mind, a synthetic *a priori* category of human knowledge. As Otto puts it: "The numinous ... issues from the deepest foundation of cognitive apprehension and, though it of course comes into being in and amid the sensory data and empirical material of the natural world, ... yet it does not arise out of them, but only by their means."[31]

This innate organizational power of the human mind was first recognized by Plato in his socratic dialogue, *Meno*. Socrates, by posing questions, gets an uneducated slave boy, Meno, to recognize how to construct a square that has twice the area of a given square by using the diagonal of the given square as a base. Socrates concludes the boy was "awakened into knowledge" that his mind already possessed. For Plato, however, this knowledge was a proof of the existence of a world of perfect Forms, the knowledge of which is implanted in our minds, a world existing beyond the world of everyday reality. But we do not have to accept Plato's metaphysics to accept with Kant a theory of the mind's innate cognitive powers. That the "Holy" is an innate category of the human mind explains why mankind everywhere and in every age has a well-developed sense of religious knowledge. A religious sense seems to be hard-wired into the human mind.

The Necessity to Choose

The first step to religious belief is the realization that comes to every individual that he or she must decide certain ultimate questions in order to live a valid life. We come into a world that is not of our own choosing, the son or daughter of parents we did not choose; at a time and a place we had nothing to do with deciding. We are literally thrown into the world and we have to make the best of it. We are used to thinking that we must make certain decisions such as what schools to attend, what work or career is best, and whether and whom to marry.

Sooner or later we also realize there are even more serious questions—ultimate questions—that we must face in our lives. We know that we will live only a finite time. We must ask ourselves: what is the meaning of my life? Is there a life after death? How can I live to fulfill my maximum potential? How should I treat other people and the world around me? There is no escape from these questions for anyone who wishes to live an authentic life.

At this point we will inevitably make some decisions about these ultimate matters; the conclusions we come to will determine our lives to a great degree. We may choose some form of traditional and established religion. Or we may choose one of the many silly new cults that have proliferated recently and are evident in every age. These are quasi-religions—really substitutes for religion—such as the Moonies, the Unification Church of the Reverend Sun Myung Moon; the Church of Scientology founded by L. Ron Hubbard; or even more pernicious alternatives such as the millennium cults founded by David Koresh (the Branch Davidians) and Jim Jones (the People's Temple) that led to violent deaths in Waco, Texas (1991) and Guyana (1978). Still another alternative many people choose is atheism, a creed for which there is no evidence; or various secular ideologies that are substitutes for religion, such as fascism, Nazism and Communism, the three curses of the twentieth century. Of course, there are also dangerous cults even within traditional religions that are attractive to some people.

It may be objected that we can legitimately forego a decision on all or some of these matters. The agnostic simply demurs and goes on with daily life. But as William James argued in his essay, *The Will to Believe*, "Our passional nature not only lawfully may, but must decide an option between propositions, whenever it is a genuine option that cannot by its nature be decided on intellectual grounds; for to say ... 'Do not decide, but leave the question open' is itself a passional decision—just like deciding yes or no, and is attended with the same risk of losing the truth." James refers to the necessity of deciding the ultimate questions of "what do you think of yourself?" and "what do you think of the world?" as "riddles of the Sphinx." He also defends the idea of making a decision even in the face of inadequate evidence: we freely admit that an act of will is necessary in certain matters such as friendship and morality without absolute evidence. We cannot judge everything by pure intellectualism. Quoting Blaise Pascal's proposition that "Le cœur a ses raisons que la raison ne connaît pas," James argues that we should let ourselves be influenced by pragmatic considerations: "[I]n all important transactions of life we must take a leap in the dark.... We stand on a mountain pass in the midst of whirling snow and blinding mist through which we get glimpses now and then of paths which may be deceptive. If we stand still, we shall be frozen to death.... Act for the best, hope for the best, and take what comes.... If death ends all, we cannot meet death better."

Yet we have free will. Our fundamental choice is to embrace or deny the innate idea of the Holy within us. In the Western tradition the two paradigm figures of this choice are Friedrich Wilhelm Nietzsche (1844–1900) and Søren Kierkegaard (1813–1855).

1. Nietzsche

F. W. Nietzsche is the classic case of an eminent and intelligent person who rejected and attacked all religions as narcotics whose purpose is to protect people from unknown forces, essentially superstitions of the pre-modern age. Raised in a strict atmosphere of Lutheran pietism, Nietzsche attacked Christianity in particular, arguing famously that "God is dead," meaning "the Christian God is no longer believable." Nietzsche was convinced that theistic explanations of reality had been superseded by the rise of science and so theism has become unbelievable. Furthermore he found that Christian values are hostile to life and health; he termed Christian ethics "slave morality" and advocated a "will to power" that affirms creativity and the imagination, a passionate commitment to ideals or art or people. For Nietzsche religious values deny life, while the "will to power" and the concept of the

Ubermensch (superman), who rises above this slave morality and exercises what Nietzsche calls "master morality," represent valid passion and an affirmation of life.

2. Kierkegaard

Kierkegaard, like Nietzsche, grew up in the Lutheran faith and shared the idea that human passions have their own indicia of truth. But for Kierkegaard passionate commitment is the path to faith and religious truth. Kierkegaard says that each individual must take a "leap of faith," a personal commitment to religion. In the realm of religion, he maintains, "truth is subjectivity" and this leap of faith must not be taken on the basis of either authority or reasoned arguments. Kierkegaard concedes this is risky but says "without risk there is no faith."[32] He offers a definition of the truth of faith as "an objective uncertainty held fast in an appropriation-process of the most passionate inwardness."[33]

Kierkegaard, like James, rejected the view that the individual may simply refrain from a religious commitment. He described two modes of being of such people: "the aesthetic" and "the ethical." The aesthetic, who lives for pleasure, will experience a life that is self defeating and meaningless; the ethical person will simply be following the common herd instead of living passionately and creatively for him or herself.

Religion and Faith: Is There a Difference?

The scientific revolutions of the past four hundred years were centered in the West where Christianity was dominant. The debate between science and religion was also until recently a Western phenomenon. Thus, philosophical and theological thinking about the nature of religious knowledge was conducted almost exclusively within the context of Christianity. Kierkegaard and James (as well as Nietzsche) were Christians, and they equated religious knowledge and faith. But since in a world of many religions, a sense of religion cannot be equated with Christianity or even with monotheism, we must draw a distinction between religion and the Christian doctrine of faith.

Assent to religious knowledge[34] is best understood as an existential choice of the entire personal self in response to our experience of the world. It is saying yes to our experience of the Holy around us. Although there is an objective element, this assent requires our active participation. In fact, our whole being must be involved for genuine assent: our reason, will and feelings. Kierkegaard is the model of such a choice, but the same idea was advanced by the theologian Rudolph Bultmann,[35] who, influenced by the existentialism of Martin Heidegger, described faith as an event, a "call for authentic decision," that affirms the truth of our own existence. Similarly, Paul Tillich finds the presence of the divine in the content of what he calls our "ultimate concern." He says, "It is a presence which remains mysterious in spite of its appearance, and it exercises both an attractive and repulsive function on those who encounter it." Tillich maintains this is an experience common to all religions.[36]

Most Christian theologians, however, find Kierkegaard and Bultmann's existential choice to be too subjective and general to be the basis for faith in the Christian God. A leading alternative, especially for Protestant denominations, is the formulation of the Swiss theologian Karl Barth,[37] who argues that God can be found not in human experience but only in the form of a gift that comes from God. Grace, he maintains, is an event that happens to us, not a knowledge that we possess. God as a *noumenon* beyond all categories of human understanding can be revealed to us only by an action of God himself. The Roman Catholic Church takes a similar position, locating faith in revelation as well as grace from God and the traditions of the Church itself. In the Jewish tradition Martin Buber[38] developed a philosophy of dialogue to reveal God as an eternal "You," present everywhere as long as we experience the world and other people as "you" not "it." Emanuel Levinas,[39] on the other hand, maintains we experience God as "always beyond" us, an ethical relationship with an incomparable "Other" revealed in the Hebrew Bible.

Mystical Experiences

The classics of Western mysticism such as those composed by St. John of the Cross and St. Teresa of Avila pose the question whether it is possible to have a direct apprehension of God based on religious experience. The skeptical answer is surely no on the perfectly logical ground that an experience of a distinctively mental kind, a feeling-state or an image cannot itself yield any information about anything except the experience. But the mystic will claim that this criterion of truth which applies to ordinary psychological experiences cannot be applied to a mystical experience of the divine, which is not an ordinary experience. But this passes the matter on to the problem of verification. Surely mystical experiences cannot be independently verified in any scientific way. Thus, they must be considered self-authenticating which again distinguishes them and puts them beyond the reach of ordinary experience. Nevertheless, direct religious experience has demonstrated power to cause behavioral changes in those who have them. This is a kind of verification although not a logical proof. Mystical experiences must accordingly remain inscrutable to those who do not experience them.

The Quest for God: The Content of Religious Belief

Even for those not blessed with mystical experiences, religious belief is a fundamental question of human life. Every person sooner or later faces the existential decision of religious belief. Should I decide like Kierkegaard or like Nietzsche? This decision is one of the most important we will ever make, comparable to selecting a marriage partner or a career, because it determines our mental outlook, our associations and our entire attitude toward our personal existence. Even mental and physical health may be at stake; experts tell us that health includes relationships, vision and values, matters at the heart of religious belief. It may be no coincidence that the intellectually gifted Nietzsche became insane and spent the last eleven years of his life in an asylum incoherently awaiting death.

What should we look for in a religion? In the West we focus excessively on doctrinal content, which, while important, is far from the most essential part of religious knowledge and experience. Religion is not a private matter; rather public participation is essential in all great religions both historically and today. Ritual and sacred places are also integral to religious practice. Religion serves an individual purpose, the private creation of self, but it is a public, participatory activity.[40]

Religion is creative of both culture and community, two essentials of human life. Throughout history religious belief has been the most important element in creating and maintaining the cultural institutions with which people can identify to give meaning and to provide aesthetic enjoyment. Music, art, architecture, literature — all of the creative arts — have been and are still profoundly influenced by religion.[41]

Religion was and is now an essential part of the creation of community for mankind. All over the world people still identify themselves by their membership or adherence to a particular religion. Within particular states a person's religious affiliation provides a powerful identity marker; and many states themselves are identified with particular religions. Religion rivals the state as the most significant human community even in the present age.

Yet despite its fundamental importance, most people, especially in the United States, are woefully ignorant of the religions of the world and, frequently, even of the religion of their own family or ethnic group. Just as most people receive inadequate educations in science, they receive little or no instruction in religion. This — despite the fact that history, culture, and philosophy — the world itself — cannot be understood without knowledge of religion. Worst of all, people are left without adequate guidance when they have to decide ultimate questions in their lives, William James's riddles of the Sphinx.

Compounding the lamentability of our ignorance is the fact that the religious heritage of mankind is one of the glories of the world. The richness of religious ideas, rituals, and values is incomparable; it exceeds even the wondrous scientific discoveries of the modern age. The great religions — all of them — give us magnificent guidance on how to formulate answers to the riddles of the Sphinx.

The great world religions have a history of 1000 years or more. Karl Jaspers coined the term "axial age" for the period about the sixth century BC when great religious teachers wrought great changes in history and civilization and established ethical values followed even today. This, however, is artificial; the age of religious thought reaches back to pre-history and continues today. Nevertheless, certain founding figures — Jesus, the Buddha, Mahavira, Zoroaster, and Confucius — lived within a relatively short period of each other. Their teachings still influence billions of people today.

In this little book we can only list the great religions and suggest their richness:

1. Hinduism

The oldest of the great religions currently observed is the connected and multifarious religions of India known as Hinduism. Not only is there no founder, the origins of Hinduism are lost in the mists of time, but extend back over thousands of years. Hinduism unfolded in stages with input from the various peoples of the subcontinent: the original stone-age inhabitants; the Indus Valley Civilization (c. 2300–1750 BCE); the later Dravidian culture, especially the Tamils, and the Aryan (Indo-European) invasions (or migrations) of the early second millennium BCE.

The earliest period — the Vedic religion named for the Vedas, the oldest religious texts in the world. The Vedas (sacred knowledge), which reflect the culture of the Aryan invaders, are myths, hymns of praise, wisdom, incantations, magic spells and prayers. They are written in the oldest of the historically sacred languages, what we now call Sanskrit. Deities invoked include not only older Aryan nature gods, such as Dyaus Pitar (Father Sky), Mother Earth, and Mitra (perhaps a sun god), but also native Indian gods: Indra, the god of storms and the mid-region of the sky; Rudra, a dread mountain god; Vayu, the wind; a number of sun gods (most prominently Vishnu); and Varuna, the god of the high-arched sky. Liturgical deities associated with worship are Agni (Fire); Soma (the juice of the soma, a magic plant); and Brahmaspati (or Brihaspati), a god who intervenes upon hearing prayer.

One of the most interesting hymns of the oldest Veda, the Rig-Veda, contains a story of creation.[42] In the beginning there was neither being (Sat) nor non-being (Asat), only the One Thing (a totally neutral principle). Then Desire (*maya*, supernatural power or magic), produced the earliest seed of spirit, which caused the world as a distinction between being and non-being.

> Whether the world was made or self-made, who really knows? Who can declare it? ... The gods were born later, so who knows? He who surveys it from the highest heaven, he alone knows ... or perhaps he does not.

By about the end of the seventh century BCE the Aryan invaders settled down to dominance and the famous Indian caste system developed. At the head were the Brahmins or priests who dominated the common people. This was the period of the Upanishads (sittings near a teacher), texts of discussions of ultimate wisdom. At this time a dualism emerges between the *atman* or human soul and *prakriti*, matter. Brahman is the limitless One, who possesses *maya* and is an all-inclusive deity, a creator god. Union with the Brahman is the highest good, but mankind's fate is *samsara*, the transmigration of souls or reincarnation, which prevents *moksha*, release and liberation by union with the Brahman. The law of *karma* (works or deeds) determines the state of one's rebirth. Sinners will experience rebirth as a lower-order creature. Asceticism and good are rewarded.

During the thousand-year period from about 300 BCE to 700 CE Hinduism became more communal with the building of numerous temples complete with images of the gods and the institution of rituals and ceremonies. Toward the end of this period new literary compositions were created:

Puranas (ancient lore), *Tantras* (threads) and various *Bhakti*, devotional poems and stories. A more complex hierarchy of four permissible life-goals was developed: (1) *Kama* (pleasure), especially through love; (2) *Artha* (power), social and material success; (3) *Dharma* (duty), attention to the religious and moral law; and (4) *Moksha* (liberation), release, the highest and noblest goal of all. Classical Hinduism recognizes three paths to salvation: the Way of Works; the Way of Knowledge (Insight) and the Way of Devotion.

The Way of Works emphasizes observing duties and rites that create favorable karma such as sacrificing, revering the gods, and keeping the moral law starting with the Code of Manu, a prescription of sacramental rituals compiled beginning about 200 BCE.

The Way of Knowledge is based on the idea that the evil of mankind's situation is the idea that each person thinks of himself as separate and autonomous when the sole being is Brahman-Atman. Salvation, which is synonymous with right understanding, is facilitated by yoga, a system of mental discipline that proceeds through the following steps: self discipline, sitting in proper posture, regulation of breathing, withdrawal of the senses, concentration, meditation, and finally *samadhi*, a trance state in which the mind is emptied of all content. This helps to free the self from attachment to the external world.

The Way of Devotion holds great appeal and dominates Indian life even today. Through devotion and theism one may attain a personal relationship with a deity as a precursor to salvation. Hinduism recognizes that God is manifest in many forms; there are many gods, and no one knows how many, but three are most revered: Brahma, Vishnu and Shiva are the cosmic manifestations of Brahama-Atman. Brahma is the creator god, the least widely worshipped; Shiva (destroyer) is the great god (Mahadeva), representing the force that rules the universe bringing both death and new life. Shiva is life itself, pure energy and force. Shiva has a consort, Parvati, who may appear as gracious or as Kali, an evil one. An associate, Ganesha, the elephant god, is helpful in overcoming obstacles as is Nandi, the white bull. Vishnu, the third member of the Hindu triad of gods, is called Preserver. In the Vedas he was a solar deity and his current role is to conserve values and divine love. His consort is Lakshmi, who is unfailingly faithful and loving.

The female principle of divine power is worshipped in Hinduism under the name Saktism. She is either the supreme deity in her own right or the consort of one of the other gods. Worship of the female harkens back to the Indus Valley civilizations and ancient times. The goddess may appear under a variety of aspects, from the terrifying Durga and Kali to the benevolent Tara.

Two of the Hindu Puranas contain epic accounts of the gods that are especially popular. The first, *Ramayana*, celebrates the happy marriage of Rama, an avatara of Vishnu, to the royal princess Sita, the ideal woman. When the demon king of Ceylon, Ravana, abducts Sita, Rama enlists the help of Hanuman, a monkey king, and rescues her. Sita endures a trial by fire to prove her fidelity and rejoins her mate. The second is the *Bhagavad Gita*, which was incorporated into the epic *Mahabharata* about the third century CE. In the *Gita*, Krishna, a lowly army charioteer, is revealed as avatar of Vishnu and the one eternal God Brahman. Krishna's advice to the fearful and uncertain warrior Arjuna confirms that, while both the Ways of Works and Knowledge may lead to salvation, the best way is Devotion, which is available to all irregardless of sex or caste: "Be Certain that no one can perish trusting me! ... Woman or man; of the Vaisya caste or lowly Sudra. All plant their foot upon the highest path."

Almost 80 percent of India's 1.3 billion people regard themselves as Hindus. Outside India the religion is growing as well. Hinduism, as we shall see, also is the source of several other religious traditions.

2. Judaism

Judaism is the second-oldest living world religious tradition. Although there are only about 15 million Jews in the world, of which about three million are in Israel and about six million in the United States, Judaism is one of the most precious heritages of mankind, the mother religion of Christianity and, to a certain extent, Islam as well.

The remarkable influence of Judaism is due in large part to the Hebrew Scriptures, known to Christians as the Old Testament, which are regarded by Jews and Christians alike as "God's word," a revelation of the will of God not only to Jews but to all mankind. The Hebrew Scriptures were compiled by various authors apparently beginning about the eighth century BCE and were organized into a canon of sacred writings at a synod of rabbis at Jamnia in Palestine about 90 CE. The Jewish canon, which is organized into books from Genesis to Malachi, contains the heart of the Jewish faith.

It is important to note that these scriptures were composed as religious, not secular, history. Nevertheless, over the last 200 years they have been subjected to minutely detailed analysis, not only textually (lower criticism) but also from a historical and literary perspective (higher criticism). They have also inspired extensive archeological research.

Judaism is historically associated with the biblical Hebrews, a nomadic Semitic people of the Middle East. These people, identifying themselves with several (traditionally twelve) tribes or family groupings, very early developed a tradition of monotheism on the grounds that their God, whom they called Elohim or YHWH (the tetragrammaton, considered too sacred to pronounce, but usually rendered as Yahweh), was superior to the gods recognized by other peoples and upon the idea that a covenant existed with their God and that they were a chosen people. Perhaps as early as 2000 BCE the Hebrew people emerged from the desert to settle near Ur of the Chaldees on the Euphrates River in Babylonia. As told in Genesis the patriarch Abraham led a migration along a caravan route to the northeast and perhaps because of unknown dangers, settled briefly in Harran, at the northern edge of the Arabian desert, before proceeding south into Canaan, modern Palestine, then dominated by Egypt. This was the age of the patriarchs Isaac and Jacob (renamed Israel). Because of famine, at some point the Hebrew tribes again relocated into Egypt proper, settling in the north, called the land of Goshen. After several centuries, however, perhaps during the reign of Egyptian Pharaoh Ramses II (1304–1237 BCE), the Hebrews—now called Israelites—were drafted into slave labor on various public works projects. This led to one of the formative events in human history, the Exodus, a miraculously successful flight of the Israelites led by Moses out of Egypt pursued by the pharaoh's army. Under Moses the Israelites spent forty years in the Sinai desert but forged a new covenant with God and received from God himself the heart of the Jewish Law, the Ten Commandments. Finally the Israelites again reached the promised land of Canaan.[43]

The Israelites, perhaps joining with other Canaanite peoples (the Habiri?), established two "states," Israel in the north and Judah in the south. At first the governing structure was dominated by leaders known as judges; this gave way to kingship, most notably King David, who unified the two kingdoms and installed the Ark of the Covenant, a wooden chest plated with gold and containing the sacred scrolls of the law, in Jerusalem, his capital. King Solomon, David's successor, built the first temple, which became the center of Jewish worship.

The two kingdoms came into conflict with the warlike Assyrians in the eighth century, and we know from independent historical sources that the northern capital, Samaria, fell after a bloody siege in 722/21. Jerusalem was besieged in 701 by the Assyrian king Sennacherib, but he was bought off by a large tribute paid by King Hezekiah. Nevertheless, in 597 Jerusalem fell to King Nebuchadnezzar II, and after an uprising in 587/86, leading Jewish families were shipped off to Babylon, to endure what is known as the Babylonian captivity, which ended only in 538 after the conquest of Babylon by the Persian Cyrus the Great.

The return from exile began the second temple period in Palestine, although remnant Jews remained both in Egypt and in Babylon. After the conquests of Alexander the Great (333), Greek influence in Palestine increased sharply, and Judah and Jerusalem become part of the Greek Seleucid (Syrian) state after Alexander's death in 323. But in the second century, a successful Jewish revolt against the Seleucid ruler Antiochus IV led by Judas Maccabeus established an independent Jewish state. In 165 BCE the temple, which had been desecrated, was cleansed and reconsecrated.

Independence lasted until 63 BCE when Judea was annexed by the Romans under Pompey the Great. During the Roman period revolt occurred in 66 CE, resulting in a total Jewish defeat and the destruction of the second temple in 70. A second revolt in 132 was also brutally suppressed. As a result of the unsuccessful revolts against Rome, many Jews left Palestine to form communities all over the Mediterranean area. A Jewish state was again established in Palestine only in 1948.

In spite of the Jewish Diaspora, Jewish communities did not melt into the prevailing culture but kept their faith. An important step in this regard was the designation of the canon of sacred scripture, three groups of ancient writings: 1. the *Torah*—the first five books dating from the fifth century; 2. the books of the prophets called the *Nebi'im*; and 3. wisdom writings known as the *Kethubim*. During succeeding centuries detailed studies of the Jewish scriptures and traditions were carried out, and these were compiled as the Talmud, which consists of the *Mishnah*, references to legal decisions of the rabbis, and the *Gemara*, further law and commentary. In the Middle Ages Moses Maimonides (1135–1204) produced a *Guide for the Perplexed*, a philosophical examination of the Jewish faith. A more mystical literature also developed called the Kabbala, which looked for hidden meanings in the scriptures and addressed metaphysical problems.

Despite unrelenting discrimination and persecution culminating in the horror of the Holocaust in the twentieth century, Judaism has endured and prevailed. Today there are several divisions of the religion, most notably Orthodox Judaism, which stresses close adherence to the Law; Reform Judaism, which maintains a more relaxed approach; and Conservative Judaism, which emphasizes the preservation of Jewish traditions. Devout

Jews pray three times a day, observe the Sabbath by going to a synagogue, keep dietary restrictions, and celebrate Jewish holidays such as Passover (commemorating the Exodus); Hanukkah (an eight day festival commemorating the victory of Judas Maccabeus); Rosh Hashanah, the Jewish New Year; and Yom Kippur, the day of atonement.

3. Zoroastrianism

The first of the prophets or holy men whose thoughts and deeds still influence our world is Zoroaster (Zarathustra), who lived in what is now northeast Iran about 1200 BCE.[44] Common people of this time and place worshipped a host of nature deities called daevas, and their religious world was very much akin to the many gods of the Rig Veda.

Zoroaster was known for his compassion, and is said to have left his family for a life of wandering to seek answers to his religious questionings. At the age of thirty he had a vision: the archangel Vohu Manah (Good Thought) appeared and conducted him to the presence of Ahura Mazda (Wise Lord). Zoroaster recounts that he could no longer see his shadow, so bright was the brilliance of Ahura Mazda and the angels who surrounded him. This was a calling to Zoroaster; he says the religion he was taught is the true and final religion. In scriptures called *Gathas,* Zoroaster sets out the teachings and devotions he learned. First, Ahura Mazda is the one supreme God, the lord of all, a creator deity "who determined the path of the sun and the stars; who made light and darkness, sleep and waking ... who made morning, noon and night, that call the understanding man to his duties." Ahura Mazda expresses his will though a Holy Spirit (Spenta Mainyu) and various other cosmic agents.

Although Ahura Mazda is supreme, he is not unopposed. There exists a fundamental dualism in the world that is a reflection of the cosmic world. For example, Asha (Right or Truth) is opposed by Druj (the Lie); and Life by Death. The source of this dualism is two primal spirits, the Good Spirit (Spenta Manyu) is opposed by Angra Manyu—the Bad Spirit. This dualism began when Ahuru Mazda created the world and bestowed free will on his creation. In later times the Bad Spirit was called Shaitin or Satan, an important character in Western religions as well.

In the moral realm this dualism means that each human being is a battleground between the forces of good and evil. Ahura Mazda gave each of us the freedom to choose between right and wrong, and we are all responsible for our own fate in this regard. In the fullness of time Ahura Mazda will triumph; evil will be overthrown. But as individuals our fate is not sure. There will be an individual judgment after we die; this will take place on the bridge of separation (Chinvat Bridge) which spans the abyss of hell, but leads to paradise. There will be a "pointing of the hand" to either paradise or the abyss below the bridge. The righteous will be saved, the evil condemned. As to the wicked Zoroaster says: "Their own soul and conscience will torment them when they come to the Bridge of Separation. For all time they shall be guests of the House of the Lie."

At the end of time Ahura Mazda will achieve his final triumph and there will be a general resurrection of the dead. Fire will test all but will burn only the evil ones; the good will find it harmless. The defeated forces of evil including Angra Mainyu will either be entirely consumed or will be hurled into the abyss of the Abode of Lies (Hell).

Zoroaster himself was uncompromising in opposing evil and promoting the good. He is said to have converted the local king by miraculously curing his favorite black horse. His vigorous promotion of his faith was met by opposition and Zoroaster was slain by his enemies at the age of seventy-seven while officiating at a fire-altar ceremony.

Although Zoroastrianism, the religion he founded, was opposed by many because it rejected the many daevas worshipped at this time, by the seventh century BC his teaching had spread across the entire Iranian plateau. Soon it was embraced by the magi, the priests of the Medes, a people closely related to the Persians who established a state in western Iran and Mesopotamia. (These are the same magi who feature in the Christian Gospel of Matthew.) When Cyrus the Great in 538 BCE established the Persian Empire by conquering most of the Middle East, Zoroastrianism spread far and wide. Although Cyrus himself also accepted (perhaps for political reasons) the Babylonian god Marduk,[45] his successors Darius and Xerxes were faithful to Zoroastrianism, which thrived during the centuries of the Achaemenid Empire until its overthrow by Alexander the Great in 333 BCE. Zoroastrianism was highly respected among the Greeks (notably Plato) and survived and influenced the Hellenistic world. Later under the Parthians — the great Middle Eastern enemies of Rome, Zoroastrianism made a comeback, and became the official religion of the Persian Sassanid Empire from 226 until 651 CE.

After the Muslim conquest and the assassination of the last Sassanid ruler, Zoroastrians were periodically persecuted. As a result many migrated to the East, to India where they are known as Parsis (Persians). At present there are about 100,000 Parsis in India and about 17,000 remain in Iran.[46]

The priests still maintain Zoroastrian fire (symbolic of God) temples in honor of Ahura Mazda (now Ohrmazd) and prayer is required five times a day. The ancient religious ceremonies are kept through rituals set out in the Avesta,[47] the Zoroastrian scriptures, which incorporate the original Gathas of Zoroaster himself. In addition to prayers and the recital of ancient texts, Parsis extract and drink the sacred haoma (soma) juice, the pith of ephedra plants, and celebrate festivals in honor of spirts such as Mithra, symbol of truth and friendship, and Favardin, the deity of departed ancestors. Parsis also traditionally dispose of their dead by placing the corpse in a dakhma, a "tower of silence," inviting vultures that quickly eat the flesh until nothing is left except the skeleton.

4. Jainism

Jainism was founded by a prince of northern India, Nataputta Vardhamana, known as Mahavira, which means "Great Man" or "Hero." Born traditionally about 599 BCE near Vaisali (modern Bihar), young Mahavira was raised surrounded by luxury and Hindu traditions. He soon reacted against the soft life of the Brahmans in contrast to the poverty of the people, and he also could not accept that the *Upanishads* were divine revelation. He believed instead in the extreme asceticism of the Hindu Way of Knowledge, known as the *Sankhya Darshana* (the view of the nature of things). According to *Sankhya* philosophy the soul is alien to the world and salvation can is possible only through the denial of worldly goods and the abnegation of worldly pleasures. Mahavira himself became an extreme ascetic, wandering naked in order to purge himself from all attachments. He is said to have finally attained moksha (deliverance) at the end of his life, after which his followers called him the Jina ("Conqueror" or the "Victorious One") and resolved to emulate him.

Jains today are about 2 million strong and are found mainly in India. They believe in an inherent opposition between soul and flesh, mind and matter. Mahavira's ascetic practices and philosophy are summed up as the Five Great Vows for Jaina monks, stressing *ahimsa* for the purpose of breaking every attachment to the world. These five vows are as follows: no killing of living beings; no lying speech; no taking of anything not given; no sexual pleasure; and no worldly attachments of any kind.

Ahimsa is a difficult ideal to meet in the modern world.

5. Buddhism

Another prince in north India (or what is now southern Nepal) was Siddhartha Gautama of the Sakya clan who by tradition lived from 566 to 486 BCE. Like Mahavira, Siddhartha was a *Kshatriya* who grew up in luxury, and his parents shielded him from all things unpleasant. However, the story goes that one day he saw three disturbing sights: an old and frail man; a dead body; and a sick person. These sights weighed on his mind, bringing on an extreme mental crisis, and he soon left home to wander about seeking some salvation. During six years of wandering, Siddhartha tried the various ways of Brahmanism, especially meditative yoga, without success. Then he tried extreme asceticism, but felt no relief.

About to despair of finding a solution to his unhappiness, sitting down under a fig tree (now famously known as the tree of knowledge, Bodhi tree or Bo-tree) at a place now called Bodh-gaya, Siddhartha began a new meditation. By tradition the demon Mara approached and told him to give up his quest and return to a life of pleasure. Siddhartha was not moved and continued to ponder how to avoid the suffering and the difficulties of human life and multiple births. Suddenly the answer came to him: suffering is caused by desire and can be eliminated only by extinguishing desire. He felt liberated by this insight; he suddenly felt no sensual yearnings, instead an ecstasy involving neither satisfaction nor dissatisfaction came over him. He exclaimed: "Rebirth (*samsara*) is no more: I have lived the highest life; my task is done; and now there is no more of what I have been." He was now Buddha or the "enlightened one."

His state of satisfaction now complete, he decided to share his insights with his fellow ascetics. He traveled to Benares where he preached his first sermon as the Buddha, now famously known as the Sermon in the Deer Park. "There are two extremes which he who gives up the world ought to avoid — a life of pleasure ... and a life ... of mortification." He called himself "*Tathagata*" — the truth-finder — and advocated that it is the Middle Path between the two extremes of pleasure and mortification leads to Nirvana (Enlightenment). His words were so convincing that his hearers readily agreed to follow this advice. This was the beginning of the *Samgha* or Buddhist community, which today comprises both monks and nuns and lay persons.

The Buddha thus successfully modified the important Hindu concepts of the Law of Karma and Rebirth. These iron laws could be circumvented by individual effort within the reach of anyone. The Buddha lived a long and productive life, preaching his message in northern India for forty-five years.

The death of the Buddha is justly famous. One day in 483 BCE he was walking toward the town of Kusinara northeast of Benares when something he ate made him ill. He lay down between two sal trees to breathe his last. Telling his companions not to grieve or weep, the Buddha said a final farewell: "I now take my leave; all being is transitory; work out your own salvation with diligence." The Buddha's death is known as his parinirvana or final release.

The Buddha's message is that we do not have to rely on devotion to the gods for salvation. And he preached against worrying about metaphysical concerns:

> I have not said the world is eternal; I have not said the world is not eternal. I have not said the world is infinite; I have not said the world is finite. I have not said that the monk who has attained the arahat exists after death; I have not said the monk does not exist after death. And why? Because this profits not and has nothing to do with the fundamentals of religion.

The Buddha's great question and concern is how can we live so as to obtain release from suffering? His first sermon advances what are known as the Four Noble Truths.

1. All of life from birth to death involves suffering;
2. The fundamental cause of suffering is unrequited desire;
3. Cessation of suffering comes from extinguishing desire; and
4. The cessation of desire is possible through following an Eightfold Path: Right Belief, Right Aspiration, Right Speech, Right Conduct, Right Means of Livelihood, Right Endeavor, Right Mindfulness, and Right Meditation.

The Eightfold Path may be summarized as the Six Perfections — morality, charity, forbearance, striving, meditation and wisdom. It involves conquering what are called the "three intoxications" — sensuality, ignorance and the thirst leading to rebirth. The idea of Buddhism is to enjoy a higher vision of calm, benevolence and serenity, a mix of understanding, morality and concentration.

In the centuries after the Buddha's death his teaching attracted wide acceptance in north India. Followers composed what are called the Pali Canon,[48] a collection of rules, discourses and stories featuring the Buddha himself. These most ancient texts are called the *Tipitaka* or "Three Baskets," said to have been written down in 29 BCE under the supervision of King Vattagamani of Sri Lanka.

In the third century BCE the Mauryan emperor Ashoka sent out Buddhist missionaries far and wide, especially to Sri Lanka and Southeast Asia. Buddhism took hold in many lands as a religion of monks clad in saffron robes who follow the same daily schedule. This is Theravada Buddhism, which emphasizes that the world is transient, the self is illusory and must be extinguished, and *nirvana* is the goal. Theravada Buddhism practices five kinds of meditations: on love, pity, joy, purity, and serenity. In addition to monasteries, Theravada Buddhism features stupas, places where relics of the Buddha may be found. Lay believers are also encouraged to take part in activities to attain Buddhahood. The Pali Canon is the authoritative scripture of the Theravada tradition and contains the key moral and disciplinary principles of Buddhism.

In northwest India Buddhism came into contact with Hellenistic culture as well as other Western influences. In this crossroads area Greek artisans were hired to fashion sculptures of the Buddha, beginning the great tradition of Buddhist art. In addition, new forms of Buddhism developed directed more toward ordinary people and those outside the monasteries. This was the birth of what is called Mahayana Buddhism, which spread west and especially east along the Silk Road trade routes. In the first several centuries CE Buddhism spread into Tibet, China, Mongolia, Korea and Japan.

Mahayana Buddhism became in time a family of religions as different conceptions of the Buddha and Buddhism itself came into being. As a figure of veneration the historical Buddha was joined by a host of additional Buddhas and Bodhisattvas (Buddhas in waiting) that voluntarily abstain from personal Buddha-hood in order to help others. Examples include Maitreya, the Buddha of the future, Avalokita, the Buddha of universal kindness, Vairocana, the cosmic Buddha associated with the sun, Bhaisajyagura, the healing Buddha, and Amitabha, who presides over the Western Paradise for those who believe in immortality.

Mahayana Buddhism also transformed itself into many different schools that emphasize different ways to Enlightenment. The earliest followers of the Buddha established a tradition of oral transmission so that new sacred texts were composed over many centuries in many countries; the most important of these are perhaps the Lotus Sutra and the Diamond Sutra.

In general, the Mahayana tradition comprises three different paths or schools in East Asia: (1) Tantrism, which emphasizes secret practices, formulas, chants, mandalas (sacred circles) and reciting sacred mantras; (2)

Cha'an or Zen, which emphasize meditation and sudden Enlightenment; and (3) Rationalistic schools which promote gradual Enlightenment through not only through meditation and chants but also through study of the sacred texts. In Tibet a distinctive form of Buddhism developed in the sixteenth century under the leadership of a monk recognized officially as Dalai Lama, a title referring to the "ocean of wisdom" of a great teacher. Upon the death of each Dalai Lama a search is instituted for a successor who is considered to be the reincarnation of his predecessors. The current Dalai Lama, Tenzin Gyatso, the fourteenth, has become through his speeches and writings a great moral leader, calling for spiritual rebirth and world peace. He was awarded the Nobel Peace Prize in 1989.

Buddhism has a long tradition of supporting the ideal ruler and righteous kingship that goes back to Ashoka, the great Mauryan ruler of North India in the third century BCE. Perhaps this explains in part its rapid success in China, Japan, and Southeast Asia: rulers and ruling elites found support in Buddhist doctrine and in turn were shaped by Buddhist practices and beliefs. In Tibet this was carried to the point where the Dalai Lama was considered the country's full secular and religious ruler. But this tradition has come to an end when the fourteenth Dalai Lama was forced to acknowledge Chinese sovereignty in 1950. He has since called for peaceful efforts to preserve Tibet's autonomy and unique culture.

Buddhism is characterized by many ancient scriptures authored by adherents during the centuries after the Buddha's death, but unlike Judaism and Christianity, there is no official Buddhist canon. Each school or sect may choose its own preeminent scriptures. The Lotus Sutra epitomizes the Mahayana tradition with a parable of the Buddha as a benign father who convinces his children, who are too young to recognize danger, to leave a burning house by promising them different "vehicles," which is meant to show that there are many ways to attain salvation.

6. Religions of China

Of the great religious traditions of the modern world, those derived from China are unique because they developed over thousands of years without significant outside influences. China is an interesting case study in the natural religious sensibilities of mankind. There is no word in Chinese for religion as we use it in the West. The nearest equivalent appears to be the word for teaching, *chiao*.

The ancient Chinese believed that the natural world is animated by spirits of many different kinds. Two main categories of spirits were active — those of heaven and of earth. Accordingly, spirits controlled the fertility of the soil, the seasons, the winds, rains and other natural processes. Spirits also animated the natural world of mountains, hills, rivers, even roads and cultivated fields. Two great energy principles maintain the physical world — the yin and the yang. These two opposite energies cause change and their interaction with the five elements — metal, wood, water, fire, and earth — give rise to myriad forms in the natural world. Yang and yin determine events as well; they are responsible for pairs of opposites such as success and failure, rise and fall, growth and decay; they determine history and give rise to time itself. The yin is feminine; it is yielding, receptive, moon, water, clouds, and even numbers. The yang is masculine; it is hard, active, red, the sun, and odd numbers.

The concepts of yang and yin gave rise to important aspects of Chinese life and thought. Various methods of divination were devised to predict the future interactions of yin and yang. The best known of these was to scrape thin a piece of shell or bone, hold it over a flame and read the resulting cracks and lines. The study of designs and forms useful to diviners in predicting the future was compiled into a famous classic, the *I Ching* or *Yi Jing* (*Classic of Changes*), produced in the first millennium (perhaps beginning about 800) BCE. A second important result was ancestor worship. Upon death, although the yin aspect of the person — the body itself — returns to earth and disintegrates, the yang aspect — the seat of the mind and conscience — ascends to the ethereal realm of heaven. Their continuing presence can be invoked through prayers and remembrances. Reverence for ancestors and the belief in their survival after death sustains the great sense of family solidarity that is such an important feature of life in China. Paradise was the abode of the Queen Mother of the West (*Xiwang mu*), beloved of all seeking immortality.

But the most important consequence of Chinese fascination with the natural world was the development of Taoism, a religious and philosophical creed that emphasizes harmony with nature as the highest good. Taoism developed into a religion that holds that the Tao is the highest principle of the universe and is also a pattern for human life — to aim for harmony with the Taoism. Yet the Tao (The Way) is mysterious and incapable of being understood. Metaphysically speaking it is the cosmic force that activates the potentiality of all existent things.

Lao Tzu, a legendary figure who apparently lived about the 6th century BCE, is given credit as one of the founders of Tao. He perhaps helped to start the compilation made in the 4th or 3rd century called the *Tao Te Ching* (*Dao De Jing* or *Treatise of the Tao and Its Power*), which is the central text that has come down to us. According to the *Tao Te Ching*: "What is contrary to the Tao soon perishes."

A second great master of the Tao is the legendary Chuang Tzu (Zhuangzi), who supposedly authored a book known by the same name in the 4th century BCE. To act according to the Tao is to be non-aggressive but firm; to be indirect in asserting one's will; to behave naturally in the sense that we should not insist that things go just the way we would like them to go. We should accept what happens and look only for indirect or natural ways to assert our own will, never acting contrary to what is natural. We must yield to nature. This is the principle known as *wu wei*, indirect assertiveness. Weak and submissive force may overcome the hard and strong. For example, water can over time wear away the hardest rock. "If nature does not have to insist why should man?"

A model of the Tao was Zhuge Liang, a great general of the Three Kingdoms period (220–265 CE) of Chinese history. Known for outwitting his enemies rather than using brute force, his exploits became the stuff of poems and stories in later times. In one battle, Zhuge, finding that he was short of arrows, tricked his enemy into firing on boats manned by straw dummies, and was able to get resupplied. On another occasion Zhuge, finding himself heavily outnumbered by the enemy, decided to leave the gates of the city undefended and open while playing chess on the city wall. His enemy, thinking Zhuge must have overwhelming force to display such confidence, withdrew without a fight.

Taoist temples were often neighborhood establishments or situated in places of natural beauty. Taoist priests and nuns practiced devotions and revered "immortals" of great age attributed their longevity to Taoist rites and magic. Taoism sponsored a vast literature of ritual and the teachings of Tao masters; art and secular literature also exhibit Tao influences.

A second great tradition in China is Confucianism, founded by the great master known as Kongzi (Master Kong). Born Kong Qiu about 551 BCE at Qufu in the state of Lu during the disorder of the Spring and Autumn period of Chinese history, Confucius (died 479 BCE), as he is known in the West, developed practices and ideas designed to bring about both social harmony and benevolent government. At the heart of his teaching is the concept of ren, translated as benevolence or humanity, in human relationships. Kongzi's ideas were elaborated by Mengzi (372–289 BCE), known in the West as Mencius, and Xunzi (ca. 310–215 BCE). Confucianism stresses the importance of rites (li), laws and etiquette to bring about social harmony. Not strictly a religion, Confucianism in China tended to blend into the practice of the Tao as well as the third great religious ideology of China — Buddhism.

According to Chinese tradition, the arrival of Buddhism was foreshadowed in a dream by the Han emperor Mingdi (ruled 57–75 CE). As testified by cave Buddhas in Dunhuang in Gansu Province, Mahayana Buddhism entered China along the Silk Road in the 1st century CE. Chinese scholars such as Xuanzang traveled to India, and translated the sacred texts. Over centuries Buddhism adapted to Chinese sensibilities. The most important schools were Cha'an Buddhism, which mixed meditation with Taoist concepts of the importance of intuition and the inability of words to express profound truths. Cha'an practice appealed to intellectuals. The common people loved the Pure Land School founded on the promise of the Buddha Amitabha to use his boundless merit to lead anyone who called his name to the Western Paradise — the Pure Land. Amitabha was assisted by another appealing figure, Guanyin, the Buddha of Mercy. Two schools founded to study the Buddhist scriptures were the Tiantai Buddhism and the Huayan School. Tiantai Buddhism promoted the Lotus Sutra as supreme; this collection of sermons and poetry stressed that salvation was open to all through the eternal compassion of the Buddha. Huayan Buddhism maintained a highly intellectual approach the study of the Flower Garland Sutra which taught emptiness and the ephemeral nature of all phenomena. Sacred mountains played a prominent role in Chinese Buddhism.

Buddhism in China enjoyed great success until 845 when the Tang emperor confiscated many monasteries and discharged over 200,000 monks and nuns. This was a blow from which Buddhism never fully recovered. During the twentieth century the Communist government suppressed all forms of religion in China, and it remains to be seen whether the traditional religious culture will be maintained in the future.

7. Religions of Japan

By tradition the Japanese have always considered their beautiful land to be alive with spirits called kami associated with nature, society and even the home. Shinto, which in Japanese means "the way of the gods,"[49] is the native religion of Japan that grew out of these traditional beliefs. Although we translate the Japanese word kami as god or gods, this does not give the exact idea of the meaning. Kami is the name for any thing or phenomenon that produces the emotions of fear, awe or respect, whether good or evil.

Beginning in the late fourth century CE, Japanese people first came in contact with Chinese influences, first coming through Korea and later from China itself. This transformed Japan in many ways. In the religious sphere Shinto was systematized to be on a par with Chinese traditions. In the *Kojiki* (*Chronicle of Ancient Events*), published in 712 CE, and the *Nihongi* or *Nihon Shoki* (*Chronicles of Japan*) of 720 a national identity and creation myth was set out to show the sacred nature of Japan and the Japanese people.

Out of primal chaos two deities interacted to produce the Japanese islands. Izanagi (he who invites), a sky-god figure, and Izanami (she who invites), an Earth-mother, descended the floating bridge of heaven, and Izanami soon bore the eight great islands of Japan. When Izanami died and went to the underworld, Izanagi unsuccessfully tried to pursue her. After returning to Earth to purify himself, Amaterasu, the goddess of the sun, was born from his right eye, Tsuki-yomi, the goddess of the moon, from his left eye and the storm god Susa no wo emerged from his nostrils. The Japanese people by this tradition are descendents of the many lesser kami of the islands. Many years later Amaterasu, seeing disorder in the islands below asked her grandson Ni ni gi to straighten things out. His great grandson Jimmu became the first human emperor of Japan by tradition in 660 BCE. It is this myth that still today sustains the present emperor of Japan as the legitimate heir of the sun-god himself. Of course, the emperor himself denied his divine origin after World War II; but the tradition of the sacred nature of Japan, the Imperial line, and the Japanese people is part of Shinto culture.

Shinto today is a religion of communal ritual and participation that honors traditional and historical areas of beauty, such as forests, mountains and the sea as well as the memories of important people such as Tokugawa Ieyasu, the first shogun of the Edo period. Myriad Shinto shrines dot Japan; they all have a characteristic gate (torii) which leads to a sacred precinct (jinja), a hall (honden) that houses the symbol of the kami and other sacred objects, and a worship area (haiden). The jinja is beautiful and peaceful in order to invite the kami's presence, and priests (shinshoku) in special dress chant prayers and tend the shrine. Members of the public may visit at will to obtain favors from the god, and community festivals center on the shrine and its god. Festivals frequently celebrate the seasons and human rites of passage such as marriage and birth. The most important shrine in Japan is at Ise, dedicated to the sun goddess and housing the divine imperial regalia given to the first emperor, the mirror, jewels and the sword. Many private homes possess a small Shinto shrine called a kami-dana (shelf for the gods).

After extensive contact with China during the Nara (710 to 784) and early Heian (784–1190) periods, Japan adopted both Chinese Tao and Confucianism and integrated their values into Shinto practices. Reverence for ancestors, for example, is characteristic of Japanese life.

Buddhism entered Japan from Korea in 552 CE by tradition when the Emperor Kinmei received a golden Buddha as a gift from the king of Paekche. Buddhism received imperial favor and was used as a means of promoting imperial power. The legendary Prince Shotoku (574–622) urged the adoption of Buddhism as a means of raising the level of Japanese culture. The prince is reported to have said, "The world is an illusion; only the Buddha is the truth"; yet he created a new Constitution of the Seventeen Articles (*junana jo no Kenpo*) that called for unification of the country under the emperor. Buddhism did not displace Shintoism, but merely added a new layer of the sacred to Japanese life.

Beginning in the Nara period Japanese scholars made regular journeys to China and the influence of Chinese Buddhism determined the course of Buddhism in Japan. In Japan, however, Buddhism was never suppressed as in China. Therefore, Buddhism today is much more vital in Japan and has been adapted to Japanese sensibilities. The main schools of Buddhism in Japan reflect Chinese influence, yet are distinctively Japanese:

- **Kegon.** One of the earliest forms of Japanese Buddhism, the most important of the schools established at the Japanese capital at Nara, was Kegon, an attempt to reconcile the leading Mahayana schools. Kegon was founded in China by Fa-shun (643–712) and arrived in Japan about 740. Its main tenet was the idea that everything in the universe is interrelated so that our commonsense view that each individual thing has independent existence is an illusion. Kegon draws its doctrines chiefly from the Avatamsaka Sutra (Buddhavatsamsaka Mahavaipulya in Pali, literally "flower wreath"), which in Japan is known as the Kegonkyo. The idea of the essential unity of all things appealed to the Empereor Shomu, who regarded Buddhism as a symbol of the unity of the Japanese people. To show his support, Shomu ordered the construction of the Great Buddha Maha-Vairocana, which graces Todaiji in Nara and is one of the important sights today in Japan.
- **Tendai.** This is the Japanese version of Chinese Tien-T'ai Buddhism. Brought to Japan by Saicho (767–822, also known as Dengyo Daishi), a confidant of emperors, this sect was established on the sacred Mount Hiei near Kyoto. Saicho preached the Lotus Sutra as

the true teaching of the Buddha and advocated the unity of Buddhism and Shinto. According to Saicho, long years of study of the Buddhist scriptures were necessary to achieve enlightenment. Followers had to promise to remain on Mount Hiei for at least twelve years.

- **Shingon.** This form of Mahayana esoteric Buddhism was founded in Japan by Kukai (774–835, also known as Kobo Daishi) in the ninth century. Shingon honors Maha-Vairocana, the great cosmic or sun Buddha, called Dainichi in Japan. Shingon, which literally means "true words," seeks enlightenment through practices that illuminate the mysteries of the body, speech, and the mind. The mysteries of the body are explained by handling sacred artifacts, exploring the ways to hold one's hands (*mudras*), and practicing various meditation postures; the mysteries of speech are attained through repeating secret formulas, incantations and mantras; the mysteries of the mind are explained by the "five wisdoms," which cannot be told conceptually, but must be transmitted through the teaching and example of a teacher. At the end of this process, according to Kukai's famous book, *Ten Stages of Religious Consciousness* (830), "the mind is filled with the mystic splendor of the cosmic Buddha."

- **Pure Land.** This school appeals to the common people. In Japan this is divided between the Jodo-shu (Pure Land sect) and the Jodo-Shinshu (True Pure Land sect). The founder of the Pure Land sect, Honen (1133–1212), taught that the Amida Buddha, a benevolent Bodhisattva (a Buddha who postpones his personal enlightenment in order to help others), has vowed to save all sentient beings. The only requirement is that they must recognize this fact. Thus, salvation and attainment of the Pure Land (the Buddhist heaven) is open to all who say the words, "*Namu Amida Butsu*" (Hail Amida Buddha or nembutsu for short) with sincerity. The True Pure Land sect goes even further with this idea. The founder, Shinran (1173–1262), maintained that trust in the Buddha is all that matters, and that even evil persons may be saved because the wisdom of the Buddha knows no bounds.

- **Zen,** which features many different sects, emphasizes meditation on natural objects, poetry and self-abnegation. One famous sect, Rinzai, which was founded by Eisai (1141–1215) and later the monk Hakuin (1685–1769), employs the technique of meditation on an insoluble puzzle, known as a koan, such as "the sound of one hand clapping." The goal of this mediation is to attain a state of "no mind," a kind of out-of-body experience like being frozen solid in a sheet of ice thousands of miles wide and deep. Rinzai maintains that through mediation under the guidance of a Zen master (moshi), the person will attain a sudden enlightenment (satori) of this kind. One of the popularizers of Zen in the West was D. T. Suzuki (1870–1966), whose book, *Essays in Zen Buddhism* (1927), set out the properties of *satori*—a non-rational, non-conceptual feeling of exhilaration that happens out of time and is completely different in nature from the rational dualisms common to Western religions and philosophies. A second major school of Zen is Soto, founded by Dogen (1200–1253), author of *Shoho Ganzo* (an untranslatable phrase given the English title *Treasury of the True Dharma Eye*). Soto employs meditation not to attain sudden insight but to make us aware of our true Buddhist nature. This requires a long period of devotion and concentration before we attain the true meaning of the Buddhist doctrine of the interconnectedness and impermanence of all being. Dogen compares this insight to being on a moving boat. At first it appears that the shore is moving past the boat, but if we concentrate on the rim of the boat, we know that the boat is moving, not the shore. Another analogy is that the moon can be reflected in a single drop of water, which can contain the entire moon without changing it in any way. Realization of the impermanence of all reality puts our desires in perspective and leads us to overcome and extinguish them. The realization that everything beautiful and desirable passes away is not, as in the West, to be lamented, but is to be celebrated.

- **Soka Gakkai.** Founded in 1930, this sect is based on the Hokke school started by the controversial monk, Nichiren (1222–1282), who advocated veneration of a mandala (the *Gohonzon*) he designed to exemplify the Buddha nature of all creatures as well as constant recitation of the first words of the Lotus Sutra: "*Namu myoho renge kyo*," as a means of salvation. Soka Gakkai emphasizes that we should not deny our earthly desires, but rather we should turn them into something that is good. For example, a person who is consumed with making money can turn herself into someone who acts with magnanimity to benefit others.

Most Japanese practice both Shinto and Buddhism to some degree and keep values from Confucius and Tao such as reverence for nature and for ancestors. Although some Japanese choose to become Buddhist monks or Shinto priests, most believe that religion can be practiced in daily life through kindnesses to others and by maintaining calm detachment toward worldly things. Many Japanese believe that upon death the soul drifts out of the body, and those who led good and blameless lives go to the *Gokuraku Jodo*, the Mahayana paradise or Pure Land, which is traditionally located somewhere in the West. The souls of those who led lives of evil become ghosts and remain forever in the Buddhist version of hell. The souls of the dead are even allowed to return for a once a year visit to loved ones on the holiday known as *bon*, which is celebrated every August in Japan.

A common prayer heard at the end of a funeral service in Japan is, "please let him [or her] attain Buddhahood!"

8. Christianity

The many denominations of Christianity together claim more adherents than any other religion in the world. The founder, Jesus of Nazareth, is arguably the most significant personage in Western culture, whose followers exhibited such zeal that Christianity replaced the polytheism of the ancient world, becoming the religion of Western civilization. From this base Christianity was extended to the New World of the Americas, much of Africa, and Australia and New Zealand. Only in Asia and the Middle East does Christianity have minority status.

Jesus of Nazareth was a Jew, born about the year 4 BCE (the date is uncertain) in Palestine, which was then part of the Roman Empire. Little is known about his early life, but at the age of about thirty, he joined his cousin, John the Baptist (who was later killed by Herod Antipas, the local governor), to wander about the countryside and small towns, preaching in the form of stories, parables, calling upon people to repent of their sins and to love others, even their enemies, as well as the poor, those afflicted with disease, and outcasts, such as tax collectors and Samaritans. His message was that the end of the world is near, although we know not the day or the time. When this day will come, there will be a final judgment of all human beings, and those who have led good lives will be admitted into heaven to enjoy eternal bliss, while those who have committed evil and are unrepentant will be cast into hell to suffer eternal punishment.

Particularly revolutionary were Jesus' ethical teachings: he preached that it was not enough simply to love those who love us, or to be good only to those who are good to us. Rather, we must love and do good even to those who are our "enemies" — the people we do not respect or openly despise. In the famous Sermon on the Mount, recounted in both the Gospels of Matthew and Luke, Jesus is quoted as saying: "If you do good [only] to those who do good to you, what credit is that...? [L]ove your enemies, do good, and lend, expecting nothing in return."* This mandate of universal love still astounds today although we have had almost 2000 years to get used to it.

Jesus attracted large crowds and a small group of devoted followers, the twelve apostles, both through his teachings and because he worked a series of "miracles": curing the sick, casting out evil spirits, and even raising the dead. But he also courted trouble by criticizing the Jewish establishment, particularly the Pharisees, who considered themselves the guardians of Jewish law.

After about three years as an itinerant teacher and preacher, Jesus suffered an extremely painful public execution by crucifixion as a troublemaker during the Jewish Passover celebrations in Jerusalem about 30 CE. Three days after his execution, he rose bodily from the dead, and once again walked, talked and ate among the living. Forty days after this resurrection, he ascended bodily to join his father in heaven.

Although these accounts of Jesus' life and death have been questioned by some, there is no dispute about the remarkable effect Jesus had on his small band of followers, who at the time of his death could not have numbered more than about one hundred. From this small beginning Christianity rose from being an illegal and persecuted sect to become, by the end of the fourth century, the official religion of the Roman Empire.

Jesus' charismatic personality and teachings inspired missionary activity to spread his message, and many letters (epistles) and gospels, fascinating narrative accounts of Jesus' life and teachings. As a result of the diligent efforts of his disciples, communities of Christians were soon established in cities of the Eastern Mediterranean and even Rome itself. Certain writings about Jesus composed in the latter half of the first century were later compiled into a canon we call the New Testament — four Gospels about Jesus' teachings and his death; the Acts of the Apostles, about the history of the early church; letters to fledgling Christian communities, the majority authored by St. Paul, the man most responsible for spreading the Christian message beyond Judaism to non–Jews, so-called Gentiles; and the Apocalypse

---

*Luke 6: 33–36.

or Revelation, about the persecutions suffered by early Christians and the ultimate triumph of good over evil.

Jesus was considered by his followers to be the messiah or "anointed one" promised to the Jewish people. Although Jesus was rejected by the Jews, his followers established many communities, churches, in Jesus' name. It was the church at Rome, the site of the martyrdom of St. Peter, which eventually emerged supreme, although for several centuries power was shared with the churches in Alexandria, Constantinople and Antioch. After the Christian faith was given official status by the empire, Christianity flourished, and in the fourth and fifth centuries, church councils defined key points of doctrine such as the nature of Christ (both divine and human), original sin and the doctrine of the Trinity, which holds there are three persons in one God.

The essence of Christianity was eloquently expounded by the Apostle Paul in his Epistles to the *Romans* and *I Corinthians*, both among the earliest Christian writings, about thirty years after Jesus's death, well before the Gospels of the New Testament. Paul maintains that our human nature is imperfect and prone to error symbolized by the "original" sin of Adam detailed in the Book of Genesis. Although we are endowed with reason and free will, our inherent weakness entails the certainty that we are overwhelmed by base desires which Paul calls the "flesh," which stands for all the many misdeeds — sins — that we commit. Although the Law of Moses was revealed by God to be a guide to the "natural law" that should govern our behavior, we were not up to the task: human beings, even God's chosen people, the Jews, failed miserably to keep the Law's commandments.

So God in his infinite love and wisdom decided to supercede the Law and to institute a plan of salvation for all mankind, not only the Jews but also the "Gentiles" (non–Jews). This plan is embodied in the life, death and resurrection of Jesus of Nazareth, the beloved Son of God. Because Jesus took upon himself human nature burdened with all the faults of mankind, and voluntarily sacrificed himself on the cross, mankind now merits the righteousness of God — the Divine Grace needed to defeat Sin and Death, which is the fruit of sin. Through the miracle of God's Grace, human beings, who are incapable of salvation by their own efforts, now have the opportunity for salvation and eternal life.

In order to participate in God's plan of salvation, each person must give his or her active consent through faith in God and Jesus Christ. This necessary faith differs from mere belief in that it is an active commitment; he or she must also have hope in the ultimate fulfillment of God's plan; and exercise love of God and his creation, especially other human beings, "neighbors." Strikingly, Pauline Christian doctrine maintains that Jesus will come again to the earth at the "end of time." This "Second Coming" will bring about God's final victory over sin and death, and all men and women will experience a resurrection of the body and a final judgment. Men and women judged worthy will gain eternal bliss while others will be condemned to "eternal fire." This view of the ultimate fate of the universe is known as the "apocalyptic" (a derivative of the ancient Greek word meaning "I reveal"). This vision apparently originated in Judaism (the book of Daniel), which influence both Christianity and Islam.

Under the aegis of Christianity new forms of culture — art, architecture, poetry, literature and music flourished and a brilliant Christian civilization developed and flourished in Europe, which was divided, mirroring the Roman world into which it was born, into a Latin culture in the west and a Greek culture in the east, centered in Constantinople. The unity of the Christian world was compromised, however, in the eleventh century when the Greek Orthodox Church split with Rome. Further splits and reforms occurred in the Western church during and after the sixteenth century with the rise of Protestant Christianity. Today Christianity is a family of hundreds of disparate religions, but all adhere to certain core beliefs rooted in the New Testament and the teachings of Jesus:

- Christians have a strong belief in a personal, loving God who is both just and merciful.
- Christians believe human beings are by nature flawed, symbolized by the original sin committed by Adam and Eve, and must depend on God's mercy and grace for their salvation.
- Christians believe in the immortality of human souls and that human life is a transition period of preparation for the eternal life to come after death.
- Christianity has a strong ethical basis replete with both rules, such as the Ten Commandments (taken over from Judaism) and the idea of love of neighbor to regulate and influence the conduct of humans toward each other.

Perhaps the most significant weakness of Christianity is the fact that it has splintered into so many different, often hostile and competing churches and congregations. As a result, Christianity exhibits significant differences of opinion and practice with regard to belief, doctrine, and ritual.

9. Islam

Muhammad, the founder of Islam, was born about 570 CE in Mecca, at that time the most important city on the Arabian Peninsula. As a caravan driver he came into contact with the religious traditions of Judaism and Christianity as well as Zoroastrianism. Mecca was also a pilgrimage center for Arab nomads who worshipped a variety of native gods. Muhammad opposed the polytheism of his fellow Arabs, and about 610 he began to experience a series of visions and revelations of the one true God. Puzzled and troubled, he withdrew from his successful business for the solitude of the desert outside the city. There he experienced what Muslims call "the night of destiny." While he was sleeping, he was visited by an angel from heaven in a dream who commanded him to "Read in the name of your Lord." Muhammad replied that he could not read, but the angel was insistent. Muhammad awoke and heard a voice calling him, saying, "I am Gabriel and you are called to be God's messenger." From that time on the angel Gabriel appeared periodically to Muhammad and dictated what we call the Qur'an, by Islamic tradition originally written on palm leaves, stones and the shoulder blade bones of camels. These revelations continued for over twenty years.

These revelations reached a climax in the year 620 during the month of Ramadan when the angel Gabriel took Muhammad on a Night Journey to heaven itself. Mounted on a flying horse named Buraq, he was taken to Jerusalem, Sinai and Bethlehem where he met Abraham, Moses and Jesus; then Muhammad rose into heaven on a ladder of light. This Night Journey is interpreted symbolically by Muslim tradition, although fundamentalists take it literally. Some scholars believe that Dante got the idea for his Divine Comedy after hearing the tale of Muhammad's Night Journey.

But when Muhammad preached his new ideas about monotheism and the repudiation of the Arab gods, he was ridiculed and vigorously opposed. This opposition caused his famous *Hijra*, an emigration to Mecca with about 70 followers and their families. At Mecca, an ancient oasis center, he won over most people expelled those who disagreed, and became a political as well as religious leader. By 630 he was powerful enough to take Mecca by force of arms. His authority was now unquestioned. On his death in 632, the stage was set for his successors and deputies to organize raiding parties, and within twelve years of Muhammad's death, his followers had occupied Egypt, Syria and Iraq, and were on the move westward to Libya and eastward toward Iran.

The Qur'an, the Muslim scripture, is central to Islam because it is considered the revealed word of God. By tradition Muhammad did not make the final compilation; this was done about 650 by his successors, the caliphs, ruling from Medina. The Qur'an consists of 114 Suras or chapters, but there is no discernable order either chronologically or by subject. The overarching theme is that there is one God, who created the seven heavens and mankind. All men will experience judgment after death; believers will be admitted into paradise, a beautiful garden, while unbelievers will be cast into hell. At the end of time there will be a general resurrection and a last judgment. Much of the Qur'an relates stories drawn from the Jewish and Christian scriptures, but these are invariably cast in a new light. For example, the flood was designed to save Noah and all who accepted God's revelation; those who were drowned were unbelievers. The Jewish and Christian faiths and biblical history prepares the way for Islam, the last revelation of God. For example, Jesus, son of Mary, states, "I am sent forth to you from God to confirm the Torah already revealed and to give news of an apostle who will come after me, Muhammad."[50] Christians are condemned for the doctrine of the Trinity, which the Qur'an interprets as belief in three gods.

Islam today claims over one billion adherents and is the fastest growing religion in the world. Muslims pray five times a day and are enjoined to keep the law (*Sharia*), which often prescribes harsh penalties, such as capital punishment for apostasy. Mecca is the holiest city for Muslims, a pilgrimage center toward which Muslims turn to pray and, at least once in a lifetime, are encouraged to make the circumambulation of the ancient Ka'ba, a cube-like shrine which houses the sacred Black Stone, probably a meteorite, the subject of Arab veneration for many centuries before Islam. Legend has it that the Black Stone was given to Abraham by the angel Gabriel.

Islam has no institutional structure and is not a church as such. Islam emphasizes the immediate relation between God and individual believers and the duties of believers to God as revealed in the Qur'an and associated traditional teaching known as *hadiths*. Unlike the two other great monotheistic religions, Judaism and Christianity, Islam is strikingly devoid of moral commands or ethical duties owed between human beings, even among the faithful themselves. Unlike Jesus and Moses, Muhammad was not a moral teacher; his mission emphasized duties owed to God. Male believers are privileged; women and non-believers are relegated to inferior positions.

Islam is unique among the great world religions in that its founder, Muhammad, from the very beginning, had an avowed political purpose: the foundation of a political community, what we call today a state. After being expelled to Medina, Muhammad mounted a successful military campaign against his former home city, Mecca. After his death, this *jihad* against unbelievers was continued by his successors. By the fourth generation after the Prophet, Islam had established an empire that extended from the Atlantic Ocean (including most of what is now Spain and Portugal) to the Indus River valley.

Much of the early political violence of Islam was directed against fellow Arabs as well as co-religionists. When Mohammad died in 632, he left no son or clear successor. His only living daughter, Fatima, was married to his cousin Ali, who was not well regarded by contemporaries. In the first three elections for caliph, leader of Islam, Ali was passed over, much to his displeasure. But in 657 the Arab army in Egypt revolted and took up his cause, marching on Medina and brutally murdering the reigning caliph, Uthman. Finally realizing his dream, Ali became caliph only to be murdered himself in 651. Then a new dynasty of caliphs, the Umayyads, seized power to rule from their capital in Damascus in Syria until 750, when they were deposed after a civil war by the Abbasid Persians, who moved the capital of Islam to Baghdad. Although the Muslims were eventually expelled from Spain and Portugal, and the Abbasids were defeated by the Mongols, who captured Baghdad in 1248, the broad arc of territory that stretches from northern Africa to central Asia remains to this day the heartland of Islam. More than any other factor, military conquest has catapulted Islam to its present position as a principal world religion.

Although all Muslims respect the same Qur'an, there are today two great sects of Islam. The majority of Muslims are Sunnis, followers of the tradition (Sunna) of the life and teachings of the Prophet Muhammad. Shiites follow this same tradition, but are followers of Ali, the son-in-law of Muhammad, the fourth of the caliphs and the first imam, who they still maintain was the rightful successor to Muhammad.

Perhaps the most appealing tradition of Islam is Sufism or Islamic mysticism, which arose as a counterweight to the practices of many rich Muslims who reaped the benefits of Islamic conquests by basking in the splendor of wealth and the pleasures of the harem. Sufis practice asceticism as conducive to personal union with God. They stress the importance of inner devotion and rely on religious experience and intense personal love of God. An important and appealing exemplar of this tradition is the sufi poet and teacher Jalahiddin Rumi (died 1273), who, after fleeing from his Bactrian homeland to escape the Mongols, settled in Iconium in Asia Minor, where he founded the Order of Mevlevi, sufi mystics popularly known as the whirling dervishes. Rumi maintained that the Qur'an was an allegory of the search for a God who cannot be found in the world but only in the human heart. He wrote in a poem about his search for God:

> I gazed into my own heart;
> There I saw Him; he was nowhere else;
> In the whirl of its transport my spirit was tossed;
> Until each atom of separate being I lost.

10. Sikhism

The Sikh faith was founded by Guru Nanak (1469–1538),[51] a holy man whose mission was to resolve the conflicts between Hindus and Muslims in India. Nanak wandered extensively throughout south Asia and the Middle East. On a visit to the holy city of Mecca, one day he fell asleep with his feet toward the Ka'ba. A Muslim pilgrim accosted him and angrily said, "You infidel! How dare you dishonor God's place by pointing at Him with your feet!" Nanak replied, "I am tired. Turn my feet in any direction where the place of God is not." When the Muslim turned his feet away, legend says that the Ka'ba also moved to demonstrate that God is equally present in every direction.

Sikhism has spread around the world, but is centered in the Punjab and the Golden Temple at Amritsar. Sikhism is strongly monotheistic and is rooted in mysticism and devotion. Sikhs reject both the Hindu caste system and the Muslim distinction between believers and infidels. He calls on Muslims: "Let compassion be thy mosque, Let faith be thy prayer mat, Let honest living be thy Qur'an."

In contrast to the Hindus, Nanak taught that mankind must seek contact with high and low castes. But Nanak retained the Hindu discipline of the body: "The five temptations (lust, anger, greed, attachment, and ego) that flesh is heir to—Make daily raids upon them." In order to implement this concept, boys and girls at about fourteen years of age are initiated into *Khalsa* (Purity) through a ceremony similar to baptism. They are then members of the Sikh community of *Singh* (lions) and *Kaur* (princesses). To remain among the pure, Sikhs pledge to keep basic rules of moral conduct and to keep their hair uncut. They must also give up all stimulants such as alcohol and tobacco. One of Nanak's hymns gives the following advice:

> Love the saints of every faith;
> Put away your pride.

Remember that the essence of religion
Is meekness and sympathy.
Not fine clothes,
Not the Yoga's garb and ashes,
Not the blowing of horns,
Not long prayers,
Not recitations,
Not the ascetic way,
But a life of goodness and purity amid the world's temptations.

Some Problems of Religious Pluralism

What are we to make of the many diverse types of religions in the world? Can we reduce them to a common denominator? Are they really one? Much as we would like to find a common thread running through them the answer is a resounding — no; there is no possibility of finding that they all amount to the same thing. Instead, what we find is the following:

- Religions are deeply creative of and embedded in human culture. Religion is perhaps the single most important determinant of culture, greatly influencing a people's art, literature, music, architecture, and way of life.
- Religions are an important determinant of people's identity and self-image even for those who are not active adherents.
- Religions to a greater or lesser degree involve and determine moral values and behavior. Religions influence human behavior in two directions: vertically, meaning rituals and honors accorded to God or supernatural powers; and horizontally, conduct toward other people. Some religions, such as Islam, emphasize vertical morality and neglect horizontal morality; others, such as Confucianism, emphasize horizontal moral behavior; while still others, such as Christianity, take both heavily into account.
- All religions deal with the problem of evil in some way: typically they offer an explanation of the origin of evil, and they envision and assure the ultimate triumph of good over evil.
- Most religions deal with the fact and mystery of death. Some religions, such as Christianity and Islam, emphasize that this life is merely a transition and preparation for the life to come after death. Other religions, such as Chinese religions and Judaism, emphasize life in the present.

- Most religions adhere to the belief that some part of men and women survives after death. Dualism — the idea that we are composed of matter — our bodies — and a spiritual part — a soul — is deeply embedded in religious belief. However, while some religions, such as Christianity and Islam, look forward to a life after death, for others, such as Buddhism and Hinduism, the goal is the extinguishing or disappearance of the self.
- Religions exhibit both doctrines of great power and profundity as well as ideas that are obvious errors and sources of evil. Although we cannot exclude divine inspiration, all religions are at least in part undeniably human creations that come from men, not from God.

The study of comparative religion and religious pluralism raises two fundamental problems: first, how can religious knowledge be equated with truth if there are not only the above described ten principal world religions but also hundreds of additional sects and sub-sects, many of dubious origin and rationality? All religions make factual claims which are often mutually exclusive. For example, was Jesus the Son of God as the Christians believe or merely a precursor to Muhammad according to Islam? Rational inquiry would deem it necessary to resolve this conflict.

Second, religion historically has probably inspired and incited more wars, violence and killing than anything else. One need only cite the long history of anti-Semitism of the Christians, the long list of holy wars of Islam, the Spanish Inquisition, the Crusades, and the wars of religion that convulsed Europe in the sixteenth and seventeenth centuries. Even today Muslim fundamentalists incite indiscriminate violence against "infidels," and incidents of religious violence and discrimination are commonplace.

The answer to both problems lies in the fundamental recognition that true and direct knowledge of God himself is impossible for human beings. All religions are attempts to know the inconceivable. All religions are very much human creations that are rooted in particular historical and cultural contexts. This is not to deny the idea of truth or to lapse into relativism; rather, it is an admission that the human mind is simply not suited to know God as He is in Himself. Just as in science we now work with concepts such as relativity and quantum mechanics that we do not fully understand, so too we have no choice but to accept the existence of disparate religious beliefs that reflect different human historical and cultural traditions.[52] Our religions are rooted necessarily in space and time even if the divine is not; and anything outside of space and time is inconceivable to us. We have no choice but to find the divine through our cultural traditions. Since human cultural traditions are often ancient and developed in space and time, they will inevitably be different and even in conflict. Without any means to resolve the inevitable differences, the best course is simply mutual respect.

There is a long history of considering God "the inconceivable." For example, St. John Chrysostom (347–407), a doctor of the church and bishop of Constantinople, distinguishes between incomprehensibility and inapprehensibility. In John's view, because of his "exceeding greatness," God escapes our mental grasp, yet we can have experience of the "wholly other" so God is apprehensible. Other religions express the same idea in different ways. For example, Hinduism can be regarded as both polytheistic and monotheistic because as far as God is concerned there is no difference between one and many. Sarvepalli Radhakrishnan , former president of India, says we are all seeking God under different banners. He calls for a sharing, a fellowship of faiths:

> The light of eternity would blind us if it came full in the face. It is broken into color so that our eyes can make something of it. The different religious traditions clothe the One Reality in various images and their visions could embrace and fertilize each other so as to give mankind a many-sided perfection, the spiritual radiance of Hinduism, the faithful obedience of Judaism, the life and beauty of Greek paganism, the noble compassion of Buddhism, the vision of divine love of Christianity, and the spirit of resignation to the sovereign lord of Islam. All these present different aspects of the inward spiritual life, projections on the intellectual plane of the ineffable experiences of the human spirit.

The Roman Catholic Church in the Second Vatican Council adopted a similar declaration of ecumenism: "The Catholic Church rejects nothing of what is true and holy in [other] religions. She has a high regard for the manner of life and conduct, the precepts and doctrines which, although differing in many ways from her own teaching, nevertheless often reflect a ray of that truth which enlightens all men."

These views of religious pluralism are much different than the tendency of people of some religions — regretfully especially the three Western monotheisms, Christianity, Islam, and Judaism — at times to regard themselves as having a monopoly on truth which meant that all other religious views are heretical or worse. This dangerous idea is far from dead as we all know. We must resist this with tolerance and the rule of law, which recognizes freedom of religion as a fundamental human right.

Religious Freedom

In our closely interconnected world of many different religious and cultural traditions, it is essential to recognize religious freedom as a fundamental human right. Fortunately the Universal Declaration of Human Rights, adopted in 1948 by the General Assembly of the United Nations, explicitly adopts this course. Article 18 of the Universal Declaration provides that:

> Everyone has the right to freedom of thought, conscience and religion; this right includes freedom to change his religion or belief, and freedom, either alone or in community with others and in public or private, to manifest his religion or belief in teaching, practice, worship and observance.

An additional fundamental human rights treaty of the United Nations system, the International Covenant on Civil and Political Rights (1966), elaborates this right with more detail, adding (Article 18, paragraph 3):

> Freedom to manifest one's religion or beliefs may be subject only to such limitations as are prescribed by law and are necessary to protect public safety, order, health, or morals or the fundamental rights and freedoms of others.

Regretfully, although religious freedom as formulated in these documents is a legally binding requirement in international customary law and treaty law, enforcement and compliance are sorely lacking. In many countries the principle of freedom of religion is violated in at least two respects: first, many governments, such as Iran, are theocracies in which the government actively promotes an established religion; second, in some countries, such as the Sudan, minority religions are persecuted and subject to discrimination.

There are two aspects to religious freedom—both go together. On the one hand, governments must allow the free exercise of religion by every person according to his own conscience and belief. On the other hand, a government should not promote or favor any one religion over another. Implicit in these two rights is the human right not to embrace any religion if this is what a person's conscience dictates.

1. Free Exercise of Religion

In the United States religious freedom is guaranteed by the First Amendment to the U.S. Constitution, part of the Bill of Rights ratified by the states in 1791. The First Amendment to the U.S. Constitution states, "Congress shall make no law prohibiting the free exercise [of religion]." The Fourteenth Amendment to the U.S. Constitution is interpreted by the U.S. Supreme Court to extend this to the states as well, but what is meant by the term "free exercise"? Does government have to accommodate every religious practice no matter what?

The free exercise problem may be analyzed on two levels. First, a law may be enacted in order to suppress or modify a particular religious practice or belief. This could be an obviously discriminatory law such as forbidding the building of mosques, which would be clearly unconstitutional; but what about a law prohibiting animal sacrifices? In *Church of the Lukumi Babalu Aye v. Hialeah*[53] a unanimous Supreme Court concluded such a law was unconstitutional because the prohibition was not "neutral and of general applicability," but rather was enacted with the intention of suppressing a religion. Although the religion involved was clearly out of the mainstream, the court held that a law squarely aimed at a religion will be tested against a "strict scrutiny" standard of validity, meaning there is a presumption that the law is unconstitutional unless the government can show some compelling interest advanced by the law. In this case neither the interests of public health nor preventing cruelty to animals were held sufficient to justify the law.

More difficult are cases of laws that do not target religious practices or beliefs but constitute incidental and unintended interference. The possible cases are legion. For example, what about military regulations specifying standards for clothing while soldiers are on duty—would this mean an Orthodox Jew could not wear a yarmulke? What about a law requiring children to attend school to age 16—could this be challenged by Amish parents who believe school attendance will destroy their way of life? Suppose government decides to ban the consumption of alcohol; can Jews and Christians who use wine in connection with religious rites and sacraments object?

Not surprisingly, when it comes to such laws such as these that incidentally impinge on religion, the justices of the U.S. Supreme Court have differing approaches and attitudes. One group, probably the majority at present, take the view that "an individual's religious beliefs [should not] excuse him from compliance with an otherwise valid law prohibiting conduct that the State is free to regulate."[54] Thus, in a case involving the use of peyote, a hallucinogen forbidden by state criminal law but used religiously at a Native American Church, the Supreme Court refused to protect the exercise of this religious practice. On the ground that accommodating every religious practice in the face of otherwise proper legal requirements is an invitation to anarchy, the court also refused to make exceptions even for matters that might be described as central to an individual's religion. The court said, "To make an individual's obligation to obey ... a law contingent with his religious beliefs ... is to permit him to become a law unto himself."[55]

A minority group of justices, however, maintains this goes too far, and that refusing accommodation to religious practices is discriminatory against minority religions.[56] These justices argue that sincere religious beliefs and practices should be exempted even from generally applicable laws except where the state's interest is "compelling."[57] Older cases favoring this approach include *Wisconsin v. Yoder*,[58] in which Amish children were exempted from compulsory school attendance laws.

Which view is best? What if fundamentalist Christian parents demand that their child be exempt from studying evolution although this is required by state standards for scientific literacy? Surely accommodation to religion would go too far if this were done on the grounds that "ignorance is bliss." Religious people should be expected to comply with generally applicable laws and regulations as long as they are not hostile to religion or aimed at suppressing religious belief. We all must accommodate ourselves to some inconvenience as a price of living in an ordered society.

2. Establishment of Religion

The First Amendment also forbids Congress or the States from "establishing" or favoring religion. In *Everson v. Board of Education*[59] the Supreme Court interpreted this prohibition to mean "at least this: neither a state nor the Federal Government can set up a church. Neither can pass laws which aid one religion, aid all religions, or prefer one religion over another." In *Van Orden v. Perry*[60] the Supreme Court described the Establishment Clause of the First Amendment as "Janislike" because "one face looks toward the strong role played by religion and religious traditions throughout our Nation's history" while "the other face looks toward the principle that government intervention in religious matters can endanger religious freedom." Thus, government must not favor religion, but should not be hostile to religious traditions.

This principle appears very clear, but many cases arise that involve an entanglement between the state and religion that is difficult to decode. The Establishment Clause was the basis on which, for example, the laws requiring the teaching of creation "science" and "intelligent design" were declared unconstitutional because they overstepped the line against favoring or "establishing" religion. In those cases the lower courts as well as the Supreme Court employed a legal test for establishment known as the *Lemon* test,[61] which looks to the purpose of the law to determine if the line against establishment is crossed. If the purpose is to advance religion, the law will be invalid; but if there is a secular purpose even if the subject matter is religious, the law will be upheld. The *Lemon* purpose test was employed by the Supreme Court majority in the 2005 case of *McCreary County, Kentucky v. American Civil Liberties Association of Kentucky*[62] to declare invalid a law requiring the Ten Commandments to be posted on the walls of all Kentucky courthouses.

However, many justices of the Supreme Court dispute the accuracy of the *Lemon* test. In another 2005 case, *Van Orden v. Perry*, a different Supreme Court majority held that a six foot high monument on the grounds of the Texas State Capital inscribed with the Ten Commandments could remain "in recognition of the role of God in our Nation's heritage." The court rejected the applicability of the *Lemon* test as "not useful in dealing with the sort of passive monument Texas has erected on Capital grounds." Obviously the difference between the Kentucky and Texas cases is very slight. Apparently the court viewed Kentucky as active promotion of religion, while the Texas monument was considered more passive in character. In addition, while the Kentucky display would have involved many sites; the Texas monument was a single display, so the two could be interpreted to send different messages about religion.

There is an undeniable split of opinion among both judges and the general public about what should be considered impermissible establishment of religion. For example, the Supreme Court has ruled that the Establishment Clause permits a state legislature to open its daily sessions with a prayer led by a chaplain paid by the state,[63] but in a series of cases also ruled that requiring school prayers,[64] a graduation prayer,[65] and even a daily minute of silence for meditation or voluntary prayer[66] are unconstitutional. As with the two Ten Commandments cases discussed above, the Supreme Court has also sent contradictory messages when it comes to public display of religious symbols. In one case the court forbade the display of a Christmas crèche inside a courthouse, but allowed the display of a menorah outside the building.[67] Yet in other cases the court has allowed outdoor displays of Christmas Nativity scenes[68] and an unattended cross in a public square.[69]

Certainly critics of the *Lemon* test are right to say that it is too simplistic to make the purpose of a law a litmus test of whether it favors religion. Where religion and religious symbolism is part of the inherent values of our public life and part of a nation's traditions and cultural heritage, they should be allowed. As Justice Kennedy has said, "Non-coercive government action within the realm of flexible accommodation or passive acknowledgement of existing symbols does not violate the Establishment Clause unless it benefits religion in a way more direct and more substantial than practices that are accepted in our national heritage."[70] Kennedy proposes a new three part test that would permit government action to advance religious values on three conditions:

- Non-coerciveness
- Accommodation or passive acknowledgement
- Similarity to accepted historical practices

This test is a good filter against objectionable favoritism of religion, but one that still would allow government to acknowledge in a public way the importance of religion in history, culture and traditions. It should be permissible for government to acknowledge the importance of religion in society and even the practice of religion without inculcation or coercion.

Summing Up: Final Thoughts About Religious Knowledge

To sum up we must address the important question — is religious knowledge truth? If so, what kind of truth?

To answer these questions we must first define again the nature of truth. Our first thought may be to say that truth is what corresponds with reality. But what is reality? In fact science shows very vividly that the correspondence or a picture theory of truth does not work. We cannot picture what the world of fundamental reality — at the scales of the universe and sub-atomic particles — is like. What looks to be solid bodies — what Aristotle called substances — are really processes driven by cosmological constants that we do not really understand. The correspondence theory of truth will not work for science, let alone for religion.

A second theory of truth we must discard is the empiricist theory that any meaningful statement about the world must be verifiable by observation.[71] Again even scientific propositions do not all pass this criterion. We accept the idea that light is both a wave and a particle even though no one has observed this directly and it is probably beyond our capacity to observe or understand. Furthermore, the empiricist theory breaks down when turned upon itself: it is self-referentially meaningless because we cannot prove it by observation.

We also cannot equate truth to sufficient evidence or even falsifiable as science does. To limit truth to what is supported by evidence necessarily eliminates much of World Three human knowledge. For example, in law, culture and the humanities — art and literature — we employ standards of truth where evidence does not come into play. We cannot give evidence that Shakespeare's *Hamlet* is a masterpiece. Evidentialism is too narrow a base on which to build human knowledge outside the sciences. Much of what we know in every field, including the sciences, is interpretative — hermeneutical — in character. This would be excluded by a strict evidentiary standard.

The best criterion for truth is simply rational belief. We can validly believe something to be true if it is rational at the time we believe it. Admittedly, this standard is quite broad; what I believe very rationally today may turn out to be wrong. But that is all right; it is better to err on the side of belief than to arbitrarily exclude many important things that may well be true. In addition to rational belief as a standard of truth, we should also judge our beliefs by pragmatism. If a belief works it may be considered true, at least until it fails the test of rationality. As pointed out above, pragmatism is extensively used even in science. For the scientist belief is not something that mirrors the world; rather it is something that works, that is useful. For example, we do not worry that Newton's laws of motion are not exactly correct; we use them anyway and they work just fine.

We also cannot equate truth with some final and fixed all-encompassing vision of the world that explains everything. Truth has always been and will always be a moving target. We also should not be epistemological individualists a la René Descartes, whose methodology was to doubt everything that he could not prove to himself. This is frankly silly; we are born into a world of traditions and belief and our duty is to make sense out of it with the help of other people. We properly must rely on authority, tradition and culture as guides.

Finally, however, we should not accept religious or any other beliefs uncritically. This leads to another important standard of truth: coherence. We must evaluate our religious beliefs critically to make sure they cohere, not only within themselves but also with other branches of human knowledge. This means for example, that our religious and scientific knowledge must cohere. Irrationality is dangerous; especially when we try to protect our religious beliefs from critical inquiry. Fortunately, in most religions —

such as Christianity and Judaism — there is a long tradition of critical examination of religious beliefs. This critical inquiry will be the subject of the next chapter.

Notes

1. Paul J. O. Tillich, *Dynamics of Faith*, p. 1 (Harper & Row, New York, 1957). Tillich states more fully that faith is "a total and centered act of the personal self, the act of unconditional, infinite and ultimate concern." Ibid., p. 22.

2. Emile Durkheim, *The Elementary Forms of the Religious Life*, 12 (1912).

3. See generally, Alister E. McGrath, *Christian Theology: An Introduction* (Blackwell, Oxford, 1994).

4. Summa Contra Gentiles; and Summa Theologiae (English translations available in many modern editions).

5. Hans Kung, *Christianity: Its Essence and History* (SCM London 1995).

6. Karl Barth, *Church Dogmatics* (T&T Clark, Edinburgh, 1939–1976).

7. Karl Rahner, *Foundations of Christian Faith* (DLT, London, 1978).

8. Rudolph Bultmann. Bultmann believed that Jesus of Nazareth taught his message using the accepted mythical and storytelling framework of his times, but that contemporary Christians must cut through and abandon this mythology to discover the real value of Jesus's teachings. See Karl Jaspers and Rudolph Bultmann, *Myth and Christianity: An Inquiry into the Possibility of Religion without Myth* (Prometheus Books, 2005).

9. Karen Armstrong, *A Short History of Myth*, chapter ii (2005).

10. Mircea Eliade, *Myth and Reality*, trans. Willard R. Trask. New York: Harper and Row, 1963.

11. Perhaps the leading exponent is Richard Dawkins, *The Selfish Gene* (1989).

12. Sam Harris, *The End of Faith*, 232 (2005).

13. John Dupre, *Darwin's Legacy*, 57 (Oxford University Press 2003).

14. Stephen Jay Gould, "Nonoverlapping Magisteria," in *Science and Religion*, Paul Kurtz (ed), 191 (New York, Prometheus Books, 2003) [emphasis in the original].

15. Address of Pope John Paul II to the Pontifical Academy of Sciences, October 22, 1996, text available at *www.vatican.org*.

16. 2 Kings 9–12.

17. Richard Dawkins, "You Can't Have It Both Ways," in *Science and Religion*, op. cit p. 207.

18. Dante Alighieri, *La Commedia Divina*, Paradiso (Italian text, Mediasoft s.r.l.), *www.mediasoft.it/Dante*, visited January 20, 2007, translation into English by the author..

19. Lucretius, *De Rerum Natura* (*On the Nature of Things*), Book 2, line 1090.

20. Notably Goethe developed a theory of colors in opposition to that of Newton.

21. Quoted in Brian Silver, *The Ascent of Science*, 71 (Oxford 1998).

22. Malthus' essay "On Population" was published in 1798.

23. Reprinted from the New York Times Service in the *Chicago Tribune*, March 7, 2006, p. 16.

24. Janet Browne, *Charles Darwin*, Vol. 2, p. 61 (Alfred A. Knopf, 2002).
25. Ibid., p. 385
26. For a complete history see Peter J. Bowler, *Evolution: The History of an Idea* (Berkeley, University of California Press, 1984).
27. Dante intended his great poem to be read also as a Christian and a moral allegory. *The Divine Comedy* may be read as an allegory of the soul's journey to God, as a moral allegory, as an allegory of love, and as an allegory of freedom.
28. As a criterion of meaning it does not even pass its own test since the proposition that something is true only if it can be verified by the senses cannot verify the logical positivist criterion of truth itself.
29. Rudolph Otto, *The Idea of the Holy*, John W. Harvey trans. (Oxford University Press, 1958).
30. Ibid., p. 40.
31. Ibid., p. 113.
32. *Concluding Unscientific Postscript* (1846).
33. Ibid.
34. Other justifications for religious knowledge are less convincing. (1) Immanuel Kant finds religious belief in our sense of morality and moral law, which he regards as based upon a priori principles. Belief in God for Kant is a "postulate" of practical reason. Kant, Groundwork of the Metaphysics of Morals. (2) Friedrich Schleiermacher finds religious knowledge in the human feeling of utter dependence and the fact that all of our spontaneous activity is utterly dependent on some (unconceptualizable) source beyond us. *Christian Faith*, Mackintosh and Stewart, trans. (Edinburgh: T&T Clarke, 1986). (3) Blaise Pascal finds belief in what he calls a wager: if God exists and we believe, we gain much; if God does not exist and we believe, we lose little. Pensees (1670).
35. Rudolph Bultmann, *What Does It Mean to Speak of God?*
36. Paul Tillich, *The Nature of Faith*, op. cit., p. 38. Tillich finds an ambiguity in the human experience of the divine: on the one hand, we seek our fulfillment in the infinite; on the other we are put off by the infinite distance between the finite and the infinite.
37. Karl Barth, *Dogmatics in Outline*, GT Thomson, trans. (New York: Harper & Row, 1959). See also Karl Barth, *Church Dogmatics* (1956–1973).
38. Martin Buber, *I and Thou*. W. Kaufmann, trans. (New York: Scribner's 1970).
39. Emanuel Levinas, "Ethics of the Infinite," in Richard Kearney, *States of Mind: Dialogues with Contemporary Thinkers* (New York: NYU Press, 1995).
40. See James C. Livingston, *Anatomy of the Sacred* (New York: Macmillan Publishing Co. 1993).
41. The reader will note my opposition not only to Nietzsche's view of religion but also Karl Marx, who believed religion was the "opium of the people" meaning that the solace provided by religion to common people was part of the alienation and exploitation of the worker in society. Karl Marx, "Preface to a Contribution to a Critique of the Political Economy," in Robert C. Tucker, *The Marx-Engels Reader* (Norton 1978). I also disagree with Sigmund Fried who called religion a "universal obsessional neurosis of humanity." Sigmund Freud, *The Future of an Illusion* (1934).
42. Rig-Veda 10, 129.
43. Many scholars regard the biblical story of the Exodus and the subsequent

wanderings in the desert as an idealized account drafted by later authors. See the *Cambridge Companion to the Bible*, 73 (1997).

44. The date is uncertain. Traditionally Zoroastra lived about 660 BCE but scholars think that is incorrect and he lived much earlier.

45. Cyrus also encouraged the Jews to rebuild the Jerusalem temple.

46. These people are referred to in Iran as Gabars, a word that loosely means infidels, because they do not share the majority faith.

47. Regretfully, much of the Avesta and the Gathas were lost as a result of Muslim persecution.

48. These scriptures, composed in Pali as well as Sanskrit, are traditionally divided into three Baskets (Tripitaka).

49. The Japanese word Shinto is actually derived from the Chinese word shentao, meaning way of the spirits or gods. In native Japanese the term is "kami no michi."

50. Battle Array, The Koran (Penguin Classics, NJ Dawood trans.), p. 391

51. Nanak's birthplace is near modern Lahore in Pakistan.

52. See John Hick, *Problems of Religious Pluralism* (New York: St. Martin's Press, 1985).

53. 508 US 520 (1993).

54. *Employment Division, Department of Human Resources v. Smith*, 494 US 872, 882 (1990).

55. Ibid. at 890.

56. For example, in *Lyng v. Northwest Indian Cemetery Protective Association*, 485 US 439 (1988) the court refused to prevent timber harvesting on national forest lands considered sacred by Native American tribes. The question can be asked, would not the U.S. Forest Service make an accommodation if such lands were sacred to Christians?

57. See the concurring opinion of Justice O'Connor, ibid., p. 894.

58. 406 US 205 (1972).

59. 330 US 1, 23 (1947).

60. 125 S.Ct. 2854 (2005).

61. This test comes from the case of *Lemon v. Kurzman*, 403 US 602 (1971).

62. 125 S. Ct. 2722 (2005).

63. *Marsh v. Chambers*, 463 US 783 (1983). [*Lemon* not applied].

64. *Engel v. Vitale*, 370 US 421 (1962) [non-sectarian prayer ruled unconstitutional even though students were allowed to remain silent or leave the room].

In *School District of Abingdon v Schempp*, 374 US 203 (1963), the court ruled unconstitutional a Pennsylvania law requiring every school day to begin with prayers.

65. *Lee v. Weisman*, 505 US (1992).

66. *Wallace v. Jaffree*, 472 US 38 (1985).

67. *County of Allegheny Union v. American Civil Liberties Union, Greater Pittsburgh Chapter*, 492 US 573 (1989).

68. *Lynch v. Donnelly*, 465 US 668 (1984).

69. *Capitol Square Review and Advisory Board v. Pinette*, 515 US 753 (1995).

70. County of Allegheny 492 US at 590.

71. See A. J. Ayer, *Language, Truth and Logic* (1957).

Chapter 5

The World of Philosophy

The Importance of Philosophy

A legitimate question is how relevant is philosophy to an examination of the relationship between science and religion? Philosophy is the search for fundamental truths about the world through rational inquiry. Religion purports to give us ultimate truth, but to some extent at least, eschews reason in favor of supernatural insight or authority. Science has its own method of attaining truth through induction and experimentation. So how does philosophy relate to either science or religion?

In traditional terms philosophy can be subdivided into four fields of inquiry. First, the most ancient branch of philosophy asks the question: what is reality? The search for reality was begun by the ancient Greeks, who founded the field of what we call metaphysics (ontology), the quest for supernatural realities.

A second branch of philosophy is epistemology — which asks and tries to answer the question, what can we know?

A third branch is logic, invented by the Greeks and part of what was studied in Medieval Europe as one of the subjects of the trivium, which is traditionally the effort to discover principles of right reasoning, chiefly deduction, the inferences which necessarily follow from necessary propositions.

A fourth branch of philosophy is ethics or moral philosophy, rational inquiry into the standards of right and wrong with respect to character and conduct.

Philosophy is useful, even indispensable in any discussion of the relationship between science and religion because philosophy can bridge the abyss separating these two fields. For there is a disconnect between science and religion: science employs methods and criteria of verifiability that by definition exclude religious concepts; religion purports to attain truths that are beyond scientific explanation and, in some instances, such as creationism, appear to contradict science.

Philosophy can help bridge this disconnect in two principal ways. First, philosophy can inquire into the nature of both religious and scientific knowledge to determine the basis of such knowledge and the limits of the knowledge each purports to acquire. Second, philosophy can be an essential supplement to both scientific knowledge and religious belief.

The necessity of supplementing religious knowledge and faith with philosophy is the official teaching of the Roman Catholic Church, the world's largest religious organization. In his 1998 Encyclical Letter, *Fides et Ratio*, Pope John Paul II condemned what he called a "resurgence of fideism (rejection of reason)" and "Biblicism," which "fails to recognize the importance of rational knowledge and philosophical discourse for the understanding of faith ... and tends to make the reading and exegesis of Sacred Scripture the sole criterion of truth."

But how far does philosophy take us? Is philosophy capable of proving the existence of God? Can we reach the divine through reason? The answer we shall see is a qualified "no": we cannot prove the existence of God, but there are reasonable ways to know the divine through myth, symbols, and analogy. But in the last instance, we shall see that acceptance of religion is not a necessary truth that we must come to if we are reasonable creatures; rather it is a free and personal act of assent on our part. Philosophy cannot compel this assent; it can only prepare it.

The Limits of Knowledge

Philosophy is a bridge between science and religion because of what it tells us about the nature of human knowledge and its limits. In common parlance we think of scientific knowledge as certain and irrefutable. Religious belief, on the other hand, is speculative and subject to doubt. This is borne out by the fact that there is general agreement on scientific truths, but no agreement on religious belief.

Yet this facile distinction is dubious: in actuality scientific knowledge, like religious belief, rests upon assumptions that are akin to faith, and there appear to be inherent limits to scientific knowledge, just as the case with religious belief.

A first article of faith we can point to in science is the hypothesis of uniformity of natural laws. All of science relies on the unspoken idea that there are unchanging natural laws that operate the same way all over the universe and have done so for billions of years, in fact since the beginning of time. But can this assumption be proved? As the Scottish philosopher David Hume (1711–1776) famously argued in his work *Enquiry Concerning Human Understanding* (1748), the answer is no. We cannot, strictly speaking prove the validity of the uniformity of nature, and we cannot even argue that it is empirically true without begging the question. We can only accept this assumption, as we all do, on a basis that is akin to faith.

The history of science also shows the limits of our scientific understanding of the world. As we have seen in Chapter 3, every field of science has undergone a series of revolutions of thinking over the past several hundred years. For example, Descartes' model of a mechanical universe of inert, insensible corpuscles was modified by Newton's dynamic universe of bodies of matter operating according to fixed laws of motion and universal gravitation. But Newton was overthrown by Einstein's theories of relativity and quantum mechanics. Similar revolutions have occurred in chemistry, astronomy, geology psychology, and most importantly, biology with the theory of evolution by natural selection. Thomas Kuhn, in his book *The Structure of Scientific Revolutions* (1963), famously argued that the adoption of a new paradigm in science involves an act of faith: the transfer of allegiance from one paradigm to another "is a conversion experience which cannot be forced" or compelled by rational analysis. Science today works within paradigms that are accepted almost without question. But history tells us that, although we have no basis for questioning them, they are unlikely to be the last word.

Another controversy in scientific knowledge has to do with whether science gives us actual knowledge of reality or merely provides useful observational evidence. The former view is known as *realism* because it posits that science is capable of providing knowledge about things-in-themselves. The latter view, the anti-realist position, is that science can never penetrate the underlying nature of reality, which will forever remain hidden from our eyes. The dominant view is the realist position, but this again must be taken on faith: if there is an underlying reality we cannot know, we have no way of knowing its existence to prove that we cannot know it.

Perhaps the major proponent of the view that there is an underlying reality, the thing in itself, that we can never know is the philosopher Immanuel Kant. In his *Critique of Pure Reason* (1790), Kant makes the case that with respect to many questions there can be "no final judgment because much must remain uncertain and insoluble" to the human mind.[1] Kant refers to these as antinomies of pure reason which are beyond the capacity of philosophy. Some additional "antinomies"—mind breakers—include the existence of the soul and immortality, the problem of evil, free will, whether the universe is infinite or enclosed in boundaries, and the existence of God or a Supreme Being, which we turn to next.

Intelligent Design: Rational Arguments for the Existence of God

Is it possible to prove the existence of God? The contemporary preoccupation of the creationists to prove the existence of God through intelligent design is not new. For centuries, beginning with the ancient Greeks (and perhaps before), philosophers and religious figures have formulated proofs for God's existence. Creationism and intelligent design are really revivals of very old proofs. How do proofs for the existence of God fare in the light of current philosophical and scientific knowledge?

There are actually three groups of rational arguments for the existence of God: (1) the cosmological proofs; (2) the teleological proofs; and (3) ontological proofs. We will define and deal with each of these in turn.[2]

1. Cosmological Proofs

The cosmological proofs attempt to prove God's existence from the reality of the world around us. The world we see must have some cause or origin, just as a statue we see in the park must have had some maker. Plato composed a story of creation to set forth his version of the cosmological argument. In *Timaeus*, Plato approaches the problem in terms of the relation between his ideal world of the perfect, unchanging Forms and the real world of changing, individual beings. He concludes that the world we see around us must have been fashioned by a divine "Craftsman" (in Greek, demiourgos) who made the individual things of our world according to the plans and blueprints of the corresponding eternal Forms. Aristotle did not accept the idea of Forms, but he kept the basic notion that since motion requires a cause, there must necessarily be some First Mover, who is responsible for setting everything going.

St. Thomas Aquinas (1224–1274) turned these tentative ideas into elegant rational proofs. This was the age of the great 13th century medieval synthesis when science, philosophy and theology all seemed to come together to point to a supreme Creator God who was all-good, all-knowing and all-powerful. Thomas employed a family of several related cosmological arguments.[3] First, Thomas argued that there must be a First Mover; second there must be a First Cause; third, since there are contingent beings there must be One Necessary Being; and fourth, since there are gradations in the world — such as hot, hotter and hottest, there is an ultimate cause of all qualities. So just as fire — the hottest thing "must be the cause of all hot things ... there must also be something which is to all beings the cause of their being, goodness and every other perfection; and this we call God."

Despite the elegance of Thomas's reasoning, contemporary science and what we know about the world demolishes these arguments. For the Greeks and for the medieval mind, motion was impossible without a cause. But Newton's First Law of Motion tells us that this is not the case. Motion does not require a cause. Furthermore, even if motion required a cause, why posit only one cause? Is it not more rational to posit many "first" causes? At least there is no reason to suppose there is only one as opposed to many. In addition, modern science has destroyed the medieval notion of a hierarchy or chain of being, an ascending order each slightly more perfect than the one before. For example, fire is not the cause of everything hot. Heat is produced by atomic and subatomic processes that we can describe but we do not fully understand. The cosmological proofs also do not lead to the idea of a loving, personal God, the concept to which many religions hold so dear.

2. Teleological Proofs

The word "teleological" comes from the Greek word "telos," which means end or purpose. The fundamental idea is that the world around us exhibits a design in that. as Thomas says, "things ... such as natural bodies ... act for an end, and this is evident from their acting always or nearly always in the same way, so as to achieve the best result. Hence it is evident they achieve their end not fortuitously but designedly." Thomas goes on to argue that since the natural objects all acting for an end lack intelligence, they must be designed and ordered by an intelligent Being whom we call God.

This argument by design is based on Aristotelian physics: all things move in order to fulfill an ultimate purpose. Violent motion is possible; therefore, I can throw a stone into the air. But natural motion, the stone falling to its place on earth, is inevitable because of design. Of course this idea of design was overthrown by the scientific revolution of the 16th and 17th centuries. It does not rain in order to make human crops flourish; rivers do not flow to the sea to fulfill their purpose. Therefore, this argument based on design is no longer credible.

Another, more powerful, argument based on design appeared in the 18th century. Most famously stated by the English theologian William Paley (1743–1805), the design argument is based on analogy: Paley points to an analogy between a watch and the works of nature. If I come upon a watch lying on the ground and examine it carefully, I am compelled to come to the conclusion that it did not just turn up. Something as complex as watch demands a designer. So too when I contemplate the design I see in nature — "in a degree which exceeds all computation" — I must conclude that there exists a designer who we call God. This argument is based on the Principle of Sufficient Reason, that nothing can exist without an adequate cause.

The intelligent design arguments put forward by those opposing evolution and Darwinism are virtually identical to William Paley's design argument. Both rely on "irreducible complexity" and the analogy between something made by design like a watch and the natural world. The answers that science provides make these arguments untenable. The doctrine of evolution does in fact tell us that the complexity of the natural world can occur through natural selection. Furthermore, random chance has the capacity to produce a stable order of things that look designed.

But Darwinism and evolution should not take the blame for demolishing the argument for intelligent design. Even on non-scientific grounds the design argument fails. David Hume, the Scottish philosopher who lived a century before Darwin, effectively put down design as a proof for the existence of God. In his *Dialogues Concerning Natural Religion* (1778) Hume exposed that the design argument is hopelessly anthropomorphic and produces perverse explanations. How can design prove what Hume called "the unity of the Deity"? After all, Hume said, "why may not several deities combine in contriving and framing the world?" As with a ship or anything in our experience, no one person is responsible; perhaps the universe was fashioned by many different designers. In addition, since there are "many noticeable difficulties" with respect to the design of our world, perhaps the designers were actually very poorly trained and prepared for the task; or maybe they were an evil bunch who made our world for their own perverse enjoyment.[4]

3. The Ontological Argument

The so-called ontological arguments for the existence of God are based on pure logic. The great medieval theologian Anselm (1033–1109), archbishop of Canterbury, formulated it first, and others such as Descartes and Leibniz had their own versions. The argument is that I have in my mind the idea of a most perfect being, a being greater than any other that can possibly be conceived. But this being necessarily exists, because if it did not, it would not be the most perfect being that could possibly be conceived; there would be another more perfect — an identical being that has existence. In other words, as Descartes[5] puts it, there can not be anything more manifest than that there is a God, "a Supreme Being to whose essence existence pertains."

Virtually no one accepts the ontological argument today, but not because of opposition from science. Rather, the argument does not hold together because, as Immanuel Kant said in the 18th century, existence is not a predicate the way red or yellow or other words that characterize reality are predicates. Thus, when I say "lions are not red," it is as if I am saying "lions exist and they are not red." If I say "a unicorn is an animal with one horn," I mean, "if unicorns exist they have one horn." But if I say "unicorns do not exist," I am not saying "if (or that) unicorns exist, they do not exist" — this would be nonsense. Existence, then, is not a real predicate and does not add any quality to a concept. Thus, existence is not a necessary attribute to my concept of the absolutely greatest being that can be conceived.

Beyond this logical and linguistic fallacy, there is real doubt that the concept of the greatest being that can be conceived has any meaning or is even possible to conceive. My concept of the greatest anything will always be limited by my experience and by human concerns. I will always end up with a very human-like Supreme Being and one who exits in absolute space and time because these are my modes of thought. We cannot define something that by its very nature is indefinable. To define is to set limits; God is beyond those limits. We cannot define God or the divine except in very imperfect and inadequate terms. Thus, human reason is not an adequate tool to capture either divine existence or essence.

A New Idea of God

Should we be troubled or upset because philosophy cannot prove the existence of God or a Supreme Being? On the contrary, we should breathe a sigh of relief. A God that is amenable to human reason or science would be necessarily all too human, rather like the Greek gods on Mount Olympus, anthropomorphic deities, or at best the abstract and distant gods of Plato and Aristotle. As the French mathematician and philosopher Blaise Pascal (1623–1662) says, "The God of the philosophers is not the God of Abraham, Isaac, and Jacob."[6] He adds that "if we submit everything to reason, our religion will have no mysterious or supernatural element."[7] Pascal's point is that we are finite creatures and we can comprehend only the finite; the infinite is necessarily beyond our comprehension. But nevertheless, reason and philosophical reflection is useful and indeed indispensable to faith because it allows us to prepare for faith, which he says is a free acceptance of God. Faith as a personal commitment is "felt by the heart, not by reason." In this context Pascal makes his famous statement, "The heart has reasons that reason does not understand."[8] He says:

> The last procedure of reason is to recognize that there is infinity of things that lie beyond it.... We must know when to doubt, when to feel certain, when to submit. He who does not do so does not understand the force of reason.... There is nothing so conformable to reason as this final disavowal of reason.[9]

In this context Pascal advocates his famous wager — that it is a better bet to believe in God than to believe the opposite. But Pascal's wager is widely misunderstood. It is not simply a coldly pragmatic calculation. The purpose of the wager is not to convince the unbeliever, but rather to shake our religious indifference and to show us that the necessary agnosticism of the human mind is a necessary precondition to belief.

What this means is that we must rid ourselves entirely of many deeply engrained misconceptions concerning God and religion. We cannot rely on rational proofs and evidence to reach God; rather passionate commitment, faith and the will to believe are paramount. We must also reject all anthropomorphisms that purport to describe the nature of God. Christians, for example, for centuries pictured a three-tiered universe, and God was of course "up there." When this conception was made untenable by modern science, God was still "out there" in the great beyond. Modern physics can surely find a place for God in one of the newly posited eleven dimensions of space-time. But all these picture ideas of reality are nonsensical. The only valid thing that we can say about God is to return to the ideas of the ancient Aryans that God is the "inconceivable" and the "inexpressible." This is the meaning intended by Rudolph Otto when he said that God was the experience of the "Mysterium Tremendum."[10]

It should not surprise us that we cannot grasp the nature of the divine or the supernatural through our human faculties. Even with respect to the fundamental nature of everyday reality, our material world of trees, rocks and stars, neither modern science nor philosophical reasoning has given us certain knowledge of the ultimate nature of reality. Consider, for example, ontology, the branch of philosophy that deals with the study of being as such. This is an ancient field with contributions by all major philosophers beginning with Plato and Aristotle. In later times ontology was defined as a "general theory of what there is," the distinction between being and non-being.

Down through the centuries many ontological debates raged concerning the fundamental nature of reality. Idealists maintained that reality consists of ideas or souls; realists maintained the irreducible reality of the world around us; atomists posited atoms — tiny little balls — as fundamental; materialists say only matter is real. All these ideas have in common the idea that reality consists of things — substances of some sort. But what twentieth century science tells us is that reality is most fundamentally not a thing at all. Substances — things — are simply the way human beings perceive the world. Fundamental reality consists of energy — ongoing events, processes and relationships. What looks to us like a solid object is mostly empty space punctuated by ongoing forces and energy. The processes that make up these forces relate to each other so as to create what looks to us like the world of substances. Somehow at the sub-sub-atomic level there are on-going events and relationships that underlie strong, weak, electromagnetic forces as well as gravity. Their interaction produces the "particle zoo" of quantum physics and more processes and interactions that we do not fully understand. Somehow at the level of reality we inhabit this translates into bodies, trees and rocks as well as stars, comets and planets. Even the world we inhabit and we think we know so well is infused with mystery and uncertainty.

Does this realization aid our understanding of the mystery surrounding the divine? At least we should rid ourselves of all the old, rationally-based conceptions of God. This is where the fundamentalists go terribly wrong: their cause is a last-ditch effort to keep the rational, traditional picture of God, the easy God to reach just by reading the Bible or the Qur'an. In reality, God and religion are much more demanding. In his classic sermon "Shaking the Foundations" (1949), Paul Tillich said God is the "infinite and inexhaustible depth and ground of all being, the depth of your life, your ultimate concern."[11] This statement is, in fact, an admission of our fundamental uncertainty about religious truth that is part of the human predicament.

Expressing the Transcendent

How can we possibly express religious truth? It would seem to be a hopeless task given our new conception of the divine. If God is "inconceivable" does this not foreclose all doctrinal content? Does it not in effect make all statements about God meaningless? Paradoxically, the opposite is true: our new idea of God is represents liberation: we are liberated from literalism, historicism and scientism in talking about God.

What this means is that, although literalism and historicism have their place, there are additional and more valid ways of expressing religious truths. These are opened up to us when we free ourselves from the traditional conception of God. Hinduism has long been accustomed to this idea. Their English overlords were astonished and aghast at the multiplicity of idols and gods. No one could even explain why or where they came from. Even animals — elephants, fishes, boars, tortoises — could be gods, and sexual intercourse could represent union with the gods. For the Indian mind, however, there was no need to take everything at face value as the English with their rationalistic concept of One God and three persons. There may be one transcendental God, but to make Him accessible and approachable, it is necessary to maintain many different points of access. Thus, for Hindus God is manifest (1) as the Supreme Transcendental One; (2) in the form of its emanations (avatara) (3) in the heart or self of each individual; (4) as controller of the universe; and (5) as the Divine Presence within a consecrated temple icon (murti). In his novel *A Passage to India*, E. M. Forster expresses exactly this point when describing a religious festival — the birth of God — taking place in a rajah's palace:

> God is not born yet — that will occur at midnight — but He has also been born centuries ago, nor can He ever be born, because He is the Lord of the Universe, who transcends human processes.

There are several ways we can express and celebrate religious truth, bridging the gap between the finite and the infinite:

1. Myth

In common parlance a myth is equated with something that is not true, but a religious myth is not necessarily a falsehood. A myth properly understood is a story about events that occur in space and time but that relate to supernatural truth. A myth is a story created not by an individual but by a community. Both stories and community are central to human needs and experience. Myths may strain credulity in their literal sense, but they are intended to illuminate human nature and truth in universal terms rather than in literal, specific ways. Myths are created to express important truths that cannot be said, only shown. Myth, like symbol and metaphor, is a way of expressing transcendental truth.

Myths are universal to all humans and pervasive in all cultures. This is because they are a means to convey truths that cannot be conveyed in any other way. Myths are unique and universal because they possess unique qualities. The truth of a myth may not be affected even if the underlying facts are shown to be wrong. For example, the flood narrative of the Book of Genesis in the Hebrew Bible cannot possibly be literally true. The text itself is contradictory as to the flood's duration and as to whether Noah brought "two of every living thing" or seven. And there is no geological evidence of any world-wide flood. Nevertheless, the Genesis flood myth conveys its own truth: the reality of divine order and justice in the world. The truth of a myth may even survive the disappearance of the religion that gave it birth. For example, the Epic of Gilgamesh composed in Mesopotamia perhaps as early as 2700 BCE still speaks to us about the futility of the quest for human immortality.

Myths can be expressive of religious truth in that they speak to us in the discourse of the time in which they were composed. Of course, we should investigate their literal meaning and truth if possible; but if this is not possible or even if they are factually not accurate, we can accept the truth they contain. For example, the miracles performed by Jesus as described in the Gospels may or may not be factually true; but this is irrelevant if we accept them as myths used by the authors to convey truths about the character of Jesus in concepts common at the time.

Without denying that Rudolf Bultmann's program of demythologizing has its place, mythic discourse is essential to our understanding of the world even today. Myths serve several functions: cosmological myths supplement and provide an antidote to our scientific rationalities and uncertainties, sociological myths support the structures of human societies, psychological myths give us truths of human nature, and moral myths teach us how to behave. Myths both delight and terrorize and are deeply engrained within all of us.

2. Analogy

As St. Thomas Aquinas[12] realized many centuries ago, it is possible to speak of God and the divine only by analogy. What does this mean? Two fundamental kinds of analogy may be distinguished: a first type we use all the time is a comparison of two different things to a third thing. For example, we might say both a mine shaft and the water in a lake are deep. This is not the type of analogy we use when speaking of God. Rather, in religious discourse we use proportional analogies. We speak of goodness, but we can imagine goodness only in a human sense. Thus, we employ human concepts with the idea that we do not mean them literally; they must be proportioned to the divine to have any real meaning.

3. Symbolism

Symbols are fundamental to religious worship and religious meaning. Religious discourse does not make sense unless we realize the importance of symbols and symbolism. What does this mean?

A symbol is a material thing that we associate with a larger idea or meaning. This can be either a religious or a non-religious concept. For example, we associate gardens with paradise, the cross with Christianity; but W. B. Yeats in his poem "Sailing to Byzantium" uses Byzantium (a non-existent city) as a symbol for immortality and eternity. A symbol should be distinguished from a mere sign or a signal. These two are merely utilitarian and prosaic. We employ them every day because we need them to live our daily life, but they do not carry any profound significance. For example, red lights make us stop; a barber pole tells us where we may get our hair cut.

A symbol, on the other hand, is more than a sign; it participates in the meaning of what it represents. For example, the flag or the cross have value and meaning in themselves, while a traffic light does not. Why is this? Symbols seem to correspond to something timeless deep within human nature. Other animals employ signs, but only humans use symbols. Symbolism is universal to the point where mankind can be defined as a "symbol-making animal."[13]

Religious symbols represent and transmit to us the world of the holy.

They are flexible and dynamic and have the power to open up levels of reality that are otherwise hidden from us. What would otherwise be dull and opaque is made vivid and real. Consider, for example, the Christian Eucharist or the many forms of the Buddha. These open up a transcendent reality that impacts our hearts and minds. Symbols play this role in other domains as well: in art, music, and poetry. We thus must recognize the power of symbolism in human life and give full credit to religious symbolism.

The essential role of symbolism is also the reason why no religion can be really understood intellectually through reason alone. Religion is highly practical and ritualistic. Only through participation in rituals and festivals can we experience the power of symbolism and its role in opening up what is otherwise transcendent and hidden. This is why all religions have festivals and rituals. In religions like Judaism, Christianity and Islam, festivals cover the entire calendar. Observance of festivals has tremendous significance and power; through symbolism secular space-time is transcended and becomes sacred space-time.

4. Hermeneutics

Hermeneutics is the study of ways to transmit the meaning of texts or spoken words. The meaning of most of what we encounter is clear to us; we can take it at face value. Religious speech and texts, however, require sometimes very sophisticated interpretive techniques that are beyond the ken of most of us.

With regard to religious texts and utterances, hermeneutical techniques are particularly valuable and essential because the person or tradition responsible for them typically left no clues as to meaning, and we are far removed from the time and place of their composition. Many times the only thing that is clear with regard to a text is that we cannot take it literally. There is a long tradition of interpreting religious texts in several different ways:

- **Literal**. This is often the first option to make sense of a text or utterance.
- **Allegory**. This is a narrative technique in which the events described are meant to refer to another simultaneous structure of meaning—historical, moral, philosophical or referring to natural phenomena. Allegory is often employed in secular as well as religious texts. St. Paul tells us, for example, that the story of Abraham, Sarah, and Hagar should be interpreted as an allegory—the two women represent two separate covenants, one bound to the law and the other

to Jesus Christ.[14] Moral allegory is frequently used in religious and secular texts to guide behavior.
- **Typology.** This method of exegesis gives a text a meaning in the context of a sacred or supernatural context. For example, Jesus is considered by Christians to be the new Adam; the Hebrew passage through the Red Sea during the Exodus is typology for baptism.
- **Anagogical Allegory.** This is an ancient method of exegesis derived from the Greek word "anagoge" which means "uplifting." The fundamental idea is to find a hidden meaning in a text that demonstrates a truth of creation or salvation of universal significance. For example, Dante used the term to describe his *Divine Comedy*, which shows the path to salvation requires both self-purification and embracing virtue.

The point of this exposition is to reiterate how different religious truth is from scientific truth. Religious truth cannot be handled as scientific truth; it is not capable of observational verification. That is not to say, however, that we are not concerned about verification of religious truth. The tools of verifying and understanding religious truth are much different than the tools of science. Verification through the tools described above obviously has limitations. But logical verification cannot be identified with the concept of proof or removal of all rational doubt. Just as in science, verification does not mean excluding all logical possibility of error, verification of religious truth means the weight of evidence is sufficient to give our assent.

The Genesis Creation Story

Since the focus of contention by those who espouse a warfare thesis between science and religion is the creation account in the Hebrew-Christian Bible found in Genesis 1 and 2, we consider this story in the light of our criteria for the truth of religious knowledge. Even a cursory reading of the text categorically excludes any literal meaning. A literal reading also contradicts accepted Christian doctrine.

To begin with the text, "In the beginning when God created (alternative translation — "In the beginning God created) the heavens and the earth, the earth was a formless void and darkness covered the face of the deep." In neither reading did God create the world and universe out of nothing — rather He started with "a formless void." Moreover, the Genesis account has God creating day and night, light and darkness, on the first day; but the sun, the moon and the stars are not created until the third day. And God created plants, trees and every kind of vegetation on the second day; but it did not rain on the earth until the sixth day, even after the creation of Adam and Eve. God is also very cavalier about creating the universe beyond the earth. There is no mention at all of the planets; and the entire region beyond the moon is reduced to creating the stars as a kind of afterthought.

Thus, without any help from science and Darwinism we can exclude the possibility of any literal interpretation of this text. The so-called Young Earth interpretation based on the idea that somehow the Earth and the universe were created by God in literally six days only a few thousand years ago makes no sense at all. The day-age literal interpretation that accepts an older date for creation and equates the days of biblical creation to ages of the earth makes no sense either. The ancient authors of this account had no idea of geological time periods. Rather, source criticism tells us that the Genesis creation account is a conflation of two ancient myths, a so-called priestly narrative and an earlier non-priestly narrative.[15]

In fact, the Hebrew text of Genesis, which is estimated to have been put into the form we read it about 400 BCE bears resemblances to creation accounts[16] current in ancient Mesopotamia as early as 3100 BCE, the time of the first writing in human history. Undoubtedly these creation stories are even older than their written form, probably going back to Paleolithic times. In the Sumerian version creation begins with a formless mass of primordial waters personified as Chaos upon which the gods work a series of separations: earth and sky; darkness and light; night and day; and waters and land, all portrayed as divine. Later accounts added favorite local gods: the Babylonian version, the Enuma Elish, makes Marduk, the god of the city, the hero who spits the monster Tiamat to create the separation between earth and sky. The Genesis account retains the starting point of creation as a formless and unbounded mass, but the dualities created are no longer deities themselves, which accords with the monotheistic idea of one transcendent creator God. Moreover, the process of separation of the primal elements does not occur through violence but rather through the power of the spoken word of God.

Once we free ourselves from the albatross of trying to make literal sense out of this account, we can appreciate it for what it is, a magnificently beautiful story in mythic form designed to convey several levels of religious truth. First, this story is what scholars call an etiology — meaning an explanation of the origin of something. In this case the six days of creation is an explanation and justification of the Sabbath, the seventh day, a day of rest and prayer in Judaism and Christianity. Sabbath observance was a sign of Israel's dedication to God and an important part of Jewish law. Second, the Genesis story of creation is an allegorical (and anagogical) account of our initial relationship with the divine and the world. God is one; there are no contesting or subordinate deities. God is a good and all-powerful craftsman; all that He creates is good and He is not responsible for evil in the world. Mankind is central to God's actions: He not only creates mankind in His image, but He provides for mankind to flourish and prosper. This is the world as it should be, an ideal realm, a gift of the highest order. In comparison with other ancient creation accounts, this is the most beautiful and the most optimistic. We rest with God on the seventh day confident of His continued loving concern — the foundations of the later doctrines of divine providence and grace.

In summary, the literal meaning of the creation story only ties us up in contradictions and causes us to miss completely the symbolic meaning of the text.

The Mystery of Existence

According to Aristotle[17] philosophy begins with "wonder" and the same may be said of religion. The origin of the universe has inspired and continues to inspire endless fascination and wonder. But another more fundamental question comes to mind that is often overlooked: why is there something rather than nothing? Why should there be a universe at all? This question may be termed the "mystery of existence."[18] Martin Heidegger in his *Introduction to Metaphysics* (1933) calls the asking of this question the most important step in the search for metaphysical wisdom. Theists such as Jacques Maritain make this question a stepping stone to God because "it is concerned with the Godhead itself, the interior life of God to which our intellect cannot rise by its unaided powers."[19] Indeed, this question is beyond science and philosophy; all we can say is that we do not know. At the same time the contemplation of this question should fill us with the deepest awe. That we can never give an answer means that reality confronts us with an impenetrable boundary, which, like our own personal death, marks a limit to the degree we can understand the world and the meaning of our life.

Ethics: How We Should Live

Most of us would subscribe to the proposition that science, for all its power and influence, cannot tell us how to live our lives. But even here, science intrudes. Evolutionary psychologists led by E. O. Wilson, the author of *Sociobiology: The New Synthesis* (1975), think that evolutionary biology may explain human behavior to such degree that ethical systems and presumably ethical philosophers would become superfluous. Their thesis, simply stated, is that evolution is centered in our genes, and that the selection of genes necessary to produce a structure like the human brain takes a very long time. Thus, our behavior is essentially a reflection of our adaptation to life in the Stone Age since our brains have not had time to catch up to modern conditions.

Needless to say, this idea of the human condition is hotly contested.[20] The vast majority of biologists reject the extreme version of sociobiology while admitting that evolution does explain certain behavioral tendencies. But we do not have specific genes for certain kinds of behavior, and the genome is only one resource for the development of behavior. We learn behavioral norms from parents, teachers, our peers and from religion and society, and we can choose to modify our patterns of behavior.[21] So the question of how we should behave has not become a scientific question and is—like religion—among the most important questions we must face in living our lives.

Ethics and Religion

All modern religions entail ethical rules and concepts, usually of three kinds: rules of devotion; rules toward the community; and rules of self control and development. The most famous example is the Ten Commandments, sacred to both Jews and Christians. In our globalized world, however, the existence of many different religious sects poses a distinct problem: unlike in past centuries when—to a great extent—we could simply accept that different ethical norms exist in different parts of the world, today we are in daily contact with people with different cultural and religious traditions from our own.

Fortunately, we can identify a common ethical principle in all religions: concern for other people. To some degree at least this idea is featured in all modern faiths. All religions foster a sense of community and ethical egotism is condemned. The epitome of this religious concern for others is the so-called "golden rule," which many identify with Christianity but actually appears as early as the 6th century BCE in ancient China. In the Analects of Confucius[22] we find this statement of the moral character of human relationships: "Never do to others what you would not like them to do to you."

In contrast to this negative statement of the rule, we find a positive statement in the Book of Leviticus[23] of the Hebrew Bible: "You shall love your neighbor as yourself."

In the Jewish tradition, Rabbi Hillel (early 1st c. CE) is said to have expanded on this to say, "What is hateful to you do not do to your neighbor — that is the whole Torah, the rest is commentary."[24] Jesus, of course, most famously quotes Leviticus according to the account in the Gospel of Matthew[25] in response to the question of one the Pharisees as to which commandment of the law is the greatest:

> You shall love the Lord your God with all your heart, and with all your soul, and with all your mind. This is the greatest and first commandment. And a second is like it: You shall love your neighbor as yourself.

Concern for others is the foundation of the great Mahayana Buddhist tradition as exemplified in the Lotus Sutra (about 100 CE), which distinguishes between the "true dharma" of compassion for all sentient beings, and the "inferior dharma" of concern for personal nirvana. The true Buddhist labors unceasingly as a bodhisattva for the liberation of all before attaining personal salvation.

Religious ethical traditions have much to offer and are good starting points for a person seeking answers on how to live. However, no religious system is sufficient to cope with the demands of living in contemporary secular societies. In contemporary life we face social, economic and moral questions upon which ancient traditions have nothing to say. Religious ethics cannot simply be accepted blindly as an excuse to avoid rational thought. Regardless of our religious choices, we need a coherent philosophy of ethics to develop fully as human beings.

To examine the basis of our ethical principles, we must turn to philosophy. Philosophy is also necessary in order to achieve a commonality of ethical beliefs to bridge the gaps between the disparate religious traditions in the world.

Systems of Ethics

We cannot avoid ethics in our lives any more than we can avoid religion. Ethics deals with values — what is important and not so important; how we should act and how we should not act. There are two distinct aspects of values we should worry about: first, what must I do to develop my own life to its full potential; and second, how should I act toward other people?

When we look to the great ethical systems that philosophers have developed in the modern history of human thought, we see two very popular sets of answers to these questions.

The first is very beloved of conservatives and moral absolutists. This is the idea that everyone should observe a code of conduct of moral injunctions. In other words we need rules to live by in order to give a moral compass to our lives. If we live by these rules we will be fine and everyone else will too.

This system of ethics is rooted in the idea of Duty — with a capital D — and is known as deontological ethics (*ta déonta* is the ancient Greek word for what is right and proper, or duty). A system of ethics rooted in duties is superficially appealing. After all, this makes ethics a system very much like law, which also sets out lots of duties. Deontological ethics also accords with the Ten Commandments and other sets of rules on how to live our lives. There are countless books using this approach, ranging from recalling the rules we all learned or were supposed to have learned in kindergarten to rules useful in business or in personal development. If we only follow the right rules, we will succeed.

The most famous proponent and the modern originator of the deontological approach to ethics was Immanuel Kant in his book *A Discourse on Practical Reason* (1789). Kant combined the idea of moral duty with belief in God to create what he called "a categorical imperative." Kant believed that we can derive appropriate rules using the test of whether they are "universalizable." For example, is the proposition "I should not kill" a universally valid duty? Kant believed that it must be since a world in which some or even one person was permitted to kill would be morally objectionable. On the other hand, the proposition "I should go to church on Sundays" is not a categorical imperative but only a hypothetical imperative — if I am a Christian, I should go to church on Sundays.

But a system of ethics based only on rules runs into several difficulties.

One is the difficulty of living by a system of rules. I might have a rule never to lie. But I will inevitably encounter ambiguous situations. When applying for that job I dearly want, do I tell them about my arrest 15 years ago for drunken driving? So I decide to make a modification to my rule: I will never lie, but I may withhold the truth. And this is just one example; all my rules may prove demanding — so I constantly make modifications and rationalizations. And I tailor my conduct so that I never cross the line, but I go right to the brink — after all, what is wrong with that?

I will be able to live close to every line as long as I am the one making all the interpretations of whether my conduct is wrongful. But I may be the CEO of Enron and involved in some questionable financial dealings. In that case I will find that the U.S. Justice Department may disagree with my interpretations and I may find myself on trial in federal court.

Living by a set of rules is also very formalistic. The rules are usually negative in character and I glean little about how to turn my life into positive directions. Even when I find some good, positive rules, the rules alone do not tell me what I must do to implement them. For example, the former CEO of the General Electric Company, Jack Welch, *Time Magazine*'s Man of the Year for 2000, gives motivational speeches about how to succeed in business. One of his rules is, "Create an open, collaborative workplace where everyone is encouraged to contribute." Now I am sure this is good advice, but the rule alone does not tell me anything about what I must do to attain this goal.

So I must conclude that rules, while essential in life, are not the key to telling me how to fashion the best life I can, to make good decisions and to get the most out of life. Even the Ten Commandments are not enough. All they really do is help me avoid huge messes. They do not tell me what schools to choose, what to study, what profession to choose, who to marry, how I should treat my friends and enemies. In short, rules set limits, they do not establish direction for my life.

A second very important ethical system is utilitarianism. Most famously espoused by Jeremy Bentham and John Stuart Mill in nineteenth century Britain, utilitarianism judges any action by the criterion of "the greatest happiness for the greatest number." This idea is to focus on the consequences of our actions — something a rule-oriented approach tends to overlook. We can make a better world if we simply create the conditions for as much happiness as possible.

This formulation also has superficial appeal. After all, who can be against happiness? Liberal thinkers in particular embrace this ideal. Rules and duty are just for show; what really counts is happiness, and we should get away from rules and focus on what people really want.

But utilitarianism is not an improvement over deontological, rule-oriented ethics. Happiness is a vague goal that is soon equated with pleasure, satisfaction and enjoyment. Is pleasure what life is all about? Some would make a distinction between the lower and the higher pleasures. Thus, we would get more credit for going to the opera instead of going to a baseball game. But who is to be arbiter of such judgments? We certainly do not want a pleasure tsar telling us what is good for us. Utilitarianism also leads us into moral dilemmas: perhaps public executions would give a lot of people something to do on their day off. How far should we go in satisfying pleasures that may be morally reprehensible? There is also the situation where my pleasure may not coincide with the happiness of the greatest number—should I sacrifice my own for the good of all? If happiness is the criterion, why should I?

Utilitarianism tends to become a system of ethics where concepts of pleasure and happiness become simply what anyone desires, no matter how outrageous. The idea is everyone should be happy and that means fulfilling desires, and who am I to judge another person's desires? So everything is permitted, we have a minimum of rules, and we allow everyone to do what he wants. This is a description of our contemporary permissive society where we do not attempt to instill values and we allow everyone to "do their own thing."

Utilitarianism quickly degenerates into the ancient ethical system known as epicureanism, after the Greek philosopher Epicurus (341–270 BCE), founder of a school in Athens known as "the Garden" where he taught that the goal of all human action should be pleasure. Epicurus distinguished between the passive (*catastematic*) pleasure of well-being in mind and body, a freedom from disturbance (*ataraxia*) on the one hand, and what he called *kinetic*, active pleasures (wine, women and song) on the other hand. He much preferred the former and so advocated withdrawal from potentially disturbing political and social commitments. Thus, Epicurus advised avoiding political life, marriage and having children as disruptive of mental well-being.

Epicureanism itself soon degenerated into hedonism, which was not what Epicurus advocated but what he stands for today. His followers became enamored of the more active pleasures of life, apparently believing they are a lot more interesting than peace of mind and well-being. A memorable portrait of a real-life hedonist was painted by Geoffrey Chaucer in his *Canterbury Tales*—the character of the Franklin, a lower ranking feudal estate-owner:

> Wel loved he by the morwe a sop in win
> To liven the delit was evere his wone
> For he was Epicurus owene sone
> That held opinion that plein delit
> Was verray felicitee parfit[26]

> Well loved he mornings to take a piece of bread soaked in wine
> Sensual delight was always his desire
> For he was Epicurus' own son
> That held the opinion that full pleasure
> Was true happiness.

Of course happiness and even pleasures have their place in an ethical system. Utilitarianism is also correct in worrying about the consequences of our actions. But we cannot make this concern over happiness and consequences all that matters any more than we should put all our faith in rules of conduct to get us through life.

A Better Alternative: Virtue Ethics

What is known as virtue ethics is a completely different orientation of human conduct from the ethical systems that emphasize pleasure and duty. The idea behind virtue ethics is that we should not worry so much about whether our actions are right or wrong; rather what is of fundamental importance is our character — good or bad. If we have the right character, our actions will take care of themselves: good actions will flow from good character. So we should work on our character.

This emphasis on good character goes back to ancient Greece and the "big three" of Socrates, Plato and Aristotle. The most important ancient formulation of virtue ethics is a little book by Aristotle that he wrote, apparently to his son, called *Nicomachean Ethics*. Like Socrates and Plato, Aristotle reasoned that every person strives for what is good as opposed to evil; and what is good for a man is to fulfill his distinctive human nature and to develop his human personality. This means the development of his natural abilities for the purpose of attaining human excellence (*eudaimonia* in Greek, usually translated as "happiness"). This distinctive human excellence — something we do not share with other animals — is the quality of mind and heart we call virtue. The development of virtue is the only way to develop what is distinctive about being human.

What virtues? Aristotle distinguished two categories: (1) the moral virtues and (2) the intellectual virtues. The moral virtues are qualities of character that can only be acquired only through training and habit. Although he lists about twelve, four became known as cardinal or of utmost importance:

- Prudence — this is the ability to choose between right and wrong
- Temperance — this allows us to enjoy pleasures but not to excess
- Justice — fair dealing and the observance of law. Aristotle further distinguished between distributive justice — the fair allocation of community privileges and goods — and corrective (commutative) justice — the justice of fair exchange and remedying grievances through compensation or punishment.
- Fortitude — mental and emotional strength in facing difficulties, dangers and temptations.

Additional moral virtues for Aristotle include proper ambition, patience, magnanimity, and wittiness. According to his famous "doctrine of the mean," Aristotle said we should conduct ourselves in a middle way between two extremes. For example, we can enjoy pleasure but not to excess; and ambition is fine, but not overwhelming ambition.

Aristotle also put a premium on cultivating intellectual virtues through education.

- Art or Technical skill — the practical skill of knowing how to do something well, from building a house to painting a picture to playing a game.
- Scientific knowledge (*episteme*) — knowledge of facts and the relationships between them, knowing biology, chemistry, literature for example.
- Practical wisdom (*phronesis*) — the ability to make wise choices.

The culmination of the intellectual virtues is the attainment of wisdom (sophia) after a certain age and experience. For Aristotle the path to virtue is not easy; many years of training and education are necessary.

Although Aristotle's scheme concentrates on the development of the individual character, he connects with social welfare through his idea of friendship. Friendship is creative of community, which Aristotle finds natural and essential to mankind. In his book *Politics*, Aristotle says that the state in some form is a natural outgrowth of the fact that man is a "political animal" and social well-being is inseparable to individual excellence. The highest kind of friendship is one that appreciates the person for his qualities of character, not for usefulness or for pleasure of company alone.

Virtue ethics in various forms remained the ideal in the West in both pagan and Christian times for several hundred years. In ancient Rome the most prominent exemplar was Marcus Tullius Cicero (106–43 BCE), the famous lawyer and politician who was murdered after a vain attempt to preserve the Roman Republic. In his essay *On Duties* (*De Officiis*), a manual of right behavior and civics addressed to his son, Cicero extends the justification for virtue practice to the idea that nature has joined mankind together in one community, and "there is a bond that links every man in the world with every other."[27] As proof of this Cicero cites the provision in the Twelve Tables, the Roman legal code, that requires any seller of real property not only to make good defects that the buyer knows about, but also any hidden problems are the seller's responsibility. Cicero also cites with admiration the conduct of the Roman consul Marcus Atilius Regulus,[28] who was captured by the Carthaginians in 255 BCE during the First Punic War, but then released on condition he would be exchanged for certain aristocratic Carthaginian prisoners. He gave his oath that if the exchange was turned down, he would return to Carthage. When Regulus arrived in Rome, he entered the Senate and reported his instructions, but upon intense questioning recommended that the Carthaginians, who were young and able officers, should not be released. When the Senate agreed, Regulus duly returned to Carthage where he was tortured and put to death. Cicero says that Regulus acted correctly and virtuously by keeping his solemn promise even to the enemies of Rome.

In the Christian Middle Ages the greatest exponent of the virtue ethics ideal was St. Thomas Aquinas, who appropriated and Christianized Aristotle's thinking. Aquinas agreed that a man's actions should be directed toward the achievement of excellence, but distinguished between excellence on the natural and supernatural levels. While Aristotle's virtues were sufficient for the natural level, a new set of virtues is called for because of mankind's supernatural purpose and these can be attained only with God's help: faith, hope and charity.[29] As for Aristotle, the chief determinant of morality is human reason, which must control the will's exercise of choice. A crucial link, therefore, between the intellectual and the moral virtues is prudence, "right reason about what is to be done ... a virtue of the utmost necessity for human life."[30]

The pervasive influence of Aquinas' scheme is evident from reading Dante's *Divine Comedy*, composed in the early 14th century. For Dante human life is a struggle to attain perfection through virtue. In the first book,

Inferno, Dante, representing "everyman" enmeshed in a midlife crisis, encounters Virgil, the great Roman poet who shows him the punishments reserved for sinners against virtue. In the second book, *Purgatory*, Dante learns how to purify himself from the seven most deadly sins by practicing their opposite virtues:

- Humility v. Pride
- Generosity v. Envy
- Meekness v. Wrath
- Zeal v. Sloth
- Liberality v. Avarice
- Temperance v. Greed
- Chastity v. Lust

In the third book, *Paradise*, Dante has to pass tests on his virtues of faith, hope and charity before he is allowed into the highest heaven to behold a vision of God and the heavenly hosts of angels and saints.

The breakdown of virtue ethics and the medieval synthesis of rationalism and theism is perhaps epitomized by the Renaissance writer Niccolo Machiavelli, who in his book of advice, *The Prince*, made the argument that moral virtues like generosity, honesty and clemency are well and good, but they must not stand in the way of the superior person who seeks to wield power and influence in society. Machiavelli's ideas presage Nietzsche's will to power and superman idea that superior men should not be constrained by moral niceties.

In the twenty-first century we live in a globalized world of many religions based on many different values. Political systems, laws, and social practices vary greatly. However, people everywhere are fundamentally the same in the sense that they want to live a full and rich life that is meaningful. Everyone needs emotional support from family and friends, meaningful work, and a participation in the larger society. Everyone wants to stand for something meaningful, something that will outlast their mortal lives. There is not and cannot be a world system of ethics, but all can agree that every individual should strive to shape his or her character to be the best person possible and to achieve excellence. Particular societies will give different emphasis to different virtues, but all should agree that reason should be our guide and that religious values must be supplemented by moral values that need to be inculcated by education and by the hard work of self-discipline and practice.[31]

Practical Reason and Objective Goods

In the modern world we are all involved in a private creation of ourselves from the beginning of our lives to the end. Whereas in former times the religious or cultural milieu we were born into was determinative, this is no longer the case. We face choices that are both exhilarating and frightening about what we should do with our lives. We have the obligation to live authentically, to engage life rather than accept the path of least resistance. Globalization has given us great choices but also the anxiety of great responsibility for what we do with our lives.

How can we assure that we will have a valuable and worthwhile life, what the ancient Greeks called a happy life? The philosopher John Finnis[32] gives us a valuable concept to work with drawn from Aristotle and Aquinas: objective goods. Finnis distinguishes between objective and subjective goods and desires. Subjective goods are goods only because I happen to desire them — like an ice cream cone on a hot day. Objective goods, on the other hand, are good independently of my momentary desires; they are intrinsic values that make life worthwhile for all human beings. Finnis identifies seven such objective goods:

- Life
- Knowledge
- Play
- Aesthetic experience
- Friendship (sociability)
- Religion
- Practical reasonableness

Finnis says these objective goods are self-evident because they are all objectively necessary for a meaningful human life. They are essential to human nature cutting across all cultures and continents. We can succeed in life if we structure our lives to gain these particular goods. "Good" for Finnis does not mean only morally good, but rather well-being or "flourishing." These objective goods are the keys to human flourishing.

Finnis does not neglect the needs of other people and of society. His concept of friendship-sociability is intended to assure a concern for others as well as for ourselves. Friendship involves caring about the welfare of another person for his own sake. Sociability involves concern for the larger community and the common good. Therefore, practical reasonableness includes not only self-preference but also the concepts of justice and law that are central to the common good. Only through justice and law can we attain the necessary stability and fairness that create and presuppose a good society and ultimately a good world order.

The rule of law is essential not only for justice but also to create a community of relationships between individual members of society. In a pluralistic society law cannot uphold any particular moral system, although there will inevitably be large areas of coincidence between morality and law. But what if our community has a rule on abortion or capital punishment that conflicts with our religious convictions? In that case we must respect the law even though as individuals we can choose to adhere to our religious morality. Of course if the law requires us to commit an act that is against our moral views, such as undergo an abortion if a family has one existing child, civil disobedience is justified; violent resistance is permissible only in extreme cases such as the death camps operated by the Nazi government during the 1930s and during World War II.

Existentialism

Søren Kierkegaard (1813–1855) is usually credited with being the founder of a philosophy called existentialism, one of the truly original ideas of the past 200 years. The basic idea of existentialism is that the attribute of existence is what is central to the life of every person. There is no overriding essence or purpose to human life that either ties us down or holds us back. We are creatures born into the world with only "being and time," the title of Martin Heidegger's famous work, which perfectly encapsulates the fundamental idea of this philosophy: we have existence and time and we make of it what we will — that is the human condition. But there are several inevitable consequences of this view:

- Our freedom to make choices is both exhilarating and a source of dread — or as Kierkegaard puts it, "fear and trembling."
- We have no excuses; we must take responsibility for what we become and what we do with our lives.
- Each of us is ultimately the creator of our own essence; we are like artists painting a picture that is not finished until the day we die.

Existentialist philosophers neatly divide into Christian and atheist thinkers; there is no middle ground because existentialism demands choice; avoidance of choice is living "inauthentically," not facing up to the human condition. This leads to radical contrasts among key figures. Nietzsche, Heidegger and Sartre are examples of atheistic existentialism. Nietzsche, echoing Darwin, maintained that purpose is lacking in nature: man "is not the result of a special design, a will, a purpose; he is not the subject of an attempt to attain an 'ideal of man' or an 'ideal of happiness' or an 'ideal of morality.'" *We* invented the idea of purpose; in reality purpose is *lacking*."[33] In *Also Sprach Zarathustra* (*Thus Spoke Zarathustra*) (1885), Nietzsche uses the religious founder of Zoroastrianism, Zoroaster, as a fictional mouthpiece for a new atheistic morality: since all values are human, the superior person — Übermensch (superman) — should reject traditional values and morality, what Nietzsche calls the morality of the (Christian) herd, and should create his own morality — Master Morality: "You yourself should create what you have hitherto called the world; the world should be formed in your image by your reason, your will, and your love!"[34]

In contrast, Gabriel Marcel (1889–1973) chose Christianity, emphasizing that the choice of certain decisions in life cannot be left to reason alone; we must reject the temptation to view ourselves as the sole giver of meaning and creator of values; and we should rely on traditional, proven values in making our own identity.[35] Marcel maintained that mankind must learn to recognize the sacred in an age of technology.[36]

The existentialist emphasis on human freedom and responsibility is itself worthy of comment. Freedom itself cannot be proved empirically or from observing the natural world. Events in nature seem to operate either deterministically according to natural laws, or randomly, by operation of chance or laws of probability. The idea of human freedom may itself be an intimation of the existence of a different dimension of reality than the empirical world of science.

Summing Up

Philosophers debate whether human life has any meaning.[37] We think of the ancient myth of Sisyphus who, because he betrayed secrets to mortals, was condemned by the gods to roll a stone to the top of a hill, from which the stone immediately rolled back down, whereupon Sisyphus would again push it to the top, and so on again and again, forever. Is this human life? We toil after goals, but all of them are destined to evaporate and to be ultimately forgotten. How can we avoid living the life of Sisyphus?

As Jean-Paul Sartre has said, existence precedes essence,[38] which means we are free to create our own essences, and we do this every day of our lives by our choices. It is our choices that fundamentally determine our values. This fundamental freedom and subjectivity also carries a terrible responsibility: there are no excuses — we are totally responsible for the success or failure of our own lives.

Two things are essential to create meaning in our lives: creativity and the impact we have on others and the world around us. We should first aspire to be as creative as possible in the sense of giving the world something new, something of ourselves. This can be a painting, a novel, a business or simply the memory of a job well done. Second, we give our lives meaning by the impact we have on other people. Each of us has an impact — good or bad — on others. Over time we affect thousands of lives or more for better or for worse. Each of the people we affect will in turn affect others so our lives have the impact of a geometric progression far into the future. We maximize the values of our lives by our effort to be as creative as possible, on the one hand, and as good as possible in terms of our impact on others, on the other.

Science is a wonderful way of viewing the world; it has given us many benefits. But science by definition objectifies the world — it provides a limited kind of truth. As the philosopher Edmund Husserl[39] put it, "The positivistic concept of science ... is, historically speaking, a *residual* concept. It has dropped all the questions which had been considered under the now narrower, now broader concepts of metaphysics, including all questions vaguely termed 'ultimate and highest.'" Science provides objective knowledge about the world, but it excludes what Husserl calls our "Lebenswelt"— the "life world" in which we live our lives.

Husserl distinguishes between the world of science that aims only at objective knowledge — the universe of realities existing in themselves — and human subjectivity in its conscious relation to the world — the people and things that motivate us "in action and passion." Human beings interact with the world subjectively and phenomenologically, and science cannot supply answers to our subjective needs. Science cannot supply values and meaning — matters that are absolutely necessary for a full human life. Husserl calls these "problems of reason" and says "it is reason which ultimately gives meaning to everything that is thought to be, all things, values and ends ... what is meant by the word 'truth'— truth in itself ... faith in the meaning of history, of humanity, the faith in man's freedom, that is, his capacity to secure rational meaning for his individual and common human existence."

In short, when we look to science for values and meaning we come up empty; we have no choice but to look elsewhere — to belief and to philosophy. Neither belief nor philosophy is subject to the verification criteria of science, but they allow us to ask questions and give us knowledge that science cannot possibly provide. Both are necessary to liberate us from the confines of definitely ascertainable knowledge. There are many questions that must remain insoluble to the human intellect, but are of the utmost interest and importance.

Religion is essential to live a fully authentic human life. In the twenty-first century for the first time in human history almost all people interact with and are influenced by people holding different religious views from their own. We must understand and tolerate these different views. We also enjoy the freedom to espouse religious views that may be different from those we were born into.

The warfare thesis between science and religion is overblown. Science has its own methodologies that are very effective for exploring the material world, but science cannot replace what religion brings to human life. It is a mistake to carry over scientific conceptions into religion, which has its own modes of thought and interpretation.

Religious belief should not become an excuse to stop thinking; we should not shut our minds to rational thought about our beliefs and our ethical values. We must think critically about what we believe and apply recognized modes of interpretation to religious mythical discourse. We should not expect to solve all questions ourselves any more than we can resolve all scientific questions alone. We must rely on experts and perhaps an institutional church for answers.

Kierkegaard distinguishes three modes or styles of human existence: the aesthetic, the ethical and the religious. The aesthetic mode emphasizes personal satisfaction and pleasures; the ethical insists on devotion to duty and principles; and the religious puts belief in God at center stage. These modes of existence are at bottom not inconsistent. We must participate in all three to be fully engaged with the world in which we find ourselves.

Notes

1. *Critique of Pure Reason*, Cambridge edition of the works of Immanuel Kant, pp. 503–504.
2. For a fuller account see John Hick, *Philosophy of Religion*, 15–29 (Englewood Cliffs, N.J.: Prentice Hall, Inc., 1963).

3. *Summa Theologica*, Part I, Questions 2 and 46, in *Basic Writings of St. Thomas Aquinas*, Anton C. Pegis, ed. (New York: Random House 1945).

4. In early Christianity the Gnostics maintained that the world as we know it is the result of error by an evil or inexperienced creator god. See the Gospel of Philip in James M. Johnson, ed. *The Nag Hammadi Library in English*, 99, revised edition (Leiden: Brill, 1996).

5. *Meditations on First Philosophy* (1623).

6. Pascal, *Pensees*, p. 273.

7. Ibid.

8. Ibid., 282.

9. Ibid., 267–68.

10. Rudolph Otto, *The Idea of the Holy*, op. cit., chapter 4.

11. Paul Tillich, *The Shaking of the Foundations*, 63 (New York: Pelican Edition, 1962).

12. *Summa Theologiae*, Part I.

13. E. Cassirer, *An Essay on Man* (1944).

14. Galatians, 4:21–5:1.

15. New Oxford Annotated Bible, p. 11 (1989).

16. Jeremy Black and Anthony Green, *Gods, Demons and Symbols of Ancient Mesopotamia* (Austin, TX: University of Texas Press, 1992).

17. *Metaphysics*, Book A, Chapter 2.

18. Milton K. Munitz, *The Mystery of Existence*, 3–10 (New York: Meredith, 1965).

19. Jacques Maritain, *A Preface to Metaphysics* (New York: Sheed and Ward, 1958).

20. See Ullica Segerstrale, *Defenders of the Truth* (Oxford: Oxford University Press, 2000).

21. See the critique of sociobiology in Richard Lewontin, Steven Rose, and Leon Kamin, *Not in Our Genes: Biology, Ideology, and Human Nature* (New York: Pantheon Books, 1984).

22. *Analects*, 12:2 and 15:23.

23. Leviticus 19:18.

24. B. Shabb, 31a.

25. Matthew, 22: 36–38.

26. *Canterbury Tales*, General Prologue, 336–340.

27. *On Duties*, III, 67.

28. Ibid., III, 97.

29. *Summa Theologiae* I a, II, at 62.

30. Ibid., 57.

31. For a contemporary exponent of virtue ethics see Alasdair MacIntyre, *After Virtue* (South Bend, IN: University of Notre Dame Press, 1981).

32. John Finnis, *Fundamentals of Ethics* (1983).

33. Nietzsche, *Twilight of the Idols* (1889), The Four Great Errors, 8.

34. *Thus Spake Zarathustra*, II, "On the Blissful Islands."

35. Gabriel Marcel, *The Mystery of Existence* (1951).

36. *The Sacred in an Age of Technology* (1964).

37. Richard Taylor, "Does Life Have a Meaning?" *Good and Evil*, 256–268 (New York: Macmillan, 1970).

38. Jean-Paul Sartre, *Existentialism and Human Emotions*, 12 (Paris: Philosophical Library, 1957).

39. Edmund Husserl, *The Crisis of European Sciences and Transcendental Philosophy*, Trans. David Carr, pp. 9, 12–13. Evanston, IL: Northwestern University Press, 1999).

CHAPTER 6

Faith and Reason

Setting the Stage

The argument has proceeded so far to say that science, while powerful in its own sphere and eminently practical, cannot lead us to ultimate truth about our values and how we should live. Science cannot even give us a complete idea of the sphere in which it operates: the material world. And the verification-falsification criterion which characterizes the scientific method itself cannot be verified, so science cannot exclude spiritual realities and values.

On the other hand, our examination of religion concluded that, despite manifest uncertainties, we must embrace one (or more) of the great religious traditions in order to have a full and complete human life.

In the last chapter we concluded that embracing a religious tradition does not obviate the need for philosophy to test and complete our values and our vision of what is a good human life. Philosophy, however, is incapable of proving the validity of any religious view or of showing the superiority of one religion over another. Philosophy can fill out our ethical views and our system of values.

Now we continue the enterprise by considering the application of reason to religion. We face, first, the threshold question whether reason has any place in evaluating religious beliefs and practices.

Pope Benedict XVI and Islam

In September 2006 the Muslim world suddenly erupted with street protests against Pope Benedict XVI. Churches were torched and Christians were attacked and killed, and the pope was burned in effigy by angry mobs carrying banners condemning the Catholic Church.

The Muslim protests were sparked by the pope's quotation of the words of an emperor of the Byzantine Empire, Manuel II Paleologus, about the nature of Islam to a Persian interlocutor in the year 1391. In the course of a wide-ranging dialogue, Emperor Manuel addressed the question of religion and violence, no doubt of high importance at the time because Ottoman Turks operating under the banner of Islam were preparing to attack and besiege the Byzantine capital, Constantinople — as it turned out unsuccessfully — from 1394 to 1402. (However, the Turks finally succeeded in taking Constantinople in 1453.)

The words of the emperor the pope chose to quote referred to passages of the Qur'an inciting "holy war" against the "infidels." "Show me," the emperor said, "just what Mohammed brought [to religion] that was new, and there you will find things only evil and inhuman, such as his command to spread by the sword the faith he preached."

The sometimes violent protests in the Muslim world were set off because the pope was widely interpreted as attacking Islam. Even in Europe and the United States commentators understood the pope this way and either praised him for being forthright or condemned his attack. Some even called upon the pope to resign. The pope himself apologized and invited Muslim religious leaders to the Vatican to a reconciliation meeting.

Lost in this melee was Pope Benedict's real point as well as the greater meaning of his speech, which was delivered to an audience of academics at the University of Regensburg, Germany. The pope's real meaning was both tremendously important and profound.

The pope's real target was not Islam, and he was not disparaging Muslims. Rather he used the quotation from Emperor Manuel II to make the essential point that violence and religion are incompatible because, as the pope went on to say, "Violence is incompatible with the nature of God and the nature of the soul."

The pope continued to quote Emperor Manuel II on this further point: "God is not pleased by blood and not acting reasonably is contrary to God's nature. Faith is born of the soul, not the body. Whoever would lead someone to faith needs the ability to speak well and to reason properly, without violence or threats.... To convince a reasonable soul, one does not need a strong arm or weapon of any kind, or any other means of threatening a person with death."

But the pope's real intent was to make an even greater point in citing this argument against violent conversion: that "not to act according to reason is contrary to God's nature." The real theme of Pope Benedict's lecture was, therefore, the relation between faith and reason. His speech was, in fact, an impassioned plea for the application of "right reason" to faith and religion.

Pope Benedict addressed this theme by recounting the long history of the intermingling of reason with faith in Christianity. In the West (and now universally) the ancient Greeks are credited with emphasizing human reason in coming to terms with the world. The Greek word *logos* means both reason and word, producing the profound meaning that reason is logic that can be communicated. Although Greek philosophy based on reason, most famously exemplified by the trio of Socrates, Plato and Aristotle, antedates Christianity, the pope makes the point that the encounter between the message of the Bible and Greek enshrinement of reason resulted in a "mutual enrichment." The prologue of the Gospel of John begins in fact with the words, "In the beginning was the word (logos) ... and the word was God." The entire New Testament was originally written in Greek, and the Hebrew Bible (what Christians call the Old Testament) was also translated into Greek in Alexandria to become what Pope Benedict calls "an independent textual witness ... that was decisive for the birth and spread of Christianity." Thus, from the beginning Christian faith and reason were not only compatible but for the pope mutually reinforcing. This was why Manuel II was able to say — joining Greek thought to faith — that not to act with "logos" is contrary to God's nature.

The further point of the pope's address was to warn against decoupling faith and reason, what he refers to as a "dehellenization" of religion. There are especially two polar dangers of such dehellenization in the modern world.

First, the pope decries the contemporary trend toward the principle of "sola scriptura," reading the scriptures literally and unthinkingly, a swipe against fundamentalism in all religions. In contrast, he maintains that much of the Bible must be read symbolically or analogically applying human reason and so continuing the interplay of faith with philosophy.

Second, the pope condemns limiting the definition of reason to what is empirically verifiable. By applying only scientific criteria of truth — the possibility of verification or falsification through experimentation — we both reduce the radius of reason and exclude religion and much philosophy, and "this method excludes the question of God, making it appear an unscientific or pre-scientific question." The inevitable result of such a reduction is that "questions raised by religion and ethics ... must be relegated to the realm of the subjective." This is the danger of extreme relativism which holds there are no absolute values.

In contrast, the pope maintains that reason must continue to include modes of thought in addition to those strictly countenanced by the natural sciences, and that this is particularly necessary in order to have what he calls a "genuine dialogue of cultures and religions so urgently needed today."

In our time we need therefore what the pope calls "the whole breadth of reason" to come to grips with the differing religious and ethical traditions of humanity. This necessity to supplement faith with reason is not new; it continues the teaching of Pope John Paul II, who in his 1998 Encyclical Letter, *Fides et Ratio*, condemned what he called the "resurgence of fideism" and "biblicism" which "fails to recognize the importance of rational knowledge and philosophical discourse for the understanding of faith ... and tends to make the reading and exegesis of Sacred Scripture the sole criterion of truth."

Critical Evaluation of Religion

Taking our cue from Pope Benedict XVI, religious values and practices developed in the pre-modern age must be subjected to critical analysis through the use of reason, because "not to act according to reason is contrary to God's nature." Even if we cannot and should not reduce the world's diverse religions to a common denominator, we can examine their doctrines, beliefs and practices with a critical eye. Values and practices that do not pass the criteria of reasonableness and coherence must be discarded. With respect to the majority of the great religions, this proposition is not contested. The great religions of the East, such as Buddhism, Hinduism and the Tao do not resist the application of reason; indeed, they are based primarily on reason as well as emotion. The religions to which the application of reason is controversial, even today, are rather the three great Western religions, Judaism, Christianity and Islam, which are "religions of the Book" because unlike other religions, they draw their primary doctrines and beliefs from scriptures composed by men who lived hundreds and even thousands of years ago under very different conditions from today.

During the last century and continuing today the Hebrew-Christian Bible in particular has been subjected to minute analysis using modern tools of historical, archeological, sociological, literary and linguistic research. Useful (although not infallible) tools have been developed to evaluate passages of the Bible. These include, for example, form criticism, the study of specific genres of oral tradition; and source criticism, the attempt to trace oral traditions to their ultimate sources. In addition, new knowledge can be derived from studying the historical context of these writings and related writings and material remains. The discovery in the 1940s of previously lost ancient writings, the so-called Nag Hammadi manuscripts and the Dead Sea Scrolls, mean that we know more now about early Christianity and Judaism than ever before.

These new tools and discoveries of course do not solve all problems; far from it — they raise more questions in an unending search for truth. But some things are clear, and it can be said that, although believers maintain the ancient scriptures are inspired by God, they are not without errors, contradictions and pronouncements that must be taken as true only in a historical sense, not as eternal truths. Two examples will illustrate my point: first, according to the Gospel of Mark, the death of Jesus occurred about nine o'clock in the morning on the day of the Passover (Mark 15:25). But in John we learn that Jesus was crucified on the day before the Passover about noon (John 19:14). John seems to have changed the date in order to promote the idea that Jesus was the embodiment of the Passover lamb that was the subject of a sacred sacrifice on the day before Passover.

A second example is the famous episode of the so-called "satanic verses" of the Qur'an. Western scholars relying on Muslim sources (the Annalist Tabari, d. 923) maintain that Mohammed early in his career countenanced pagan polytheist rituals, a fact evidenced by an apparent editorial amendment to a revelation contained in Sura 53, The Star. In a key passage of this Sura Mohammed mentions three pagan goddesses: "Have you thought on Al-Lat and Al-Uzza, and on Manat, the third other?" (53:19–20). Then apparently came a passage later excised: "These are the exalted cranes, and their intercession is to be hoped for." This continues to create a stir today because it appears that Mohammed was recognizing and calling upon three pagan goddesses to be intermediaries between God and man. This would of course compromise the strict monotheism of Islam, and so we find inserted immediately after the mention of the goddesses: "These are but names that you and your fathers have invented; God has vested no authority in them" (53:23).

We know that the Qur'an was dictated by Mohammed over a period of about twenty-two years, from revelations received from 610 to 632, but the first manuscripts were not edited until about 650, well after the prophet's death. Of many existing manuscripts the reigning Caliph selected and edited one as authentic; all the rest were destroyed.

These are but two examples; many more could be added of such textual problems and contradictions in the Scriptures of all three religions. This is not to condemn or even question the fundamental quality of these works. The Hebrew Bible, the New Testament and the Qur'an are all precious texts of undeniable beauty and power; but they must be read and debated critically with all the tools of modern research. Of course many, if not most problems will never be definitively resolved. But we have the responsibility to try if we are to avoid what Pope Benedict calls a "clash of cultures" because we now live in a world that has become a village where people of very different cultures and religions are in constant contact. Even within one state this is true; few nations today are homogeneous. We cannot create a peaceful society on the global level or on the level of an individual state unless people are willing to use reason to deal with religious doctrines and issues that have the capacity to deprecate or provoke others.

In evaluating the sacred texts we must realize that they were composed and edited by men (regrettably there is no record of a woman), not some divine agency, and they are subject to being affected by human foibles. We know that the Hebrew Bible was composed over many hundreds of years and edited by many hands mainly from the sixth to the second century BCE. The New Testament was composed between about the year 50 to perhaps 100. The principle writings dealing with the life and ministry of Jesus, the four Gospels, date from after about 70, almost forty years after Jesus' death. The Qur'an, as we have seen, was composed over many years as random notes that were not edited into a book until many years later.

Even believers have a duty and responsibility to examine critically the content of these writings using the powerful tool of human reason, for as the Emperor Manuel II said, approved by Pope Benedict, "Not to act according to reason is contrary to God's nature." The tradition of relying on reason to evaluate religious truth harkens back to Aristotle, who maintained that reason (nous) is the "best thing in us — the most divine element in our nature."[1] Aristotle puts it this way: "If the gods have any care for human affairs, as they are thought to have, it would be reasonable both that they should delight in that which was best and most akin to them [i.e., reason] and that they should reward those who love and honor this most, as caring for the things that are most dear to them and acting most rightly and nobly."[2]

Religion and Values

Why is there a clash of cultures based upon religious beliefs? Certainly this clash is not new — it has existed perhaps as long as people of different religious beliefs began to come in contact with each other. In his essay "Ideas That Have Harmed Mankind," the English philosopher Bertrand Russell lumped religion together with superstition as ideas that have caused the most suffering and death in the world. Why has there been and does there continue to be so much bitter debate and violence over religion?

We find the answer in Plato's *Euthyphro*, composed in the early fourth century BCE. This work is a dialogue between a young Greek noble, Euthyphro, and Socrates, Plato's hero and erstwhile mentor and teacher. Socrates and Euthyphro meet by chance in the vestibule of the king archon in Athens. Both men are involved in legal matters: Socrates is responding to a complaint of impiety that will ultimately lead to his execution; Euthyphro is there to lodge a complaint against his own father for murder because his father had punished one of the family's servants who had killed a man by putting him in chains and throwing him in a ditch, which resulted in his death. Socrates is surprised that Euthyphro would take such an action against his own father, and the two have a conversation about justice and morality.

Socrates first poses the question, "What sort of differences of opinion make us angry and set us at enmity with each other?" After some discussion, Socrates says the answer lies in the distinction between matters of fact and matters of value. If there is a difference of opinion over a fact, the question can be settled quite amicably by simple verification. If two people disagree, for example, over a measure of grain, they can weigh the amount to see who is right. But Socrates points out that a difference over values — about what is good and evil, just and unjust, honorable and dishonorable — cannot be settled by verification. And so, he says, "about these people dispute; and so arise wars and fighting among them."

The point is relevant because Euthyphro is convinced that what his father had done was evil and required punishment. His father had committed an act of impiety, an evil deed. Euthyphro is a religious person — today we would call him a fundamentalist in religion — who is absolutely convinced that he is acting correctly in indicting his father because he believes his action would be condemned by the gods. His father was guilty of impiety because he offended the gods.

This makes Socrates pose a further question: "Is the pious or holy beloved by the gods because it is holy; or holy because it is beloved by the gods?"

Socrates is raising a classic issue: the divine command theory of moral behavior. Euthyphro is acting out of a conviction that his father's action has displeased the gods, and that something is holy because it is beloved by the gods, and is impious if not.

Socrates employs his questioning technique to show Euthyphro that he is wrong. He gives some examples: "A thing is not seen because it is visible, but, conversely, visible because it is seen. Nor is a thing led because it is in the state of being led, or carried because it is in the state of being carried, but the converse of this.... And my meaning is that any state of action or passion implies previous action or passion. It does not become because it is becoming, but it is in a state of becoming because it becomes; neither does it suffer because it is in a state of suffering, but it is in a state of suffering because it suffers. Do you not agree?"

Euthyphro says "yes." Then Socrates adds: "And the state of being loved follows the act of being loved, not the act the state?" Euthyphro has to agree. Then Socrates gets Euthyphro to admit that it must follow that something is loved because it is holy and not holy because it is loved. Therefore, it cannot be the gods' love which causes a thing or action to be holy. Euthyphro has admitted he was wrong.

This is a convincing refutation of the divine command theory of morality. God's command is not what makes an action or thing right or just. The religious person must not blindly follow what he thinks is God's command. This point is often lost. But consider the classic case of Abraham's willingness to sacrifice his beloved son Isaac as recounted in Genesis 22. We learn from the beginning this was just a test and that God did not really want Abraham to kill Isaac. But what if God had allowed Abraham to go through with this deed? Would this have been a morally good action? And suppose sacrificing the first born child was commanded to be done by all Jews and Christians? Would such a command make this good?

For Muslims, we can pose the question, what if the Qur'an in fact contained the so-called satanic verses commanding polytheistic worship? Would polytheism be good and right?

Socrates convincingly makes the point that God's command cannot change concepts of right and wrong. Values therefore are not valid simply because they appear in a sacred religious text. We may derive many of our values, such as the Ten Commandments, from religious sources, but their fundamental validity does not depend on the command of God.

This insight is very important; for if our values do in fact derive solely and completely from our religions, and if they come solely from God's command, there would be no possibility of dialogue between different religious viewpoints. There would be no debate, no possibility of changing one's point of view or accommodating other viewpoints. In fact, this is the attitude of some even today, especially in the three great Western religions, Judaism,

Christianity and Islam. This is extremely unfortunate and regrettable, because it is a recipe for unending conflict and even a war of civilizations and cultures.

But happily this is not the case, and if people come to this realization, people of different religious beliefs can enter into dialogue and live peacefully together. There is still the possibility of conflict, however; and here Socrates' first point in *Euthyphro* is relevant: we fight among ourselves over values not facts because, unlike the case with matters of fact, when it comes to matters of value, there is no way to verify who is right and who is wrong. But is this the case? We may not be able to verify values the way we verify matters of fact, but are there not objective criteria for the validity or non-validity of values? This is the question to which we now turn.

Theories of Right Action

Regretfully, experts on ethics and values, try as they may, cannot come up with any fool-proof touchstone of right action. It is safe to say that we search in vain for a test of what is right that will never fail us. But we should not despair; there is a multiplicity of candidates to help us decide what is right. We just have to determine how to use them.

First, it is clear that consequences matter when evaluating any action or behavior. What will be the result if I choose to have an abortion? If I donate my kidney to a relative in need? At first glance it would seem that consequences are the key, and all behavior can be evaluated on this basis. This indeed is the utilitarian viewpoint — that we should always try to maximize good consequences, which they define as the greatest pleasure (or happiness) for the greatest number.

There are, however, two main problems with relying exclusively on consequences as criteria for evaluating what is right. First, we can imagine situations where the good consequences would be very great, but our moral sense tells us that our action would be wrong. For example, it may be the case that holding public executions would attract great television ratings and therefore give pleasure to millions; would this make it right? Or we can imagine a case where an ethnic minority is causing unrest among the majority population somewhere in the world. Would it be right to relocate (or kill) the minority for the sake of improving the happiness of the greater number? Obviously, in some cases, consequences must not be the only consideration. We admit this in the maxim, "the end does not always justify the means."

A second objection to consequentialism is that it is not always clear what it is we should try to maximize in terms of consequences. Various alternatives include pleasure, happiness, and "the good." But all of these terms are vague and require definition and elaboration. People also will disagree on what is "the good" and on what makes — or should make — people happy.[3]

The main alternative to consequentialism as the standard for ethical judgments is the recognition of moral duties and the necessity of action on principle out of a good will. This theory presents the question of how are principles derived to create duty and will. The answer comes from an application of the principle behind the Golden Rule that any moral proposition that is universalizable — applicable to all and even to myself — must be right and correct. This would rule in not only the Ten Commandments but also principles like promise-keeping and respecting other people's rights and doing all I can to help someone in need.

Neither consequentialism nor duty-based principles, however, are capable of resolving moral dilemmas that arise in close cases. Difficult cases arise when competing moral principles are involved. In such instances we commonly weigh competing considerations, a mix of consequences and principles. To give a mundane example,[4] if my wife and I are going out to meet important guests, and it is important for both of us to wear appropriate attire, suppose she arrives just before we are due to leave, and she is inappropriately dressed. When she asks me if all is in order for our appointment, I am faced with competing choices of principle and consequence: (1) It is impolite and a breach of courtesy to be late. If we are late, there may be bad repercussions to our discussions. (2) I must not lie to my wife and tell her she is appropriately dressed when she is not. Lying would be a clear breach of ethics. (3) To tell her she is poorly dressed may cause her distress and damage our relationship. What should I do? My conduct faced with these choices must be decided based upon weighing and balancing the principles and consequences in question.

The same is true with regard to more controversial moral choices, such as abortion and bioethical cases. The reason reasonable people differ is that there are competing considerations and arguments, and people weigh these differently. This is not to say that values are relative; even with absolute values we face competing choices and we may balance them differently. The fact that there are in many cases competing considerations that people of good will balance differently is one of the main arguments for tolerance of the opinions of others.

Fortunately, however, not all moral choices are difficult. Most cases we are faced with on a daily basis are clear and we can agree on a course of conduct. Let us examine three of these easy cases in the context of contemporary religious views: (1) religious violence; (2) suppression of minorities; and (3) suppression of women.

Religion and Violence

People like Bertrand Russell who indict religion as harmful point to the wars, genocides and other atrocities committed in the name of religion throughout the history of mankind. Certainly it is true religious believers have committed countless crimes in the name of their faith, and this continues today in many parts of the world. Why is this so? History shows that almost all religious violence stems from the three monotheistic Western religions, Judaism, Christianity and Islam. Is there some characteristic of these three religions that makes their partisans prone to violence? Two factors suggest themselves that are unique to these three religions: monotheism and the fact they are all "religions of the Book." Monotheism seems to play a role because adherents to a monotheistic faith by definition believe themselves to be uniquely in possession of Truth (with a capital T). Thus, by definition as well, all those who do not share their religious convictions are either knowingly or unknowingly bearing false witness. Furthermore, such people are dangerous because they may not simply mind their own pathetic business but may seek to infect those in possession of the true faith as well. Thus, it follows that all who are outside the pale of the truth constitute a threat, and the next step, of course, is that it is justifiable to take even violent action against them.

The second powerful incitement to violence is the sacred book that is the foundation of the faith of believers. In the sacred writings of all three religions there are passages that call for or condone religious violence. For example, in the Book of Deuteronomy (20:11–15) we find the following divine command:

> When you draw near to a town ... offer it terms of peace. If it accepts ... and surrenders to you, then all the people in it shall serve you at forced labor. If it does not submit to you peacefully ... then you shall besiege it; and when the Lord your God gives it unto your hand, you shall put all its males to the sword. You may take as booty the women, the children, livestock ... and everything else in the town.

A subsequent passage in Deuteronomy cautions the Jews against cutting trees when they besiege a town because they may need them later. In actual practice, however, biblical Jewish leaders frequently invoked what we would today call executive discretion to override the subtleties of the divine command. For example, when Joshua took the city of Ai at God's command, the Hebrew Bible (Joshua 8:24) records that he slaughtered all the inhabitants, including women and children, and burned the whole town, leaving it a "heap of ruins."

The New Testament may be devoid of divine commands to engage in slaughter, but the accounts of Jesus' death unjustly heap blame upon the Jews as a people—"His blood be on us and our children" (Matt. 27:22)—while the Romans who were actually in charge get off rather too easily. These Gospel accounts soon gave rise to virulent anti–Semitic tracts in later so-called Gospels, such as the Gospel of Peter, penned in the early second century, which highlights Jewish responsibility for Jesus' execution. As a result there is a shameful record of anti–Jewish violence perpetrated by Christians for centuries down to our own time. Moreover, Christian religious violence encompassed much more than the Jews. We need only mention the Crusades against Islam, the Inquisition, and the Wars of Religion that took up much of the sixteenth and seventeenth centuries in Europe and especially Germany.

While Jewish and Christian leaders now eschew and condemn religious violence, Islam retains an ambiguous policy on the matter. On the one hand, a verse in the Qur'an, Sura 2, apparently written early in Mohammed's career, says very cryptically, "There shall be no compulsion in religion" (2:256). On the other hand, the famous "sword verse" of Sura 9 reads: "After the sacred months are over, slay the infidels wherever you find them. Arrest them, besiege them, and lie in ambush everywhere for them" (9:5). This and other verses in Sura 9 are the basis for *jihad*, meaning struggle or holy war against non–Muslims. At various times throughout history Muslim armies have waged holy war, particularly against Christian states and peoples. The great majority of Muslim leaders today disavow holy war, but many preach that Muslims have the right to defend themselves. Of course this right of defense plays into the hands of *jihadists* who maintain their terrorist and other attacks are only defensive.

Even more of a concern is the classical doctrine of Islamic tradition (*hadith*) that the world is divided into two hostile camps, the sphere of Islam (*dar al-Islam*) and the sphere of War (*dar al-harb*). There will be *jihad* between these two spheres until the dar al-harb either submits or converts to Islam. In any case, Muslim doctrine assures the ultimate triumph of the *dar al-Islam*. Those who die in the "path of God" in this *jihad* will immediately see paradise without waiting for resurrection or the Day of Judgment. This fanatical doctrine constitutes one of the main threats to world peace in the twenty-first century.

Suppression of Minorities

A second worrisome religious doctrine common to Judaism, Christianity and Islam is that non-adherents to the majority faith are at best second class members of society. This tradition begins with Judaism and the doctrine of the "chosen people." The Book of Deuteronomy (28:1) states that God has set the Jews "high above all the nations of the earth," beginning a religious tradition that God favors some over others. This is continued by Christianity: in his Epistle to the Romans, St. Paul (10:12) says "there is no distinction between Jew and Greek," but in Hebrews (12:24) we learn that Jesus is the mediator of a "new covenant"; now the Christians are favored by God, and the Jews will "receive mercy" according to Paul (Romans 11:26–27) because "all Israel will [eventually] be saved."

These sentiments are now disregarded by most Jews and Christians, although some still believe these concepts in their hearts. Islam also contains similar sentiments, and they are more widespread. In the Qur'an we find a so-called tribute verse that reads:

> Fight those who believe not in God and the Last Day ... such men who practice not the religion of truth, being those who have been given the Book, until they pay tribute out of hand and are utterly humbled.

This verse (9:29) is usually interpreted to mean that the People of the Book—Jews and Christians—will not have to convert to Islam as long as they are subdued and pay a special tribute, presumably to Muslim authorities. This offer of toleration is contingent upon their acceptance of inferior status in Muslim society.

The Status of Women

A supreme irony of the pre-modern world is that, although no ancient society appears to have granted women any formal or legal status or rights, women nevertheless played leading roles, and all accounts of the ancient world are full of depictions of strong and interesting women. The Hebrew Bible and the New Testament are no exceptions to this rule. In fact, women dominate many of the biblical stories of the Judeo-Christian tradition.

Jews and Christians today, it is fair to say, no longer take seriously the various biblical passages that call for less than full equality for women. Christians in particular emphasize St. Paul's observation (Galatians 3:28) that the Christian Gospel transcends all differences, male and female, slave and free, rather than his instructions that women should cover their heads (I Corinthians 11:2–16) and be silent in church (I Corinthians 14:34); and should be subject to their husbands (Ephesians 5:22–23).

The Muslim world, for the most part, however, takes seriously and literally the passages in the Qur'an that command the subjugation of women. One particularly problematic verse is as follows (4:34):

> Men have authority over women because God has made the one superior over the other, and because they spend their wealth to maintain them. Good women are obedient. They guard their unseen parts because God has guarded them. As for those from whom you fear disobedience, admonish them, forsake them in beds apart, and beat them.

This is a particularly disturbing scriptural passage because it advocates domestic violence against women. This verse and others in the Qur'an concerning women are the basis for widespread denial to women in the Muslim world of basic rights of education, ownership and social and legal equality. While countries that are majority Muslim are diverse in their treatment of women, in all such countries women are to some degree denied rights guaranteed by international law.

The foregoing are but three salient examples of religious practices and doctrines that do not withstand scrutiny in the modern world. Certainly we must tolerate and even welcome cultural differences and the profound insights and practices of the great religions of the world. Nevertheless, all believers have an obligation to scrutinize their own religion carefully and to measure practices and doctrines against the standard of right reason, and further, to engage in theological discussions with people of other religions to hear objections and to resolve possible conflicts. Only such an interfaith dialogue will allow people in our globalized world to live in peace.

Can the sacred texts of the People of the Book be reinterpreted to allow this change? For Muslims the Qur'an has sacred meaning that goes beyond what Jews and Christians believe concerning their scriptural texts. While Jews and Christians believe that their scriptures were inspired by God, they were authored by men and not directly by God. And Jews recognize that the Hebrew Bible was composed by as many as 500 hands; Christians know the New Testament had many authors. In both traditions there are also disputed ancient texts referred to as apocrypha. But Muslims believe the Qur'an was directly revealed by God through the angel Gabriel to Mohammed who merely was the human agency for the composition of the heavenly text.

For Muslims to reinterpret the Qur'an, therefore, it may be necessary to invoke the doctrine of the satanic verses as has been done for Sura 53. In this instance the reference made by Mohammed to allow for the intercession of pagan gods was interpreted to be a verse inspired by Satan in an effort to corrupt the word of God. If this was done in Sura 53, the question can be asked, what other "satanic verses" remain in the Qur'an and have yet to be uncovered? Certainly Pope Benedict's point is relevant here that not acting according to reason is contrary to God's nature. The further point is that principles of morality cannot rest on God's command alone. If it appears that God has commanded a practice contrary to reason, we have an obligation to examine and possibly change that practice to accord with right reason.

The idea that religion must be tested by reason is embedded in Muslim tradition. Great Muslim figures of the past pioneered the analysis of religion using philosophy and reason. According to the Spanish Muslim Ibn Rushd (Averroes, 1126–96), the Qur'an is not opposed to philosophy and we can know its meaning only through philosophy, since it is the function of philosophy to lead men to God.[5] Another medieval Muslim thinker, Al Farabi (870–950), argued that Islam and reason go together because religion presents in symbolic form truths that philosophy gives more adequately and universally. As he puts it: "Both comprise the same subject and both give accounts of the ultimate end for the sake of which man is made—supreme happiness.... Philosophy gives an account ... as perceived by the intellect ... [while] religion gives an account based on imagination."[6] Ibn Sima (Avicenna, 980–1033) also maintained that reason must have the final say with regard to any conflict between faith and philosophy.[7]

Religion and Law

Religious law plays an important role in the modern world. All major world religions seek to enforce codes of conduct to some degree, but the most important traditions of religious law come from the West, from Judaism, Christianity, especially Catholicism, and Islam. While Jewish and Canon (Catholic) Law have played important roles historically, they now directly affect only religious adherents that choose to keep their rules; they are now largely voluntary and have very little impact on civil society. There are, of course, some exceptions to this statement: For example, the Jewish Law of Return determines citizenship and residence rights in the State of Israel. But the Law of Return does not apply to non–Jews or to persons of Jewish descent who have converted to another faith. The State of Israel itself has no constitution, and Israeli law provides for freedom of worship, which is generally observed by authorities. Nevertheless, the Basic Law describes Israel as a "Jewish" and "democratic" state, and observers such as the U.S. Department of State[8] have identified instances of discrimination on the part of both the Israeli government and the private sector against non–Jews, particularly against Arab Israelis. Christian countries have a better record of allowing religious freedom, and in Europe, the historical heart of Christendom, international religious freedom and non-discrimination standards are monitored by the European Commission of Human Rights and redress may be obtained by individuals who are allowed to make a complaint against a government in the European Court of Human Rights.

The preeminent set of religious laws in the world today is the Shari'a, the law of Islam. The source of Shari'a is the Qur'an so Islamic law is considered divine and co-eternal with God himself. The Shari'a was derived by legal scholars from the injunctions of the Qur'an itself through analogy and syllogisms, but the effort was not to make law, but to understand the law as it is deemed to exist laid down by God. Nevertheless there are various schools of Shari'a, at least four Sunni schools of jurisprudence and one Shi'a school. The dominant school in the Middle East is the Hanafi school, which was the official school of the Abbasid Caliphs and later the Ottoman sultans. The Shari'a concerns three primary areas: marriage, divorce and inheritance law; criminal law; and laws of personal conduct regarding eating, drinking and the making of contracts. The actual practice and application of Shari'a belie its theoretical foundations, however, because the law differs greatly among the different schools and as enacted by Muslim countries. Extreme cases make international news. For example, in Nigeria in 2002 a woman named Anna Lawal was sentenced to death by stoning for adultery under the Shari'a laws enacted in Katsina state; however, this harsh sentence was reversed on appeal. Nevertheless, harsh and discriminatory laws are in force in many Islamic states. Death by stoning, amputations of hands and feet, and flogging are relatively common punishments; many sexual offenses are punishable by death; and women must wear the *hijab* (veil) or a tent-like *burqa*. Yet there are relatively great sexual rights for men, including temporary marriage and polygamy. In some countries a man cannot be convicted of rape except upon the testimony of at least four women; and the testimony of a woman carries only half the legal weight as that of a man. The Shari'a is capable of change despite its religious roots: in former times both slavery and concubinage were permitted and regulated by the law. Happily, this at least has died out.

The Concept of Law

Law can be defined as a system of rules, principles and procedures established by a community to govern the relationships between its members and with the community.

What is the function of law and what should be the relationship between law and religion in society?

To understand the role of law we must start with the philosopher David Hume's (1711–1776) famous distinction between "is" and "ought": while a factual proposition is an "is"—a statement about what is existing in the world, we should not confuse an is with an ought. An "ought" proposition is not necessarily factual, but is rather about what we think should happen or should be the case. A law is in the category of an "ought" proposition rather than an "is" proposition. We say the law is *normative*, about what should be the case but may not necessarily be the case.

But what is the difference between law and morality? Morality like law is normative and is designed to govern human relationships. There seem to be two essential differences between law and morality. First, law is established by an authority, and for the law to be legitimate, the authority establishing the law must have legitimacy. Second, law carries some sanction or some means of enforcement; it is not voluntary. A moral rule may be extremely important, but it is voluntary in the sense that an infringement of a moral rule will not as such carry any formal sanction or enforcement mechanism. Thus, we can say that law constitutes an external control while morality is an internal control system with regard to human behavior.

What is the difference between religious law and civil law? Both religious and civil law derive from authority and both carry some enforcement mechanism or sanction, so in this respect they are similar. The difference lies in the community that is the lawgiving and enforcement authority: in the case of religious law the community is a church or religious officials; in the case of civil law, the authority is the state or other recognized civil authority.

Three Conceptions of Law

Law as an important feature of human life has a long history. Law codes are among the earliest documents that have come down to us from Sumer and the other Mesopotamian civilizations that first established what we call cities based upon widespread irrigation agriculture in the fourth millennium BCE. Law and human community seem to be coextensive; Aristotle's observation that "man is a political animal" captures the idea that it is impossible to have a human community without law. Yet we can identify three very different conceptions of law in the ancient world.

The earliest idea of law to develop we can call legalism — law in the service of the ruler. An outstanding example from the Middle East is the Code of Hammurabi, the sixth of eleven kings in the Old Babylonian (Amorite) Dynasty, who reigned from 1728 to 1686 BCE. The Law Code[9] was apparently handed down at the beginning of his reign to establish order in his kingdom. This code is a comprehensive document covering criminal law, property rights, and commercial and family relations. Harsh punishments — usually death — are prescribed for offenses, signaling a strong effort by the government to control society. Few articles are devoted to procedural matters, but the code presumes a system of courts and judges and testimony by witnesses.

In China and the Far East legalism was the dominant legal tradition into the twentieth century. The beginning of legalism can be traced to a group of philosophers and scholars associated in the key Chinese state of Qin in the second century BCE. During this time — known as the Warring States Period (475–221 BCE) China was enveloped in seemingly endless war as various feudal rulers vied for control and territory. Scholars led by the Confucianist Hsun-tzu developed an authoritarian conception of control of human behavior. Since human nature is prone to evil, they argued, order and security can be established only through a system of severe laws and harsh punishments administered by the state. A law code should therefore establish a clear system of punishments and rewards, and people should be dealt with according to their actions. In this conception law is simply what the ruler desires, and absolute obedience is required of the people. The success of this legalism was assured when the man known as the first emperor of China, Shihuangdi, the ruler of Qin, employing a shrewd mixture of diplomacy and war, eliminated all opposition, and by 221 B.C.E. established complete control over China. During the next eleven years until his death Qin Shihuangdi, as he is known, created a centralized administration that built roads, standardized Chinese writing and weights and measures, extended the Great Wall, and subdivided China into 36 administrative units.[10] This was the beginning of the Chinese Imperial System that was to last over 2000 years. Chinese legalism and the imperial tradition have had widespread influence in Asia, and legalism spread and became dominant in the region. As a result, law in Asia has usually been associated with absolutism, and the rule of law is still sometimes viewed with suspicion.

The second tradition of law to develop was religious law, as we have already seen. The earliest system of religious law that has come down to us is Jewish law of the Torah, the first five books of the Hebrew Bible, the Pentateuch, composed probably beginning about 1000 BCE, but there were undoubtedly other Near Eastern legal systems in Egypt and Mesopotamia. The purpose of the Torah was to make Israel a holy nation (Deuteronomy 33:4), and belief in the divine origin of the Torah remains the touchstone of Orthodox Judaism. In India the Laws of Manu, the legendary Hindu primeval man, were compiled about the first century CE and set out in detail the Hindu caste system and the duties religious men and women should follow, including the famous four stages of life: (1) *bramacharya*, the period of being a celibate student; (2) *grihastha*, the period of being a householder and raising a family; (3) *vanaprastha*, when parents should withdraw to the forest to engage in religious contemplation; and (4) *sannyasa*, an optional stage of life, complete renunciation of society for a life of wandering the countryside teaching, learning and debating. Of course, as we have seen, the most widespread and vital system of religious law today is the Shari'a, the law of Islam.

The third system of law is the Western tradition of civil law that begins with the ancient Greeks. The law developed by the Greeks was very much influenced by the development of what we call the city-state (polis) as the main political unit. The Greek city-state was a small area that typically included both a fortified city with residences, political buildings and shops concentrated in a commercial area (agora), and a religious center (acropolis) together with the surrounding countryside where most of the inhabitants engaged in farming. Although the population of such areas were small enough so that every face was a familiar one, Greek city-states were first dominated by a few leading families. But periods of unrest and rebellion led to legal reforms that broadened participation in government institutions. Legendary reformers of this type included Solon (early sixth century BCE) in Athens and Lycurgus (late seventh century BCE) in Sparta. In Athens as well as most other city-states by the fifth century there was a firmly established tradition that the laws of the polis were to be developed by the active participation of all citizens, restricted to adult males who met certain residence qualifications.

The ancient Greeks first developed the unique idea of the rule of law over civil society and the right of all qualified citizens to have a voice in making the laws and rules that applied to them. Although religion and morality were important to the Greeks, their legal tradition was distinct. The Greek concept of law was transmitted to the Romans who looked to Greek models when they developed the Twelve Tables after sending a delegation to Athens in the mid-fifth century BCE. The Greek participatory model of civil law separate and distinct from religious law survived the Roman Empire to be transmitted to Western Europe beginning in the medieval period. From Europe the concept of the rule of law as the indispensable basis of civil society spread across the globe until now it is the dominant conception of law for most nations of the world.

Which Is Best?

There is little question that in the modern world the only acceptable choice of a legal system is a secular civil law system according to the Western model in which laws are made with the participation of the governed. A top-down legal system according to the legalist model is out of the question because it is totalitarian and absolutist in nature. A religious legal system is also unacceptable because of its appeal to religious authority and because all states today have citizens of different religions, and enshrining the religious law of the majority population creates second-class citizens and is intrinsically unfair. As Plato puts says in *The Laws*, penned about 350 BCE, "[W]e maintain that laws which are not established for the good of the whole state are bogus laws, and when they favor particular sections of the community, their authors are not citizens but party-men."[11] Moreover, the operation of a modern state requires law that derives its validity from secular institutions in which all citizens have the right to take part. In such a legal system, however, the question remains, what role should religion and morality play in a secular legal system? Before addressing this important issue, however, we must consider a threshold question: what is the function of law in society?

The Function of Law

Law plays an indispensable role in human society. We can identify four crucial functions:

- Law allocates rights and duties in any society; these are both horizontal — between individuals (including business persons such as partnerships and corporations) — and vertical — between individuals and the state. In doing so the law binds everyone together into relationships. Thus, law is in fact creative of human society;
- Law provides a blueprint for political compromises to solve societal problems;
- Law provides a forum and procedures for the settlement of dispute and in this way precludes the option of the use of force to solve differences; and
- Law is the societal instrument to do justice, both distributive and corrective, in order to give every person his or her due.

The Constraint of Natural Law

Are there any constraints the law must respect — considerations of natural law or morality? There is a long tradition in Western law to posit a divine or religious law that serves as a measuring rod or a test for the validity of man-made laws. This is the tradition of natural law, which begins with the Greeks.[12] Roman law too maintained the natural law tradition: Cicero, the most famous lawyer of antiquity, believed in the existence of what he called a universal law — right reason in agreement with nature, eternal and unchangeable, authored by God.[13] The most famous codification of Roman law, the Institutes of Justinian, compiled in the sixth century, also says there is a universal law established by divine providence for the benefit of all people.[14] In the Middle Ages Thomas Aquinas posited the existence of both an eternal law, the rational guidance of all created things by God, and a natural law, norms of right conduct known to all out of the application of reason. Thomas believed that human law should be subordinated to natural law.[15] According to this natural law tradition, human law that does not measure up to natural law and divine law is not law.

Enter Positivism

This natural law tradition, which was accepted without question for over two thousand years, was undermined by two main developments occurring ironically in the Age of Reason in the seventeenth and eighteenth centuries and culminating in the nineteenth century. An opening shot was fired by Thomas Hobbes (1588–1679), who, having suffered through the terrible unrest of the English Civil War, formulated a theory of human nature that left little room for an unchanging, benevolent natural law based upon reason. Hobbes famously believed that the nature of man was totally and irredeemably selfish; that we act only out of self-interest; and that in a "state of nature" the natural condition of mankind is a "war of every man, against every man." Under these conditions, therefore, the life of men is necessarily "solitary, poor, nasty, brutish and short" since every person, following his self-interest, is engaged in constant warfare against his or her fellows.[16]

In Hobbes' view there is one "Fundamental Law of Nature"[17] and that is survival. The impetus to survive is what leads people to accept the idea that human conduct must be restrained by law, and so they are willing to accept a "Leviathan"—law and a state to act as a "Common Power" to lay down rules of conduct. Thus, for Hobbes there is no natural law based upon reason; rather, mankind depends on a human lawgiver and human acceptance of law for essentially selfish reasons. Law in this view is a mechanism to attenuate the destructive self-interest drive of mankind. Hobbes' theory of law and the state, which is known as the social contract, has been extremely influential. The social contract was the basis of the political philosophies of a long line of thinkers, including John Locke and Jean-Jacques Rousseau, who refined and reshaped it. The social contract continues to have wide influence to this day.

The second idea key to undermining the natural law tradition was the general acceptance of the idea that we should not look to metaphysical or spiritual entities or explanations for human and physical beings or events. In the fifteenth century the philosopher William Ockham had formulated a version of this idea known as Ockham's razor, and the Age of Reason enshrined this as a general truth. Once again, we can look to Thomas Hobbes for an unflinching formulation of this idea: "[T]he whole mass of all things that are, is corporeal, that is to say, body...; and that which is not body is no part of the universe; and [hence] nothing." For Hobbes, therefore, all is corporeal, and there is nothing in the world that is universal but "names," the universal concepts human beings use for convenience of communication. What we call by the same names are not universals but individual existing things.[18] Universals do not exist so there cannot be any universal natural law.

The social contract theory of law and the denial of metaphysical explanations caused an intellectual revolution of the idea of law. In the nineteenth century lawyers and philosophers led by Jeremy Bentham (1748–1832) totally repudiated the natural law tradition in favor of what is now called positivism. According to this conception law is a totally human creation; there is no supernatural or metaphysical component of the law.[19] What is law depends totally on the "will of the lawgiver" and is totally distinct both from any metaphysical concept of reason and from religion and morality. This conception of law is the current accepted paradigm that dominates in the Western world today. This paradigm is typified by the system of law outlined by the Oxford law professor H. L. A. Hart in his brilliant book, *The Concept of Law* (1961). Hart conceives of law as a system of social rules: "[T]wo minimum conditions [are] necessary and sufficient for the existence of a legal system.... These are ... rules of behaviour which are valid according to the system's ultimate criteria of validity ... and its rules of change and adjudication ... effectively accepted as common public standards of official behaviour by public officials."[20] Hart's formulation assumes the necessity of three kinds of so-called secondary rules which underpin the validity of the system. First, there must be what he calls a rule or rules of recognition, some constitutional formulation that confers legitimacy on the legal system. Second, there must be rules to govern how changes are made in the law and how disputes are handled. Hart assumes that law and morality are completely separate, and there is no place for natural law, with one exception. Harking back to Hobbes, Hart concedes that survival is an overriding concern for human beings; thus, he is willing to accept the "natural necessity" for certain minimum forms of protection for persons, property and promises.[21] This is his idea of a "minimum content" of natural law. There is no suggestion, however, that the law is derived from moral principles or that there is any conceptual link between law and morality.

Hart's concept of law squarely raises the question whether law can or should be entirely separated from morality.

A New Concept of Natural Law

The positivist tradition of law is on firm ground in rejecting the idea that there exists somewhere a metaphysical code of unchanging natural law to which human law must conform. Positivism also is correct in its rejection of any particular form of religious law or any particular code of morality as a necessary background to civil law. In our diverse world where there are people of differing religious and cultural traditions in different states but also within single states, we cannot tailor law or enforce moral principles derived from a single religious tradition. No state should enshrine religious law or a religious code, whether derived from Christianity, Islam or Buddhism. Yet this separation of law and religion need not abolish all connection between law and moral values. The key to a system of natural law that is divorced from religion but not from values, even values shared by religions, is to look for principled ways of injecting value into law without resorting to any one religious tradition. So the question is — can we posit moral values as a necessary content of law?

The necessity of values in the law is highlighted by a case[22] arising in Germany after World War II, the prosecution of a woman who, wishing to rid herself of her husband, denounced him to Nazi authorities. The husband had in fact violated Nazi laws forbidding criticism of the Third Reich, so the woman's defense was that what she did was fully in accord with German law as it existed at that time. Nevertheless, the Court of Appeal upheld the conviction of the woman for unlawfully depriving her husband of his freedom, an offense under the German Criminal Code of 1871, which had never been repealed and was still in force. The court stopped short of declaring that the Nazi laws were not law, but rejected the woman's defense because the Nazi laws were "contrary to the sound conscience and sense of justice of all decent human beings."

This statement seems to inject natural law into the proceeding. Under a strict positivist approach, the woman should not be convicted; her defense is that her act of denunciation, while not compelled by law, was in accord with the law. Hart suggests that this in fact should have been the result, although he admits this to be distasteful. Alternatively, he suggests that the woman be convicted under a new law passed with retroactive effect. Although he is troubled somewhat by the idea of convicting someone of a crime under a frankly retrospective law (this is prohibited under the U.S. Constitution and the constitutions of most democratic states), Hart presents this as the best alternative,[23] a judgment that appears to be highly questionable.

How can we establish a basis for natural law if we do not use religion? Three separate ways suggest themselves.

First, a basis for natural law can be found in reason, a value as old as the Greeks, and an insight of the Greco-Romans that remains valid. The most important recent partisan of reason in legal ordering was Lon Fuller, professor of law at Harvard who famously debated H.L.A. Hart over positivism versus natural law. According to Fuller, although reason cannot give us a code of substantive rules that all will subscribe to, reason does determine objectively how we must deal with each other from a procedural point of view. Fuller posited eight criteria that all laws have to meet: laws must be promulgated in a general form applicable to all; they must be public; sufficiently prospective; clear and intelligible; free of contradictions; sufficiently constant through time so that people can plan their relations accordingly; not require the impossible; and be administered in a fair and objective manner.[24] Fuller calls these principles the "inner morality of law." Fuller's principles are a good start, but more is needed than a few procedural standards, much as these are welcome.

For a second justification of natural law, we can consider whether human nature is a source of human rights. According to the social contract theorists, especially John Locke, the source of human rights is the contract itself. The idea behind this conception is that all human beings in a state of nature possess all rights, in the sense there are no legal restraints on their behavior. But this, as we have seen, produces a state of war or anarchy, and is unacceptable, so, the theory continues, men and women accept the "coercive power" of law and the state — as Hobbes puts it — a rational person recognizes that he must "lay down his right to do all things; and be content with so much liberty as he would allow to other men." Thus, all men and women retain a modicum of their rights; this was the theoretical origin of human rights for the founding fathers of the United States, as reflected in the U.S. Declaration of Independence and the Bill of Rights.

But the necessary existence of inalienable human rights can be derived without acceptance of the social contract theory. The existence of human rights flows from the concept of the moral equality of all human beings and from the idea of justice that is a necessary result of this moral equality. The idea of moral equality is a fundamental truth that rationally must be accepted by all peoples. The principle of equality holds that no person or group of people has any inherent right to dominate or enslave any other, and that all are equal before the law. This appears to be a fundamental natural principle that all must accept. From this flows a further principle of natural justice that is captured by the philosopher John Rawls' First Principle of Justice[25]: "Each person is entitled to the most extensive system of equal basic liberties compatible with a similar system of liberty for all." This principle is similar to the social contractarian rights principle, but we can derive it without the necessity of positing a putative social contract that appears never to have actually taken place. The equality theory, then, seems superior to the social contract theory as a justification for human rights.

The meaning of this principle of justice is that certain civil, political, economic and social human rights must be recognized by all peoples and be featured in the laws of all states. So that they cannot be abridged even by a majority, such human rights properly should be entrenched in a constitutional order where they receive special legal protection. For the substantive content of such rights we should look to the United Nations Declaration of Human Rights,[26] which was adopted by unanimous vote in the General Assembly of the United Nations and is accepted by the international community as international law.

A third source of natural law is the concept of justice posited by the eighteenth century Scottish thinker Francis Hutcheson (1694–1746). In contrast to Thomas Hobbes, Hutcheson's examination of human nature turned up the existence of a moral sense that naturally directs our actions.[27] Hutcheson believed that we are constituted by nature to favor actions which stem from love and benevolence: there is "in human nature a disinterested ultimate desire of the happiness of others, and our moral sense determines us to approve of actions as virtuous which are apprehended to proceed from such a desire."[28] If Hutcheson is correct — and he is supported by contemporary empirical research — the idea of law as totally a restraint on our natural self-interested behavior as Hobbes believed is wrong. Rather, the law, while it must restrain self interest, must also serve the natural benevolence of our natures which seeks the best for our fellow men and women, even those we do not know personally.

But how do we translate this benevolence into natural law? The answer is that we cannot derive precise and particular propositions of law from this general characteristic of human nature. We can, however, state the appropriate goals that the law should fulfill. We cannot do better than to repeat John Finnis' formulation (discussed in the previous chapter) of the intrinsic objective goods that are needed by all persons to live a full life: law should enhance the values of life, knowledge, play, aesthetic experience, friendship, religion, and practical reasonableness for people.[29]

This tripartite conception of natural law sees natural law not as a code of laws existing in some metaphysical realm but rather a set of fundamental propositions that law must observe to be worthy of the name. Natural law of this kind does not enshrine any particular system of morality or religion, but does posit important moral values that are common to all the religions of the world. Finally, this system of natural law does not supplant or conflict with positive law; rather natural law is a necessary supplement that ultimately must be implemented through positive law.

This conception of natural law has great limitations, but this is for the best. Natural law cannot serve as a litmus test to solve the particular moral dilemmas that exist as burning issues at any particular time or place in society. The issues change with the times, but some perennial moral issues include abortion, stem cell research, the definition of marriage and the family, sexual conduct, pornography, environmental ethics, animal rights, and privacy. All of these issues are controversial because competing values and moral principles are intertwined in their solution. Natural law can provide only general guidance with regard to such issues, not the solution.

How should such questions be handled? First, here the distinction between law and morality is relevant. The law should respect moral values but cannot enshrine a particular religious moral code. In a pluralistic society, therefore, the law on these issues should be decided by the political process through democratic action. Since these issues do not for the most part relate to entrenched rights, they should be left as legal matters to be decided by the majority, and the minority on whatever question is involved should respect the decision taken. Of course, members of the minority can observe behavioral norms themselves that are consistent with their moral beliefs, and can continue to try to reshape the law accordingly.

Summing Up

Only through the application of reason can religions adapt to each other and to living together in the modern world. Reason is the handmaid, not the enemy, of religion. Acceptance of dialogue based upon reason with people of other religions will not endanger religious belief. Living in a secularized world with people who have differing values does not mean abandoning principles of morality and value. Positive law must reflect moral values, but the derivation of such natural law is not without difficulty. As Jacques Maritain[30] says on this subject, "Natural law is not written law. Men know it with greater or less difficulty, and in different degrees, here as elsewhere being subject to error. Natural law is the ensemble of things to do and not to do which follow by virtue of human nature [and] which reason can discover and according to which human beings must act to attain the necessary ends of being human."

Notes

1. *Nichomachean Ethics*, 1177a, 13–16.
2. Ibid., at 1177a, 25–32.
3. The founding fathers of utilitarianism include Jeremy Bentham, who regarded pleasure as the greatest good; John Stuart Mill, who preached happiness and somewhat snobbishly distinguished between higher and lower pleasures; and GE Moore, who called for the "good" and distinguished between various types of good, such as aesthetics, knowledge and so forth.
4. This example is taken from Jonathan Dancy, "An Ethic of Prima Facie Duties," in *A Companion to Ethics*, Peter Singer, ed., 219, 223 (Ames, IA: Blackwell, 1991).
5. See Max Charlesworth, *Religion and Philosophy*, 31 (2002).
6. L. Gauthier, *Ibn Rochd*, 34 (1948).
7. Charlesworth, op. cit. at 31.
8. The Human Rights Report on the State of Israel is available at http://www.state.gov/g/drl/rls/irf.htm.
9. For a complete English translation see James B. Pritchard, ed., *The Ancient Near East* (Vol. I) 138 (1958).
10. See John K. Fairbank, Edwin O. Reischauer, and Albert M. Craig, *East Asia*, 53–55 (1978).
11. *The Laws*, 1715b.
12. L. Weinreb, *Natural Law and Justice* (1987).
13. *De Republica* III, 22.
14. *Institutes* I, 2.
15. *Summa Theologica Qu.* 90–91.
16. *Leviathan*, 82 (1651). Carrying this idea forward, some have concluded, like the Marquis de Sade, that "nothing is forbidden us by nature, nor has she dictated us laws." Quoted in Taylor, *Sources of the Self*, p. 336.
17. Ibid., 222–223.
18. Ibid., 19.
19. *Of Laws in General*, Hart, ed. (1970).
20. *The Concept of Law*, 113.
21. Ibid., 176.
22. Judgment of July 27, 1949, Oberlandesgericht, Bamberg.
23. *Positivism and the Separation of Law and Morals*, 71, Harv. L. Rev., 593–629 (1958).
24. Lon Fuller, *The Morality of Law*, 2d ed. (1993).
25. J. Rawls, *A Theory of Justice*, 179 (1970).
26. Available on the United Nations Website, *www.un.org*.
27. "An Inquiry into the Original of Our Ideas of Beauty and Virtue," in

Schneewind, ed., *Moral Philosophy from Montaigne to Kant*, p. 510 ff. (Cambridge: Cambridge University Press, 2002).
  28. Ibid.
  29. J.Finnis, *Natural Law and Natural Rights* (1980).
  30. J. Maritain, *Man and the State* (1951).

Concluding Remarks

To summarize the argument, the world of science and the world of religion are two very different but essential human-created worlds, each in response to very different needs and purposes. Each has its own criteria of what is knowledge and truth. Since they are human artifacts — magnificent as they are — both are subject to errors and excesses. Furthermore, both are incomplete and ongoing creations of the collective human condition. We can confidently predict that the effort to complete these bodies of knowledge and belief will never end as long as there are human beings on the planet.

Philosophy and reason can bridge these two very different worlds, but only in part. Philosophy can analyze the essential claims of both, but cannot totally reconcile contrarieties and contradictions. This may be because human knowledge and reason has inherent limits: philosophy can neither prove the existence of a supreme being nor prove that science gives us absolute truth. This is the human condition, and we have no choice except to bow before it and do the best we can. Belief in the coexistence of the incompatible is not wrongful and is even required. Absolute and final truth and understanding lie beyond our grasp.

At the beginning of the twenty-first century, more than at any other time in human history, science presently commands our awe and respect. Not only do we now possess unprecedented and innumerable technologies that have transformed our lives, but we know more about the world and the human condition than ever before. We can pinpoint (at least within a few billion years) the beginning of the universe; we know the origin of our solar system and our planet; we understand that we live in an obscure corner of a vast expanse of hundreds of billions of galaxies, each containing perhaps a hundred billion stars; and we know that human beings are very recent additions to this marvelous cosmos. What is more, scientific discoveries have given us the laws that operate this universe from the minutest to the largest scales. These laws even include us, chance products of the process we call evolution.

This powerful vision of reality, which is the product of only the past few hundred years, seems to exclude much of what was important to human beings for many millennia — belief in the spiritual realities that mark the world's great religions. If science provides all the answers, what need is there for religion? Science not only explains all the old religious mysteries such as the creation of the world and of man, but scientific criteria of truth — limited to what is verifiable by our senses — seems to exclude all religious doctrines and explanations. Instead of a corruptible body and an immortal soul, science tells us that although we have no soul, the matter that makes up our bodies will survive our deaths according to the principle of the conservation of matter and energy. And the centerpiece of scientific debunking of religion is Darwinian evolution which undermines the idea that human existence has special meaning and that our individual lives have a higher purpose.

Fortunately, this sterile vision is unwarranted; the person who accepts only the scientific point of view in making sense of the world is guilty of an unjustifiable leap of faith that transforms science into a religion. Such a leap of faith equates scientific findings with ontological truth, a totally false supposition.

Science gives us undeniable but incomplete truth about the world.

First, scientific theories and findings are inherently limited by the bounds of our human senses extended by our instruments and machines. Science is limited to a human point of view; it is incapable of giving us a God's eye view of reality. We can appreciate this if we think of how a bat would do science if its brain were as powerful as ours. It would perceive reality in a different and incomplete way. We too cannot assume our point of view is all-encompassing; in fact we know it is not. For example, we perceive the world as "naïve-realists" in our daily lives. We live in a world of absolute time and space in which the shortest distance between two points is a straight line. But the theories of special and general relativity tell us that the way we perceive the world is not ontologically correct. The world of absolute time and space does not exist. And how can we be sure the world of relativity is ontologically correct? We cannot; in fact the history of science creates the distinct probability that it will be displaced by another theory. Even if this never happens we cannot rest easy; we have no independent check on ontological truth and falsity.

Second, even when a scientific truth operates with seemingly perfect predictive and experimental validity, this is no guarantee that it describes a complete picture of reality. For example, Newtonian physics is still relied upon for millions of applications of science and technology all over the world, although we know Newton's laws are not ontologically true. Can we be sure this is not the case with other scientific theories, including Darwinian evolution? Our best view of scientific truth is that it is pragmatically useful and technically sound; we have no right to leap to the conclusion that science is ontologically correct.

Third, scientific laws and mathematical formulas give certain truths limited to how natural phenomenon behave; they do not provide information on the intrinsic characteristics that make them behave in the way we experience them. Our scientific laws give us perfect predictive success, but this does not mean we understand what is going on. An example of this is gravity: Newton regarded gravity as an occult force because it operates at a distance. Even Einstein's concept of gravity in the context of general relativity does not explain why matter has this characteristic.

Fourth, many scientific theories, including our most advanced concepts of the way the world works, rest on certain assumptions that are not logically deduced but rather simply adopted as a last resort because they correspond to how the system in question appears to operate. Examples of this include the constant speed of light in relativity theory and Planck length in quantum theory. The necessity of using an assumption is an indication that a scientific theory may accord with our experience of the world without being ontologically correct. For example, Euclidian geometry works perfectly based on the assumption that parallel lines never intersect. But we know this is a false assumption in the sense that this is not true in the real world. Newer forms of non–Euclidean geometry work out the implications of removing this assumption.

Fifth, as is well-known, science cannot give us a picture of reality in the sense we see the universe as a complete and objective whole. We cannot picture the atom; we are reduced to resorting to probability theory. We cannot really picture how relativity or the quantum world operates, and string theory is a metaphorical attempt to describe what is essentially beyond human comprehension. We will probably never be able to describe much of what science tells us is true except mathematically and metaphorically.

Sixth, the folly of placing our faith in science as an ontological system is readily demonstrated by the history of science, which is the story of findings and brilliant insights and discoveries that were overthrown or later demonstrated to be only partially correct. Science is best considered as an evolving, imperfect and corrigible endeavor of great but limited value.

This is not to deprecate the great value of science in human life but only to put it in its proper place. Science cannot give us a final answer as to the ultimate nature of reality. Science deals with phenomena we can observe with our senses and with scientific instruments and machines. Science cannot provide ultimate answers about the nature of physical laws, where they come from, and why they operate as they do. For all its power and predictive success, scientific reasoning cannot supplant long-standing human needs and traditions. Science gives us reality, but one that is bounded and incomplete. Science gives us valid but imperfect truth. Science does not substitute for the necessity of finding truth intuitively through our knowledge and experience of human nature and what it means to live an excellent human life. Reason and science lead to impasse and contradiction. Since all human knowledge is imperfect, there still exits the possibility of religious faith and belief—we are compelled to use additional methods to deal adequately with the human condition.

Nevertheless, religions as they exist in their many-splendored variety in the modern world are also human institutions that are in need of reforms. The great world religions in particular should reform certain aspects without overturning the core areas of belief or their ancient traditions. Four reforms in particular are sorely needed: (1) the establishment of full and equal participation of women; (2) the renunciation and condemnation of religious violence; (3) the condemnation of doctrines relegating non-believers to inferior status; and (4) the separation of secular law and religious morality and law.

Of course, there is no one religious leader who speaks for all of the world's religions. Because of historical reasons there are only three religious leaders who have global authority and a world following—(1) the pope, who is both head of state and leader of the Roman Catholic Church, (2) the Dalai Lama, who has gained world-wide respect as a Buddhist moral leader; and (3) Archbishop Tutu of the Episcopal Church, one of the leaders against apartheid and racism who has spent his life combating hatred and violence. These three men should lead a joint initiative that can encompass all religions and eventually include all religious leaders in order to reform the religions of the world. Let us earnestly hope this process will begin.

Of the great religions of the modern world, one stands out in special need of reform—Islam. While other religions, notably Christianity, have renounced their sometimes bloody and discriminatory past, Islam stands unreconstructed, and while most Muslims do not endorse extremism, official doctrine in Islam, which stems from the Qur'an, is commonly interpreted to endorse discrimination and even violence against non-believers, the suppression of women, and the enforcement of religious law by the state. This state of affairs has its most damaging impact in the Muslim world itself. According to the human rights organization Freedom House, the largest deficits in human freedom and human rights in the world occur in predominantly Muslim countries.[1] Of the forty-one such countries in the world, only eight, led by Turkey, can be considered even partly free. Almost all Muslim countries are guilty of repressing human rights and human freedoms in the name of religion. This is, perhaps, the greatest single world problem of the twenty-first century.

Note

1. *www.freedomhouse.org*, visited October 17, 2006.

Bibliography

Armstrong, Karen. *A Short History of Myth*. New York: Canongate, 2005.
_____. *The Great Transformation*. New York: Knopf Publishing, 2006.
Barbour, Ian G. *Religion and Science*. San Francisco: Harper San Francisco, 1997.
Behe, Michael J. *Darwin's Black Box: The Biochemical Challenge to Evolution*. New York: Simon & Schuster, 1996.
Black, Jeremy, and Anthony Green. *Gods, Demons and Symbols of Ancient Mesopotamia*. Austin: University of Texas Press, 1992.
Bodanis David. *E=mc²: A Biography of the World's Most Famous Equation*. New York: Walker, 2000.
Bowler, Peter J. *Evolution: The History of an Idea*. Berkeley: University of California Press, 1984.
Brooke, John Hedley. *Science and Religion*. Cambridge, UK: Cambridge University Press, 1991.
Brown, Peter. *Augustine of Hippo*. Berkeley: University of California Press, 2000.
Clayton, Philip. "Theology and the Physical Sciences." In *The Modern Theologians*, edited by David F. Ford. London: Blackwell, 2006.
Dawkins, Richard. *The Selfish Gene*. Oxford, UK: Oxford University Press, 1976.
_____. *The God Delusion*. Oxford, UK: Oxford University Press, 2006.
Deane-Drummond, Celia. "Theology and the Biological Sciences." In *The Modern Theologians*, edited by David F. Ford. London: Blackwell, 2006.
Dembski, William A. *Intelligent Design: The Bridge Between Science and Theology*. Downers Grove, IL: InterVarsity Press, 1999.
Dennet, Daniel. *Darwin's Dangerous Idea*. New York: Simon & Schuster, 1995.
Dupre, John. *Darwin's Legacy: What Evolution Means Today*. Oxford, UK: Oxford University Press, 2003.
Gould, Stephen Jay. *Rocks of Ages*. New York: Vintage Books, 1999.
Greene, Brian. *The Fabric of the Cosmos*. New York: Knopf, 2004.
_____. *The Elegant Universe*. New York: W. W. Norton, 1999.
Gribbin, John. *Science: A History*. London: Penguin, 2004.
Harris, Sam. *The End of Faith*. New York: Norton, 2005.
Herrin, Judith. *The Formation of Christendom*. Princeton, NJ: Princeton University Press, 1987.
Hosle, Vittorio, and Christian Illies, eds. *Darwinism and Philosophy*. Notre Dame: University of Notre Dame Press, 2005.

Hume, David. *Dialogues Concerning Natural Religion* (1779). London: Penguin.
Husserl, Edmund. *The Crisis of European Sciences and Transcendental Phenomenology.* Trans. David Carr. Evanston, IL: Northwestern University Press, 1999.
John Paul II. *Fides et Ratio (Papal Encyclical).* The Vatican: Libreria Editrice Vaticana, 1998.
Johnson, Phillip E. *Darwin on Trial.* Downers Grove, IL: InterVarsity Press, 1993.
Kane, Gordon. *Supersymmetry: Unveiling the Fabric of the Cosmos.* New York: Perseus, 2001.
Kierkegaard, Søren. *Concluding Unscientific Postscript.* Princeton, NJ: Princeton University Press, 1944.
———. *Either/Or.* Princeton, NJ: Princeton University Press, 1959.
Kuhn, Thomas. *The Structure of Scientific Revolutions.* Chicago: University of Chicago Press, 1962.
Kurtz, Paul B., ed. *Science and Religion.* Amherst, NY: Prometheus Books, 2003.
Larson, Edward J. *Summer for the Gods: The Scopes Trial and America's Continuing Debate over Science and Religion.* Cambridge, MA: Harvard University Press, 1998.
Lindberg, David C., and Ronald L. Numbers, eds. *God and Nature: Historical Essays on the Encounter Between Christianity and Science.* Berkeley: University of California Press, 1986.
Livingston, James C. *Anatomy of the Sacred.* 2nd ed. New York: Macmillan, 1993.
MacIntyre, Alasdair. *After Virtue.* Notre Dame: University of Notre Dame Press, 1984.
Nietzsche, Friedrich. *Thus Spoke Zarathustra.* Walter Kaufmann, trans. Viking Portable Nietzsche. New York: Viking, 1974.
Numbers, Ronald L. *The Creationists.* New York: Knopf, 1992.
Otto, Rudolf. *The Idea of the Holy.* John W. Harvey, trans. Oxford, UK: Oxford University Press, 1923.
Oxtoby, Willard G. *World Religions: Eastern Traditions.* 2nd ed. Oxford, UK: Oxford University Press, 2002.
Pais, Abraham. *Subtle Is the Lord: The Science and Life of Albert Einstein.* Oxford, UK: Oxford University Press, 1982.
Popper, Karl R. *In Search of a Better World.* London: Routledge, 1992.
———. *The Logic of Scientific Discovery.* New York: Harper Torchbooks, 1959.
Quine, W. V. O. *A Logical Point of View.* 2d ed. Cambridge, MA: Harvard University Press, 1961.
Ruse, Michael *Can a Darwinian Be a Christian?* Cambridge, UK: Cambridge University Press, 2001.
Schmidt, Roger, et al. *Patterns of Religion.* Belmont, CA: Wadsworth, 2005.
Scott, Eugenie C. *Evolution vs Creationism: An Introduction.* Westport, CT: Greenwood Press, 2004.
Silver, Brian L. *The Ascent of Science.* Oxford, UK: Oxford University Press, 1998.
Singer, Peter, ed. *Ethics.* Oxford, UK: Oxford University Press, 1994.
Trigg, Roger. *Rationality and Religion.* Oxford, UK: Blackwell, 1998.
Young, Matt, and Taner Edis, eds. *Why Intelligent Design Fails.* New Brunswick, NJ: Rutgers University Press, 2005.

Index

Adam and Eve 54, 77, 78, 118
Ahura Mazda 101–102
Al Farabi 181
Alexander the Great 100, 102
American Civil Liberties Union 12–13
Analogy 146
Angels 79
Anselm 141
Antimatter 48
Aristotle 26, 28, 30, 78, 130, 139, 150, 169
Ashoka 107
Astronomy: cosmology 52; galaxies 51; stars 50; supernova 51
Atomic physics: beta decay 46; Bohr's model of the atom 40, 44; Dalton's theory 39; nuclear fission 43; nuclear fusion 43; quarks 47; radioactive decay 42; Rutherford solar system model 44; standard model 47–48; strong force 46; uncertainty principle 44; weak force 46
Atomic theory 38
Avogadro, Amadeo 39–40

Bacon, Francis 27
Barth, Karl 73, 93
Becquerel, Henri 42
Behe, Michael J. 3, 19
Benedict XVI (Pope) 167–169
Bentham, Jeremy 189
Bhagavad-Gita 98
Big Bang 8, 48, 52–53
Bohr, Niels 40, 44
Boyle, Robert 30
Boyle's Law 30
Brahe, Tycho 29
Branch Davidians 90
Brownian motion 42
Bryan, William Jennings 13
Buber, Martin 93
Büchner, Ludwig 35
Buckland, William 54
Buddha 95, 104–105

Buddhism 104–107, 152, 170
Bultmann, Rudolph 73, 93, 145

Cannizzaro, Stanislao 39–40
Canon Law 182
Carlyle, Thomas 83
Chain of Being 79
Chaucer, Geoffrey 155
Chemistry 40–41; bonds 41; reactions 41
China: religions of 107–110
Christianity 3, 115–118, 170, 175, 179, 190, 200
Chuang Tzu 109
Church of Scientology 90
Church of the Lukumi Babalu Aye v. Hialeah case 127
Classical physics 28; laws of motion 29; laws of planetary motion 29; universal gravitation 30, 31
Confucius 95, 109, 152
Copernicus, Nicolas 26, 28
Coulomb, Charles 32
Creation myths 74
Creation science 15
Crick, Francis 59
Curie, Marie 42
Curie, Pierre 42
Cuvier, Georges 56, 80

Dalai Lama 107, 199
Dalton, John 39
Dante 78–79, 158–159
Dark energy 48, 88
Dark matter 48, 88
Darrow, Clarence 13
Darwin, Charles 1, 7, 8, 55, 57, 81–85
Dawkins, Richard 2, 77
Dead Sea Scrolls 171
de Broglie, Louis 44
Deism 31, 79–80
de Maillet, Benoit 54
Democritus 38
Dennett, Daniel 2

205

Descartes, René 26, 28, 29, 31, 137, 141
Design 80–81
Diamond sutra 106
Diderot, Dennis 31
Dirac, Paul A.M. 45
Dupre, John 76
Durkheim, Emile 72

Earth sciences 53–55; catastrophism and uniformitarianism 70n80; pangea 55; plate tectonics 55; Vulcanism and Neptunism 54, 80
Edwards v. Aguillard case 17–18
Einstein, Albert 36, 37, 38, 42, 43, 44, 45, 137
Eisai 113
Electricity 32–33
Electromagnetism 33
Elijah (prophet) 77
Enuma Elish 74, 149
Epicureanism 155
Epperson case (*Epperson v. Arkansas*) 15
Everson v. Board of Education case 128
Evolution 7; Cuvier's theory 56–57; Darwin's theory 58–62; Lamarckian theory 57; mankind and 62–63; teaching of 8, 14
Existentialism 161–162

Faraday, Michael 32
Fatima 121
Feuerbach, Ludwig 35
Finnis, John 160
Flood geology 16
Forster, E.M. 144
Franklin, Benjamin 32
Franklin, Rosalind 60
Freedom House 201
Fresnel, Augustin 34
Fuller, Lon 191

Galileo Galilei 9, 29, 77, 79
Garibaldi, Giuseppe 40
Gassendi, Pierre 39
Gell-Mann, Murray 47
Genesis 148–149, 174
Gilgamesh, Epic of 145
God, proofs of existence: cosmological 138–139; ontological 139–140; teleological 139–140
Goethe, Johann Wolfgang von 88
Golden Temple 122
Gospel of Mark 171
Gospel of Peter 178
Gould, Stephen Jay 9–10, 76
Greek Orthodox Church 118

Hakuin 113
Harris, Sam 2, 76
Hart, H.L.A. 189, 190, 191
Hebrew Bible 77, 93, 149, 169, 172, 177–178, 180

Heidegger, Martin 93, 150
Heisenberg, Werner 44
Heraclitus 1, 39
Hermeneutics 147–148
Higgs boson 47–48
Hinduism 95–98, 125, 144, 178
Hobbes, Thomas 188–192
Holocaust 100
Honen 113
Hubbard, L. Ron 90
Hubble, Edwin 51, 52–53
Human rights 191–192
Hume, David 31, 137, 140, 181
Husserl, Edmund 163
Hutchinson, Francis 192
Hutton, James 54, 80
Huxley, Thomas 83
Huygens, Christian 26

Ibn Rushd (Averroes) 181
Ibn Sima (Avicenna) 181
Indus valley civilization 95
Inherit the Wind (play) 14
Intelligent design 8, 18–20, 138, 140
Islam 3, 119–122, 167, 170, 175, 178, 181, 190, 200

Jainism 103
James, William 91–92
Japan, religions of: Kegon 112; Pure Land 113; Shingon 113; Shintoism 111; Sokkai Gakkai 115; Tendai 112–113; Zen 113–114
Jaspers, Karl 95
Jesus of Nazareth 95, 115–117, 120
Jewish Law 182, 185
John Paul II (Pope) 4, 76, 170
Johnson, Phillip 18
Jones, Jim 90
Joule, James Prescott 31
Judaism 3, 98–101, 170, 190

Kabbala 100
Kant, Immanuel 89, 137–138, 153
Kepler, Johannes 29, 79
Kierkegaard, Søren 91–92, 94, 161–162, 164
Kitzmiller case (*Tammy Kitzmiller v. Dover Area Board of Education*) 8, 11, 19–20
Korea 112
Koresh, David 90
Kuhn, Thomas 65, 137
Kukai (Kobo Daishi) 113

Lamarck, Jean-Baptiste 57
Lao Tzu 108
Laplace, Pierre 31, 61
Law 182–193
Lawal, Anna 182
Laws of Manu 185
Leclerc, Georges-Louis (Comte de Buffon) 54

Legalism 184–185
Leibnitz, Gottfried 26
Lemon v. Kurzman case 16, 129
Leucippus 38
Levinas, Emanuel 93
Light 33; speed 34, 36; as wave 34; wave/particle duality 44
Linnaeus, Carl 56
Locke, John 30, 191
Lotus sutra 106, 107, 114, 152
Lucretius 80
Lyell, Charles 58, 70, 80

MacIntyre, Alasdair 165
Magnetism 32–33
Mahavira 103
Maimonides, Moses 100
Malthus, Thomas 58
Manuel II Paleologus (Emperor) 168
Marcel, Gabriel 162
Maritain Jacques 150
Marx, Karl 35
Maxwell, James Clerk 33; equations 33, 34
McCreary County, Kentucky v. American Civil Liberties Association of Kentucky case 129
McLean case (*McLean v. Arkansas Board of Education*) 16–18
Mencius 109–110
Mencken, H.L. 13
Mendel, Gregor 59
Mendeleev, Dmitri 40
Minorities, suppression of 179
Moleschott, Jacob 35
Moon, Sun Myung 90
Moonies 90
Muhammad 119, 121, 124, 171
Mystical experiences 93–94
Myth 73–74, 145–146

Nag Hammadi manuscripts 171
Nanak 122
Napier, John 26
Napoleon 31
Natural law 187–188, 190–194
Natural selection 7, 82–84
Natural theology 80, 85
Naturphilosophie 80
Nazi laws 190
New Testament 169–170, 172, 178, 180
Newton, Isaac 9, 29, 30, 31, 33, 39, 79, 80, 137
Nietzsche, Friedrich Wilhelm 91–92, 94, 162

Ockham, William 188
Oersted, Hans Christian 32
Otto, Rudolph 88–89, 143
Overton, William R. (judge) 16

Paley, William 80, 140
Parsis 102–103

Particle physics 26
Pascal, Blaise 91, 142
Pendulum clock 26
Periodic table of the elements 40–41, 51
Philip II of Macedon 25
Philosophy: epistemology 135; ethics 135, 151–159; logic 135; metaphysics 135; realism 137
Pius XII (Pope) 76
Planck, Max 43
Plato 24, 89, 138, 169, 173–174
Pompey the Great 100
Popper, Karl 23–24, 64, 86
Positivism 188, 190
Ptolomy 28, 78

QCD (quantum chromodynamics) 46–50
QED (quantum electrodynamics) 45–46
Quantum mechanics: Copenhagen interpretation 44, 66; Planck's constant 43
Qur'an 2, 119–120, 122, 168, 171–172, 174, 178–179, 180, 182, 200

Radhakrishnan, Sarvepalli 125
Radioactivity 42
Rahner, Karl 73
Ralston, John T. (judge) 13
Ramayana 98
Randomness and chance 80–81
Relativity: general 35–36, 37–38; special 36–37, 38, 43, 45, 137
Religion: definition 72; establishment 128–130; the Holy 88–90; knowledge 72–73, 92, 130–132; and law 181–183; pluralism 122–123; religious freedom 126–128; ritual 74–75; and science 75–77, 85–88, 198–199; and values 172–175; and violence 177–179
Right action theories 175–177
Risorgimento 40
Roemer, Ole 34
Roman Catholic Church 77, 125
Rousseau, Jean-Jacques 188
Rumi 121–122
Ruse, Michael 9–10
Rutherford, Ernest 42

Sacred Places 75
Saicho (Dengyo Daishi) 112
St. John Chrysostom 125
St. John of the Cross 93
St. Paul 117–118, 179, 180
St. Teresa of Avila 93
St. Thomas Aquinas 138–139
Saktism 97
Sartre, Jean-Paul 162–163
Satan 78, 101
Satanic verses 171, 174
Schelling, Friedrich 56
Scholasticism 27

Schrödinger, Erwin 44
Scientific materialism 35
Scientific method 26–28
Scientific truth 64–67
Scopes case (*Scopes v. State*) 8, 12–14
Shari'a 182–183
Shotoku, Prince 112
Sikhism 122–123
Social contract 189
Socrates 89, 173–174
Spencer, Herbert 61
String theory 48–49
Supersymmetry 48–49
Sutton, Walter 59
Symbolism 146

Tamils 95
Tantrism 106
Tao 108–109
Ten Commandments 151
Theology 73
Theory of everything 49
Thermodynamics laws 31–32
Thomson J.J. 42
Tibet 107
Tillich, Paul 93, 143

Unification Church 90
Ussher, James 54
Utilitarianism 155–156

Van Orden v. Perry case 128
Viete, Francois 26
Virtue ethics 156–159
Volta, Alessandro 32

Wallace, Alfred Russel 7, 58
Watson, James 59
Welch, Jack 154
Wheeler, John 37
Wilberforce, Samuel 83
Wilson, E.O. 61, 151
Wisconsin v. Yoder case 128
Women, status of 179–181
World soul 80–81

Yeats, W.B. 146
Young, Thomas 34

Zen 106
Zeno 38
Zhuge Liang 109
Zoroaster 95, 101–102
Zoroastrianism 101–103

www.ingramcontent.com/pod-product-compliance
Ingram Content Group UK Ltd.
Pitfield, Milton Keynes, MK11 3LW, UK
UKHW041959140426
5217IPUK00015B/888